LIBERALISM AND NAVAL STRATEGY

By the same author

Imperialism and Social Reform (1960)

Jamaican Blood and Victorian Conscience; the Governor Eyre Controversy (1963)

Occasional Papers of T. R. Malthus (ed., 1963)

The Rise of Free Trade Imperialism (1970)

Elie Halévy's *The Birth of Methodism in England* (trans. and ed., 1971)

The Methodist Revolution (1973)

Marxism and the Science of War (ed., 1981)

John Stuart Mill and the Pursuit of Virtue (1984)

LIBERALISM AND NAVAL STRATEGY

Ideology, Interest, and Sea Power during the Pax Britannica

Bernard Semmel

State University of New York, Stony Brook.

Boston

ALLEN & UNWIN

London Sydney

**Allen & Unwin, Inc.,
8 Winchester Place, Winchester, Mass. 01890, USA**

Allen & Unwin (Publishers) Ltd,
40 Museum Street, London WC1A 1LU, UK

Allen & Unwin (Publishers) Ltd,
Park Lane, Hemel Hempstead, Herts HP2 4TE, UK

Allen & Unwin (Australia) Ltd,
8 Napier Street, North Sydney, NSW 2060, Australia

First published in 1986

Library of Congress Cataloging-in-Publication Data

Semmel, Bernard.
Liberalism and naval strategy.
Bibliography: p.
Includes index.
1. Great Britain – History, Naval – 19th century.
2. Liberalism – Great Britain – History – 19th century.
3. Naval strategy – History – 19th century. I. Title.
DA88.S45 1986 941.081 85–28603
ISBN 0–04–942200–6 (alk. paper)
ISBN 0–04–942201–4 (pbk.: alk. paper)

British Library Cataloguing in Publication Data

Semmel, Bernard
Liberalism and naval strategy: ideology, interest and sea power during the Pax Britannica.
1. Great Britain, *Royal Navy* – History
2. Naval strategy – History 3.
Liberalism – Great Britain –
History
I. Title
359.4'3'0941 VA454
ISBN 0–04–942200–6
ISBN 0–04–942201–4 Pbk

Set in 10 on 12 point Baskerville by Computape (Pickering) Ltd,
N. Yorkshire
and printed in Great Britain by Anchor Brendon Ltd, Tiptree, Essex

To Stuart

Contents

Preface

This study will explore the role played by liberal doctrine (political, economic, ethical), frequently in association with economic interest, in the making of British naval strategy during the period of the Pax Britannica. Ideological considerations, even when allied to economic interest, did not always carry the day, yet they at times shaped critical choices.

British military and naval history, especially of the decade before 1914, has in recent years received the attention of a number of specialists. The subject of this book, however, though touched upon, has not been elaborated. While making no claim to expertise in military or naval affairs, this study seems a natural extension of my earlier books on the relationship between British internal and external policy during the past two centuries. I have discussed closely related issues in previous works, one on the politics and economics of social-imperialism in the decades before 1914, and another on the economics of Britain's early free trade empire; parts of my books on Methodism and on J. S. Mill discussed aspects of these questions, although their titles may not reveal this. I have also written on the efforts of Marxist ideologists and strategists to create a "science of war" conforming to their doctrinal system.

The research for this book overlapped my writing of an extended essay on J. S. Mill. Indeed, the original conception for a study of liberalism and naval strategy grew out of my acquaintance with Mill's 1867 parliamentary speech on the subject. I again thank the Guggenheim Foundation for the fellowship granted me for work on the Mill essay. I delivered a paper in 1979 at the annual meeting of the American Historical Association on the "maritime revolution" of 1856.

I should like to thank friends and colleagues in my department and elsewhere with whom I have discussed certain ideas of the book. Among them are Franklyn and Alice Prochaska, in whose London house the research for this study began, and Brian and Marion Wilson in whose it was completed. A particular debt is owed to Paul M. Kennedy of Yale University, Frank E. Myers of the State University of New York at Stony Brook, and David F. Trask of the US Department of Defense who read all or parts of the manuscript and made useful suggestions, many of which I have incorporated.

I have an obligation also to the librarians of several collections in England and the United States. Among the British collections consulted were those of the British Library, the Public Record Office, the National Maritime Museum, and the Historical Manuscripts Commission; among the American were those of the Library of Congress, the New York Public Library, and the libraries of Columbia University and the State University of New York at Stony Brook.

My debt to my wife Maxine is, as always, my greatest and also the most difficult to describe. It may be enough for a preface to record that without her loving encouragement and patient attention to the minutiae of life (and those of producing a manuscript), nothing would have been accomplished. I have dedicated the book to my son Stuart, always a good companion and, increasingly, a perceptive critic.

Stony Brook, New York Bernard Semmel
July 1985

[1] Sea Power, Commerce, and Liberalism

> Even from the economic standpoint of profit and loss, which the Pacifists always apply, an all-powerful British Navy by assuring the future is an asset of incomparable value. If our position at sea were in doubt, Consols would fall to 50 or 60.
>
> *National Review*, 1911

> Only here among the Great Powers in Europe has pacifism flourished, only in nineteenth-century England could Mill have written his *Essay on Liberty*, which rests on the unconscious assumption that the British Navy ruled the seas ... Since the days of Bright even questions concerning our own security have been debated as moral problems. As a result our most typical vice is thought abroad to be hypocrisy; and at home the first of our national pleasures was for long moral indignation.
>
> Noel Annan, 1959

In early 1915, in the first year of the war of Britain and France against Germany, articles on British "navalism" appeared in the American press. Their writers sympathized with the German position that the Central Powers were fighting to protect freedom of the seas against the arrogant ambitions of the Royal Navy. Since the Allies had declared their enemy to be Prussian militarism, the navalism of the Pax Britannica seemed an appropriate counter-charge. In the United States, this awakened historical memories of the War of 1812, and of the American resistance to England's claim of a peacetime right of search in the Royal Navy's campaign against the slave trade during the previous century. American papers raised the standard of Grotius, the seventeenth-century founder of the doctrine of freedom of the seas, and denounced Great Britain for having been for three centuries the major offender against maritime liberty. The newspaper articles provided the occasion for a worried discussion by the British cabinet, which saw American friendship as essential to a successful war, and the charge of navalism as the "strongest card in the German Propaganda game."[1]

In reply to this charge, Julian Gorbett, a well-known English naval historian and strategist, wrote an article for an American newspaper to dismiss "the bugbear of British navalism." "For a full century, during which British naval supremacy had been almost undisputed," Corbett declared, "the world, as a whole, had quietly acquiesced in it," for "abundant trial had proved it was a menace neither to freedom of trade nor to national independence." English sea power had saved Europe from Napoleon's militarism in the early years of the century. "Under the inspiration of America and the shield of British naval supremacy" the South American republics were born. By restraining the continental despotisms, the Royal Navy had given Greece and Italy the opportunity to achieve their independence and to acquire liberal institutions. Far from being a menace to freedom of trade, the policy of British naval predominance was to permit free commercial access to all England's colonies, and to maintain the "open door" in the Far East. Great Britain had worked to restrict no trade except the slave trade, Corbett concluded, and the suppression of that inhuman commerce had been characteristic of the unselfish efforts that "marked the zenith of our naval power."[2]

The 1914 to 1918 contest between Prussian militarism and British navalism appeared to be a repetition of an ancient pattern. Many writers through the centuries had called attention not merely to the geopolitics of the conflict between land and sea powers but also to its moral aspects. Thucydides, for example, described the maritime society of a democratic and cosmopolitan Athens, which prized individual liberty and commercial enterprise, at war with an agricultural, xenophobic Sparta which stressed the disciplined subordination required by a landed, military society.[3] In modern times, an insular Great Britain became the model of a free, maritime society engaged in what seemed a continuous struggle with the despotic, military powers of the continent. England had defended herself and the independence of the smaller European states against the armies of the Bourbons in the seventeenth and eighteenth centuries, and against first Napoleon and then the ambitions of the Russian tzars in the nineteenth. In the second decade of the twentieth century, she saw herself at war with the autocratic Hohenzollerns not only in behalf of her own but of the world's liberty.

Corbett wrote in his 1915 article of "the mysterious power" which affected "the men who go down to the sea in ships," and of "the free-spirit of the sea," which he declared the British and Americans but not the Germans could understand. Imperial Germany had assembled a considerable merchant marine and a powerful navy by 1914 but Corbett insisted that she continued to have the outlook and drives of a land power. The France of Louis XIV and of his finance minister Colbert had thought it possible "artificially" to create sea power, and had undertaken a state-organized and financed construction of new port cities at the end of the seventeenth century. The result was failure.[4] The French historian Elie Halévy argued that England's eighteenth-century superiority at sea derived not from the superiority of her ships – he thought those of France better designed – but from the character of her sailors, and the great popular favor they inspired.[5]

England possessed, as did Holland, but as France did not, a maritime culture, one which had overcome the atavistic dread of the oceans, as well as, and perhaps more importantly, the xenophobic fears of the persons, products, or ideas from overseas to which a relatively open society exposed her. The German economist Friedrich List wrote in the 1840s of navigation as the most demanding of "industrial pursuits," and of overseas commerce as requiring "energy, personal courage, enterprise and endurance," qualities which could "only flourish in an atmosphere of freedom."[6] Half a century later, the American naval historian Captain A. T. Mahan was to agree that the members of a sea-directed culture were enterprising, ready to risk their ships, their goods, and their persons in the venture for profit – with great gains as a reward for great risks; they were a "patient" people prepared to take profits by labor rather than by the sword. A maritime society, Mahan also observed, was a free society, while landed states tended toward autocracy.[7]

Both List and Mahan were convinced that sea power was decisive in international affairs. List saw England's maritime supremacy – her great Navy as well as her control of the narrow seas at such choke-points as Gibraltar and the entrances to the Baltic – as the basis not only for her colonial empire and her commercial and industrial predominance, but for her ability to impose her will on other nations. He urged Germany to follow the British example and turn to the sea.[8] In 1890, in his epoch-making work *The Influence of Sea Power*, Mahan argued that throughout the course of history, from Roman times to the present, that nation which possessed command of the sea exercised the dominant role in world affairs.[9] England was Mahan's particular model and he was convinced that a maritime United States, perhaps in association with Britain, would be the heir to this authority. Mahan's ideas were to be influential not only in his own country and in England, but even in a landed Germany, where Kaiser Wilhelm II and his naval aide Admiral von Tirpitz became his disciples.

In 1900 the American lawyer and historian Brooks Adams sounded a warning to the maritime societies. From the time of the Crusades until about 1870, in good part as a result of the invention of the compass and the quadrant, the maritime system had had the advantage over "the Continental system" based upon the network of roads which Rome had built. Although London was for some time at the center of this maritime system, England did not achieve an "undisputed economic supremacy" until about 1835. This was the period when she was the "workshop of the world," and the guardian of liberalism and of free trade; it was "the age of the Manchester School, of Cobden, of Bright, and of Mill." More recently, the railroad, by greatly reducing the cost of land transport, was pressing sea-haulage severely. Adams saw the United States as sharing England's maritime interests in opposition to the continental ambitions of France and Russia in the nineteenth century; and now it was Germany which sought to impose a land and railway-based control over the natural and commercial riches of Eurasia. But with England weakened, "the old equilibrium has failed," Adams concluded, and America would have to fight on her own for the maritime system against that of the continent.[10] The British geographer, Halford J. Mackinder, in his "The geographical pivot of history" published in 1904, spoke in similar but even less hopeful terms, forseeing the victory of the landed, continental powers.[11]

Liberal pacifism

Since the end of the eighteenth century, European and American liberals have believed that the growth of an international economy would bring about an era of universal peace. Commerce would supplant war, and a world of hostile states would give way to a cosmopolitan republic of mankind. This vision grew out of the struggle between two world-outlooks, one that of the traditional landed, military community of pre-industrial times, and the other of a modern commercial and industrial society – and the anticipated inevitable victory of the latter. The heyday of this dream was the nineteenth century, when because of a British commercial, financial, industrial, and naval pre-eminence, indeed for a time, predominance, there evolved a "Pax Britannica" which many liberals in England and elsewhere saw as a step toward this goal.

That international commerce would destroy all motives for making war was widely accepted at the turn of the twentieth century, even as Europe prepared for fighting. In 1909, for example, the British liberal writer Norman Angell argued that not the new dreadnought battleships but "better and cheaper goods" would give one nation a genuine superiority over another. England and Germany, Angell concluded, were each other's best customers, as they both well knew, and neither would be so foolish as to make war on the other.[12] The American philosopher William James contrasted the industrial with the earlier military society in a well-known essay in 1910, and suggested that trade was "the moral equivalent" of violent conflict. Modern man had inherited all "the innate pugnacity and all the love of glory" of his progenitors, but seeing how expensive war was, he had turned to commerce as "a better avenue to plunder." James saw war as merely "a transitory phenomenon in social evolution."[13] There were others who were less sanguine, but they were dismissed as men of "reactionary" sentiments. Some of these argued that man's "innate pugnacity" found commerce insufficiently satisfying, and others, like Brooks Adams a decade earlier, that war was "the ultimate form of economic competition."[14]

The philosophical case that a progressive commercial civilization would necessarily turn from destructive war and establish a perpetual peace was put forward by the German philosopher Immanuel Kant at the end of the eighteenth century. Kant elaborated a position that went beyond Enlightenment idealism, and anticipated that peculiar combination of protestant conscience and laissez-faire economics that shaped British Radical liberalism. For Kant's argument bore the marks not only of French revolutionary republicanism, but also of a pietistic belief in moral duty, and a vision of a socio-psychological process (resembling Adam Smith's defense of the free market) that found in a selfish human nature the means to secure the end of war.

Kant argued that both individual and national self-interest would necessarily bring about a perpetual peace. In 1784, he took note of the "unsocial sociability" that drew men into social relations which their propensity ("obviously rooted in human nature") to secure "honour, power or property" led them to resist. Nature had a "hidden plan" whereby men might master their "self-seeking animal inclinations." Civilization had sufficiently advanced that a state could neglect the "internal culture" and civil and religious liberties of its citizens only at the expense of its external power, since any injury to the diffusion of knowledge and freedom undermined all trades and industries and the armies and navies dependent on them. (This was the "great benefit which the human race must reap even from its rulers' self-seeking schemes of expansion.") In a Europe "closely linked by trade," war would become "a highly artificial undertaking," one so "extremely uncertain in its outcome" as to become "a dubious risk."[15] In 1793, in a variation of Adam Smith's "invisible hand," Kant insisted that a natural providence would compel men, given by nature to the use of force and to pursuing selfish ends, to do what they might not individually choose to do. Because of the "sheer exhaustion" of profitless wars, and supported by a human nature sufficiently "animated by respect for right and duty" and not too "deeply immersed in evil," "practical moral reason" would triumph and states would submit to the public laws of a "lawful *federation*" of nations.[16]

Kant prefigured almost all the liberal positions on war and peace of the following century: a non-interventionist, anti-militarist, and anti-imperialist, he called for a voluntary submission to international law, and the establishment of a cosmopolitan federation of states. An admirer of Rousseau, he was convinced that a republican constitution for each state was essential to a perpetual peace; autocratic rulers might see wars as "a kind of amusement" at the expense of others, but if war depended on popular consent, citizens would be reluctant to embark on "so dangerous an enterprise." The German philosopher called for the abolition of standing armies: voluntary military training of citizens for defense was acceptable, but to hire mercenaries meant to use men as "mere machines and instruments" and not as ends in themselves. He deplored the fact that international jurists like Grotius, Pufendorf, and Vattel were cited to justify the right to engage in certain forms of aggression, though no state thought it necessary to refrain from activities those jurists condemned, and insisted that no state had a right to interfere in the government of another. He denounced bond-slavery in the Americas, and European conquests in Asia and Africa which had led to oppression, wars, and famines, all this being the work of powers who saw themselves as "chosen believers while they live on the fruits of iniquity."[17] The liberal philosopher rejected the argument that wars bringing an advanced culture to backward peoples were justifiable: for him, "supposedly good intentions cannot wash away the stain of injustice from the means which are used to implement them."[18]

In 1798, Kant argued that human progress depended not on an increase of man's moral capacities – only a "new creation or supernatural influence" could accomplish this – but on the readiness of men to submit to the duty of obedience to law. Such an improvement, coming partly from "a love of honour" and partly from self-interest, would "ultimately extend to the external relations between the various peoples, until a cosmopolitan society is created." The "*spirit of commerce*" which "sooner or later takes hold of every people" was in opposition to war, making the duty to work for peace "more than an empty chimera." Gradually, "war, the greatest obstacle to morality and the invariable enemy of progress, first becomes gradually more humane, then more infrequent, and finally disappears completely as a mode of aggression." While finding all passion "blameworthy," Kant urged a "true enthusiasm" directed to the achievement of this moral ideal; this required a "greatness of soul" that had already been revealed in the early wars of the French Revolution when the people had risen up to defeat "the old military aristocracy's concept of honour."[19]

Kant's philosophical speculations were translated into social and economic analysis by late eighteenth- and nineteenth-century liberals. Many of these may never have read the German philosopher, but their convictions like his were shaped by the politics of the enlightenment and the moral presuppositions of the Reformation. For the classical political economists, following Smith and Ricardo, the self-interest of the industrial classes led them to seek peace even as the interests (and psychological proclivities) of the quasi-feudal landed governing classes directed them to violence and aggression. Such a view of politics and society became a central part of the creed of Victorian liberals, and particularly of the more doctrinaire Radical liberals.

Radical politicians and writers were to describe the contest between industrial and landed society as a kind of class struggle. The Manchester manufacturer and Radical and pacifist leader Richard Cobden spoke of two contending parties, "the commercial interest" as the party of peace, and "the territorial interest" as that of war: "the middle and industrious classes of England can have no interest apart from the preservation of peace," Cobden asserted in 1836; "the honours, the fame, the emoluments of war belong not to them; the battle-plain is the harvest field of the aristocracy, watered with the blood of the people."[20] Leoni Levi, a Radical economist at University College,

London, wrote of "the mercantile element" and "the military element": the latter favored "triumphs and adventures," while it was a sober, rational, and pacific commerce and industry that paid the burdensome costs of war.[21] The liberal historian W. E. H. Lecky was confident in the 1860s that the "spirit of rationalism," as well as that of democratic liberty, had undermined any interest in conquest in the modern world.[22]

"We may safely say," the Radical historian H. T. Buckle optimistically observed in the mid-1850s, "that, in our country, a love of war is, as a national taste, utterly extinct," for the industrial and intellectual classes of the advanced nations were establishing a rule of public opinion that would make war impossible. For Buckle, who had read Kant, war was the second greatest evil known to humanity – the first being religious intolerance. The growth of knowledge, not "moral teachings," had vanquished intolerance; now knowledge assisted by the economic interest of the industrial classes would bring about the end of war. Progress in the sciences had increased "the authority of the intellectual classes," and sharpened the conflict between them and "the military class": in barbarous countries, "the only merit [was] personal courage," but this primitive "dominion of force" was giving way in advanced societies to the "authority of thought." War was doomed, Buckle wrote, because there existed "certain classes of society which have an interest in the preservation of peace, and whose united authority is sufficient to control those other classes whose interests lie in the prosecution of war." The "antagonism" between the liberal industrial classes and the feudal class was one "between thought and action, between the internal and the external, between argument and violence, between persuasion and force; or, to sum up the whole, between men who live by the pursuits of peace and those who live by the practice of war."[23]

Buckle noted the antagonism between "the internal and the external," the former the preserve of liberal society, and the latter of feudal. For the British advocates of economic rationality, internal structure shaped by economic interest in the long run determined foreign policy. The historians of nineteenth-century Germany, notably Ranke and his followers, whose country possessed a very different social and political base and geopolitical position, saw considerations of power among nations as primary. Even after Germany became fully industrialized (albeit under Junker control), the historian Otto Hintze, despite a sensitivity to social forces, would in 1906 call it a liberal and socialist delusion "to consider class conflict the only driving force in history." Conflict between nations had been "far more important"; "it has even often suppressed internal strife or forced it into compromise." "Throughout the ages, pressure from without has been a determining influence on internal structure," Hintze observed, noting that the necessities of warfare would determine, as they always had, "the form and spirit of the state's organization": Land forces gave a "military cast" to the state, while sea power, lacking "feudal vestiges," served commercial and industrial interests and, because of the importance of capital and technology to its development, stood with the "progressive" and "modern forces of life."[24]

Certainly Britain's naval predominance rested in good part on her considerable capital. A Liberal ex-prime minister, Lord Rosebery, was to declare in 1900 that his country had "two supreme assets, to a degree which no other country in the world possesses": "they are our navy and our capital – weapons of enormous importance in time of war and instruments of enormous weight in times of peace."[25] Britain's capital resources, among their many uses as tools of power, served to intimidate potential naval rivals. That England was the richest country in the world persuaded them that she would always be able to keep ahead in naval construction. On the other hand, an industrial Britain was on principle frugal, frequently parsimonious. Liberals in office were determined to cut expenditures in all areas, and the Radicals regarded the services as the devil's playground. Britain's status as an island, however, freed her from the necessity of maintaining a large and expensive army, and since her continental rivals had to provide first of all for their military establishments, this left England able to concentrate her available resources on ships.

The Pax Britannica and the phases of development

It is customary to think of the Pax Britannica as extending from the victory at Waterloo in 1815 to the beginning of the First World War. It can be argued that the time of a British economic and naval predominance may have begun earlier, and not have lasted quite so long. A French writer has not hesitated to speak of much of the eighteenth century as one of "la prépondérance anglaise,"[26] but this was hardly a time of peace but one of commercial wars waged on a world-wide scale. During the so-called Pax, of course, there were more limited wars on the continent, and also scores of minor conflicts in colonial areas. Most Liberals, though not always Radicals, considered these non-European engagements as legitimate efforts to crush barbarism and to enter into a trade forbidden by selfish and despotic rulers. (Although initially, as in the 1839 Opium war with China, the Tories objected to the waging of a war in the interest of merchants,[27] they came to accept such actions.) What further distinguished these conflicts from the wars of eighteenth-century mercantilism, of which later liberals strongly disapproved, was Britain's nineteenth-century interest in imposing not commercial monopoly but rather a free trade for all nations.

We may outline – somewhat simplistically – a three-fold division of England's economic and political development from the fifteenth century through the time of the Pax. First we have a largely traditional society (that is, land-based, quasi-feudal, and hierarchical); this was followed, between the sixteenth and eighteenth centuries, by a mixed landed-mercantile society, one more and more infiltrated though not entirely dominated by a bellicose commerce; and, finally, we have the relatively pacific industrial society of the Pax Britannica, with the abolition of the corn laws in 1846 by an alliance of the industrial and commercial classes serving as a symbolic date for the defeat, but hardly extinction, of the earlier, more traditional society and governing class. It has sometimes been assumed that in the feudal and mercantilist eras, power was the strongest motive of political conduct, that in the modern, liberal era which extended into the twentieth century, rational, economic interest became preponderant, and, in more recent decades, that ideology has occupied an increasingly influential position. But periods during which a particular motive was believed preeminent cannot be precisely marked, and other motives have always demanded and received consideration and on occasion assumed control. A concern for power, for instance, continued to exist in each period, possessing a social base and at times reinforced by only partially-repressed instinct. Attitudes toward power were necessarily affected by changes in the perception of interest and ideology: for example, while politicians and merchants of pre-industrial times understood that to increase the national wealth significantly meant depriving other countries of trade by effective competition, or force, or both, the new industry made significant, absolute increases in the production of goods possible; consequently Adam Smith's view in 1776 that the ability of a nation to defend itself was more important than an increase in its wealth marked the beginning of a time when an observer might envision a serious discrepancy between the two.

But the new industrial era, beginning in the late eighteenth century, was hardly all of one piece, and a number of economists and political scientists have employed the Kondratieff cycle to describe its stages. The major portion of the period of this study is included within three fifty-five year Kondratieffs. A critical element in differentiating these may be the readiness to assume risks, which Mahan saw as characteristic of maritime society, and the Austrian liberal economist J. A. Schumpeter, in his various writings, saw as defining the stages of capitalism.[28]

The first of the three Kondratieffs extends from 1787 to 1842: we may call it "entrepreneurial," for this was the time of innovation and expansion, as Schumpeter noted, when the industrial classes were most ready to take the risks of enterprise. These risk-takers were no longer merchant-adventurers gambling on the success of a voyage, as in the previous mercantilist period, but sober workmen (frequently protestant Dissenters from the established church) determined that their industry and frugality would bring them success. The second, from 1843 to 1897, Schumpeter labelled "bourgeois." It was a time of self-confident laissez-faire and free trade, one of consolidation, the extension at home and abroad of a previously developed technology in undertakings whose profitability was already proved; this was the era that Schumpeter called "the railroadization of the world," a task pioneered by British capitalists. The third stage, the half-century after 1897, which Schumpeter described as "neo-mercantilist," was one in which innovative entrepreneurship was discouraged (by a slothful readiness to enjoy the profits of already established businesses, egalitarian *ressentiment*, and so on), and risk-takers were replaced by a new managerial class even less prepared to gamble than the owner-conservators of the bourgeois stage.[29] Laissez-faire and free trade came under attack: groups of industrialists demanded tariff protection to lessen the perils of German and American competition; others turned to programs of social reform to fend off possible revolution.

We may see these economic stages, broadly and with qualification, as having given their character to the general political outlook of the time, as well as to the naval strategies that prevailed. The mercantilist period before the 1780s, one of trade innovation and political risk-taking (the establishment of colonies and trading posts, as well as of readiness to seize a rival's profitable colonies and trade), was a time when trade, war, and piracy appeared not dissimilar, and, as we shall see, when naval strategy amalgamated the three. In the following entrepreneurial period of industrialism, with the quasi-feudal landed classes still in political ascendancy, the traditional strategy of sea power was retained, though directed after 1815 to accommodate the moral values (and interests) of the commercial and industrial classes, not merely to continuing a war against piracy, but to extirpating a sinful slave trade. In the succeeding bourgeois stage, a group of pacifistic Radicals, seizing the moral initiative, condemned the use of force even to end slavery, agreeing with Kant that "supposedly good intentions" could no longer "wash away the stain of injustice" of violence. A liberal nation convinced that trade was replacing war now favored the maritime policies which legitimated most neutral commerce with belligerents, and saw the traditional naval strategy of commercial war as immoral, as well as injurious to its economic interests. Shipowners and merchants, anxious to secure themselves further against the risks of war, soon called for immunity from capture of all private property at sea, even that of the enemy. (Schumpeter wrote of the Liberal prime minister Gladstone's development of "that consistent policy of *détente* which in England has never been seriously challenged since ... and which could be shown to be the most perfect expression of the economic and cultural structure of capitalist society.")[30] Finally, in the neo-mercantilist period, Tories warned the nation about increased political dangers from abroad, and called for a more powerful fleet, and the revival of a strategy of commercial war. When Radicals opposed naval expansion and urged, instead, domestic reform, Tories saw them, and liberalism generally, as wedded to peace even at the risk of national catastrophe. The liberal concern with the rational and internal again confronted the conservative perception of the threat of irrational and external power.

We wish to investigate how liberal ideology, and commercial and industrial interest (so closely allied in rationale and historical association with liberalism), helped to shape Great Britain's maritime and naval policy and strategy from the end of the eighteenth to the early twentieth century. By strategy, I mean how a state intends to employ power – economic, or military/naval – not merely to defend itself against attempts by others to impose their will, but also to enforce its own position when necessary. For Radical liberals, antagonistic to the exercise of power on principle, an uninhibited ability to sail the seas and to trade with whom one pleased was a right established on natural justice. For most liberals, however, questions such as the rights of neutral vessels when England was at war appeared more those of policy which statesmen – weighing both moral and practical considerations – must decide. For many Tories and naval officers, liberal efforts to secure the protection of neutral trade or immunity from maritime capture of private property by international agreement overlooked vital strategic considerations and endangered the nation's existence. During this time of the Pax Britannica, a liberal naval policy often came into conflict with what many saw as sound naval strategy.

The early nineteenth-century German military strategist Carl von Clausewitz, in a spirit very different from that of Kant whom he otherwise admired, wrote slightingly of "self-imposed" limits on the use of force called for by international law as "hardly worth mentioning."[31] But Germany in Clausewitz's time had not undergone the economic and cultural changes that the industrial revolution and the liberal-democratic ethos were effecting in Britain. By the end of the eighteenth century, England had begun this momentous transformation even as she became the world's greatest naval power. Strategy in a liberal and industrial society had to take into account the moral factor, upon which rested the social cohesion of a people. Democratic electorates needed to be persuaded that a war morally justified the sacrifice of its sons and the expenditure of its subsidies.[32]

Separately and in tandem, industrial and commercial interest and liberal ideology sought to restrain the state's use of physical force abroad, and thus to counter the call to aggressive instinct by an appeal to rational interest and to moral duty. Radical liberals were the enemies of strategy, which they identified with the exercise of sinful power, and saw preparations for war as engineered by the landed and military classes to further their selfish interests. Although sea power had helped maritime states to foster a profitable trade and free institutions, by the middle decades of the nineteenth century a pacifistic liberalism came to think of its advocates as enemies of liberty, and Britain's exercise of sea power beyond the minimum necessary for defense as wicked – an atavism that threatened both peace and a commerce that had acquired an ideological mission.

Forces of ideology, interest, and power which had been in symbiotic harmony in the eighteenth century, now appeared in hostile contradiction. In a world in which the nature of men and of nations had not altered as much as Victorian and Edwardian optimists believed, the Radicals charted, and a liberal England seemed at times prepared to follow, a course which assumed the imminence of a perpetual peace. Even a "hawkish" nineteenth-century Liberal prime minister, Viscount Palmerston, somewhat bemused by the glow of "progressive" opinion and made heady by the mounting profits of trade, was for a time to support a change in maritime policy that he would later describe as "suicidal." Maritime society, in classical dialectical fashion, seemed to bear the seeds of its own demise, or so some commentators saw the matter in the years before 1914. That Great Britain managed none the less to survive the crisis of a world war was owing, in part at least, to what liberals called the atavistic survival of "reactionary" ideas and conduct.

[2] The Fierce Trident

Non illi imperium pelagi saevumque tridentem,
Sed mihi sorte datum.
(The fierce trident and the empire of the sea
Have been given by fortune not to him but to me.)
Virgil, *Aeneid*, quoted by Viscount Sidmouth, House of Lords, 1809

Krieg, Handel und Piraterie,
Dreieinig sind sie, nicht zu trennen.
(War, Commerce, and Piracy,
Three-in-one are they,
Never to be parted.)

Goethe, *Faust*, Part II, Act V

The pope in 1493 divided the South Atlantic and Pacific oceans and the Asian and American lands washed by these seas between Portugal and Spain. A century later a commercial and maritime Holland sent merchantmen into the waters assigned by the pope to Portugal, and in 1604 the Dutch East India Company commissioned the jurist Hugo Grotius to prepare a brief justifying the Company's right to trade in the seas that the Iberian powers claimed as their monopoly. A part of his brief entitled *Mare Liberum*, the Free Sea, was to prove not merely the legal framework for the Dutch challenge to the Catholic Powers, but a foundation stone of international law.

Grotius appealed to natural law "innate in every individual" and "derived from nature, the common mother of us all," in this tract that established the liberal view of freedom of the seas. God had ordained that nations would possess different products so that a mutually beneficial trade "free to all men" would be the basis of international friendship. How, then, could any nation prevent other nations "from selling to one another, from bartering with one another, actually from communicating with one another?" The commercial interests of the Dutch in the East Indies were therefore "bound up with the advantage of the whole human race." The sea was "common to all," and God would not "prosper the efforts" of those who violated nature's laws, nor permit the triumph of men who "for the sake alone of private gain oppose a common benefit of the human race." It was before the courts of conscience and of public opinion that Grotius brought his indictment against the engrossing mercantilism of the Spaniards and the Portuguese, proclaiming that the just and "powerless" must always appeal to these tribunals against the powerful who would otherwise perpetrate injustices at will.[1]

Grotius would be cited in the following centuries as the founder not only of the doctrine of freedom of the seas, but of what was to be known as the "old rule" which permitted the capture in time of war of enemy goods even aboard neutral vessels. Grotius's principal successors in the development of international law, notably Pufendorf and Vattel, accepted this rule. Enlightened opinion in the eighteenth and nineteenth centuries would, however, regard the right of capture as a violation of the freedom of the seas and no more than piracy. Grotius's name would therefore be invoked not only by liberal advocates of maritime freedom and the "new rule" of "free ships, free goods," which prohibited the capture of enemy goods aboard neutral ships, but also by defenders of the old rule, principally the statesmen of Great Britain. For by the middle of the eighteenth century England had replaced Holland as the strongest maritime and naval state, and she wished to make full use of the belligerent right of capture that she believed necessary to the effectiveness of her sea power. Great Britain was determined to wield what Virgil had called "the fierce trident."

The old rule and the new

In 1753 the Duke of Newcastle, on behalf of the government of King George II, dispatched a defense of the old rule in a letter to the king of Prussia. The Prussian king had charged a belligerent England, when she was at war with France several years earlier, with having taken illegal action on the high seas against a neutral Prussian merchantman, and he expropriated British assets as compensation for damages. The Newcastle reply, largely the work of the solicitor-general William Murray (who as the Earl of Mansfield was to become an ornament of the common-law bench), argued in support of the belligerent maritime rights of the old rule, already seen as the palladium on which British security depended. The letter's arguments were accepted by the leading international lawyers of the day as well as by the French political theorist Montesquieu.[2]

In time of war, the Newcastle letter declared, citing Grotius and his successors, a belligerent had the right to capture enemy ships and enemy property on the high seas. From this general principle, the international jurists had deduced others:

> That the Goods of an Enemy, on Board the Ship of a Friend, may be taken.
>
> That the lawful Goods of a Friend, on board the Ship of an Enemy, ought to be restored.
>
> That Contraband Goods, going to the Enemy, tho' the Property of a Friend, may be

> taken as Prize; because supplying the enemy, with what enables him better to carry on the War, is a departure from Neutrality.

In order to determine the nationality of a ship and the ownership of its cargo, the law of nations had granted to belligerents a right of search, and all ships were liable "to be stopped, and examined" to discover "whether they are carrying Contraband to the Enemy." Britain conceded that particular treaties – for example, the Anglo-Dutch treaty of 1674 as well as that of Utrecht in 1713 between France and England – had inverted the generally accepted rule, making neutral goods aboard an enemy ship a prize of war, while enemy goods on a neutral ship were free. (This somewhat weakened the force of the British argument, and this inversion of the old rule was to be followed by the French maritime courts until the middle of the nineteenth century.) None the less England, dismissing the Prussian assertion "that the Sea is Free," rejected the new rule of free ships, free goods.[3]

The Newcastle letter also rejected Prussia's claim to the jurisdiction of her own courts in cases where Prussian property was at stake. The British government insisted that jurisdiction belonged to the admiralty courts of the country whose subjects had made the capture, a position that favored England, the predominant naval power and the state that would most often be the captor. Of course, the courts of the captor country had to decide such cases according to the accepted law of nations, and enemy property on the high seas could not be claimed as a prize without a "regular judicial Proceeding" in which both parties were heard and all the evidence (ship's papers, testimonies of ship's masters and officers on oath, and so on) scrutinized. If a seizure were made "without probable cause," the captor, more often than not a privateer (a former merchantman now armed and sailing under letters of marque) was obliged to pay costs and damages.[4]

This encounter between England and Prussia was an early skirmish in a century-long battle in which the weaker maritime powers and the neutral merchants acted in alliance. If the new rule were to prevail, France would be able to compensate for her weakness at sea in time of war by enlisting vessels of neutrals to supply her with the goods she required from abroad, without fear of their capture by British warships. The Prussians, the Russians, the Scandinavian powers and, most particularly, the Dutch (who possessed the most considerable carrying trade among the neutrals) all favored the new rule, for their merchants wished to enjoy the profits of a trade with the belligerents during the wars for empire between England and France.

With the renewal of war between France and England in 1756, the so-called Seven Years' War, France again adopted the strategy made necessary by her inferiority at sea. The French fleet withdrew to home ports where they could be protected by shore fortifications against British naval guns. A portion of the British navy kept watch on the French ports to make certain that this enemy fleet-in-being did not make a surprise sortie. Once more France called on neutral ships to maintain not merely the commerce with French overseas colonies, upon which colonial economic well-being and political contentment depended, but even the busy coastal trade between one French port and another. The British responded by promulgating "the rule of 1756," forbidding to neutrals in time of war the coastal and colonial trades which French mercantilist regulations denied them in peacetime. Ships of the Royal Navy as well as privateers proceeded to cruise the seas, and to profit by capturing prizes not only of enemy vessels, but also of goods to or from France or her colonies carried by neutral ships.

In 1757, the barrister Charles Jenkinson, the future first Earl of Liverpool, wrote an often reprinted tract defending the rule of 1756 against the attack that it was an illegal innovation. "It must always be the interest of England to protect the just rights of commerce, and to support those principles which promote the labours of mankind, since she herself can only be great from the virtuous industry of her people," he observed. But under neutral flags, French colonial commerce "would have passed safe and unmolested through our fleet, if Britain, again raising her spirit, had not resolved that by this means her naval power should not be rendered useless." Even Grotius, who had written "so nobly on the freedom of navigation" and "laboured to give the greatest extent to the rights of commerce," had conceded that a neutral flag could not protect enemy trade. England's admiralty courts, finally, were "more wisely calculated to preserve the freedom of navigation, than those of any other country," and in them foreign traders had "in favour of their property all the security which the nature of the thing will admit." Jenkinson concluded that the rule of 1756 was entirely consistent with prevailing attitudes toward trade and power[5] – which were of course those which Adam Smith was later to describe as mercantilist.

Shelburne and Fox: from expediency to ideology

A naval strategy based on the old rule and the rule of 1756 helped to bring victory to England in the Seven Years' War, but also made enemies of the neutrals and stirred a French desire for revenge. After the American colonies declared their independence in the 1770s, the French entered the war on the side of the rebels, and England returned to her traditional strategy, though at this time she refrained from invoking the rule of 1756. None the less, British naval interference with neutral commerce proved sufficiently irksome to spur the formation in 1780 of a League of Armed Neutrality, whose members included Russia, Holland, Sweden and Denmark, under the leadership of Catherine the Great. The League wished to impose a decisive change in international maritime law. The government of Lord North determined not to submit to any of the League demands, a decision that disturbed the leaders of the opposition.

Among these were a group of Whigs formerly associated with the elder William Pitt, the Earl of Chatham, England's charismatic leader during the Seven Years' War. These Chathamites found Lord North's inflexibility a sorry contrast to the adroit management of Pitt, and feared disaster. In June 1780, the principal spokesman for this group, the Earl of Shelburne (who three years later as prime minister negotiated the Treaty of Paris that recognized American independence) rose to move a vote of censure.

Shelburne found "alarming" a passage in Catherine's manifesto that called for the new rule, a change in international law that would "terminate in the ruin of Britain, or at least in the overthrow of her naval power." If France and Spain could obtain vital naval and military stores in neutral ships, "then, farewell for ever to the naval power and glory of Great Britain!" England must remind all the European nations, especially the Dutch, of the danger to Europe if "so formidable and ambitious" a nation as France should add the "dominion of the sea" to her land power. Yet Britain's "bullying and oppressive" conduct on the seas had alienated her long-time friend, Holland; the North government had in fact broken the treaty of 1674 which permitted the Dutch to continue their carrying trade to all countries, even to Britain's enemies. If Britain did not quickly restore these Dutch rights and stop the wholesale seizure of neutral goods, this as a temporary concession, the neutral powers, encouraged by France, meant to call a congress at The Hague to frame a maritime code based on the new rule and binding upon the belligerents. Britain would then be forced either to accede, or to go to war with all of Europe.[6] Another Chathamite, Lord Camden, also warned his countrymen that "our seas, as well as the ocean, would soon be visited by powerful squadrons" if Britain persisted in her rigid and arrogant behavior.[7]

Viscount Stormont, one of the principal secretaries of state, defended the ministry's strategy. "Placed as it were by Providence, between the northern and southern parts of Europe," England would have deserved blame if she had not "cut off those sinews of war" by stopping the supplies of naval stores destined for Brest, France's principal Atlantic naval station. Stormont dismissed the possibility of Europe uniting to impose a new naval code since the interest of Russia and England in containing French power was the same.[8] (Shelburne's motion was lost.[9] But after the fall of the North government in 1782, Shelburne, as the prime minister, suspended the right of search so as to avoid war with Russia.)

The opposition in 1780, as we have seen, did not attack the old rule, but rather its inflexible enforcement. They did not advocate capitulation to the League, but compromise. There was "a medium to be taken," the Duke of Grafton argued, for England could cut off a substantial portion of naval and military stores bound for France without indiscriminate interference with neutral commerce. "All parties [might] rest contented when the principle of right was not strictly contended for," he observed.[10] The basis of the opposition arguments was pragmatic not ideological. The opposition was prepared to trim Britain's maritime principles to fit the circumstances of the moment, without yielding anything that might prove advantageous in the future.

During the following decade and a half, maritime law became even more of a muddle as states contracted treaties whose provisions first accepted the universality of the old rule and then made particular exceptions. England herself in a treaty with the United States in 1794 agreed to allow the ships of America, which was becoming a great carrying nation, the privilege of trading with the colonies of France, with whom England was then at war, this on the model of privileges granted to the Dutch in 1674. But events were moving towards a new crisis. In the 1790s Britain began what was to become nearly a quarter of a century of war with France. England found herself hard-pressed by the end of that decade as French revolutionary armies were imposing their will on the continent. Once again, Britain determined to strike at France by crippling her commerce.

As in earlier conflicts, Great Britain's indiscriminate policy of search and seizure of merchant ships on the high seas antagonized neutrals. In 1799 a frigate in the convoy of a Danish man-of-war refused to be stopped and searched by a British cruiser. The Danish government protested this insult to the convoying armed-ship, insisting that its presence alone ought to have been a sufficient guarantee of the neutral nationality of the merchantman and of its being free of contraband. Denmark's protest on behalf of the rights of neutrals was taken up by Sweden and Russia, and a new League of Armed Neutrality, like that of 1780 under Russian direction, was formed in 1800. This confederacy of Baltic powers threatened war if England did not moderate her conduct.

There were several parliamentary debates in the early months of 1801 in which a number of the more properly ideological arguments of the new liberalism made their first appearance. The principles of the French Revolution had had an impact on a small but articulate minority in both houses, particularly on that group of Whigs that supported Charles James Fox. Moreover, there were now politicians of both parties who were partisans of the new liberal economics of Adam Smith. We must remember that the dominant doctrine of mercantilism saw commerce as a species of war, and that in the eighteenth century English merchants and shipowners often favored wars as opportunities to enrich themselves – to gain prizes at sea and to capture foreign and colonial markets. America was the harbinger of a new liberal era: with a large merchant marine and no effective navy, the United States intended that her wealth proceed by commerce not war. The American example, Smithian economics, and the political principles of the French Revolution all had an influence on a burgeoning English maritime liberalism.

No less important was the recognition that the United States was determined to defend the rights of neutrals.

The chief exponent of the new liberalism in the upper house was the Earl of Shelburne, now the Marquess of Lansdowne, who had long been a follower of Adam Smith. Neither the old nor the new rule was inherently more just, Lansdowne began, in pragmatic vein; it was a question not of law but of power. England possessed a maritime preponderance which made the old rule more convenient, but conditions were changing. The rise of the United States with its considerable merchant marine was the great new fact in international commerce and politics. America was already a champion of neutral rights at sea, and since 1783 England had driven an increasingly profitable trade with her former colonies which she did not wish to endanger. "Was it possible to prevent America from carrying any kind of goods as a neutral nation?" While it was "unpleasant to lose the power once possessed," yet if "obliged to forego the maritime code," England might turn its energies to profit "by other forms of wealth."[11] (This was the liberal reply to the Tory Lord Eldon's forthrightly mercantilist defense of the right of search, in an earlier debate, as "the foundation of our naval glory, our commerce, and our wealth.")[12] "Peace alone would raise our commerce," not "the assertion of rights whose basis was power," Lansdowne concluded in the authentic accents of nineteenth-century liberalism; "commerce was a vast organisation which one nation could not violate without injuring the whole system."[13] A leader of the Whigs in the House of Commons, Charles Grey, argued along similar lines: the new rule, he declared, would be "most favourable to that power which has the most commerce," that is to Great Britain.[14]

The Tory prime minister, the younger William Pitt, a son of Chatham, rose to defend the old rule in the lower house. Although like Lansdowne a disciple of Adam Smith, Pitt chose to deal with the question in the traditional context of power. The new Armed Neutrality was attempting "arbitrarily to force upon Europe ... Jacobinical principles" – that is, the new rule. The prime minister peremptorily dismissed demands that the right of search be suspended when an armed neutral convoy guaranteed that there was no contraband in the cargo. Nor was he more sympathetic to the neutral demand that a blockade had to be effective – unlike Britain's "paper blockade" of the time – to be legal. Pitt called on his countrymen to resist the neutral demands "to the last shilling and the last drop of blood." Why ought they "to sacrifice the maritime greatness of Britain at the shrine of Russia?"[15]

Pitt's long-time parliamentary rival, the liberal Whig Charles James Fox, cautiously replied that he had no wish to give up "the benefit of maritime preponderance," which he conceded would be "wholly lost" if neutrals were granted the privileges they sought. Such a course would be "at variance with common sense." Yet it was "repugnant to reason" that "mere naval superiority should despise every rule of relative justice, and by bare-faced power, make its own will the law of the ocean." There was a "true medium" between a neutral shamelessly supplying one of the belligerents with the materials of war, and a belligerent "insisting upon a universal right of search" and "making innocent commerce the sport of its whim, in express contempt of specific regulation." The latter had unfortunately become British practice. Why could not England exercise the right to search only "upon lawful or urgent suspicion" instead of "subjecting the commerce of the world to vexatious and insulting interruptions and injuries without stint or distinctions"? That Prussia was indulged in her hostility to the old rule while Sweden and Denmark were not proved that Pitt was ready "to give everything to force and nothing to reason." Fox predicted that force would not extinguish neutral claims, for these would be revived when neutrals became sufficiently strong to renew them. The natural direction of affairs was moving toward "the general freedom of commerce."[16]

Henry Addington, the chancellor of the exchequer and soon to become Pitt's successor as prime minister, defended England's belligerent rights at sea on geopolitical grounds. "The true interests of Europe" would be injured if "maritime and continental superiority should be engrossed by the same power." English "naval preeminence" during the war had protected European commerce from piracy and the nations of the continent from French despotism. Addington urged the northern powers to consider their conduct carefully, for by "abridging our power" they would "diminish their own security."[17]

Refurbishing the old rule

In 1800 Pitt's foreign secretary Lord Grenville commissioned a young barrister Robert Ward, the author of a history of international law published five years earlier,[18] to frame a reply to the legal claims of the Armed Neutrality. When the tract appeared in late March 1801 it was handsomely praised by Sir William Scott, later Lord Stowell, a judge of the high court of admiralty whose decisions were to be widely regarded as models of impartiality. Ward was to receive a more practical expression of appreciation in 1804 when he was named under-secretary of state for foreign affairs.[19]

In his 1801 tract Ward observed that the new rule found widespread support not because it represented a "natural system" of justice but because of the advantages it offered to the strategy of the weaker belligerent and to the greed of neutral merchants. French policy was, as would "always be [the case] with the inferior Belligerent at sea, to turn the whole of their marine resources into the means of offence;" and French support for neutral interests was not based upon liberal doctrine, but was rather a "usurpation" designed to secure "unlawful advantages" and the "total deprivation of the lawful means of defence to us." The neutrals argued, following Grotius, that the sea was free to all and that the right of men to conduct a peaceful commerce and to profit by their industry were principles grounded in nature. But if the right of navigation were "sacred" and "founded upon the absoluteness of the freedom of the sea, and the entire want of dominion, and consequent jurisdiction of the ocean," how could a ban on contraband, or a blockade, or an embargo be justified? How could England wage maritime war at all? Such a view was consequently "visionary, partaking of little less than the original Jacobinical madness." Reasoning from "principles of general equity," the authority of Grotius and Pufendorf, and the provisions of treaties, Ward concluded that "the natural right is on the side of the Belligerent" and that "the neutral claim, where allowed, is a matter of the purest convention." England "must contend to the end of her resources" for her maritime rights "or cease to be a nation that has any resources at all."[20]

On 2 April 1801, shortly after the publication of Ward's tract, England made a reply of a different order to the threats of the Armed Neutrality. A British fleet under the command of Admiral Lord Nelson surprised and destroyed the main body of the Danish navy off Copenhagen. Since the blow was struck without warning at a nation with whom England was still at peace, it was hardly Nelson's or his country's finest hour. Yet the strike proved effective, so much so that it was to be repeated in 1807, and a century later there would be talk about "Copenhagening" the German fleet.

The Addington government in the last months of 1801 negotiated with Russia a Convention on maritime rights that sought to compromise differences on maritime policy. The supporters of the new ministry, also a Tory one, praised the Convention's "judicious mixture of firmness and moderation."[21] Its critics, the recently deposed Pittites, were unhappy that the ministry had not made better use of Nelson's victory.

The former foreign minister Grenville complained that "our system of maritime laws [was now] . . . shaken, its exercise embarrassed, and its clearest regulations made matter of eternal dissension and contest." Russia would be permitted to carry naval (though not military) stores to France, and to buy goods in one French port and sell them in another. Neutral vessels might now be manned by crews up to one-half of whom were enemy subjects, instead of the previous limit of no more than one-third. Were these harmless concessions as the ministry insisted? It was not wise "to purchase present ease by the sacrifice of future strength," for the principles of the British naval code must be regarded as "fixed and permanent." Grenville urged no turning away from "the immutable principles of natural law, or from the long-established usage of civilized societies" to "the fleeting dreams of modern speculation."[22]

In reply Lord Hawkesbury, the foreign secretary and the son of Charles Jenkinson who had defended the rule of 1756 nearly a half-century earlier, argued that by making the exercise of their maritime rights "as little vexatious as possible, we might prop them up more effectually." The Convention "contained an ample recognition of all that was essential to us as the first maritime power on the globe," and England had gained "all that justice, all that policy required."[23] The admiralty judge Sir William Scott supported the government, noting that the right of search, "one of the pillars of our maritime strength" without which "all the rest were almost useless," had been preserved.[24] The Earl of Darnley, opening the debate in the upper house, rejoiced that Addington unlike Pitt had not continued "to bully and insult" the powers of Europe.[25] Eldon, now lord chancellor, observed that by not insisting on "trivial points" England displayed that she was "not intolerant in her power," while still maintaining her traditional positions that free bottoms did not make free goods, that ships of war (though, because of a "false philanthropy," no longer privateers) had the right of search, and that a blockade of ports was acceptable practice.[26] Lord Cathcart similarly delighted in the frustration of the new maritime code which, he noted ironically, was "to dignify this age of reason."[27]

All but one of the peers praised Admiral Nelson's performance at Copenhagen, and in the debate in the upper house Lord Nelson gave his support to the Convention. It was a triumph to have destroyed "a proposition so monstrous" as the new rule, Nelson declared. If the northern powers had not yielded in this matter, England ought to have fought "while a single man, a single shilling, or even a single drop of blood remained in the country."[28] The lone critic of the Danish exploit in the House of Lords was the liberal Whig Lord Holland, a nephew and admirer of Charles James Fox. Holland dismissed England's defense of her maritime rights as unimportant, and the attack on Copenhagen as having "idly wasted the blood and treasure of the country in a war ... merely to maintain a speculative point."[29]

The merchants versus the mercantilist war against commerce

After a brief peace with Napoleon signed in the early spring of 1802, Britain once more found herself at war the following year. Pitt returned to office. Both parties were now convinced that given the restless ambitions of the Emperor there could be no lasting understanding with France. After Pitt's death in 1806 a coalition government of Pittites and Whigs, headed by Grenville and with Fox as foreign secretary, issued orders-in-council that sought to prevent neutrals from supplying France by sea. Napoleon responded by the Berlin and Milan Decrees of 1806 and 1807, and initiated the so-called "continental system" to block British goods from Europe. Even more stringent English orders-in-council were promulgated in retaliation; the rule of 1756 was invoked as it had been in the Seven Years' War, and a blockade designed to restrict the trade of neutrals was instituted.

In an extraordinary departure from international law, England insisted that all neutral vessels call at a British port to purchase a license before journeying to their European destinations. The purpose of certain of these regulations was to force British manufactures on the continent – a perversion of the idea of blockade and perhaps the epitome of a mercantilist strategy. The Royal Navy employed the right of search not merely to uncover contraband and unlicensed cargoes but to seize and impress into service seamen on American ships who were alleged to be of British nationality. Neutral trade was plagued by the conduct of both belligerents, but since her maritime predominance gave her better means of enforcing her policy, England proved the more troublesome, particularly to the United States.

There was a debate of some years duration concerning the orders-in-council, and the Whig barrister Henry Brougham became the spokesman for those who wished to eliminate those parts of the regulations that most troubled America. A polymath – a fellow of the Royal Society at the age of twenty-five and an editor of the *Edinburgh Review* – Brougham made his mark in the Scottish bar before becoming counsel for the Liverpool merchants who petitioned parliament against these restrictions on trade. So much of English commerce had become dependent on the exchange of American agricultural products for British manufactures that the merchants felt a great stake in preserving peace.

James Stephen, an admiralty lawyer and a master-in-chancery, led the defense of a mercantilist naval strategy against enemy commerce. After some years in the West Indies, Stephen had entered parliament under the sponsorship of the Tory Evangelical Spencer Perceval, who was to become chancellor of the exchequer from 1807 to 1809, and prime minister from 1809 to 1812. Stephen, too, was an Evangelical, as was his brother-in-law William Wilberforce, best known for his leadership of the Evangelical campaign to abolish the slave trade. At the exchequer, Perceval played a prime role in promulgating the orders-in-council, and Brougham was to describe Stephen (a "man of very considerable powers, combined with great firmness of purpose and unquenchable ardour") as the principal force behind the chancellor.[30] A secular-minded Brougham was taken aback by his Evangelical opponent's conviction that the misfortunes of the wars with France were "a punishment inflicted by Providence, because England had more than once rejected the measure for the abolition of slavery!"[31]

But the principal thrust of Stephen's appeals to the public on naval policy and strategy were of a more terrestrial – not to say maritime – order. His two tracts of 1805 and 1807 argued that Britain must either reassert her full maritime rights or perish. Without the economic pressure exerted by British maritime superiority, Stephen insisted in his 1805 tract (written before the erection of the continental system), Napoleon would achieve a "universal empire." England had been able to defeat the House of Bourbon in the past because she could "impoverish our enemies": "We distressed their trade, we intercepted the produce of their colonies, and thus exhausted their treasuries." This British strategy at sea had compelled France to maintain distant fleets and convoys, whose capture not only enriched England but obliged the French to make expensive replacements. This was how "the masters of the sea" had triumphed in the preceding century, "more than by naval victories or colonial conquests." But England had departed from this strategy, and her recent laxity in enforcing her maritime rights allowed France to wage a "war in disguise." By failing to apply the rule of 1756 rigorously, England permitted the French to use neutral shipping fraudulently to carry her commerce.[32]

Stephen excoriated the English "idolators of the neutral flag" (and merchants with an interest in the American trade) who winked at allowing neutrals to profit immorally from the war. American merchantmen habitually abused the spirit of the treaty of 1794, which permitted the carrying of French or Spanish colonial goods to the United States, by making brief, formal stop-overs at American ports before proceeding with their cargoes to Spain or France. By entrusting her colonial commerce to neutrals, France might employ all her fighting ships for offensive war; meanwhile enemy colonial planters, whose produce was transported by neutrals not obliged to pay the higher war insurance premiums imposed on belligerent vessels, were able to compete unfairly with British planters. The high wages offered by an expanding American merchant marine, moreover, attracted British seamen, all the more easily seduced because of the scarcity of legitimate prizes of war on the seas. The Liverpool merchants warned of the danger of war with America, but Stephen insisted that the United States understood that "we alone, of all the nations in the old world, now sustain the sinking cause of civil liberty." Americans would hardly ally themselves with "a military despotism . . . which aspires to universal domination," and were not so foolish as to think the Atlantic "a sufficient rampart" against a France which was "lord of the navies, as well as the armies, of Europe."[33]

Stephen justified the strategy of the orders-in-council by mercantilist theory, and argued that England's industrial pre-eminence would protect British markets against neutral reprisals. France had three times yielded her colonial and coastal trades to neutral shippers simply "to suit her convenience" as a belligerent. This was why England must call upon the just and necessary rule of 1756. Experience had proved that in peacetime the French "attachment to the principle of the colonial monopoly is as strong, nay stronger, than ever." Despite her pretenses in time of war, France had not the slightest intention of permanently opening her colonial trade to foreigners. Nor ought the Liverpool merchants to worry about a loss of the American trade, for English manufactures would continue to be "in demand all over the globe, for their superiority in quality" and "in cheapness." "Take care of your maritime system, and your commerce will take care of itself."[34]

As an appendage to France's new "liberal" colonial policy, Stephen continued, Napoleon now spoke of liberty and equality on the seas as the foundation for a future "pacific system" established on the new rule. This was to be the "maritime code of the nineteenth century." Britain must not be deceived, for what France really wished was a system "for ruining the commerce and marine of this country." England must retain and enforce not only the old rule but also that of 1756 if her commercial and maritime superiority, and with it her security, were not to be undone. "Let us not, therefore, abandon the best means of defence" God had given England, "her navy, and her maritime rights."[35]

Stephen's warnings to his fellow-countrymen bore a different complexion in a neutral United States, which had rebelled against mercantilism a generation earlier, and now saw herself a victim of that system's naval strategy. An anonymous reply to Stephen's tract appeared in America in 1806; its author Gouverneur Morris was a prominent Federalist, which was the pro-English party in his country. Morris accepted the legality of the old rule but believed that Stephen and the British government were giving their undoubted rights "an extravagant extension [which] transgress the bounds of reason and justice," not to speak of the long-accepted law on the matter. The rule of 1756 had no standing in international law, and Britain's licensing system was a dangerous innovation. Certainly there were neutral merchants who engaged in a fraudulent trade; by all means, punish them. But it was necessary to "respect the principle of Justice" and not charge "on all the guilt of a few." Britain wished "to fasten on the necks of other nations, the yoke of her commercial monopoly," Morris charged, and "would grasp at all trade, while complaining that, for the protection of what they already possess, the navy of Britain must be spread over every sea." But "neither the ocean, nor the commerce borne on its bosom, can be considered," as Stephen apparently did, "the private property of any one nation."[36]

Another anonymous rejoinder to the extension of British belligerent rights was published in 1806 by the American secretary of state James Madison. Madison argued, as had Morris, that neither the writings of the international jurists nor the evidence of treaties justified the rule of 1756. Britain herself opened her ports in the West Indies to neutrals in time of war, and Sir William Scott's defense that this privilege had not been granted because of the superior naval power of the enemy only revealed that "the *true* foundation of the principle ... [was] *a mere superiority of force*." Was international law and world commerce to depend not on "any fixed principle of justice, but on the comparative state of naval armaments"? England must not forget the transience of power and her own dependence on supplies from abroad: "her fleets may be called home from the protection of commerce to the defence of the state"; "her harvest may fail, her existence may depend on foreign food" brought by neutrals in a commerce not open to them in peacetime. The progress of civilization ought to favor "the rights of those remaining at peace." Madison somewhat ingenuously observed that since war imposed "a variety of privations and embarrassments" on neutral traders, it was reasonable that they enjoy "the advantages which may happen to arise."[37]

In a second tract, published in 1807, James Stephen cautioned British merchants and manufacturers against yielding to neutral arguments or to Napoleon's peace overtures. The French emperor would use peace only "to replenish his treasury and restore his marine," and thus to dispute again England's "undivided possession of the sea." With the machinery of the continental system now in place, Stephen observed that if peace were restored Napoleon would exclude British goods from the European continent by treaties imposed on satellite governments. The French emperor held "the continental gates of the market"; "in war we command all the roads that lead to it, and can therefore starve him into the admission of our trade: in peace, the roads will be free to him, and he will still command the gates." Britain would in peacetime no longer have the power to counter the commercial regulations of the continental system by "the pressure of our hostilities by sea." Other maritime countries would then more easily compete with an encumbered England. Only a maritime war waged against French commerce, Stephen concluded, could defeat Napoleon and preserve British merchants from ruin.[38]

In December 1807 the United States Congress passed an act forbidding American ships to sail for any European port. America hoped that an embargo would enlist the support of British and French merchants on behalf of neutral rights. British commercial interests groaned at the loss of their American trade, and in early 1808 Brougham presented a petition of complaints from the merchants of London, Liverpool, and Manchester at the bar of the House of Commons. This petition and Brougham's arguments revealed the naked self-interest of the commercial classes, before it became embellished by pacific sentiment and liberal rhetoric.

There had been much said about maintaining the predominance of England's sea power, Brougham observed to the Commons, but English merchants and manufacturers had no wish to vaunt "the powers and glories of the British Navy" in the "most remote corners of the earth," as one minister had suggested. Brougham's mercantile clients preferred to consider "their plaguy account books and dry details of profits and loss." ("We are plain men – merchants, manufacturers, and workmen," their petition stated, "and we care not if one half of Europe never heard of the British Navy ... nay, nor knew that there was such a country as England – provided that half were consuming our produce and wearing our manufactures.") America could only pay for the goods she imported from England out of the profits of her trade with the continent. If the Royal Navy succeeded in cutting off American trade with Europe, the United States would use the £8 million she owed British merchants to begin to manufacture for herself. "You will find raised up by your jealousy and violence," Brougham warned, "a rival to your prosperity," capable of becoming "the first manufacturers in the world."[39]

Parliament failed to respond to these entreaties, and the American trade embargo continued. England experienced difficulties: one MP noted that England had "shut the door against the supply of the granaries, by their conduct toward America," and the price of bread rose sharply.[40] But the embargo was proving more injurious to the United States than to the belligerents, and after two years was replaced by a non-intercourse act which banned trade only with England and France. The conduct of the Royal Navy toward American shipping did not improve.

In a House of Lords debate in February 1809, Lord Grenville, whose government had issued the first order-in-council in 1806, publicly changed his mind. America had offered to withdraw her embargo against England if both the orders-in-council (with their licensing provisions) and the rule of 1756 were abandoned. Grenville urged that this offer be accepted. While prepared to wage "a just and legitimate war" in defense of "the maritime rights and the maritime superiority" of England, he believed these could best be preserved by conciliating the United States. America had every reason to resent British efforts to reduce her once again to humiliating dependence. England needed American markets for her manufactures, he reminded the peers, and was dependent on American corn and cotton. Perhaps most revealing of Grenville's change of mood was his reference at this time to Nelson's "ill-advised and unjust" expedition to Copenhagen.[41]

In early March, the debate moved to the lower house. The Whig brewer Samuel Whitbread denounced the unjust orders-in-council, and called for healing the breach with America. The ministry was foolish to believe that Napoleon's armies would mutiny "for want of coffee or tea for breakfast!" The American embargo had made cotton mills in Manchester idle and soon "we shall have a whole nation calling for bread;" on the other hand, "with America by your side, you may defy the world."[42] The Whig Alexander Baring, a member of a prominent merchant-banking family with considerable American interests, spoke in support,[43] as did the Irish leader Henry Grattan. By excluding colonial luxuries from the continent, Grattan declared, "you may barbarize Europe, and in a degree martialize her," but this would prove no advantage to England. Was it a wonder that America resented England's wish "to compel her to come over to this country, and pay a tax to us for allowing an independent country the privilege to trade! to pay us a tax for carrying on her own trade!" By her conduct, England would "make the enemy a nation of soldiers, and America a nation of manufacturers."[44]

Foreign secretary George Canning and James Stephen led the response to this attack. Canning acknowledged that the ministry had not acted upon "the poor pretense of the existing law of nations" when it issued the orders-in-council. Rather, it based its conduct upon "an extension just and necessary" of that law.[45] James Stephen was prepared to explain, once more, the nature of this justice and necessity. Without the orders-in-council, Napoleon's continental system would have deprived Britain of all her overseas trade and threatened "our utter annihilation as a mercantile country." War with America was better than such a fate. Stephen fumed at the "insolence" of France which did not dare "show a single flag on the ocean" and yet declared the ports of "so superior a maritime power [as England] in a state of blockade." If England accepted the American offer and the embargo were lifted against England but not France, how could the admiralty know that a ship leaving the American harbor was not secretly headed for enemy ports?[46]

England's maritime policy was vulnerable not only to attacks by liberal merchants, but also to those by long-time defenders of traditional belligerent rights at sea. In the upper house in 1809, Viscount Sidmouth, the former Henry Addington, argued that by taxing colonial cargoes carried by neutral ships and selling licenses to trade with the continent, the government had erected an extra-legal system of "pernicious indulgence." England must give up the system of paying for war by taxing trade with the enemy, and revert to the full force of England's maritime rights, no more and no less. Sidmouth called for a complete blockade of France, since this was "a legitimate application of our naval superiority." In pursuing a policy of full-scale enforcement of England's traditional rights, Britain might interfere even more severely with neutral trade, but at least she could defend herself on grounds of accepted international law.[47] This was also the position of Joseph Phillimore, a judge of the court of admiralty of the Cinque Ports as well as regius professor of civil law at Oxford. In his tract of 1811 Phillimore denounced the "dangerous innovations" introduced by the orders-in-council, particularly England's illegal efforts to force her products on Europe. By her extraordinary system of licenses, Britain permitted Dutch and Hanse merchants, subjects of Napoleon, to carry on a commerce that British cruisers would otherwise have intercepted.[48] The orders-in-council were "illegal, immoral, and unjust," the regius professor declared the following year, for "it must still ever be the true policy of a Maritime State, to maintain and uphold the equal and unvarying administration of Maritime Law."[49]

By 1812 British mercantile and industrial interests had suffered so much from the American non-intercourse act that even the ministry was convinced that

England's policy would have to be revised. Still, it hesitated. In June Henry Brougham, newly elected to the lower house and now able to address it from the floor and not as a petitioner from the bar, again called for the repeal of the orders-in-council.

Brougham warned the House that the policy of the ministry was sacrificing the American trade to "pure whimsies, I can call them nothing else, respecting our abstract rights." England's "paper blockade," the "right to blockade, by a few lines in the Gazette," entire continents "without sending a single sloop of war to enforce the order," could not be legally justified. Nor was it proper to blockade "for purposes, not belligerent but mercantile," in an effort to prevent neutral trade with the enemy in order to secure it for England. The American trade was one "in comparison of which, whether you regard its extent, its certainty, or its progressive increase, every other sinks into insignificance," and England must not make "a new enemy, America, on our flank." If Britain now prudently and expediently set aside her maritime rights, this would not prevent her from reasserting them in the future: though she had always rejected the new rule, and "we deem our denial the very cornerstone of our maritime system," yet she had agreed to this principle at Utrecht in 1713, and had yielded the rule of 1756 during the American War and again in 1794; this had not prevented James Stephen's first tract – a book which "I deeply lament ever saw the light" – from having successfully urged their revival. How then could one argue that if England refrained from exercising her maritime rights they would forever lapse? "Keep fast hold of your rights" but "do not play the part of madness" and insist on their exercise when this "will infallibly work your ruin," Brougham concluded. Let practical considerations dictate whether British maritime rights ought or ought not to be asserted.[50]

In the debate that followed, Brougham received support as usual from Alexander Baring, who stressed that America did not dispute England's legitimate maritime rights,[51] and from Samuel Whitbread.[52] Even the liberal Tory George Canning, no longer in office, urged the revocation of the orders: he did not approve "some late attempts at converting a measure of political retaliation into a commercial monopoly for ourselves."[53] The foreign secretary Lord Castlereagh trod an uneven course between defending the orders and urging the conciliation of America. In the end, Castlereagh agreed that Britain ought to suspend the orders in the hope that the United States would then suspend its non-intercourse act.[54] The widespread economic distress and the threat of war with America clearly compelled a drastic change of policy.

"The repeal of the Orders-in-Council," Brougham was to observe in later years, "was my greatest achievement." "It was second to none of the many efforts made by me, and not altogether without success, to ameliorate the condition of my fellow men." What Britain ought to have done after Napoleon's 1806 Berlin decree, he believed, was to permit France to incur the enmity of the neutrals by her attack on their rights, and to rely on smuggling to sell British goods to the continent. But "our rulers" had determined on retaliation by a counter-blockade and a licensing system, both proceedings out of line with international law. "No doubt France had by the Berlin Decree grossly violated neutral rights," but that was "no justification of the course taken by England." "Such a wanton outrage against the rights of neutrals never before was perpetrated."[55]

What triumphed in parliament in 1812 was not liberal principle, for which no case had been made in either house since 1801, but expediency. Brougham stood for a pragmatic policy against those who insisted upon England's "abstract rights." Nor had anyone in these later debates questioned the legality or desirability of the old rule. What they criticized were the innovations introduced by the rule of 1756 and the licensing provisions of the orders-in-council. But the British government had delayed too long. Before the news of these concessions could be received in Washington, the United States had declared war in defense of her maritime liberties, and in anger at the continued impressment of her seamen.

Only one voice was raised in the Commons to oppose the government's 1812 reversal of policy. The leader of the struggle against the slave trade, and now against slavery itself, the Tory Evangelical William Wilberforce had "doubts as to the propriety of abandoning the Orders in Council."[56] Brougham in his remarks to the House "hailed the absence" at this debate of Wilberforce's brother-in-law and fellow abolitionist James Stephen. "It was evident," Brougham remarked, that Stephen "had not been able to bring himself to witness the death of his darling offspring – the Orders in Council."[57] Both Wilberforce and Stephen had special reasons, we shall see, for regretting this yielding of British maritime pretensions.

[3] Christianity, Liberalism, and the Trident

One whom he [H. L. Mansell, a mid-nineteenth-century Oxford philosopher given to puns] was showing around St. Paul's complained of the heathenish character of the monuments. "Just look at *that* now," – (pointing to a huge figure of Neptune). "What has *that* got to do with Christianity?" "*Tridentine* Christianity perhaps," suggested Mansel.

J. W. Burgon, *Lives of Twelve Good Men*

For the King and Founder of this city of which we speak has in Scripture uttered to His people a dictum of the divine law in these words: "God resisteth the proud, but giveth grace unto the humble." But this, which is God's prerogative, the inflated ambition of a proud spirit also affects, and dearly loves that this be numbered among its attributes to "spare the meek and crush the haughty." And therefore ... we must speak also of the earthly city, which though it be mistress of the nations, is itself ruled by its lust of rule.

St Augustine, *The City of God*

In the years following Waterloo, Great Britain undertook a policing of the oceans – the guardianship of a maritime Pax. The Royal Navy sought to eliminate not merely piracy, a serious problem in the Indian Ocean and China Seas where merchant ships were sailing in greater numbers, but also the trade of the slave ships, regarded as no better than pirate vessels, in the waters of the South Atlantic and Caribbean. The powers at the Congress of Vienna had denounced the slave trade as unChristian, and pledged themselves to its destruction. An England which possessed naval supremacy, and many of whose leaders believed the Almighty willed the immediate end of slavery saw herself as uniquely fitted to carry through this judgment.

To accomplish this, England seemed interested in converting her belligerent rights of search and seizure into peacetime rights. It would prove difficult to oppose these pretensions of the pre-eminent naval power, particularly when put forward in religio-philanthropic garb. In the end, however, the Royal Navy's *mission civilisatrice* fell victim not only to the resentment of rival nations, but also to the growing strength at home of a Radical liberalism antagonistic to the use of force for any reason.

The Evangelical plan

The Evangelicals – Anglicans belonging to the "low church" which shared the puritanical and evangelistic fervor of the Dissenters – had for some time campaigned to end slavery. In 1806 the Evangelical leader William Wilberforce assigned to his brother-in-law James Stephen a leading role in advising the prime minister Lord Grenville on this issue, and Grenville was ready to receive such counsel.[1] After Grenville left office later that year, Stephen corresponded along similar lines with Spencer Perceval, the new chancellor of the exchequer and, as already noted, an Evangelical himself. In 1807 Wilberforce succeeded in persuading parliament to abolish the British slave trade, and the Evangelicals set their sights on its extirpation throughout the world. In this we may find a good part of the explanation for Stephen's fervent advocacy of British belligerent rights at sea.

In late 1807, Stephen warned Perceval against any attempt by the ministry to conciliate America "by a sacrifice of all our old & *new* maritime rights."[2] Although the naval system erected by the orders-in-council might cause some temporary commercial losses, British merchants would be ready to accept this "necessary sacrifice," confident in a future increase in their trade, and in the use of the system to promote Christianity. For a "wise, righteous & wonderful Providence" had so arranged events as to bring about the "compleat deliverance" of the blacks along with "the triumph of British commerce & British power." By exercising her naval rights, England might expiate past sins of slave-trading by ending that commerce in men utterly. God approved Britain's assertiveness at sea, for Stephen believed the recent successful display of naval strength against the Danish fleet was providential. Immediate naval action must also be taken against the Portuguese slave traders and their commercial settlements along the African coast. "Would that you were Dictator," the Evangelical barrister wrote to the chancellor, "& I your sole adviser." Stephen would then "cry in your ear incessantly" that Perceval had the "most glorious game to play that ever presented itself to the ruler of a great nation."[3]

When the war was over, England negotiated treaties with America and France directed to the abolition of the slave trade. The United States had outlawed the trade in 1808, and by the Treaty of Ghent in 1815 England and America agreed to work jointly to suppress the commerce in men. In 1794, France had abolished the slave trade, though Napoléon was to reinstate it in 1799; in 1815, the France of the restored Bourbons once again abolished the trade, and entered into a convention with England similar to that signed by America.

Much to the unhappiness of the philanthropic enemies of the slave trade, British admiralty courts inhibited an early effort to make a wartime right of search a peacetime right as well. In 1817 a British man-of-war captured the

Louis, a French slaver en route from Martinique to Africa, and a British admiralty court in Sierra Leone condemned the ship under the 1815 convention with France. Upon appeal, however, the high court of admiralty in London, with Sir William Scott presiding, reversed this decision, declaring that the right of search had not been specifically granted by that convention. "No authority can be found which gives any right of visitation or interruption over the vessels and navigation of other states, on the high seas, except what the right of war gives to belligerents against neutrals," Scott declared. No nation, "on the pretence of an eminent good," had the right to trample upon the independence of other states. The Royal Navy might not "press forward to a great principle" like the ending of the slave trade, "by breaking through other great principles." "If this right be imported" from war "into a state of peace," the only course must be by specific treaty.[4]

Britain then turned to a strategy of bilateral treaties. Spain, Portugal, and Holland in 1817 granted England a limited right of search, and set up mixed courts to preside over cases of seizure of slave ships. Although these treaties specified a mutual right of search, it was clear that England, whose men-of-war were to be found on every ocean and whose naval supremacy was unchallenged, would in almost every case wield this power. Spain and Portugal had long been engaged in the slave trade, and these countries became principal targets of British philanthropists. By mid-century, England had "compensated" Portugal with nearly £3 million and Spain with over £1 million to sign treaties that granted the Royal Navy the right to seize slave ships flying their flags. But the Iberian countries had been virtual English dependencies ever since Wellington's armies helped to liberate them from Napoleon's grip. Other nations – particularly the United States and France – were more cautious about treaties granting a mutual right of search, even though they possessed navies which gave some force to the idea of reciprocity.

In late 1821 the leading opponent of the wartime orders-in-council Henry Brougham wrote an article in which he traced "the intimate connexion between slave-trading, and all the atrocities of a piratical life," and called upon America and France to agree to a mutual right of search. Wartime excesses had given "a bad name" to the exercise of this right; indeed, Brougham reminded his readers that he himself had deplored the conduct of the Royal Navy during the recent conflict. But matters were very different now. In peacetime, this right of search would be in every way mutual, a proceeding of "perfect reciprocity." "England harbours not a thought of visiting the ships of any power which shall not have the self-same right to visit hers."[5]

In the years following, England attempted to secure some kind of international reciprocal right of search, but without success. At the Congress of Verona in 1822, Great Britain urged the powers to denounce the slave trade as piracy, an act that would enable British cruisers to capture slavers without specific treaty permission. But the nations of the world were wary of surrendering their maritime rights to the Royal Navy for any reason. They, and most particularly America, continued to suspect that under cover of philanthropy and mutuality the British intended to wield in times of peace "the fierce trident" that she had employed in recent wars.

The United States had fought in 1812 against what secretary of state John Quincy Adams in the early 1820s described as the "gross perversion" of the right of search in time of war. When the British minister to America asked Adams whether there could be a more dreadful evil than the slave trade, the secretary of state replied it was that of "admitting the right of search by foreign officers of our vessels upon the seas in time of peace; for that would be making slaves of ourselves." "If the freedom of the seas is abridged by compact for any new purpose," President Monroe declared in 1823, "and if its operation is extended to a time of peace, as well as of war, a new system will be commenced for the dominion of the sea." The "abuses" into which such a system might lead, he added, might "eventually" come to "confound all distinction of time and circumstances, of peace and war, and of rights applicable to each state."[6]

Despite such strong reservations, hatred of the slave trade brought Monroe and Adams to agree in 1820 and 1821 to the co-operation of the American and British fleets off the African coast, but not to a peacetime right of search. But anti-slavery sentiment pushed matters still further. In 1824, the United States signed a convention with England which granted a qualified, reciprocal right of search, provided ships seized were tried by the courts of their own country rather than the mixed courts the British favored. When this agreement was submitted for the Senate's approval in April 1824, it was substantially qualified by amendments. One that exempted American waters from this right of search led to England's refusal to accept the accord.

England, however, was more successful in her diplomatic courtship of other nations. A treaty between Britain and Sweden in 1824 established the mutual right of search between those countries, as did one with Brazil in 1826. In 1831, England and France established a geographically-limited mutual right of search, and this was followed in subsequent years by similar treaties with Denmark, Sardinia, the Hanse cities, and Naples. English and French efforts to secure American adhesion to their 1831 treaty failed, however, in good part because of the hostility of the Southern states; and in 1833 the United States refused to entertain a belated English acceptance of the amended convention of 1824. When English men-of-war exercised searches of American ships, supposedly to verify their nationality, the result was ill-feeling, protests, and demands for reparations.

Central to the naval crusade against the slave trade was an African Squadron that maintained a watch off the western shores of that continent to capture slave ships and to liberate their cargoes. This proved a great expense;

not only was it costly to keep men and vessels so occupied, but the government awarded head-money of £15 per rescued slave to the squadron's crews as a spur to their enterprise, converting the wartime prize system to the uses of philanthropy. Since there was no financial inducement for the capture of the slave ship itself, except in special instances, critics charged that the officers and crew of a cruiser of the Squadron had an interest in permitting a slave ship to reach Africa and take on a cargo of blacks before seizing it, rather than in preventing the embarkation of slaves in the first place.

By the late 1830s, after almost a generation of diplomatic and naval efforts, it was clear that the vicious trade had substantially increased, as had the anguish of the human cargo. Greater numbers of slaves were transported under conditions of more intense hardship, with a higher rate of profit for the traders because of the greater risks of capture. Very narrow ships were built to secure maximum speed so as to facilitate escape from British cruisers, and the resulting cramped quarters were brutally hard on slaves in mid-passage. Furthermore, if a British cruiser were sighted, the captain of the slave ship would throw his cargo overboard rather than risk capture with the living evidence of his crime. All in all, many Englishmen were becoming convinced that British meddling not only cost the taxpayer a handsome sum without tangible results, but also increased the sufferings of the blacks.[7]

This was not the view of the African Institution, founded in the early years of the century as the principal organ of Evangelical opposition to the slave trade. In an 1837 tract, the Institution sought to spur the government to greater efforts. These philanthropists knew that matters had not gone well; that, for example, the pursuit of slavers as pirates had in many cases made them in fact pirates. But they saw the increase of naval pressure as the only practical solution, and complained that the African Squadron was composed of too small a number of largely ineffective vessels. The Evangelicals, like Stephen and Wilberforce a generation earlier, appealed to Britain's national pride: the slave runners "insulted the flag of Great Britain when unfurled on board her ships of war!" they charged, and the government passively accepted such indignities. For the sake of its honor, the Navy had to undertake punitive action. Why did England permit Spain and Portugal to encourage piratical acts, even after having paid them huge sums to end the wicked commerce?[8]

In May 1837 one of the Institution's leaders, the philanthropist Thomas Fowell Buxton who had led the abolitionist campaign to a successful conclusion in 1833 when slavery was outlawed throughout the British empire, wrote to the Whig foreign secretary Viscount Palmerston, another long-time foe of the trade. Buxton informed the foreign secretary of a motion he intended to introduce in the Commons which would denounce Portugal for violation of treaties, and threaten her with punishment.[9] In early 1838 the Institution again professed "our astonishment" at the British people "tamely submitting to be cheated" by Spain and Portugal, and called for steamers to enforce England's treaty rights.[10]

Naval war with Portugal and Brazil

The Portuguese slave trade had been frequently discussed in James Stephen's letters to leading politicians in the first decade of the century. The Portuguese, at that time the principal purveyors of African blacks, were dependent on British support against Napoleon's armies, and in 1807 Stephen urged that England exact the end of Portugal's slave trade in exchange for continued aid.[11] When the Portuguese royal family fled to Brazil later that year, Stephen could only regard it as "a striking retribution to the Power which next to Britain has been the greater, & is now the only oppressor of Africa!"[12]

After Waterloo, England had signed a treaty with Portugal whose terms outlawed the slave trade, and the Iberian state received financial compensation from England in exchange for the Royal Navy's right to search Portuguese ships suspected of slave running. Yet slave ships under Portuguese ownership, and at times flying Portugal's flag, continued a profitable trade despite the efforts of the African Squadron. Britain believed, with some evidence, that contrary to its treaty commitments the Portuguese government was turning a blind eye to these illegal activities. The philanthropic opponents of the slave trade were particularly irritated that so puny a power as Portugal could dare to deceive the might of England.

Early in 1838, the leading liberal Whig opponents of the orders-in-council, Henry Brougham and Alexander Baring, who had denounced the arrogance of British naval power thirty years earlier, called upon the government to take vigorous action against Portugal, as well as against Brazil and Spain. These nations, the most active slave traders, were also those "with whom our commerce is the closest, and over whom our influence is the most commanding," Brougham, now Lord Brougham, observed in the upper house. In the past, England did not "shrink from our duty through delicacy or through fear," yet now "when the millions of Africa look up to us for help, we pause and falter, and blanch and quail before the ancient and consecrated Monarchy of Brazil, the awful might of Portugal, the compact, consolidated, overwhelming power of Spain!"[13] Alexander Baring, now Lord Ashburton, was astonished that while an English fleet had shelled the fortifications of the pirate Bey of Algiers, yet she "suffered the Kingdom of Portugal to stand a nuisance on the ocean."[14] Lord Glenelg, the Whig secretary for war and colonies and a member of a prominent Evangelical family, supported Brougham and Ashburton.[15] The following month, Brougham privately proposed that parliament unilaterally declare slave-running to be piracy, which would mean that the Royal Navy might summarily execute slave traders as pirates. The foreign secretary Viscount Palmerston, to whom this proposal was addressed, thought it "impracticable" for "no nation would consent to render its subjects liable" to the "yardarm justice ... of the Naval officers of other nations."[16]

Palmerston, himself a keen opponent of the slave trade, determined on another course of action. In 1839, the anti-slave trade treaty between England and Portugal was due to expire, and the Portuguese government refused to renew it. Palmerston came before the Commons in March of that year in support of a bill to make it possible to impose on Portugal the terms of the unrenewed treaty, and to give to British cruisers statutory authority to search Portuguese vessels, and to British admiralty courts the right to condemn those found to be slavers. This legislation would protect officers of the Royal Navy from suits for damages in English courts.[17] Liberals and Evangelicals happily supported this "more vigorous course," thus exercising English influence "for higher purposes," in the words of the Evangelical Sir Robert Inglis.[18] Sir Harry Verney insisted that the government enforce the treaties on the slave trade "even by war if necessary," observing that England might be compelled to violate existing international law in order to further a more lofty injunction.[19] It would be unfortunate if other nations saw this effort to wipe out the slave trade as one designed merely to give "increased ascendancy to our maritime power," Dr Lushington, an Evangelical barrister, declared, but Britain must take this risk.[20] The lower house overwhelmingly approved the course of the Whig government.

In the upper house, however, there was discontent among the Tories. When the Whig Earl of Minto, the first lord of the admiralty, declared it "too much to be endured that the efforts of this country in the cause of humanity should be frustrated by ... a single nation,"[21] the Duke of Wellington, the Tory leader in the Lords, urged caution lest there be "a quarrel to the death with our ancient ally" Portugal. If Portugal had violated treaties, Wellington argued, let England negotiate with her before the eyes of the world, not wage an undeclared war in order to impose a treaty. If the government thought war necessary, let war be declared in "the old constitutional mode." Did England intend that "the vessels of any or all the powers of Europe might be detained and searched, and afterwards allowed to proceed on their voyage, whether we had slave-trade treaties with those powers or not?" If so, "such a law would be quite a novelty."[22] The prime minister Viscount Melbourne replied that the government was "bound in point of duty and in point of honour" to compel Portugal to fulfill the commitments she had entered into, and for which she had already received financial compensation. Since the lower house had passed the bill without debate, Melbourne was "surprised" to find any difference of opinion on the subject.[23] The House of Lords rejected the government's bill by a vote of 38 to 32, with Tories and Whigs divided along party lines.[24]

Here was an extraordinary reversal. The Whigs (on their way to becoming Liberals), contrary to the party's position three decades earlier, supported high-handed naval action, while the Tories called for caution and invoked the constitution and international law. Because of the anti-slavery campaign, liberalism and what England's rivals would term maritime aggression were neatly linked for much of the first half-century after 1815.

But the last word on the Portugal Bill had not been spoken. Lord Brougham was not present on the night of the vote in the Lords, but a week later he moved an address to the Queen in an effort to salvage the situation. The address urged that the Queen give such orders to British cruisers "as may be most efficacious" to halt the slave trade, particularly that portion carried on by Portuguese and Brazilian ships.[25] The Marquess of Lansdowne, a son of Shelburne and the lord president of the council, asked for support of the government in its "lawful exercise, of the whole power of this country to perform one of the greatest acts of moral justice which any country was ever called upon to perform."[26] Melbourne, the prime minister, called the passage of Brougham's proposal necessary to counteract the "severe blow on the foreign policy of the country" which the Lords had administered the previous week, one "most injurious to the great cause of humanity."[27] Wellington continued to object,[28] as did the Tory Earl of Ripon.[29] In a later debate on a revised bill, Wellington declared that France and the United States would never give to England the power of visit and search.[30] Lord Ellenborough agreed. "There was a feeling of universal jealousy on the part of all maritime powers," Ellenborough warned, and these powers possessed "a determination to maintain their rights by war," if necessary.[31] Brougham ignored such cautions and merely noted that given Portugal's dependence on England, the Tagus might be regarded as "a British stream," and England as more Portugal's "mistress than ... her friend."[32]

When the House of Lords finally passed the Whigs' Portugal bill, its Tory opponents issued a manifesto of protest that predicted that "the probable resistance and retaliation of Portugal and other powers" would endanger "the innocent and defenceless commerce of her [the Queen's] subjects in all parts of the world."[33] In presenting a revised bill to the House of Commons, Palmerston denounced Portugal's "obstinate and rigid determination not to make any treaty with us." Though the Tories might say "that this was waging war against the world," he could not see "how any nation could complain."[34] The lower house passed the revised bill without difficulty.[35] Portugal in the end yielded to British intimidation and renewed her treaty with England.

In July 1845, the liberal Tory prime minister Sir Robert Peel, who was his party's leading spokesman for the commercial interest, asked parliament for authority to use against Brazil powers much like those that Palmerston had employed against Portugal in 1839. Like Portugal, Brazil refused to renew a treaty that granted Britain the right to search Brazilian vessels to determine whether they carried slaves. England now argued that since Brazil had contracted to abolish the slave trade, the Royal Navy could continue to enforce its earlier right even without formal agreement. Palmerston, on behalf of the Whigs, pledged his support to the Tory government. This time the Tory peers were silent.

The Radical free traders, not the Tories as in the case of the 1839 Portugal bill, now led the opposition to the proposal. The leading spokesman during the debate on the Brazil Act was a wealthy and socially prominent Manchester MP, T. Milner Gibson. Gibson, the son of an army officer and a former Tory member for Ipswich, was a convert to Radicalism and served as one of the leading parliamentary advocates of the abolition of the corn laws. He denounced Peel's bill as "nothing short of a declaration of war," adding that such an action would seriously injure England's trade with Brazil. Gibson also protested against England's discriminatory tariff against cheap, slave-grown Brazilian sugar, this in the interest of discouraging slavery. Radicals regarded such an intervention into commercial relations between nations as a reversion to an exploded mercantilism and not justifiable for any reason – even that of a supposed philanthropy. Brazil had threatened to retaliate against this tariff by a duty on British manufactures that might prove harmful to British industry. "How long were the great manufacturing interests of the country to be jeopardized," Gibson asked, "how long were the property and lives of British subjects to be endangered, in order to carry out the peculiar views of a small section of the anti-slavery party in this country?"[36] (Other Radicals, including W. H. Hutt,[37] Sir Thomas Wilde,[38] and G. F. Muntz supported this position, the last warning that the passage of the bill "would produce a general war.")[39]

None the less, conscious of Britain's duties as the maintainer of the maritime Pax, Peel determined to use the Navy to scatter the forces of anarchy and impose the will of a divine providence – regardless of the petty interests of merchants and manufacturers. A great power like France could not perhaps be compelled to renew a treaty, and America had yet to accept a proper one, but Portugal and Brazil might be put under a civilizing discipline. Since piracy was a crime against international not merely municipal law, Peel argued, and since Brazil had declared slave trading to be piracy in its earlier convention with Britain, Brazil had given England special rights to deal with that crime. Peel proclaimed Britain's over-riding policy was not so much "to further the commercial prosperity of this country," as Radicals seemed to believe, but rather to advance "the interests of humanity."[40]

The Times, which had not always been friendly to the philanthropists, supported Peel on this issue. While conceding that Britain's insistence on the right of search was in this case "something more than a belligerent right," the paper none the less contended that England might "feel no more compunction" in its proceedings against Brazil than in waging war against the Barbary pirates. While *The Times* was "not insensible to the claims of British mercantile interests" that there would be injury to the Brazilian trade and therefore a "private inconvenience and loss," yet "where a great principle is to be maintained and a right exercised these objections cannot prevail."[41]

Three years earlier, in 1842, in a reply to an address presented to him by opponents of the naval war against the slave trade, Palmerston had observed that "the Power & Influence of England is greater ... than many Persons in this Country are aware of," and that if this power were "steadily and vigorously exerted," and "supported by public opinion & national Feeling," England could secure "a faithful and complete Execution of the Engagements" into which foreign powers had entered. But England "must be firm and decided," we "must not care for giving offence to the guilty Parties," and finally "we must not be stopped by the Clamour raised against us." Crossed out in an early draft of this reply, but still legible, was Palmerston's rejoinder to those who believed his 1839 position on Portugal in violation of international law: "we must not strain theoretical Doctrines to a degree of inapplicable Refinement so as to prevent us from taking Measures best calculated to accomplish the great & humane Purpose we have in view."[42] In a private memorandum written during the Brazilian affair, Palmerston noted that "Power is valuable only in its employment" and he could not "conceive any Pleasure greater than Employment of Power to put an end to [the] Slave trade."[43]

Radicals versus the naval philanthropists

The Birmingham Quaker and Radical Joseph Sturge, a leading member of the British and Foreign Anti-Slavery Society, was determined not only to oppose slavery but also, and more immediately, to end the British naval war against the slave trade. The Radical industrialists of the Society, often Dissenters, belonged in spirit not to the risk-taking, entrepreneurial period, but to the succeeding quasi-pacifist one of bourgeois consolidation. They shied at risk and saw the use of force as sinful and dangerous. Economy in government was a by-word for them, and they were dismayed at the expense of maintaining the African Squadron; they believed that the naval effort to end the slave trade had failed, for the trade was growing not declining. This proved to Sturge and his Radical supporters that it was futile "to promote philanthropic ends by violence and blood." Only "moral, religious and pacific means" to abolish slavery were justifiable. England ought to act to persuade, not to compel by force, the slave states to give up the wicked and, as these Radicals believed, thoroughly unprofitable institution.[44]

These Radicals, followers of the pacifist free-trader Richard Cobden, were determined opponents of the politics of war and empire that they identified with the aristocratic heirs to a decadent feudalism, concerned with glory and positions in the armed services or colonies. One of the chief targets of the Cobdenites (about thirty strong in the lower house by the middle decades of the century) was Viscount Palmerston, who as both foreign secretary and prime minister pursued a vigorous foreign policy. Palmerston was prepared to employ naval power on behalf of constitutionalism and national self-determination on the European continent and, as we have seen, to run the risks of war with Portugal and Brazil in order to wipe out the slave trade. While most of the liberal middle classes cheered Palmerston's defense of British moral and political principles, the pacifistic Cobdenites detested his provocative rhetoric and behaviour which they believed alien not only to the values but to the interests of English merchants and manufacturers.

In June 1845, the Radicals of the Anti-Slavery Society brought a motion before the Commons to withdraw the African Squadron. W. H. Hutt, the Radical member for Gateshead, a prominent free trader and a future vice-president of the board of trade, denounced the blockade of the West African coast as based on "erroneous principles" and "mistaken humanity." "I deny entirely," Hutt declared, "that we are under any kind of moral obligation" to "assume the task of extirpating the crime" of the slave trade or "patrolling the world to put it down." England's naval methods were "very expensive," costing over half a million pounds a year, were "destructive of the enterprising and gallant men" of the Royal Navy, struck down by the unhealthy African climate, and yet had proved quite useless. Furthermore, high-handed conduct at sea had brought Britain "into collision with jealous and powerful nations," thereby "hazarding the peace of the world." An England that thought itself "more virtuous" than others mistakenly believed that it could teach foreigners "morality with fire and sword." "Withdraw your cruisers," he urged; and then let the inevitable slave insurrections do the work of abolition in Brazil, Cuba, and the United States.[45] Viscount Howick, a former Whig colonial secretary, agreed, urging reliance upon Brazilian and Cuban public opinion to undo slavery.[46]

The Evangelical merchants of the African Institution thought themselves better representatives of the moral values and economic interests of the middle classes than the Cobdenite manufacturers of the Anti-Slavery Society. They had established the Institution in the first decade of the century with two objectives – first, to destroy the slave trade, and, this accomplished, to open Africa to a civilizing commerce. The Institution had for decades supported the strategy of employing the Navy to enforce the abolition laws of all states by a peacetime visitation and search.[47] From its earliest years, the Institution had seen the slave trade as the "only impediment" to the civilizing of Africa. That trade "at once turned aside the attention of the natives from the more slow and laborious means of barter, which industry presented, to that of seizing upon and selling each other."[48] When the pro-slavery West India interest accused the members of the Institution of caring more for their private commercial interests in Africa than for the abolition of the slave trade, one of its early stalwarts, the Evangelical barrister James Stephen, replied in 1817 that nothing was so "likely to promote so much the purposes" of England and of the Institution "as the success of individuals who engaged in its [Africa's] innocent commerce."[49]

In 1840, the Evangelical T. F. Buxton re-stated the determination of the African Institution to use the Royal Navy's blockade of the African coast to wipe out the slave trade and to protect "innocent commerce." A number of persons associated with the Institution had established plantations along the African coast, and Buxton envisioned a free black population engaged in tillage at home instead of being forcibly transported to cultivate the lands of the western hemisphere. If the African Squadron were to abandon its patrol of the coast, as its opponents demanded, the act would serve as "a signal to the chiefs of the country to prosecute the horrid traffic with even more than their usual energy." "While we act under the impulse of charity," Buxton concluded, "we are also obeying the dictates of the most farsighted policy," for by "leading Africa to grow at home, cheaper sugar than Brazil, and cheaper cotton than the United States, we are renovating the very sinews of our national strength."[50] Given such frankness, it was hardly surprising if foreign nations concluded that England sought to establish profitable colonies under the protection of a supposed philanthropy.

There was some discomfort – particularly among Tories – at reports of irregular conduct by the Squadrons. In the early 1840s, British men-of-war raided the African coast at points where slaves were herded into barracoons to await shipment. Seamen were put ashore, released the slaves, and burned the barracoons, proceedings hardly justifiable by international law. Peel was unhappy with this adventurist strategy, and sought to negotiate treaties with tribal chieftains that granted permission to the Royal Navy to seize and destroy slave barracoons. England must always act "by means recognized and sanctioned by the Law of Nations," he declared.[51]

But was a naval blockade of the African coast permitted by that law? Peel's foreign secretary, the Earl of Aberdeen, observed that strictly speaking Britain was not blockading any coast, for "a blockade was a belligerent right": the Navy was merely engaged in "a strict watching of those vessels, belonging to countries which had bound themselves to England by treaties, and which vessels they, by the Law of Nations, as well as by the municipal law of this country had a right to visit and detain."[52] Lord Colchester, a navy man, was glad that the foreign secretary had made this distinction since "the word 'blockade' led to great misconceptions abroad."[53]

There was a debate among politicians and naval men in the 1840s and 1850s as to whether a close blockade or distant cruising would be the more effective strategy for the African Squadron to pursue. This formed a curious echo of a similar controversy among the admirals in the 1790s, at which time a close blockade of the French coast had proved superior. The philanthropists favored the concentration of a strengthened Squadron's forces off the African coast rather than distant cruising. Buxton suggested the blockade's extension by the use of small steamships to explore rivers and harbors that sailing ships could not enter, and of black seamen, more accustomed to the climate.[54] The Tory government of Sir Robert Peel accepted this course in the early 1840s. Palmerston, now in opposition, argued that a part of the British naval force should also blockade Havana and Rio de Janeiro,[55] and Peel assured the lower house that England would continue to station men-of-war in both Cuban and Brazilian waters.[56]

The naval professionals on the whole approved the activities of the African Squadron, and favored the Squadron's new system of close blockade; they rejected the narrow commercial principles of the Radicals. In the Commons, Peel's senior naval lord of the admiralty, Admiral Sir George Cockburn, defended the abandonment of haphazard "cruising about,"[57] as did another naval veteran in the lower house, Admiral Sir Charles Napier, the Whig MP for Marylebone. Referring to the losses of life among the crews of the Squadron, Napier observed that "if we only lost 4 or 5 per cent of the men employed, the experience gained by the officers and men on the coast would well repay that small loss of life."[58] Among men on the active naval list, Captain Denman defended the close blockade and wrote of the "strange perversity" of free traders who talked of "the rights of mankind" in Hungary and Italy but not in Africa. To withdraw the Squadron because of "a perverted application of free-trade principles, and a narrow and short-sighted economy" would work "equally to the injury of our naval *prestige*, and of our national character."[59] Commander H. J. Matson, supporting Denman, derided the "Liverpool merchants" who wished to withdraw the Squadron in order to "carry out the principle of free trade in its most unlimited sense,"[60] and Lt. Henry Yule was equally dismissive of those in the Anti-Slavery Society who were "infected with a morbid and exaggerated aversion to everything of warlike hue." Why did they not extend "to the gallant cruisers of our maritime policy" the support they gave to the London bobbies?[61]

The differences between the naval philanthropists and the pacifist Cobden ites were sharp. The African Institution was prepared to use the navy not only to make war on slavers but also to encourage and protect trade and investment along the African coast, very much in the pattern of eighteenth-century mercantilism; moreover, under the flag of a liberal philanthropy, blacks rescued from slave ships were sent as contract laborers to British Caribbean colonies badly in need of hands, particularly after the abolition of slavery in 1833. The philanthropists defended themselves against Radical charges that they wished to employ devices that smacked of the old colonial system for selfish reasons, and denounced "the ultra-economists and free traders" so ready "to sacrifice the interests of humanity and the honour of their country" to "a favourite theory or crotchet" (in this case "their dogmas of political economy").[62] The Anti-Slavery Society, on the other hand, noted not only "the utter inefficiency" of both cruising and close blockade but the immorality of the Navy's use of force.[63]

The right of search: Cass, Tocqueville, and Mill

In 1841, England, France, Russia, Prussia, and Austria signed the so-called Quintuple Treaty declaring the slave trade to be piracy, and granting to the men-of-war of each of the signatories a reciprocal right of search. The United States immediately denounced any application of the treaty to her ships. The American minister to Great Britain protested the treaty as confirming "the right of placing British cruisers on any part of the ocean that Her Majesty's government may select, and prescribing the terms upon which other nations are to participate in the freedom of the seas"; this was "in effect a claim of jurisdiction over the whole of the African coasts and seas."[64] French opinion could not, if honor were to be preserved, fail to be roused by what America saw as an offense to her national sovereignty; France would never ratify this treaty, in part because of a persuasive letter sent to King Louis Philippe by the American minister to Paris, Lewis Cass, a long-time opponent of British maritime pretensions. The French jurist Cussy, agreeing with Cass, warned his countrymen that if the powers too readily adopted measures England saw as "most efficacious," they would usher in "a system for the dominion of the seas."[65]

In a tract in 1842 on the right of search, Lewis Cass cautioned the maritime nations against permitting England to exercise the "police of the Ocean, searching it and seizing it at pleasure," a role she might use to interrupt the trade of others to her advantage. Such a reciprocal right of search would give to Britain "the virtual supremacy of the seas," because in practice it would be British cruisers that would search the ships of other countries. If the powers indulged England in this matter on philanthropic grounds, England would escalate her pretensions, "till the British flag rode triumphant over the waters of the earth." Might England then not next seize such slave-grown products as rice, coffee, cotton, and tobacco as "contraband of peace"? When in 1842 Lord Ashburton, long an advocate of American interests, negotiated a treaty with secretary of state Daniel Webster by which the United States and England agreed to patrol the African coast jointly so as to avoid the subjection of American ships to a British right of search, Cass denounced Webster for having yielded to England even to this extent.[66] Cass's campaign against British maritime policy helped to make him the Democratic party's nominee for the presidency in 1848.

Nor was the effort of Ashburton and Webster to bury this explosive issue in Anglo-American relations to prove altogether successful on the British side. In early 1843, Sir Robert Peel insisted on a formal distinction between the belligerent right of search and a peacetime right of visit. "The right we claim," the Tory prime minister declared, was "to know whether a vessel pretending to be American, and hoisting the American flag, be *bona fide* American." Even a slave ship whose American nationality was clearly established would be permitted to continue its voyage. Britain merely wished to secure all maritime nations against fraud, and "I am surprised the United States should contest this."[67] The former Whig premier Lord John Russell was to speak in similar terms two months later.[68]

The Quintuple Treaty came under a spirited attack by the French liberal historian and political theorist Alexis de Tocqueville in the Chamber of Deputies in January 1843. Like Cass, Toqueville declared it not "fitting for a great people" to besmirch its "maritime pride" and endanger its sovereignty by granting to "the armed force of one nation the exorbitant right to arrest the criminals of another ... on the solitude of the Ocean, there where one can do anything one wishes." The treaty if ratified would place French subjects under the jurisdiction of an English court, "so contrary to the customs of all civilized nations." Though an opponent of the slave trade, Tocqueville warned England that the 1841 treaty could lead only "to recriminations ... violence, and finally war."[69]

Tocqueville's attack irritated Lord Brougham, who in an impassioned reply in the House of Lords in early February denounced "the contentious spirit" of certain Frenchmen who wished only to excite hostility to England. Brougham reminded French critics that he and Ashburton had taken "the low view of maritime rights" over thirty years earlier and opposed the orders-in-council, "the favourite measures of those who maintained the maritime supremacy of England." The Whig party to which he belonged had always favored the rights of neutrals against belligerents and consequently was attacked "as un-English, as anti-national." Yet it was the Whigs, because of their hatred of slavery, who now most actively supported the right of search while the Tories ("with one or two exceptions"), who a generation earlier had claimed maritime supremacy, cared "not a straw" for the right of search because they were "indifferent about the slave trade." Of Tocqueville, "a worthy friend of mine," Brougham could only observe that the historian possessed a "marvellous ignorance of the whole question."[70]

Tocqueville was disturbed by what he described as Brougham's "crude and violent sortie." The French liberal found Brougham's charge that he had "a marvellous ignorance" of the issue galling. There was certainly no evidence to justify such an accusation, he insisted, in a letter to his English friend the

Benthamite liberal John Stuart Mill,[71] already a well-known writer and soon to become a leading spokesman of Victorian liberalism. The French historian also wrote a letter to Brougham in which he asked the Whig peer to withdraw his charge that Tocqueville wished to embitter French opinion against England.[72] To support his French friend, Mill wrote a defense of Tocqueville's integrity – but not his views on the right of search – in the London *Morning Chronicle*, [73] and Tocqueville, jealous of his English reputation, was appeased.[74]

Mill himself shared the views of Brougham and the philanthropists on this matter, rather than those of Tocqueville and the Radicals. In 1839, for instance, Mill wrote to another French friend that while Palmerston's Portugal bill and the undeclared naval war against the Portuguese slave trade could not be defended on principles of international law, he believed that Portugal's systematic disregard of her treaty obligations might justify British conduct.[75] When the Radicals attacked the African Squadron and its blockade of West Africa in the 1840s, Mill again took up the position of the naval philanthropists: "I do not think the coast blockade so ineffectual as it is represented," he observed in May 1849; "& at all events, to abandon it would be understood throughout the world as the abandonment of our anti-slavery policy & by its moral effect would I believe increase the amount of slavery tenfold." While Mill did not think that the African blockade should be "persevered in for ever," he "would not give it up until something more effectual" was "actually in operation."[76] This continued to be his view of the matter into the 1860s.[77]

American public opinion, of course, supported the Radical position on maritime and naval policy. Brougham's attack on Tocqueville was seen in the United States as directed against Lewis Cass as well, and Cass again became the subject of eulogies. A journalist in the *Washington Globe* who signed himself Americanus dismissed Brougham's "parliamentary billingsgate." Had France ratified the Quintuple Treaty, England would have been "so emboldened in the pursuit of her long-cherished aim of undisputed supremacy on the ocean" that America single-handedly would have had to go to war against "the greatest maritime power in the world" in defense of "the liberty of the seas." America, the writer concluded, had "staked her character and her fortunes" on this "vital question of the freedom of the seas."[78]

Britain yields

What was to bring the issue of the right of search to a head in the late 1850s was the demand of anti-slavery die-hards like Charles Buxton, the son of the abolitionist, that the Royal Navy be employed against Spanish Cuba. Only if the slave trade were put down, Buxton told the lower house in July 1857, could Africa be turned to the growing of cotton. To end that trade, he called for the continuance of the Navy's "in-shore system" of blockading Africa, and demanded that British cruisers also be dispatched to blockade Cuban ports.[79] In the months ahead, British ships in the Caribbean arbitrarily stopped and visited vessels flying the United States flag to determine if they had a legal right to do so. In 1858, the American secretary of state, at this time Lewis Cass, instructed the United States minister to England to protest against this "systematic practice" of Great Britain "which would establish over the commerce of an independent community a system of foreign police."[80]

In 1858, a Conservative government under the Earl of Derby was briefly in power, and few Tories, as Brougham had observed earlier, were supporters of the peacetime right of search for philanthropic purposes. (It is noteworthy that in the twenty-eight years between 1846 and 1874 the Tories enjoyed only short periods of office, a total of fewer than five years.) The Earl of Malmesbury, the Tory foreign secretary, had long had doubts about the peacetime right of search,[81] and on receiving Cass's complaint referred the question to the legal officers of the crown. The law officers concluded, much as had Scott in the case of the *Louis* forty years earlier, that such a visit and search was illegal except by treaty agreement. Though Malmesbury continued to maintain that some means of "verifying the nationality of a vessel, suspected, on good grounds, of carrying false colours" was "most indispensable to the interest of civilisation, and the police of the seas,"[82] he gave way.

It was with a sense of relief that the Conservative government abandoned the pretensions that now defined the peacetime right of search, and a number of peers, in the upper house, contentedly pronounced the obsequies. Aberdeen, who had been Peel's foreign minister, acknowledged that "the zeal of our cruisers has converted into a rule that which was only intended to be an exception," and urged that what remained of this right be exercised "cautiously and prudently."[83] Aberdeen was joined by a former Tory lord chancellor, Lord Lyndhurst, the Massachusetts-born barrister and son of the painter John Singleton Copley. "We have surrendered no right," Lyndhurst told the Lords, for "no such right as that which is contended for has ever existed"; England had merely abandoned "the assumption of a right," and in this had acted "justly, prudently, and wisely." "Whether they be strong and powerful, or weak and imbecile, all are on a footing of perfect equality" on the high seas. "What right has the ship of one nation to interfere with the ship of any other nation, where the rights of both parties are equal?"[84]

The American minister in London was jubilant because of the Tory retreat. In a letter to secretary of state Cass, he told of the many messages of congratulations received from his diplomatic colleagues who all appeared "to regard with pleasure every check given to the maritime insolence of England." "There is no country in Europe," the minister concluded, "which does not look upon the right of search as a weapon in the hands of a single bully –

especially since your famous letter which stopped Louis Philippe signing the Quintuple Treaty."[85]

There were protests by leading Whigs. Both Lord John Russell and Palmerston argued that if the flag alone granted immunity from visit, piracy would become rampant on the seas.[86] In the Lords, the Bishop of Oxford and Lord Brougham insisted, at the very least, on the maintenance of the right of search when permitted by treaty, and continued to urge the government to continue its efforts to bring Spanish Cuba to heel.[87] J. A. Roebuck, a liberal MP from Sheffield, who supported a policy that would enlist Britain's naval power to further her interests and ideals, was exasperated at the abandonment of a noble cause:[88]

> I say that we, acting as a great people, have only the desire to put down a great blot upon humanity – I mean the slave trade ... I believe that our officers have merely done their duty ... Sure I am, that the people of England wish to employ their great power – and we have a great power, though we do not wish to boast about it ... in the service of mankind ... Sir, the people of England will maintain that great position which they have ever held; they will not be bullied out of their rights; they do not wish to maintain a power which they ought not to have ... but they will take care of their own honour.

The following month, Roebuck complained of England's having "truckled" to America.[89]

The naval philanthropists were fearful and the Radicals hopeful that the yielding of the right of search would be followed by the recall of the African Squadron. A spokesman for the foreign office, Seymour Fitzgerald, reassured the philanthropists that while Britain would withdraw its cruisers from seas which were "the highway of American commerce," the African Squadron would remain at its stations.[90] But the Radicals persisted in their attack. John Bright approved Malmesbury's concession, but demanded the end of the African blockade.[91] The following month, W. H. Hutt introduced a motion to abandon any effort to suppress the slave trade by armed force, a tactic that risked "angry collision with powerful maritime states."[92] Hutt received the support of the Cobdenite Milner Gibson who derided the apparent conviction of the philanthropists that England "monopolized all the moral feeling of the world."[93] Another Radical Charles Gilpin demanded the repeal of the Brazil Act of 1845, asserting that he did not believe in "the Christianity that was propagated by the guns of cruisers."[94]

But the moderate Whig and former Tory adherents of Peel as well as the Evangelical and Tory supporters of the African Squadron held firm against the Radical onslaught. A Tory backbencher denounced the commercial principles of Hutt and his party: "the love of money" that was "carried on under the name of free trade," he observed, "really ate out of the country anything like moral or religious feeling."[95] Both the Peelite liberal Edward Cardwell, a future war secretary, and the Tory first lord of the admiralty Sir

John Pakington praised the Squadron's support of "Commerce and Christianity."[96] Palmerston argued that if the motion succeeded, the slave trade would become "rampant to the utmost degree."[97] Charles Buxton struck a more practical note. Dismissing the relatively small expense of the African fleet when "our cruisers, after all, formed a constituent part of the defences of the country," he observed that should war break out, "we should have ships ready equipped and ready manned, the crews all the better for having had active service, instead of merely loitering about the Mediterranean or elsewhere."[98]

"There are those who believe," Viscount Palmerston declared in a remarkable peroration on this occasion, "that the world is governed by a Divine Providence," that nations suffered for "their misdeeds" and were rewarded for "the good deeds which they perform." Was it not "a curious coincidence" that "from the time when this country first began to abolish the slave trade" and "to use its influence for the suppression of the slave trade elsewhere," England "has prospered to a degree which it never experienced before"? "If the English nation were now to recede from its high position" of war against the slave trade, "I think it is not assuming too much the functions of a prophet to say that the crime would be visited upon the people of this country in a manner which would lead them to repent of having been guided by the counsels" of men like Hutt and Gibson and Bright.[99]

The Evangelical vision of James Stephen and William Wilberforce now appeared to be that of the country. The House of Commons was too firmly committed to thinking England an instrument of divine providence to hoot. When Christian philanthropy and liberal sentiment were so well-mated with British maritime and imperial pretensions, they could be challenged only by threats of a greater force. The Radical motion was defeated by a vote of 223 to 24.[100]

With Malmesbury's concession, Tory doubts concerning the peacetime right of search prevailed against Liberal pretensions. In 1858 an American writer observed that the United States always had an easier time negotiating with Tories on maritime questions "than with those who have pretended to a greater liberality in their political creed."[101] The French *Revue des Deux Mondes* declared that same year that "the Tory ministry and the Radicals are agreed" that it was futile to attempt "to impose by force their moral ideas on nations that will not adopt them"; the yielding of the right of search reflected a "vast change" in public opinion against "that police of the sea, which England had usurped" as well as against the "intermeddling obstinacy" of Lord Palmerston.[102]

In 1856, two years before Malmesbury's retreat, England had accepted the foremost demand of the Armed Neutralities of 1780 and 1800 – that of free ships making free goods. The main body of moderate Whigs led by

Palmerston joined the Radicals who had long urged such a course. The Tories, on the whole, continued to be opposed. While prepared to abandon the provocative enforcement of a peacetime right of search exercised in the interest of philanthropy, Tories believed that any yielding of England's belligerent maritime rights, and thereby her traditional naval strategy, would threaten the country's safety. But the liberal climate of the time, allied to what English merchants and manufacturers saw as their interest, overwhelmed what had come to be regarded as the exploded strategy of the mercantilist era.

[4] The Maritime Revolution

> The Athenians ... spoke as follows: "... and it was not we who set the example, for it has always been the law that the weaker should be subject to the stronger. Besides, we believed ourselves to be worthy of our position, and so you thought us till now, when calculations of interest have made you take up the cry of justice – a consideration which no one ever yet brought forward to hinder his ambition when he had a chance of gaining anything by might. And praise is due to all who, if not so superior to human nature as to refuse dominion, yet respect justice more than their position compels them to do."
>
> Thucydides, *The Peloponnesian War*

> How far are the rules established by the British maritime Courts in the last war applicable to the present state of the world, transformed and enlightened as it is by nearly half a century of peace, prosperity, and progress? ... The doctrines which regulate our commercial policy are totally inverted ... and the Ministers of the Crown have shown an earnest and intelligent desire to adapt the exercise of our belligerent rights to the present condition of the world.
>
> Henry Reeve, *Edinburgh Review*, 1854

In the late 1780s, the liberal philosopher Jeremy Bentham wrote a *Plan for a Universal and Perpetual Peace* that anticipated the Radical world-view of the following century. While later Cobdenites were to invoke Christian morals as the basis for their outlook, Bentham's standard was utility – what was useful in securing the greatest happiness for the greatest number. To attain a perpetual peace, he urged disarmament and the emancipation of colonies; and since the English were "the strongest among nations" as well as "the greatest sinners," they must take the lead in unburdening themselves of both their overseas possessions and their powerful fleets. For a considerable time, Britain had had force but not justice on her side, and "it is your force that has been the main cause of your injustice," Capital not conquest was the true foundation of national prosperity, and men would soon see that "all trade is in its essence advantageous," and "all war is in its essence ruinous." It was "not the interest" of Great Britain to maintain a navy greater than what was necessary to defend her commerce against pirates, for with trade free and colonies set at liberty (and therefore the causes of war removed), naval force could have no other purpose. Bentham lauded the "reasonableness" of the new rule of free ships, free goods which all the maritime powers but England supported. This rule was one "not of ambition, but of justice – a law made in favour of equality, a law made for the benefit of the weak."[1] A decade after the adoption of free trade, Englishmen were prepared to accept the new rule.

Nineteenth-century British Liberals and Radicals saw themselves constructing a cosmopolitan order based on free trade and an international division of labor, and on Christian ethics. For Richard Cobden and the Quaker cotton manufacturer John Bright and many of their followers of the so-called Manchester School of Radicalism, free trade was both economically and morally sound. To buy in the cheapest and sell in the dearest market, Cobden once disingenuously proclaimed, was the nineteenth century's version of the Golden Rule;[2] and a universally-adopted system of free trade would be the first step in the turning of swords into plow-shares. For most British liberals, free trade was first of all a matter of self-interest: free traders welcomed the import of cheap foreign corn not only to provide agricultural nations with the means of purchasing British industrial goods, but also to make possible the cheap food that would keep British factory wages low and competitive. It was the primary appeal to interest that distinguished moderate liberalism from a cosmopolitan and pacifistic Radicalism and from Tories who stressed national power.[3]

In the 1830s and 1840s John Stuart Mill looked to the landed classes as a social base for other than the short-term materialistic values of the bourgeoisie.[4] Tory landowners saw themselves as guardians of the honor and permanent interests of the nation, and were convinced that the liberal commercial and industrial classes and the doctrinaire Radicals were leading the country to disaster. The future Conservative prime minister Benjamin Disraeli observed in 1838 that it was "a delusion" to believe that if only England permitted the free entry of foreign corn, other countries would permit her to monopolize the world's industry.[5] Such "arrogant aspirations" were founded on abstract theory and a "profound ignorance of human nature," he noted two years later, and would court catastrophe.[6] When the liberals – the Whigs, Radicals, and followers of the liberal Tory prime minister Sir Robert Peel – who repealed the corn laws in 1846 over the opposition of the bulk of the Tory party wished to do away with the navigation acts, which since the seventeenth century had protected British shippers against foreign (primarily Dutch) competition, Disraeli proclaimed "the empire of the seas" in danger.[7] The shipping interest – which had backed the abolition of the corn laws – also came to the support of the navigation acts. A Durham MP, H. T. Liddell, a spokesman for the shipowners, warned that if England were to be made "merely the workshop of the world," she could not recruit an army or equip a navy from "the stunted population of our manufacturing districts."[8] Even the free trader Lord Brougham, invoking the authority of Adam Smith who had favored the navigation acts,[9] defended protection for British shipping as necessary to the "best interests of the country, her defence, her very existence," against a "sect" of "ultra free-trade men" who were now exposing the empire to "ruin."[10] The navigation acts were none the less repealed by a liberal majority in 1849.

Having achieved free trade and the abolition of the navigation acts, the radicals charted their next objective – the abandonment of England's traditional naval policy and strategy. Historians have not appreciated the importance Cobden, Bright, and their followers attached to this goal. For the Radicals and for many other liberals, by the mid-nineteenth century, England's reliance on an outmoded mercantilist strategy that depended on using naval power to halt the trade of the enemy, whether in its own or in neutral vessels, was both immoral and opposed to her true interests. Only a free commerce, not force, as Bentham had argued, would enrich England. Liberals had long dreamed of the preservation of a commercial peace even when nations were at war, and in the 1850s they took what they saw as the first step toward this goal.

Crimean War and maritime policy

Throughout the nineteenth century, the Turkish empire stood in danger of disintegration, and Russia was prepared to deliver the decisive blow and collect the spoils. England was determined to prevent Russian expansion into the Balkans, and to block a Russian control over the Dardanelles that would challenge the Royal Navy in the Mediterranean. In 1854, Britain and France went to Turkey's assistance against a Russian threat. In office at this time was the liberal coalition of the Earl of Aberdeen composed of Peelites (former Tories who had voted for the abolition of the corn laws), and of Whigs like the Earl of Clarendon, the foreign secretary, and Palmerston, now the home secretary. (By the end of the 1850s, a new Liberal party was to emerge from a coalition of Peelites and Whigs, to be joined by the Radicals, whose pacifist leaders Cobden and Bright condemned this war with Russia.)

The Aberdeen coalition, by a series of orders-in-council in early 1854, adopted a naval policy like that which the Armed Neutralities of 1780 and 1800 had vainly sought to impose on England. The new technological, economic, and political circumstances of the mid-nineteenth century, the government maintained, made naval enforcement of the old rule impracticable. Acceptance of the new rule did solve a number of immediate difficulties. French maritime law called for the confiscation of neutral goods on an enemy ship, while the British code stipulated their restoration. An Anglo-French compromise, with France yielding this point to Britain while England accepted the new rule long maintained by France, reconciled these differences. The Aberdeen cabinet decided to mount a blockade against imports reaching Russian Baltic ports but none to cut off Russian exports, since only a small part (1/78) of British exports was bought by the Russians while England relied on exports of cheap Russian grain. No privateers were dispatched.

The coalition wished to disturb peacetime commercial arrangements as little as possible lest British merchants lose their primacy in the Russian trade. English factors (but not English ships) were permitted to engage in commerce with the enemy; as the Peelite president of the board of trade Edward Cardwell observed, "the moment that the trade of neutrals with the enemy is recognized, the justification for prohibiting it to our own subjects is gone." Moreover, if the commerce with Russia which British merchants controlled fell into neutral hands, "our own resources and not those of Russia" would be damaged.[11]

This proved to be a policy that would satisfy most liberals. While Cobdenites opposed the naval blockade of Russia's ports as mercantilist regression, they welcomed the temporary adoption of free ships, free goods. Not only did Peelite spokesmen for commercial interests approve the new departure, so also did more traditional Whigs like Russell and Palmerston, both of whom took a forceful view of the peacetime right of search.

The first stage in the acceptance of the new maritime policy was made in response to a motion by the Cobdenite Milner Gibson in March 1854 urging that British cruisers be instructed not to interfere with neutral merchantmen carrying enemy goods other than contraband. Gibson avoided a doctrinaire position. "I do not ask the House to commit itself to any abstract principle," he insisted; "I do not propose to give up any of our maritime rights." But the exercise of such rights under present circumstances would injure British commercial interests without impairing Russia's capacity to wage war; and the enforcement of the old rule would provoke the hostility of the United States, whose friendship was essential. Perhaps the time had come, he suggested, when the nations of the world should consider "a general negotiation" on maritime policy.[12] John Bright supported Gibson in more ideological terms, observing that the old rule had been made by the powerful naval states concerned not with justice but the imposition of their selfish will. The "true and permanent and future interests" of England like those of the United States lay in a peaceful commerce.[13] Lord John Russell, a minister without portfolio in the Aberdeen cabinet, agreed.[14]

In July 1854, Henry Reeve, the editor of the Whiggish *Edinburgh Review*, argued that the old rule had been made impractical under *all* conditions – not merely those that prevailed in the war with Russia – by decades of "peace, prosperity, and progress." Free trade and the networks of railroads and the telegraph united nations by "a thousand ties" of commercial interest and humanitarian sympathy; and "the dread of public opinion" was now a powerful restraint upon "the abuse of superior maritime power," as was the increasing naval strength of neutrals. Privateering was "a remnant of more barbarous times," "utterly at variance with the more enlightened principle, that war should be exclusively carried on by the regular forces of the belligerents." Once England recognized the right of neutrals to trade with the enemy, Reeve concluded, it was easier to accept the justice of Englishmen doing the same, thus establishing "a partial commercial peace in the midst of a political war."[15]

Later that month the Benthamite first commissioner of works, Sir William Molesworth, revived for the Commons the argument outlined by the utilitarian philosopher in the 1780s. Speaking for the government, he declared that the old belligerent rights at sea had become "obsolete, in consequence of the progress of humanity and civilization." The old rule had neither legal nor moral justification; neutrals had submitted to "acts of violence" when compelled but resisted "wherever strong enough to defend their rights." It was therefore foolish to cite the authority of Grotius or Vattel and fallacious to assume "that what is law ought to be law." The "tendency of civilisation" had been to "enlarge the rights of neutrals, and to protect weak neutrals against the tyranny of strong belligerents." Certainly, no belligerent, no matter how strong, was "entitled to issue . . . commands to free and independent nations, and to punish the disobedient as if they were his subjects." "The sea is free," and "the abolition of private war on the ocean" was a "step in civilization," and a "benefit to the human race."[16] It was now clear to the House – though Molesworth did not say this explicitly – that the government was not merely refraining from exercising England's belligerent rights on this occasion. It was prepared to yield them forever. What had seemingly begun as a pragmatic response to a particular situation had become principle.

There were objections by British ship-owners who felt themselves injured by the prohibition of the Russian trade to British ships though not to British merchants. Was this not an "absurd principle" helpful only to neutral shippers, a Radical from Dundalk inquired. Why not let British vessels trade with the enemy?[17] But the government was not prepared to go so far. In February 1855 the shipping interests, in exasperation, demanded the complete stoppage of Russian trade, a fully effective blockade, rather than see the enrichment of neutral ship-owners. Later there was talk of a blockade of Prussian ports through which overseas goods, mostly in the hands of British merchants, were making their way to Russia, or of a search of Prussian ships, thus calling Prussia to account by the rule of 1756. Such moves, however, did not comport with the ministry's determination to avoid antagonizing neutrals. British trade with the enemy continued unabated in neutral vessels.

The sons of Joseph Phillimore, the Oxford professor of law mentioned earlier, defended the old rule and the traditional position of the international jurists as their father had done during the Napoleonic Wars. The barrister J. G. Phillimore, the Whig member for Leominster, warned that the new rule increased the probability of war "by making it the harvest of neutral nations." Critical of the "benevolent, though . . . very mistaken principles" of Cobden and Bright, he saw it as a "mistaken humanity" to believe "that a nation could carry on a maritime war, and at the same time allow their enemy the advantages of peace."[18] His brother R.J. Phillimore, the Whig MP for Tavistock who succeeded his father in 1855 on the admiralty court of the Cinque Ports, confessed to having an "unenlightened mind," one not "illuminated by those great modern lights" and content with "groping in the dark" with the masters of international law Grotius and Vattel. Was it not "a little strange" that the "Liberal principles" now maintained by the government were "the doctrine which the Autocrat of All the Russias had insisted upon in 1780"? The Armed Neutrality of that year had not been "influenced by any abstract love of justice," but by a desire to injure Britain.[19]

The government's policy of what Reeve called "a partial commercial peace in the midst of a political war" also distressed a Plymouth barrister, later to become a Liberal attorney general, R. P. Collier. In a debate in the lower house in early 1855, Collier denounced the existence of a wartime trade with Russia. "Was it to be said that they would take every measure for the purpose of prosecuting the war with vigour, except one, which was likely to injure their commercial interests?" If this was the spirit in which they wished to wage war, the English "were rightly called a nation of shopkeepers, and they had better stay at home." In response, John Bright shouted "Hear, hear!"[20]

The Declaration of Paris

The Aberdeen coalition was followed in February 1855 by a Whig government led by Lord Palmerston; it was Palmerston who brought the Crimean War to a close. The Whig Earl of Clarendon, England's foreign minister and plenipotentiary at the treaty-making, signed in May 1856 the Declaration of Paris which made permanent the wartime revolution in maritime policy. The Declaration provided for the end of privateering, insisted that a blockade be effective if it were to be binding, and endorsed as both just and progressive the principle that free ships made for free goods, except in the case of contraband. The French foreign minister proclaimed that just as the Congress of Vienna had outlawed the slave trade, so did the 1856 Conference at Paris take a great step forward in the march of civilization by placing war at sea on an equitable footing. The new rule had triumphed.

The circumstances that led to this revolution in policy are not fully clear. The French foreign minister Drouyn de Lhuys suggested that the British government, knowing the advantages of the new rule to England under modern conditions, wished to give up the old. Yet the Whig ministry feared "d'abandonner, *en face du pays*, les règles inviolables de son vieux droit maritime." The old rule, after all, was regarded for over a century as essential to the security of an insular England. In March 1854, Clarendon wrote in a private letter of his desire to "pay homage to the civilisation of the times we live in" by bringing British law and practice "more in harmony" with those of other maritime nations.[21] (One historian has suggested that Milner Gibson and Sir William Molesworth had converted Clarendon to this position.[22]) During the negotiations that led to the Peace of Paris, Clarendon urged the new rule upon a hesitant Palmerston. If England returned to "our ancient doctrine" it would be "under pain of having all mankind against us," he explained. Why not volunteer "as a benevolent act" making "permanent the principle" on which Britain had acted during the war, on the condition that all the powers, most importantly the United States, give up privateering?[23]

The Declaration of Paris was promulgated at a time when the optimistic views of the Cobdenite Manchester School were generally accepted by liberals. Since peace was in the best commercial interest of all nations and war would soon disappear, and since Britain saw herself as more likely to be neutral in a future European war than belligerent, no English liberal could object to a rule that would both benefit neutral commerce and advance the cause of civilization. Even Palmerston, whom the Cobdenites thought a sword-rattler, was convinced in the mid-1850s that this liberal Utopia was coming to pass. The prime minister's support of the Declaration hampered Tory opposition since, as one Victorian historian suggested, "there was no public man, not even Lord Derby, who could plausibly pretend to be more warlike than Lord Palmerston."[24]

None the less in May 1856 the Tory peers initiated a parliamentary assault on the Declaration. Lord Colchester, in moving a censure of the Whig government, argued that the new system would only prolong wars because the stronger belligerent would be deprived of "the power of reducing his enemy to sue for peace in consequence of exhaustion." The weaker belligerent would merely turn its commerce over to neutrals and use all its seamen and ships for war. The principle "identified with her [Britain's] national Greatness" had been accepted by "the most eminent Jurists of all Ages," and to abandon it was "a serious injury to a Power whose main reliance is her Naval Superiority." How could the British plenipotentiaries at Paris "sign away the law of the land without the consent of Parliament"?[25] The Earl of Carnarvon saw the old rule as embodying "the principle of self-preservation and legitimate self-defence"; since England was more often a belligerent than a neutral, she ought to hold more firmly to her belligerent rights.[26] The Earl of Hardwicke wondered whether with such a Declaration in force a future war could "ever be terminated." The new rule might bring to an end the system of prizes of war, "that legal system of gain" for naval officers and men "procured by their own exertions," and consequently make it more difficult to find men for the Navy.[27]

The former Tory prime minister the Earl of Derby made the most spirited attack on the Paris agreement. Derby was content "to class myself in the same line of barbarians with Canning, Pitt, Lord Hawkesbury, and Lord Shelburne," who had all favored the old rule. England possessed only her navy to counterbalance the French army and "the more you circumscribe the power of that navy the more you weaken the strength and influence of the country." In the event of a war with France, England's only hope was "closing her up hermetically, and stopping her commerce." With the new rule, France could simply turn her merchantmen into war ships and let neutrals carry her trade. If the new principle were accepted, why not in good logic declare that enemy merchantmen, "unarmed and engaged merely in the prosecution of commerce," were private property and similarly immune from capture? "I defy you to draw the line." (The Radicals, we shall see, would agree on this point.) "My lords," Derby declared, "I look upon this act of the Government as cutting off the right arm, as it were, of the country." Without her belligerent maritime rights, England could no longer be "the mistress of the seas," and would fall "immediately and naturally into the position of a third-rate Power." Derby could only hope that circumstances would arise to enable the country to repudiate "the humiliating Clarendon Capitulation of Paris."[28]

The Earl of Clarendon, replying, declared the principle that free ships made free goods to be one of "reason and justice" which had long been accepted as "the rule of civilized nations." Having waived her belligerent rights during the Crimean War, "was it possible, or was it prudent" to revert to them? If Britain continued in a course not only "contrary to the public opinion of the world" but also "hostile to commerce, and as unfavourable as possible to a mitigation of the evils of war," she would be at war with every maritime power, most particularly America. In exchange for accepting the new rule, England had secured the abolition of privateering, and he noted that even one steam-driven privateer could wreak the greatest destruction on Britain's merchant sailing-ships. England had given up both tariff protection and her monopoly on colonial trade, Clarendon concluded, "those pretended rights and claims – each of which has been in turn a British palladium and bulwark," and had not suffered thereby; indeed, she had greatly profited.[29]

Other Whig peers joined in the defense. Her acceptance of the new rule, the Earl of Harrowby noted, was a demonstration that England was not "a selfish asserter of extreme claims" to be enforced by her maritime power. "The real strength of England" consisted "in her reputation for justice as well as for power."[30] The Earl of Albermarle saw the old rule as "a law of the strong against the weak"; as a "step in the progress of civilisation," the "last and highest" of all the rules of war was free ships, free goods.[31] Earl Grey declared that no nation could stand against "the public opinion and general intelligence of the world,"[32] and the president of the council Earl Granville announced that at this "time of England's greatest strength" the acceptance of the new rule was a concession which could be made "without destroying for ever the naval supremacy of England."[33] The Duke of Argyle complained that the Tory opposition had shown but scant regard for the views of "the great commercial classes of the country," and insisted that the power of blockade, which England possessed because of her naval superiority, was "infinitely more effective" than the stopping of neutral trade on the high seas.[34]

The motion of censure failed in the House of Lords on a largely party vote.[35] Bentham's dream of the previous century had come to pass.

Radical MPs in the coming years were to propose motion after motion calling for the immunity from capture at sea of all non-contraband private property – even enemy merchantmen. These motions were withdrawn before a vote could show how few MPs supported them. Much to the irritation of the Radicals, a few members of both parties took the opportunity provided by these debates to denounce the Declaration of Paris.

Lord John Russell, for one, was no longer convinced in 1857 – as he had been in 1854 – by his party's maritime policies. He had come to believe that the Declaration undermined "our maritime supremacy" and "ought to be altered." England's strategy in past wars with France had been to destroy the enemy's trade and to disorder their finances so as to make them sue for peace. Now the enemy would not be distressed by such economic reverses. "We might gain naval victories" and "drive all their vessels of war from the seas," all without gaining "an honourable peace." The situation was "very alarming," but Russell could not bring himself to recommend "a breach of faith" by a unilateral denunciation of the Declaration.[36]

Others were better prepared for such a one-sided breach. In the 1857 debate a Tory member, G. W. P. Bentinck, called on England to renounce the Declaration "at any cost," even "that of the reputation of this country for integrity"; the alternative was the destruction of "the maritime supremacy of this country."[37] The Whig Admiral Napier, MP for Southwark, agreed. If Britain stood by the treaty and there was war with France, England must blockade every enemy port not by "a mere paper, but an efficient blockade." Were the Royal Navy three times its present size, this would prove impossible. "Diplomacy had drawn us into a very impolitic engagement," Napier concluded, and "some clever diplomatist" had "to get us out of it."[38] In a later debate, in 1862, the Earl of Malmesbury, who as foreign secretary in 1858 had yielded to America on the right of search, argued that though the Declaration was "extremely creditable to Christian feeling and philanthropy," not a single article would be "carried out when a great war should take place," for "human passions were too strong."[39]

There were others outside of parliament who rejected the new rule. Most active in this cause was David Urquhart, who initiated a nation-wide campaign against the Declaration of Paris. Both Karl Marx and John Stuart Mill accepted the validity and urgency of Urquhart's position.

Urquhart, Mill, and Marx

Urquhart, an Oxford-educated Scotsman, participated as a young naval lieutenant in the Greek struggle for independence. In 1831 he joined the staff of England's ambassador to Turkey, and in his two years in Constantinople became an ardent Turcophile and, necessarily, a fierce enemy of Russia. An anti-Russian pamphlet that he published in 1833 was to bring a rejoinder two years later by Richard Cobden. Cobden was persuaded that a relatively progressive and Christian Russia was a more suitable candidate for British political support and commercial penetration than a backward and pagan Turkey.[40] Urquhart, on the other hand, was convinced that Russia was England's most dangerous rival and that the Russian tzars, despotic rulers of their own peoples and suppressors of Polish liberty, were implacable enemies of progress. These views were widely shared by continental revolutionaries and liberals, particularly after Russia's suppression of the Hungarian uprising in 1848.

During the 1830s, 1840s and 1850s, in the pages of his periodical the *Portfolio*, and from 1847 to 1852 from his seat in parliament, Urquhart worked to persuade his countrymen that for well over a century Russia had been engaged in a grand effort at world conquest. To further Russia's purpose, newspapers and politicians throughout Europe had been hoodwinked or bribed. Most prominent among these suborned statesmen, Urquhart insisted, was Viscount Palmerston, whose whole career the Turcophile agitator saw as devoted to the service of Russian ambitions. Like the Radical pacifists Cobden and Bright, Urquhart opposed the Crimean War, persuaded that Turkey was strong enough to fight her own battles without the dubious help of the western powers. He saw behind England's war against the tzar a Palmerstonian plot to advance Russian interests.

When the Liberal government subscribed to the Declaration of Paris in 1856, Urquhart had proof that Palmerston's pro-Russian plot had succeeded. Had not Russia, the leader of the Armed Neutralities of 1780 and 1800, finally gained her objective? Urquhart ascribed the half-hearted character of the war, as displayed by the concessions to neutral shipping, to collusion between England's and France's aristocratic and middle-class politicians and the tzar. Only the enforcement of England's belligerent rights at sea might still prevent the realization of Russian plans for world conquest; only a union of the Crown and loyal British working men could save England and the cause of European liberty. In the late 1850s, and in the 1860s and 1870s, Urquhart presided over a "national Movement," as he called it, to encourage working men to study foreign affairs. A Maritime League was also formed under Urquhart's auspices to secure the repudiation of the Declaration of Paris.[41]

Urquhart believed that the history of the world for the previous three generations could be understood only in terms of the belligerent right of search – the sole power which England possessed against insatiable Russian ambitions. England's real power at sea was "not in her line-of-battleships" but in her cruisers: "The power of seizing your enemy's property upon the high seas ... constitutes metaphorically the trident of Great Britain." Without that right, Britain would "sink to a fifth-rate power at once," for there was no medium for "an island State" between "absolute maritime supremacy and entire domestic and territorial subjugation." The "holder of the trident" might protect "the oppressed or extinguished nations" of Europe, and even if the maintenance of naval supremacy proved a burden to taxpayers and if Britain's insistence on her maritime rights were to lead to "a combination against us of the whole world," "we must still endure it" for the sake of liberty and progress. The threat of British privateers was "the greatest of Russian fears," and Clarendon and Palmerston, by yielding both privateering and the old rule in 1856, revealed themselves to be Russian agents or dupes.[42]

Urquhart encouraged his committees of working men to oppose Palmerston's pro-tzarist foreign policy. One Urquhartite working man who signed himself 'A Journeyman Shoemaker' in a series of letters to a Nottingham weekly declared that by the Declaration of 1856 England had "transformed itself from a great naval to a small military power"; for when she yielded the right to halt neutral trade with the enemy, Britain endangered the precious right of blockade. A neutral would think it a "mockery and equally illogical and unjust" for England to grant him a right to trade with the enemy, and then by blockade "withhold his right to finish the last mile of his voyage." The Shoemaker was shocked that citizens of belligerent states might continue to trade with the enemy, as English merchants had done in the Crimean War, "in spite of all antiquated notions about treason": "the Queen's cause will not be ours; the Queen's enemies will not be ours." The end of the right of search had brought about "the sudden exposure of the country to invasion."[43]

Perhaps it was John Stuart Mill's association with the East India Company – his job was to oversee the external policies of the states of British India – that made him, almost uniquely among Radicals, a defender of power properly used. Mill's friend Alexander Bain described him as "a Greece-intoxicated man,"[44] and Mill saw the role a democratic Athens played in the ancient world as similar to the one played by England during the Pax Britannica. "Under the protection of the powerful Athenian navy," Mill observed in 1853, the states of Greece "enjoyed a security never before known," and were able to make great strides toward both liberty and improvement. Athens' "ambitious external policy" was "perversely misjudged and misunderstood." Not that the Athenians were "exempt from the passion, universal in the ancient world, for conquest and dominion," and judged by "the universal standard of right," this was undoubtedly "a blemish." But given Athens' "vocation as the organ of progress," it was "most beneficial to the world." Rather than denounce the Athenian maritime empire, those subjected to it had "cause to lament" that it did not last long enough to protect them against the cruder rules of Macedonia and Rome. The lesson was plain. Power in the right hands was critical to the progress of civilization. There could be no possibility of "permanent improvement for mankind," unless "intellect ... asserted its superiority, even in a military sense, over brute force."[45]

Mill was critical of the policy of non-intervention which the Cobdenites championed. In 1859, he praised England as more dedicated to "the service of others, than of itself," for she always stood ready "to procure the abandonment of some national crime and scandal to humanity." Yet continentals could not accept the selflessness of English policy, her readiness, for example, to spend £20 million to abolish the slave trade; they were persuaded that England was "reaping some inexplicable advantage." The expansion of British power in India was also the "discharge of an imperative duty". Was it not better for barbarians to be "conquered and held in subjection" than for them to massacre each other and threaten the peace? As the foremost liberal power, Britain had a duty to defend, by armed intervention if necessary, the liberties of the submerged and suppressed nationalities of Europe menaced by "a coalition of Continental despots." When the Russians had marched into Hungary in 1848, Mill believed that it would have been both "honourable and virtuous" if England had helped the rebels, a policy of "intervention to enforce non-intervention."[46]

A number of Urquhartite working men wrote to Mill in 1866, when he was Liberal MP for Westminster, to press their views on the Declaration of Paris. Mill, as an advocate of a peacetime right of search to end the slave trade and a defender of the repressed peoples of the continent, was prepared to listen sympathetically. In a reply to one Urquhartite, Mill described the "relinquishment by the naval Powers" of the old rule, "their most powerful weapon of defence against the great military Powers," as an error,[47] and noted that no nation had the right "to bind itself and its posterity permanently" by treaty.[48] What might be done? Mill could not agree with the Urquhartites that Napoleon III, at last realizing that France, too, was a maritime power, would join an awakened England in repudiating the Declaration, for he remembered too well how French governments "prided themselves on vindicating against us what they call the liberty of the seas." He hoped, however, that Disraeli might reopen the question of the unwise surrender of the old rule.[49]

It was Mill himself who reopened the question in a speech before the Commons in August 1867 calling for the resumption of England's belligerent rights. England had been since 1856 condemned to see "great international iniquities perpetrated before our eyes, and our expressions of deprecation, even of reprobation, passed over with civil, or scarcely civil contempt." The renunciation of the old rule was a consequence of liberal self-deception. Liberals in fact showed "less knowledge" and "less understanding" than did Conservatives: fresh from the triumph of free trade and the enthusiasm of the Great Exhibition of 1851, they believed war "alien" to "the modern spirit" of science and saw "the universal substitution of commerce for war." But "we were mistaken," said Mill, thinking no doubt of Prussia's recent wars against Denmark and Austria, for "wars of conquest and annexation" had been renewed. Though "'the light that led us astray was light from Heaven,'" England must "shake off" her self-forged chains and "resume that natural weapon which has been the main bulwark of our power and safety in past national emergencies." The utilitarian philosopher defended this course on "no narrow grounds of merely British patriotism" for, as "the elite of Europe" would agree, "the safety, and even the power of England, are valuable to the freedom of the world, therefore to the greatest and most permanent interests of every civilized people."[50]

The great issue was the balance of power which Radicals mistakenly decried as a fallacy. To weaken the "essentially defensive" naval powers who in both ancient and modern times were the "cradle and the home of liberty" was to add to the strength of "aggressive" military nations. Were the leading naval powers – Britain, France, and the United States – rendered impotent, two or three military monarchies would divide Europe among them, and then "desolate the earth by fighting for a re-division." It was ludicrous for the British to have freed the navies of their enemies, no longer needed to protect their own commerce, to bring troops to English shores. Britain was now committed to an expensive program of fortifications to protect herself against the despotic continental powers that "we justly feel to be a danger to us." These powers maintained "gigantic and ruinous" military establishments as much for internal as external reasons, and the relatively small population of Great Britain could not cope with "this mad rivalry."[51]

Some advocates of the Declaration of Paris wished to proceed further and declare all non-contraband private property at sea free from seizure, Mill continued. This would be a serious mistake. We would then see "nations at war with nations, but their merchants and shipowners at peace," and conducting a profitable trade with their country's enemies. Would this be a "gain to humanity" as the advocates of immunity maintained? If war were confined to such "a duel between Governments," commerce and industry would lose nothing by such conflicts and consequently have "no pecuniary interest" in preventing them. This would constitute a considerable setback to the cause of peace.[52]

The Radicals were shocked, for Mill had been a friend to every cause they held dear. Instead of joining their campaign to extend immunity to all private property, Mill urged the repudiation of the Declaration of Paris.

Even mainstream Liberals and a liberal-minded Tory foreign secretary were disappointed with such an unprogressive position.

Lord Stanley, the Tory foreign secretary in the cabinet of his father the Earl of Derby (who we know was a foe of the Declaration), ignored the tribute Mill bestowed on the treaty's Conservative opponents. Stanley belonged to the liberal wing of his party, and like the Cobdenite Radicals was strongly opposed to English interventions abroad. (In 1878, he resigned from Disraeli's cabinet and later joined the Liberals because he disapproved of the activist imperial policies of the Tories.) Perhaps the Declaration of Paris *had* deprived England of her natural weapon, Stanley granted, and made it more difficult for her to intervene in continental affairs. But "the power to intervene effectually is a temptation to do so," and if England were restrained by the 1856 Declaration "from mixing ourselves up with Continental complications with which we had nothing to do," this was a good thing. The foreign secretary conceded that "the necessities of self-defence" overrode all compacts, but unless England lived up to the agreement the world might again – as in 1780 and 1800 – rise up in arms against her. Up to now England as a neutral in continental quarrels had benefited from the 1856 arrangements. In any event, she had urged other nations to adhere to the Declaration, and was morally bound herself.[53]

Finally, we turn to David Urquhart's convert and follower, the socialist economist Karl Marx. Marx was to write his friend Kugelmann in 1869 that Urquhart's interpretation of international affairs was essentially correct, though somewhat spoiled by "the crotchets of the great 'David.'"[54] Yet the German socialist shared many of these crotchets. Marx saw a "secret and permanent collaboration of the cabinets at London and St. Petersburg" since the time of Peter the Great and, for Marx as for Urquhart, Palmerston was a Russian agent and consequently a great villain. Marx lauded Urquhart as Palmerston's "indefatigable antagonist" who could not be "intimidated into silence, bribed into connivance, charmed into suitorship."[55]

Marx also shared Urquhart's (and Mill's) less eccentric view of the perils posed by Britain's adoption of the Declaration of Paris. "By the Paris Peace Treaty of 1856, England disarmed herself," Marx wrote to Kugelmann in 1870. "England is a sea power," possessing "only the weapon of naval warfare as a counterweight against the great continental powers"; her "infallible method" was "to destroy or bring to a standstill, the overseas trade" of her enemies. To do this, however, she must "enforce the principle of seizing enemy goods in neutral vessels." But England had foolishly surrendered this and other maritime rights in 1856. Why? "Clarendon did this at the secret order of the pro-Russian Palmerston," Marx charged. However the Paris Declaration had never been ratified by parliament, and the continental despots were "reckoning without their host" if they believed "the bourgeois weak-mindedness of a Gladstone" would "at a decisive moment keep John Bull from casting overboard" these self-imposed restraints. When war came, England would destroy Russian–German overseas trade and starve out her continental enemies, and then the world would see "the disconsolate faces of the Petersburg and Berlin diplomats."[56]

Echoes

In an 1871 debate in the Commons, there was a confrontation between the two most considerable parliamentary gladiators of Victorian England. Benjamin Disraeli, the leader of the Conservative opposition to the government of W. E. Gladstone, proclaimed that Britain's adherence to the Declaration of Paris was "a most impolitic step, calculated to cripple the powers of this country," and urged that "we must emancipate ourselves from its fatal trammels." What did it matter if the old rule had vexed neutrals? "I am afraid that the exercise of power at all times, is not agreeable to those who experience its force and influence."[57] Other Tories supported Disraeli, two enlisting the authority of Mill's 1867 speech, which Serjeant Simon, the Tory MP for Dewsbury, described as having been "received by a thrill of amazement throughout the country."[58] The Liberal prime minister Gladstone replied, in a different spirit, that the traditional belligerent rights at sea had long been "totally isolated from the actual living sentiment of the civilized world." Under those circumstances, England had no choice but to accept the new rule.[59]

Four years later in 1875 a Tory government was in power, and it became clear that Disraeli's anxiety to emancipate England from the "fatal trammels" of 1856 was largely rhetorical. Tory backbenchers might initiate motions to withdraw from the Declaration, as did Baillie Cochrane on this occasion, but the front bench was silent. "No fortifications, no torpedoes, no ironclads, no increase of our Army or Navy," Cochrane argued, "could give us the power that we should derive from the right of seizing enemy's goods at sea in time of war." "Unless we were to adopt for ever a principle of selfish isolation, we should do everything to maintain the maritime greatness of this country."[60] Serjeant Simon once again invoked the authority of Mill, who had died in 1873 – "a great philosopher, whose whole life was devoted to the study of what was best calculated to promote the freedom and the happiness of mankind." Mill had understood that England's mission was "to spread the blessings of liberty," and perceived that by accepting the Declaration we "weaken our power for good."[61]

It was left to the barrister Sir William Harcourt, a future Liberal chancellor of the exchequer, to defend the 1856 agreement in the debate. England was no longer in the position when "by the genius of Nelson and the valour of her sailors" she ruled as "mistress of the seas," he declared; moreover, under the new rule a neutral England, in the course of the European and American wars since 1856 had virtually "monopolized the carrying trade of the world" and enjoyed its considerable profits. "Yet we were asked to repent of the obligations under which we derived such advantages"! Were the Declaration repudiated, he suggested, with somewhat specious strategical reasoning, "our enormous foreign trade, which was 30 times as great as in the days of Nelson, would be at the mercy" not only of privateers, should Britain be at war, but of "every South American Republic" which thought fit to exercise belligerent rights. More realistically, Harcourt noted that the Declaration left intact a right "most valuable to a maritime Power," that of blockade.[62]

Ideology was a central issue in an 1877 debate on maritime policy. The Hon. Percy Wyndham, a Tory back-bencher and opponent of the 1856 Declaration, blamed England's unhappy naval position on "the teachings of the Manchester School" which "had penetrated the middle classes of this country, and had largely affected the upper classes."[63] Defenders of the Declaration hastened to confirm this linkage; one saw Adam Smith as the first defender of neutral rights,[64] and another the repeal of agricultural protection in 1846 as the irretrievable break with the past that had made the adoption of the new rule necessary. "We cannot, at the same time, have the advantages of being dependent on, and independent of, the whole world," he concluded.[65] To complete the proof, John Bright's brother Jacob again recited a central doctrine of the liberal catechism: "when commerce was made free ... it was destined to destroy war."[66]

On this occasion, Liberals and their opponents also differed – on ideological grounds – on the hoary question of defensive or offensive war. The Tory Lord Eslington, a defender of the old rule, protested that Liberals wished to confine war only to defensive operations: you might as well "tell a man engaged in a duel *à outrance* and with a rapier in his hand that he must content himself with parrying and not attempt to thrust."[67] On the other side, Lord Edmund Fitzmaurice wished to affirm that "the 'meteor flag of England,'" would remain as "every great statesman of the country desired ... a warning to the privateer, the slaver, and the pirate," but not "what the members of the [Urquhartite] Maritime League wished it to be – the dread of the defenceless trader and the terror of the unarmed merchant."[68] Some Liberals sought to confine contraband to arms and munitions since such a limited definition, as M. E. Grant Duff, a Liberal MP and a future governor of Madras, argued, was to the advantage of a trading nation like England. Grant Duff saw something both immoral and dishonorable in a war against commerce: "Our present naval officers" regarded the Navy's job as the defense of England against invasion and the restriction of enemy ships to their home ports, a "class of duties" far preferable to those performed in earlier wars against trade, which had "many features in common with piracy."[69]

Radicals believed themselves the spokesmen not only for reason and morality, but also for British interests. They viewed the House of Lords as well as the greater part of the House of Commons – whether Conservative or Liberal – as still too much influenced by an obsolete mercantilist economics and quasi-feudal politics which thought first of power not of well-being. While it was their devotion to the establishment of a universal peace that inspired Radicals to work so enthusiastically for freedom from maritime capture for all private property, they also argued that immunity served the interests of British trade and shipping. Though successive Liberal and Tory governments and their admiralties were ready to accept the principle of free ships, free goods as compatible with both England's commercial and strategic interests, they strongly resisted the Radical effort to extend this immunity from capture to enemy merchant ships.

[5] The Cobdenite Conscience: National War and Commercial Peace

War then is a relation, not between man and man, but between State and State, and individuals are enemies only accidentally, not as men, nor even as citizens, but as soldiers; not as members of their country, but as its defenders. Finally, each State can have for enemies only other States, and not men ... A just prince, while laying hands, in the enemy's country, on all that belongs to the public, respects the lives and goods of individuals ... These principles are not those of Grotius: they are not based on the authority of poets; but derived from the nature of reality and based on reason.

Rousseau, *The Social Contract*

Radicals agreed with Rousseau that war was a relation "not between man and man, but between State and State,"[1] and cheered the possibility of a commercial peace even when nations were at war. As early as the 1820s, the Benthamite Radical James Mill – the father of John Stuart Mill – had defended freedom of trade in all goods, in war as in peace, by the standard of utility, the greatest material happiness of the greatest number: "all nations gain by the free operations of commerce," he observed; if one nation's riches were "increased by freedom of commerce, so are those of its antagonists." Mill went beyond the doctrine of free ships, free goods. Not merely the importation of provisions but even that of instruments of war should "upon the principle of utility" not be interfered with; the abolition of the concept of contraband would spare the neutrals "the annoyance of search, the loss by detention, the occasion of quarrel," all "evils of no ordinary magnitude." (The only exception to the rule of freedom for wartime commerce would be in the case of ports "actually blockaded.") Mill had also called for the establishment of an international tribunal, whose sole sanction would be the public opinion of the world, as a more proper place for settling maritime differences than national courts of admiralty.[2]

In his 1867 address advocating repudiation of the Declaration of Paris, and also citing utility as his standard, J. S. Mill called on a bourgeois England to restore to herself the instruments of naval power that his father James and the

Radicals had condemned. Some thirty years previously, Mill had regretted that, with authority passing from individuals to masses in modern industrial society, all ranks were no longer exposed "to the spectacle of harshness, rudeness, and violence, to the struggle of one indomitable will against another, and to the alternate suffering and inflicting of pain"; with the progress of civilization men had given up "the love of active virtue," and now desired only to increase their wealth. If they had in their character "much more of the amiable and humane," they had "much less of the heroic." Mill complained that "there has crept over the refined classes, over the whole class of gentlemen in England, a moral effeminacy, an inaptitude for every kind of struggle"; "they shrink ... from everything which is troublesome and disagreeable," and are "sluggish and unenterprising."[3]

What helped to make so many Victorian liberals shrink from struggle and violence, indeed become quasi-pacifist during the nineteenth century, one may argue, was the dissemination, as well as the secularization, of the doctrines of Dissent.[4] Dissenters were convinced that God – and secular Radicals that historical progress – intended a millennial reign of peace, and that this new era was at hand. To prepare for war displayed an unredeemed nature. The true enemies of peace and progress were not France or Russia, but the feudal classes (in alliance with the masses, still psychologically dependent on them), who were selfishly prepared to welcome a satanic reaction. The Radicals dismissed the politics of the past, based on instinctual aggression and irrational appeals, and worked to loosen the ties of traditional dependence, and to attain a sense of autonomy, a self-discipline established – in the mode of the Dissenting sects and Kant's philosophy – in the individual conscience.[5] For the religious, the psychoanalyst Sigmund Freud speculated, conscience might assume the position of an exacting God who judges sinful inclinations as well as actions, giving rise to heightened feelings of guilt; such feelings were clearly in evidence among Radicals, whether formally religious or not, who were only too aware of the impossibility of perfectly fulfilling the commands to love their neighbors as themselves and to entrust vengeance to the Lord.[6] They were persuaded that it was the survival of the feudal ethos that delayed the final victory of the spirit over the flesh. The stimulation of the aggressive instinct that would accompany war would threaten not only the newly acquired sense of autonomy of the middle classes, but might also restore the feudal governing class to its former power.[7]

Radicals, capitalists, and immunity

Cobden and Bright, we know, were opposed to the rules on naval war set forth by the international jurists. As pacifists they were convinced that the principle of immunity for private property at sea would not merely soften the rigors of war but help to bring war as an institution to a speedier demise.[8] The ultimate Cobdenite standard was not Benthamite utility nor international law but Christian morality. "The 'law of nations,' is not my law," Bright declared in 1854 in a letter to a correspondent who had invoked the authority of Vattel; for international law was founded on custom and "the will of the strongest" and not on that of the "higher morality."[9] The Radicals saw themselves as the Christian conscience of modern, liberal society.

In defending the government's maritime policies during the Crimean War, the Benthamite Molesworth, invoking both morality and utility, had called for "the abolition of private war on the ocean."[10] Other Radicals were to make similar suggestions. With the war barely a year old, T. E. Cliffe Leslie, the professor of political economy at Queen's College, Belfast, in 1855 observed that merchants had done "more than all others to promote peace," and had secured for England both "maritime power" and a "high place among nations." Had they thereby "only established a claim to be the chief sufferers in every struggle?" Given her vast merchant marine, Britain stood most to gain from the adoption of the principle of immunity which, moreover, would make it unnecessary to bear "the cost of maintaining an enormous fleet."[11] A tract that same year by J. L. Ricardo, the nephew of the economist, pronounced the "Pufendorfian rights of war" dead. To "destroy trade" had "affected but a few" in the past, but "to disturb it now, is to attack the whole fabric of our social economy." That an England with her large mercantile marine and carrying trade, an England which had grown "powerful, not by conquest, but by commerce," should hesitate to free trade from "the evils of war" was "an incredible anomaly to perplex and amaze the future historians of our time."[12]

But Cobden's agenda went beyond that of James Mill, Molesworth, Leslie, and Ricardo. While earlier Radicals recognized the legitimacy of blockade if naval force was to have any meaning, Cobden in an 1856 letter proclaimed the "Blockade laws" to be "about as rascally an invention as the old Corn Laws."[13] (Some observers, indeed, feared that the Paris Declaration already undermined the mounting of an effective blockade.)[14] Changes in traditional methods of naval warfare were for Cobden "the necessary corollary of the repeal of the navigation laws, the abolition of the corn laws, and the abandonment of our colonial monopoly." The system of capture and blockade was absolutely "incompatible" with free trade. Though once useful, blockades now inflicted "greater injuries on an unoffending neutral community than on a belligerent." And Britain had become "the great neutral power." A maritime war fought by the traditional strategy would jeopardize the course Britain had undertaken in 1846 to permit "the indefinite growth" of a population dependent on overseas food. "We have thrown away the sceptre of force to confide in the principle of freedom – uncovenanted, unconditional freedom," a "new *regime*" that had brought prosperity without precedent.[15]

Cobden prayed that "the intercourse of nations, as well as individuals may some day be brought into harmony with the precepts of the New Testament."[16]

In 1856, the American secretary of state W. G. Marcy rejected the Declaration of Paris; since her public navy was so small, the United States refused to give up privateering until all private property was free from capture at sea – and the Radicals were ready to meet Marcy's conditions. "I tell you candidly," Richard Cobden wrote to a political associate at the end of August 1856, "I want to see war brought as much as possible to a duel between Governments and their professional fighters, with as little stimulus from the hope of plunder and prize-money as possible." Cobden observed that "the proposal of the American Government carries out my wishes completely."[17]

What was extraordinary in this heady year of liberal optimism was that the prime minister Viscount Palmerston was for a time in agreement with his old enemy Cobden. In November 1856, Palmerston delivered a speech to the merchants of Liverpool, a commercial community, he noted, whose interests "flourish in peace and are likely to be crippled by war." During the recent war, the government had made "relaxations in the doctrines of war" to ease the pressure upon commerce, and this was done without weakening England's power against Russia. The Declaration of Paris had ratified these changes. The prime minister then suggested that such relaxations "may perhaps be still further extended": in time, "those principles of war" which applied to hostilities on land might also apply at sea, "so that private property shall no longer be the object of aggression by either side." History proved that no "powerful country was ever vanquished by losses sustained by individuals." "It is conflicts of armies by land and of fleets at sea that decided the great contests of nations," Palmerston concluded, and it was desirable that "these conflicts should be confined" to "bodies acting under the orders and directions" of the State.[18]

There were surprising adhesions to Palmerston's position. A few days after the prime minister had spoken, a far from pacifistic *Times* wrote approvingly, noting that – as the workshop of the world – "we fight our battles far less with fire and sword, with gabion and howitzer, than with calico and scissors, with coal and with iron."[19] Even Lord Brougham, who had voted against the abolition of the navigation acts in 1849, and who like Palmerston had favored the use of naval power against Portugal and Brazil, supported the prime minister and the Radicals on the question of immunity. But the trial balloon set afloat at Liverpool was not generally well-received. Palmerston reported "so many remonstrances against giving up the *palladium*, &c. &c.," Brougham was later to write to a correspondent, "that he told me when he returned to London that the pear was not ripe, and that we must give public opinion a little more time to become reasonable."[20]

The Radicals were determined to bring the public to reason. Cobden's method was to convince practical businessmen that Radical doctrine served their interests. Radicals argued that the principle of immunity, long a part of the pacifist platform, had become an economic necessity for the shipping industry. Though a step forward for a pacific commerce, the provisions of the Declaration of Paris threatened the prosperity and even the existence of the British carrying trade, for if England were at war insurance premiums on goods transported by British ships would go up so substantially that merchants would prefer to use neutral carriers.

In early July 1857, Cobden wrote to W. S. Lindsay, the MP for Tynemouth and one of the spokesmen for the ship-owners in parliament, observing that it was "mere childishness to go on talking, as Urquhart and others do, about the unconstitutional and illegal way in which Lord Clarendon surrendered our maritime rights at Paris." Let the House of Commons either repudiate the concession or affirm it and then proceed "like statesmen and men of business TO CONSIDER WHAT, UNDER THE ALTERED CIRCUMSTANCES, IS BEST FURTHER TO BE DONE."[21] In case of war, English ship-owners would be obliged to sell their vessels to foreigners, and the English mercantile marine – the greatest in the world – would be ruined. Ten days later, in response to Cobden's proddings, Lindsay moved in the Commons that Britain support the inviolability of private property at sea, arguing that if British shipping were to pass to neutrals "we should become a sixth-rate Power."[22] In reply, a more cautious Palmerston spoke of the difficulties of accomplishing this "at once."[23]

Cobden also worked to persuade the shippers that their interests no longer lay with the advocates of a big navy. When members of the governing class spoke of "naval supremacy," Cobden wrote to Lindsay in 1860, "their minds are filled with the traditions of 1810." They believed naval superiority would secure all the advantages to commerce that it had conferred a half-century earlier when in the wars against Napoleon British cruisers prevented neutral ships "from performing *their* [the French] carrying trade." But advances in technology had made a revolution. With the coming of railways, commercial blockades had lost their formerly critical importance. Were England now at war with France, the Navy could only protect Britain's shores against invasion, while Americans and other neutrals took over the British carrying trade. Of course, "naval men" would oppose the end of commercial blockades "because it will deprive them of prize money." "*Governments* also instinctively oppose it," for "what excuse would they have for maintaining a costly navy if it were agreed that private property at sea should be free from molestation, and therefore require no protection?"[24] The problem was that governments, controlled by the aristocracy, preferred war to peace.

"Nothing could be so foolish, nothing so mad, as a policy of war for a trading nation," John Bright declared in 1858, adding that "any peace was better than the most successful war." The prime interest of the United States was trade not war, as the American middle classes who actually governed the country and were conscious of their own interests understood. Bright believed that America was the model that first England, and then other European countries must and would follow. The English middle classes did not as yet see their overriding interest in peace, which was why a majority of them supported interventionist policies, most recently in the Crimean War. The interest of the aristocracy, on the other hand, made it favor violent conflicts, though this class usually masked its selfishness by a pretended principle. At one time, the English ruling classes defended the Protestant interests, now they spoke of preserving the liberties of Europe. Their real concern was jobs in the army and navy for their sons, "neither more nor less than a gigantic system of out-door relief for the aristocracy of Great Britain." For these reasons, the governing aristocracy fostered England's "perpetual delusion that it is about to be attacked."[25]

What the Cobdenites envisioned was a struggle between classes, not one between capitalists and proletarians in the Marxist mould, but rather between what they labelled the governing or ruling class – the aristocracy and landed gentry who dominated parliaments and cabinets – and the commercial and industrial middle classes. The rhetorical technique to be employed was suggested to Cobden by a leader of the pacifist movement Henry Richard: this was to convince the middle classes that they were exploited by the landed aristocracy – in Richard's words, "to make the commercial & industrial classes feel they are really befooled by the 'Services' & the aristocracy, that they may be used as mere beasts of burden upon whose back any amount of taxation may be placed." Cobden thought there was "great shrewdness" in this plan. Such arguments proved persuasive for, as Cobden wrote to Bright in 1861, men like Lindsay and the Baptist building and railway contractor S. M. Peto were now "gradually occupying the ground which you & I stood upon almost alone a few years ago."[26]

Despite their appeal to capitalist interests, Cobden and Bright found the selfishness of the commercial classes repugnant. The Radical leaders spoke for the pacific concerns of humanity and Christian civilization in opposition to the feudal barbarism of a bellicose aristocracy. The problem, Cobden wrote Bright, was how to advance those principles when the only politically feasible allies were the commercial and manufacturing classes, the basis for such "a party as Gladstone might lead." If "a progressive & more rational policy" could not find support from these classes, "it is useless in our day to look for such change." In their narrowness and selfishness, the commercial classes "may not be all that you & I wish," Cobden continued, but they offered the only hope for an effective "counterpoise to our ruling class." The way to curtail "the emoluments of the ruling class" was by "rousing the opposition of the same power in the State as that which formed the strength of the [Anti-Corn Law] League." This was the only practical method to bring about "a reduction of armaments, or a reform in international law affecting belligerent rights." With this in mind, Cobden warned Bright, who was given to demagogic hyperbole, "not to encourage a feeling of alienation from the capitalist class."[27]

Cobden and the US Civil War

In 1861, Cobden saw his opportunity in the difficulties produced by the Union naval blockade of the cotton ports of the South. With Lancashire's cotton industry desperately in need of raw material, textile firms facing bankruptcy, and thousands of workers unemployed, Richard Cobden had a crisis not unlike the harvest failures of the 1840s that had compelled Peel to repeal the corn laws. In a letter to Bright in October 1861, Cobden described "this pinch in Lancashire" as the occasion "to commit all parties, & to compel the government to assent, to the doctrine of free seas & free ports." If successful, he continued, this "*could have immense bearings on future discussions on our armaments*."[28]

Cobden's objective, as he noted the following year, was to persuade the government to adhere "to the *principle* of the abolition of commercial blockades for the future," something "our antiquated Palmerstons and Russells are not prepared to do." These men foolishly believed in "the efficacy of blockades as a belligerent weapon," failing to understand that it was "a two-edged sword, which cuts the hand that wields – when that hand is England's – more than the object it strikes."[29] Only if Manchester and Liverpool mobilized to demand a liberal maritime policy would "the 'Services'" and "our ruling classes" respond.[30] Cobden urged Bright to "try to induce" the chambers of commerce "to take up the question of Belligerent Rights." With the stoppage of cotton exports, "I should think that Liverpool without distinction of parties would now go against blockades."[31]

Very soon, the economic crisis was to turn into a political one as well, enhancing Cobden's moment of opportunity. In late 1861, a United States warship stopped the British mail-steamer *Trent*, claiming belligerent rights, and seized two Confederate diplomatic agents on board. This was in violation of maritime law, and the foreign secretary Lord John Russell protested, reversing the usual positions of the two countries by taking up the neutral cause against America. Both English and American public opinion became highly excited, and for a time war between the two countries seemed possible.

Soon after the incident occurred, Cobden wrote a series of letters to his friend Charles Sumner, the Republican Senator from Massachusetts, a long-time abolitionist and pacifist and at this time the chairman of the Senate's foreign relations committee. Cobden urged Sumner to use the *Trent* imbroglio to "emancipate the commerce of the world" from the old code of maritime law, and to demand not only immunity but also the abolition of commercial blockades.[32] Cobden saw Sumner as a fellow Radical: "We are I think both more Christians & Cosmopolitans, than British or Yankee."[33] It was in this Christian spirit that he hoped to enlist Sumner's help in carrying out a "revolution in maritime law" against a British governing class whose "favorite plea when we vote the Navy Estimate is that they are necessary for the protection of commerce."[34]

In later letters to Sumner, Cobden begged that the United States not act "in opposition to the spirit of the age," observing that America had always opposed commercial blockades. Such blockades had never brought about a nation's defeat. The world had "in truth outgrown them," for millions of workers now depended for their jobs on overseas raw materials, "to say nothing of hundreds of millions of capital" invested in machinery.[35] If "with your naval resources you are permanently destroying the great arteries of commerce" in the South, "it will put you in wrong with the whole world."[36] If reason proved unavailing, Cobden reminded Sumner, expecting him to share the letter with the American president, that "we, in England, have ready a fleet surpassing in destructive force any naval armament the world ever saw," that governments always wished "to use such armaments by way of proving that they were necessary," and that following the Declaration of 1856 the Royal Navy would find it "very easy" to prove "that along your thousands of miles of coast *access* is possible" and the blockade therefore ineffective and illegal.[37]

Following Cobden's advice, Sumner worked to win over President Lincoln's cabinet as well as his colleagues in the Senate. The two Southern emissaries must be returned, Sumner insisted, and Lincoln, with some reluctance, was persuaded. In an address to the Senate supporting the return of the rebel diplomats, Sumner noted that if the United States yielded her belligerent rights, "the sea-god will in future use his trident less," thus "rendering the ocean a highway of peace, instead of a field of blood." The United States will have secured the "triumph of their principles," which were also those of the continental states "smarting for years under British pretensions on the sea." He called for the inviolability of private property at sea, as well as the abolition of the concept of contraband of war,[38] but not for the lifting of the Northern blockade, much to Cobden's disappointment. Sumner took the threat of British naval action against America seriously, fearing lest "perhaps Copenhagen be enacted anew." In a letter to Bright, he warned that if England chose "to take advantage of our present misfortune & to attack us," it would "leave behind an ineradicable sting."[39]

British commercial circles were hesitant about the maritime program that the Cobdenites were proposing to the chambers of commerce, as were Liberals generally. Henry Reeve of the *Edinburgh Review*, for example, representing a moderate mainstream Liberalism, was ready to yield the right to expropriate contraband on neutral ships, a change advantageous to

England when as in the American war she was neutral. The search for contraband, moreover, alienated neutrals without having much effect on the waging of war, given the possibilities of railway transport. But Reeve was not prepared to support immunity; the 1856 Declaration made it possible to "maintain the trade of England" in wartime "under whatever flag," and by its provisions England would be able to "stand unshaken for an indefinite period against the world." This was sufficient.[40] The commercial classes hesitated to go further. T. B. Horsfall, Liverpool's Radical MP, reported that his city's chamber of commerce did not think it a good time to take up the reform of maritime law – as Cobden unhappily informed Bright in early 1862.[41]

At the end of January 1862 Cobden was still hopeful that if the Americans made a grand maritime "offer" and the Continent accepted, "*we* can compel *our* aristocracy to come in." Otherwise, "our governing classes will resist a clean sweep of *Vattel & Co.* because they help to keep up the services, & supply an occasional war."[42] If no American offer were forthcoming, Cobden still hoped to use the Anglo-American difficulties as the impetus for a full-scale parliamentary debate on immunity. Such a debate would, of course, give the Tories and the Services the chance to argue for the repudiation of the 1856 treaty; this was particularly true of "that Gorilla, big Ben," meaning Disraeli, and the Whig admiral "old Charley Napier."[43] The government would "resist as much as possible," yet they knew "they are in a mess on this subject." The Whig government had adopted the 1856 Declaration "without exactly knowing what they were doing, & now they are between two fires": they do not wish to meet the objection of the shippers, since this would be "distasteful to their order & the 'services,'" but virtually nobody thought Britain could repudiate the Declaration. A debate would compel the government "to declare itself."[44]

The 1862 debate on immunity

In mid-March 1862, the Radicals in the lower house mounted their most far-reaching debate on immunity. T. B. Horsfall, the Liverpool MP, invoked Palmerston's 1856 speech to the merchants of Horsfall's constituency;[45] and along similar lines, G. H. Liddell, an M.P. from Northumberland, making the Radical appeal to class hostility, pleaded for the "mitigation of the asperities of war, which pressed not on the governing classes who were responsible for the war, but on their unoffending subjects, the ship-owners and merchants." In a less divisive tone, Liddell remarked that it was in the national interest that "we should carry our commerce during the war in our own ships."[46] Future naval wars would be settled by "a collision between hostile forces," not by attacks against trade or private persons, the Liberal

MP from Salford, W. N. Massey, declared.[47] After W. S. Lindsay cautioned that under modern conditions it would prove impossible for the Navy "to assure complete safety upon the high seas to our vast commercial shipping,"[48] Massey also observed that the "old system of convoys was exploded," for how could slow sailing ships be convoyed by steamers? Since no future war would last more than one or two years, he optimistically concluded, it was hardly "worth our while to provide for the destruction of the enemy's commerce."[49] John Bright, even more sanguine, believed the time close at hand "when the commercial interests of mankind will assert the superiority to which they have a right over these tendencies to war."[50]

Liberals opposed to immunity necessarily spoke more in strategical than ideological terms. Palmerston's attorney general Sir William Atherton, while conceding that the Declaration of Paris gave an advantage to neutral carriers, made a critical exception: "where the belligerent was a strong naval Power," "especially where she was mistress of the seas," her "fleet, as in former wars, would effectually protect her mercantile marine."[51] To yield the right to capture enemy ships, added the secretary of state for war, Sir George Cornwall Lewis, would be "almost like interdicting ourselves from the use of gunpowder or heavy ordnance in time of war."[52]

Sir Roundell Palmer, the Liberal solicitor general, stressed that this "momentous question" of immunity required them to make concessions not to neutrals but to enemy belligerents: "You cannot make war upon the Government and have peace with their people." While not subscribing to the view that merchants were "the least patriotic class of men in the world," Palmer feared that "if merchants' interests were separated from the general interests" – especially given the fact that profits of ship-owners rose in wartime – it would be a temptation to the commercial classes to seek war if they were protected against its consequences. To insist on a blockade only of military ports and armed fleets would reduce "the efficacy of a naval Power to very narrow limits," producing "a sort of stalemate." Palmer further observed that in wartime belligerents would undoubtedly renounce any commitment to immunity.[53]

Viscount Palmerston, the prime minister, declared that the increased strength of such neutrals as the United States had compelled Britain's acceptance of the 1856 Declaration. But Palmerston had changed his mind on immunity. An earlier reliance on commercial logic had yielded to strategical reasoning. Since England was "the most powerful naval State," enemy ships would either be "confined to their ports" or "come out and suffer defeat"; consequently, after England established her sea supremacy, the danger to her merchant shipping would be considerably diminished. Since Britain's insular position made it necessary that her navy destroy enemy commerce and ships, "deeper thinking" convinced Palmerston that immunity was only superficially plausible. Indeed, it was "a dangerous doctrine," for its acceptance would make impossible a commercial blockade, an essential instrument of British strategy. If the House accepted the principle of immunity, Palmerston warned, "you would be guilty of an act of political suicide."[54]

The leader of the Conservative opposition, Benjamin Disraeli, chose this occasion to denounce both the 1856 Declaration and immunity, and to stress the perils of preferring economic interest over national power. The Radical principle of a peace for commerce while the nation was at war "may make rich societies, but will surely make weak states," he observed. "In some part of the world, some man of force, some conquerors with some new system of tactics or some new kind of artillery" would "take advantage of such a flourishing but dead community," which would then be forced to "give place to a society established on very different principles from those which have now the ascendancy in the excellent town of Liverpool." The question of immunity affected "the disposition of power throughout Europe and the world," for with its adoption would come the end of commercial blockade. It would then be "inevitable that your naval power must cease to be an aggressive power, and must exist only for defensive objects." In a war with a great continental state "we should sink into utter insignificance" for "we should have no power to assert our authority."

England had long maintained her influence because of the enforcement of the old rule, Disraeli continued, and yet Clarendon and Palmerston had foolishly yielded it. How could "so experienced a statesman" as Palmerston, "born and bred in the school of politics that attached so much importance to this point of our maritime code, the school of Liverpool and Canning," suddenly find "abstract arguments against its existence." At the city of Liverpool in 1856, Palmerston had even argued, again on abstract grounds, that immunity for private property at sea was a natural consequence of the Declaration of Paris. Now the prime minister had changed his mind. "For forty years" – as secretary of war, foreign secretary, and prime minister – Palmerston must have been "meditating and manipulating" just such subjects, yet he had just a few years earlier urged a principle that he was now ready to admit to be perilous to England. How was such a metamorphosis possible?[55]

Horsfall withdrew his resolution before a vote,[56] knowing how few would be its supporters. In the following years, the Cobdenites moved other bills calling for immunity, in efforts to influence public opinion. In 1866, 1867, 1871, 1875, 1877, and 1878, there were to be debates on the principle in the lower house, with the arguments substantially as they had been in 1862. In each of these cases, the bill was withdrawn before a division.[57] The nation seemed quite prepared to leave the commercial and shipping interests, in Lindsay's phrase, as "truly between the horns of a dilemma,"[58] approving of the Declaration of Paris when Britain was neutral but fearful of its consequences when she was at war.

Angered at Radical efforts to yield further Britain's maritime rights, David

Urquhart at the time of the 1862 debate professed himself unaware of "the accidental qualifications" by which the members of the Manchester Chamber of Commerce, "collectively or individually, have mastered the science of strategy." The Declaration of 1856 was "coining the blood of Her Majesty's subjects into mill-owners gain." If the manufacturers, merchants, and shipowners were now to seek their profits by supplying the enemy in wartime, as their support for immunity would suggest, Urquhart warned that the result must be civil war. Always ready to spot a conspiracy, Urquhart now believed that Palmerston and Cobden had pre-arranged the *Trent* incident to secure a back-handed parliamentary ratification of the Declaration of Paris.[59]

Radical parsimony and the Navy

But wartime trade was not the sole economic motive of the commercial classes; another was their interest in a parsimonious state. In 1848 the editor of the Radical *Economist*, James Wilson, wrote that "exorbitant taxation, to make preparations for a war that never arrives, though the preparations invite and provoke it, grinds down the people, and turns their heart from their rulers." For Radicals, to prepare for war was not to maintain peace, as traditional wisdom held, but to make war more likely. Since the "best defence of the country is an attached population," Wilson continued, the governing class must maintain "a parsimonious state or the populace would invite" a foreign invader.[60]

What might have been derided as mere parsimony was lifted to the plane of high economic strategy. Cobden called on the Commons in 1859 to follow the example of America, "aloof from the politics of Europe – and no expense for armaments," a circumstance that made the United States better able to compete with English industry. Only the "territorial interest" in Britain, concerned about jobs in the army and navy, wanted to raise the service budgets.[61] Speaking as a member of "the party of financial reform" and representing "the trading and manufacturing interests," Cobden observed in 1863 that "economy and frugality" in admiralty expenditures were essential to permit "our constituents" to "apply their industry, and to compete with the rest of the world."[62] Nor was it reasonable to expect war with France, England's only serious maritime competitor, Cobden noted in 1859, anticipating Norman Angell's argument half a century later, because "we stand at the head of the list of the customers of France."[63] Why, then, did England require a large and expensive navy?

But Cobden, though a pacifist, remained – rhetorically, at least – a champion of the fleet. In an often quoted peroration in 1862, he declared that were there "a real danger" to the country, were it revealed that "a neighbor is clandestinely and unduly trying to change the proportion which its forces should bear to that of this mercantile people living in an island," then he "would willingly vote £100,000,000 of money to protect our country against attack." It was not true that the free traders wished to "leave the country defenceless." But there was no immediate danger.[64] The Radical leader understood that the Navy was so much the darling of the nation that voters would reject a party that cut its strength too severely. Yet it was not merely a prudential regard for the electorate that kept Cobden a defender of the Navy. He saw it as the ideal instrument of a free, commercial, and sea-going people. "I am not speaking now in the spirit of one bearing hostility to the navy," Cobden observed in 1863: Liberals "always avowed an attachment" and had "no traditions hostile" to the Navy, for unlike the army the Navy had never been used "for repressive purposes in internal struggle." An effective Navy would make unnecessary a system of conscription, with its curtailment of liberty, Cobden declared, and "make these islands invulnerable" at the least cost.[65] Since reliance on the Navy was cheaper than the enlargement of the military (either as a prime or an auxiliary instrument) and the building of fortifications, the Radicals, not unlike the later blue-water school, insisted that only a naval force could protect Britain from invasion and her worldwide commerce from attack.[66]

Radical efforts to whittle down naval and military estimates, an irritation to both Liberal and Tory governments, were often well-directed. In 1863, for example, Cobden protested the admiralty's readiness to retain in service over a thousand "obsolete" wooden ships with their full complements of officers and men, since such ships, as the American war confirmed, could easily be destroyed by the new combustible missiles. Still anxious to avoid waste, he suggested that these vessels might be "serviceable in barbarous and uncivilized regions" as "a sort of police of the seas."[67]

Cobden described three efforts made by the governing classes to "panic" the country into naval expansion and the building of fortifications by entirely unfounded fears of an imminent French invasion. A proposal to increase the income tax by 5*d* in the pound ended the first panic of 1847 and 1848; and an alliance between France and England against Russia dissipated the second of 1851 to 1853. The third panic of 1859 to 1861, the most serious, produced a call not only for greater military and naval expenditures, but for the volunteer and rifle corps movements. During this last scare Cobden was negotiating a free trade treaty with France. "Reflecting men began to ask themselves," he wrote, "if it could be possible that the most logical people [the French] were contemplating at the same time a policy of free trade and of unprovoked hostile aggression." It was plain, Cobden concluded, that the British governments of the day had engineered these panics as excuses to increase armaments.[68]

What, then, could Radicals do when both Liberal and Tory governments submitted bloated naval estimates? "During my 21 years of experience in Parliament," Cobden wrote a Lancashire friend in 1862, "I never knew an

Estimate altered by an opposition vote"; indeed, "the oldest member never witnessed such an event." To continue to fight and be defeated "makes any cause ridiculous."[69] The previous year Disraeli had called upon the Palmerston government to eliminate obsolete wooden ships: "that was a bold bid for office to the Manchester school," Cobden observed at this time.[70] The course for Radicals, for whom peace was the prime interest, must be "to withdraw their support from the [Liberal] government, & let it be overthrown on the first chance by their opponents avowedly on the ground of its extravagance."[71]

Though a pacifist ideologue like Cobden was ready to defeat even a Liberal government for the cause, the men of commerce whom he sought to attach to his camp were not prepared for such a risk. Therefore Cobden's letters to businessmen were not so much appeals to pacifist sentiment as to suspicion of sinister interests. A policy of non-involvement in continental affairs was the Radical ideal. In 1864, Cobden argued that England must "give up" such "antiquated hobbies" as the Balance of Power and the Eastern Question and realize that her prime concerns were at home. Only a "strictly defensive" war could be justified.[72] That political risks were to be avoided made sense to businessmen increasingly reluctant to take economic risks.

In 1900, Brooks Adams was to attribute the moral "decay of England" to bourgeois timidity – and this at a time when Great Britain was still regarded as the richest and most powerful nation. Like Mill at the beginning of the bourgeois period, Adams remarked on the decline of such virtues as courage and honor, lamenting in particular the waning of "the martial and adventurous temperament." "The 'Industrial Revolution' began about 1760," he wrote, and "may be said to have ended toward 1840." After this time, "personal strength and courage ceased to be qualities which commanded the highest rewards at nature's hands, and, on the contrary, those qualities which had long condemned their possessors to inferiority had risen to preeminence with the rise of Manchester and Birmingham." As this "timid social stratum" rose to power, the aristocratic caste which saw "courage as an essential quality in a ruling class" was for all practical purposes "eliminated." Before the 1840s there had been three generations of Englishmen who personified "energy" in all fields, "in war, in commerce, in intellectual activity, in industry, in invention." But by mid-century the British had lost their "initiative," and become "dilatory" and self-indulgent. The Boer War displayed an England bereft of martial vigor. To Englishmen living at the turn of the century, Adams observed, the generation of the 1840s and earlier appeared almost a mythical race of supermen, in their industry and frugality, as well as in their initiative and enterprise.[73]

Mill had anticipated Adams's critique in the 1830s, and in his 1867 address, he saw liberal naval policy as the consequence of excessive bourgeois caution.

In this address, Mill had scouted the idea of immunity, only to dismiss it as no "gain to humanity" and perhaps even a setback since the commercial classes would have "no pecuniary interest" in preventing war. The following month, Mill wrote to the political economist J. E. Cairnes that "almost every one" among his Radical friends seemed to agree that if England did not "go back, we must go farther, and exempt private property from seizure"; he observed more specifically that Lord Hobart, a Radical and one of Mill's political allies, wished also to abolish commercial blockades. Mill expressed no agreement with this Radical evaluation. Indeed, he reiterated his fear that as a consequence of the Paris Declaration "the naval powers would be unable to defend themselves against the military," and that England might be conquered by a continental enemy. Under such circumstances, he concluded, somewhat ironically, Britain's independence "could perhaps only be preserved by our joining the American Confederation."[74] After Mill's death, the Cairnes letter was to become the basis for the myth that the liberal philosopher had come to accept the principle of immunity.[75]

Upon returning from a continental assignment in 1874, an admirer of Mill, the diplomat Sir Robert Morier, wrote to Disraeli's foreign secretary – Lord Stanley, now the Earl of Derby, who had been Mill's opponent in the 1867 debate – in favor of immunity. English public opinion would distrust such a proposal if advocated by Liberals in "a humanitarian, philanthropic, and *esprit de siècle* garb," a "mummery peculiarly hateful, and rightly so to every well-constituted mind." Morier therefore urged Derby to make immunity a Conservative policy, and to present it as one of the "logical consequences" of the 1856 Declaration, which, as Mill unfortunately had "entirely ignored," "pensioned off" the old right of capture "without the slightest hope of its ever being again introduced into active service." By relieving the Royal Navy of the duty of defending British commerce, Morier concluded, immunity would "treble the efficiency of our fleet," and enable England "to concentrate our forces on blockading and naval battles."[76]

In the last quarter of the nineteenth century, Liberal supporters of immunity adopted this more pragmatic defense. Persuaded of the obsolescence of the Navy's traditional strategy of exerting economic pressures on the enemy, they saw only a duel between fleets as decisive. Strategy and the liberal ideology were thus to be brought into harmonious alignment. For "the first time in the annals of the world," as Cobden had observed in 1856, wars would become exclusively conflicts between governments, and "we shall have one pretence less" for increasing the naval estimates.[77] Such a view, we will see, was to be widely accepted, even in admiralty circles.

The last decades of the nineteenth century, however, were to see a renewal of serious thinking about naval strategy. The revival in the 1880s of the primacy of a war against commerce by French naval strategists was hardly reassuring to the admiralty, particularly when its advocates suggested that belligerents would certainly jettison the Declaration of Paris. Strategists began a long debate as to whether a duel between rival fleets or a war against enemy commerce would prove decisive in a future naval war.

[6] The Strategists: Naval Duel or Commercial War?

You, you *if* you should fail to understand
  What England is, and what her all-in-all,
On you will come the curse of all the land
  Should this old England fall
    Which Nelson left so great.

His isle, the mightiest Ocean-power on earth
  Our own fair isle, the lord of every sea ....

Her dauntless army scatter'd, and so small,
  Her island-myriads fed from alien lands –
The fleet of England is her all-in-all;
  Her fleet is in your hands,
    And in her fleet her fate.

Lord Tennyson, *The Fleet*, 1886

Whether a war against commerce would again play a critical (or an honorable) role in a naval conflict became a pivotal question for statesmen and writers on strategy in the decades before the war of 1914. Not only Radicals, but moderate Liberals and Tories shared the view that such a war was now obsolete. Many free traders, caught up in the millennial strains of Victorian Radicalism, denied its legitimacy or utility, a number of professional sailors thought it unchivalrous, and certain admiralty strategists doubted its feasibility. A duel between battle fleets appeared the most sure and the most economical means of arriving at a decision.

A number of forces converged to create this consensus. The enormous increase in international trade appeared to compound the difficulties of effectively attacking commerce; moreover the adoption of the new rule in 1856 eliminated much of the world's commerce from the sphere of maritime war. Radicals believed that a war against trade was no better than piracy, and would prove more injurious to England, with her commercial preeminence, than to her enemies. There was a lack of assurance about the meaning of the technological changes that had taken place both in sea and in land transport, and in naval weaponry. There had been, furthermore, a re-shaping of international power relationships, dramatically evident in the growing naval and industrial strength of an America determined to maintain neutral rights.

By the 1890s a revival of a pre-industrial mercantilism, with its stress on power and not profit or economic welfare, was accompanied by a heightened interest in a strategy of commercial war. This had the effect of diluting without entirely dissipating the earlier naval consensus, and made for some ambiguity in the thinking of strategists. Admiralty planners seemed uncertain as to how much of England's naval superiority ought to consist of men-of-war to do battle with enemy fleets, or of cruisers to protect British commerce or to prey on enemy merchant ships.

Neatly expressing the Victorian strategic consensus of the decisive naval duel was Henry Reeve, whose writings on naval policy were highly regarded.[1] Reeve, no Radical but a moderate Liberal, had lost the illusions of the 1850s when, as he wrote, "a millennium of trade, unbroken by the clang of arms" persuaded so many "that Europe would never again hear the tread of great armies in the field."[2] Yet he saw no possibility of return to the traditional strategy. England was no longer mistress of the seas, he wrote in 1876, but if she were, a war against the enemy's trade, "the old system," would prove "a double-edged weapon, of which the keener blade is directed against our own commerce." Such a strategy was based on a mercantilist "fallacy [that] has now been totally exploded." It was because of a "strange confusion of ideas" that John Stuart Mill had thought otherwise since England's maritime strength so clearly depended on "the principles of commercial freedom, both in war and peace." Without either conscription or a large standing army, Britain could not rival the massed armies of the continent, but she could wage war until the military powers found their "armed millions an intolerable burden." By the 1856 Declaration, Reeve further observed, England had secured her commerce and her supply of food and raw materials by freeing neutral vessels for these tasks; as a considerable naval power, she could then rely on success in what would be a decisive engagement between her navy and that of her enemy.[3]

Some observers, and not merely the Radicals, went beyond Reeve in their distaste for the traditional strategy of a war against trade. For example, Sir Stafford Northcote, the civil service reformer and a future Tory chancellor of the exchequer (though of a Gladstonian bent), argued in 1862 that the fleet ought "not to be frittered away" in protecting British vessels or "in making prey" of enemy merchant ships, but ought to do "the proper work of the navy." This was to battle the fleets of the enemy.[4] One Liberal observed that "modern warfare" held in contempt the earlier "trifling kind of warfare" of "petty and quasi-*piratical* captures," or "the hardly more glorious duty of acting sheep-dog to our own commerce."[5] Now that privateering had been labelled a species of piracy, even career naval men found a war against enemy commerce wounding to professional pride. They wished to fight as Jervis had at Cape St Vincent and Nelson at Trafalgar.

Yet did not the parliamentary opposition to the principle of immunity suggest support for the efficacy of a war against enemy commerce? Not necessarily. Public opinion, as Palmerston discovered, would as a matter of patriotic sentiment rather than careful analysis resist further dilution of the traditional strategy. And even those ready to dismiss the usefulness of a war against trade might oppose immunity lest the commercial classes, reassured by a paper guarantee, should no longer feel committed to maintain a strong navy. Most parliamentary supporters of the Paris Declaration, furthermore, regarded a military blockade of enemy ports as decidedly useful to a naval power like Britain, and thought immunity would make all blockades difficult if not impossible. Equally chilling was the view that immunity would make it possible for enemy merchant ships to return safely to port to be outfitted as men-of-war. The right to capture enemy private property was not to be yielded lightly, despite the prevailing opinion that a strategy of commercial war could not in itself bring victory.

Early parliamentary critics of the consensus

Many of those who contributed most ably to the naval debates of the 1860s and 1870s were not professional sailors, but politicians who held or would hold high cabinet office. Among the most perceptive of these were Sir Roundell Palmer, first Palmerston's solicitor general and then his attorney general in the 1860s, and the future Liberal chancellor Sir William Harcourt. Both were critics of reliance on the strategy of the duel between fleets.

Despite the Declaration of 1856, Palmer insisted that a war against enemy trade was not an exploded fallacy. When Northcote in 1862 pronounced the traditional strategy of war against commerce outmoded,[6] solicitor general Palmer replied that if navies were to confine their activities to military and not commercial blockades, this would reduce "the efficacy of a naval Power to very narrow limits indeed," and might only produce "a sort of stalemate." The only way to injure the enemy mortally and to bring him to terms was to attack not merely his armed ships but also his merchant vessels.[7] Palmer denounced Radical efforts to secure immunity. "Great battles . . . might have to be fought between the contending fleets," Palmer, now attorney general, observed in 1866, but what if it were not "the policy of the enemy to fight such battles"? The Royal Navy must then respond by a commercial blockade and a war against enemy merchant ships. Such forms of war were directed not so much at the private property of individuals, as the Radicals argued, but at "the general public and national resources" and "the general commercial interests" of the enemy.[8] Palmer agreed with the Tory Viscount Cranbourne – the future Marquess of Salisbury and prime minister – who earlier in this debate had observed that a war against enemy commerce at sea was as much designed "to exhaust the enemy" as Sherman's march though Georgia;[9] and the attorney general praised the effectiveness of the Union's blockade of Southern ports in bringing about a Northern victory.

Britain must decide, Palmer continued, whether she would agree "to cripple" her "warlike power in time of war," or whether she would "submit to a temporary, though it may be a serious interference" with her trade. It would be ignoble if England thought primarily of the commercial profits of neutrality. "Let us not impose fetters upon ourselves on that ocean where hitherto we have been supreme." By bringing pressure on the enemy's commerce, the war would end sooner: "in this way commerce works as an antidote to war."[10] In 1867, Palmer observed that the Declaration of Paris had not introduced "so great a difference as some people supposed," for contraband was still contraband, both before and after 1856, and the possibility of action by the superior naval power to exclude contraband would prove a powerful weapon.[11] In 1871, he suggested that English merchant vessels might arm themselves, "to a moderate extent," in the event of war[12] – an open revival of mercantilist heresy.

An equally firm opponent of exclusive reliance on naval duel was the Liberal Sir William Harcourt, a barrister who wrote on maritime questions[13] and was appointed Whewell professor of international law at Cambridge in 1869. In an 1865 talk, Harcourt warned that the adoption of immunity would hamper commercial blockades, which he described as "one of the most powerful engines of maritime warfare that England may ever have to wield."[14] In 1875, in the lower house, he argued that the Declaration of Paris had been useful to England for two reasons: first because privateering, now outlawed, was "a thorn in the side" of the great naval powers and, secondly, because the treaty vouchsafed what was for England the vital right of a commercial blockade.[15] Harcourt repeated these arguments in 1877.[16]

In an address to the Commons in 1878, Harcourt speculated that if the immunity principle were accepted, and the two belligerent fleets set upon each other "as though they were in a cockpit," what would occur? If "pretty evenly matched," then "a good deal of entertainment" would be given to neutrals; if "unevenly matched," then the weaker power would keep her ships in port, and there would be "a nautical stalemate." There was only one effective strategy for a great naval power: "as far as you could and as soon as you could – to sweep the enemy from the seas," both her armed ships and her merchantmen. For only so could England "cope with the great territorial armies of the Continent" and make any war waged against her "a terrible scourge."[17] (In this debate, in similar vein, the Tory attorney general Sir John Holker reminded the Commons that "owing to our ideas with respect to liberty" and the voluntary principle on which Britain's military was recruited, England had "no better weapon" than commercial blockade and the seizure of contraband: "Were we," he asked, "for the sake of chivalry, to forego all the advantages which we had in case of war, and to rely simply on our pluck and valour"?)[18]

The Colombs: command of the seas and the protection of British trade

In the 1870s and the 1880s, the Royal Navy possessed a diminished sense of mission. It was widely believed that steam power had deprived Britain of her insular invulnerability. After the French war scare of 1859 volunteer militias were raised and trained, and fortifications planned and erected to defend the country against invasion, very much in the continental manner. For this mid-Victorian generation, no longer naval but military force became the bedrock of national and imperial defense. The widely accepted opinion of the Navy's helplessness in protecting England's widespread commerce was another symptom of this mood. These were the circumstances from which there emerged a school of strategists that sought to reestablish the Navy in the mind of the nation as the chief and most efficient instrument of British power. If the Royal Navy achieved a maritime predominance, these writers argued, invasion would prove impossible and British merchantmen would have little to fear.

The Colomb brothers were the founders of what was to become known as "the blue-water school." Sons of a British general, both brothers made careers in the services. The elder, Philip Howard, spent much of his early life in naval actions against piracy in the China Seas and the slave trade in the South Atlantic.[19] The younger, Captain John C. R. Colomb, served with the Royal Marines before becoming associated with naval intelligence and strategic planning. While Liberals like Reeve wished to rely on neutral carriers to keep up the wartime supply of England, and Radicals and ship-owners sought immunity for private property, the brothers Colomb saw the solution to England's dependence on overseas commerce in a Royal Navy strong enough to establish "command of the seas."

The Colombs were not prepared to argue that sea command by itself would protect all British trade.[20] Nor were they more ready than other naval writers at this time to insist on the primacy, or practicality, of British naval action against enemy commerce. The lessons of the Crimean War were otherwise. Still, the brothers were intent upon awakening England to the enormous usefulness of sea power. By a military (not a commercial) blockade of enemy naval ports, both Colombs believed, the warships of a continental foe would be prevented from either assisting in an invasion of England or interfering with British commerce. In his 1878 Naval Prize Essay, P. H. Colomb argued that the Navy did not need to attempt the impossible job of protecting British ships everywhere, only "to keep open the great sea-routes to and from the heart of the Empire – the islands of Great Britain."[21]

In an 1881 tract, Captain J. C. R. Colomb regretted that English public opinion no longer thought of sea power as decisive for her own and the empire's defense. He particularly lamented the dearth of works on naval strategy. What was needed was a return "to a calm quiet contemplation of the grim realities of modern maritime war," so that, if there were a naval conflict, England might secure "the safety and freedom of the seas." British ships were everywhere, "carrying *foreign* food to British mouths, material to British manufactories, and goods to British warehouses." How could such a vast and widespread commerce be protected? Convoys by warships might prove inadequate, and Colomb believed that England must be prepared to arm "every ocean-going British steamer." But the best means of defending British trade was a full military blockade of the enemy's coast. "Advancing science and modern appliances" had no doubt reduced the chances of making such a blockade "effectual and complete," and hostile cruisers might evade it and do dreadful damage. Yet only a blockade of naval ports would offer a practicable course. If enemy cruisers evaded such a blockade in wholesale fashion, invasion might be unnecessary to secure "our complete subjugation," for the crushing of British sea-borne commerce would have the same effect. The tract's immediate purpose was to urge "the trade and shipping interest" to press for a well-financed intelligence section in the admiralty.[22] But for the most part, the early writings of the Colombs went unnoticed.

Mahan's rebuttal to the Jeune Ecole

In the 1880s and 1890s, the British public was dramatically alerted to the danger of naval attacks on England's trade by the "Jeune Ecole," a group of younger officers of the French Navy who enjoyed the support of at least two admirals, Aube and Bourgeois. The first popular exposure of their doctrine of a commercial war against Britain was in articles by Gabriel Charmes on "La Reforme Maritime," first published in 1884 and 1885. The aim of the attack on commerce, Charmes argued, was not so much to starve England, which would require a prolonged operation but, by making necessary the raising of insurance rates on British shipping, to produce economic panic. Indeed, the purpose of maritime warfare, the Jeune Ecole would insist, was not the destruction of the enemy's naval power, as the then dominant British opinion would have it, but – as in England's traditional strategy – "the annihilation of its [the enemy's] financial and commercial power and riches."[23]

"A war of pursuit" – a *guerre de course* – "will, therefore, necessarily, fatally, definitely, replace squadron warfare in future conflicts between maritime nations," Gabriel Charmes declared. Naval battles by themselves were nothing more than "fictitious tournaments" or "passages-at-arms as fruitless as they would be sanguinary." No nation would give up the destruction of the enemy's commerce and merchant marine merely "to prove the superiority of numbers, and the infallible power of great squadrons." To do this would be to wage war by England's rules and to England's advantage. To persist in the financially-draining efforts to build ships with ever thicker and more costly defensive plating was similarly to play the game of a capital-rich England.

The Jeune Ecole wished the French navy to emphasize not unwieldy and expensive battleships, of which France could have but a few, but rather, many speedy and relatively inexpensive and less vulnerable small boats designed to destroy merchant vessels by torpedo. The French strategists would "cover the coasts and commercial routes with hundreds of boats that could not be destroyed in a single fight." They called for a revival of the struggle for "the commercial supremacy of the sea" like that waged in the mercantilist wars of the eighteenth century, and even for a return to privateering, a form of warfare for which "the monster" (that is, the battleship) "is useless."

Likewise in the mercantilist manner, the Jeune Ecole refused to recognize any distinction between private and public wealth, observing that if a nation wished "to divert some great commercial resource from a country," she "must unflinchingly attack private property, and aim at destroying its [the enemy's] general prosperity by a series of individual disasters." The Declaration of Paris, in its free-trade idealism, had condemned privateering and, by implication, the *guerre de course*, but "vainly do philanthropy or international rights attempt to oppose the natural course of events." A *guerre de course* had "its own rules": "to fall without pity on the weak; and without false shame, and with all possible speed, to fly from the strong." "Let not short-sighted philosophers tax us with barbarism," Charmes noted, for British naval defeat would mean a victory for liberty and "the triumph of equality" since Britain's "sceptre" would be shattered "to be apportioned in fragments to the whole universe."[24] In 1890, a British journal quoted Admiral Aube's view that French ships ought to be prepared to destroy unarmed merchant vessels by torpedo. "Others may protest," Aube declared, "for ourselves, we accept in these new methods of destruction the developments of that law of progress in which we have a firm faith"; for Aube, "the final result would be to put an end to war altogether."[25]

In 1890, a retired American naval captain, Alfred T. Mahan, provided reassurance to the world's greatest naval power. Mahan's study of British naval history from 1660 to 1783 had satisfied him that a nation like Britain which possessed command of the seas had nothing to fear from a *guerre de course*. The American naval historian described two national naval strategies, one pursued by the British during the eighteenth century and the other by the French. While the British sought battle, the French employed their navy not so much to fight the enemy fleet as for such "ulterior objects" as commerce destruction. "It is instructive" to see "how strong a hold tradition has over the minds of men, that a body of highly accomplished and gallant seamen should have accepted, apparently without a murmur, so inferior a role for their noble profession." Moreover, the French frequently had dispatched single ships as cruisers to prey on enemy commerce instead of more properly concentrating their forces for battle, he noted, translating the French military strategist A. H. Jomini's warning against dispersal of forces on land to war at sea. The French posture in time of war was "habitually defensive," one intent on avoiding an engagement of fleets, consequently permitting the English Navy "with impunity to range the seas." In this way, the French Navy had lost the eighteenth-century struggle for empire. Were English wealth concentrated in a few treasure galleons like that of Spain in earlier centuries, "the efficacy of commerce-destroying as a main reliance in war" might well have proved itself. But when Britain's wealth was "scattered in thousands of going and coming ships, when the roots of the system spread wide and far, and strike deep, it can stand many a cruel shock and lose many a goodly bough without life being touched." To think otherwise was "a delusion, and a most dangerous delusion." Only if a rival maritime nation achieved "command of the sea by prolonged control of the strategic centres of commerce" could it succeed in destroying the extensive British trade. "Such control can be wrung from a powerful navy only by fighting and overcoming it."[26]

Mahan reinforced the view of the blue-water school which insisted that so long as Britain maintained command of the sea, she need fear no enemy. The Colombs had anticipated Mahan's doctrine in some respects, but had not fully embraced it in their earlier works. In the 1890s, they became its most strenuous advocates. "Keep command of the sea as you value the national life," the now vice-admiral Philip Colomb proclaimed in 1893: "With it you can do everything. Without it you will be speedily blotted out from the list of great countries."[27] A year previously, a prominent Liberal politician Sir Charles Dilke, in collaboration with a young journalist Spenser Wilkinson, who became in 1895 the military correspondent of the Tory *Morning Post* and in 1908 the first Chichele professor of military history at Oxford, produced a book on imperial defense. The collaborators proclaimed "the primacy of the navy," and exulted that "the ocean is, in fact, a British possession." So long as Britain maintained her superiority at sea, Dilke and Wilkinson declared, neither England nor any part of the Empire, except Canada and India, need fear invasion.[28]

There were other journalists who wrote on naval strategy, and described themselves as students of the Colombs and Mahan. The "commercial sensitiveness" of the English, one of them, J. K. Laughton, observed in 1890, had brought the nation to dread the *guerre de course*; Mahan had brought a message of confidence.[29] J. R. Thursfield, the naval correspondent of *The Times*, another admirer of both Mahan and the Colombs, warned the French in an 1893 article that a *guerre de course* would "never overthrow the strategic supremacy of a Power which holds the command of the sea." In fact, powers with overseas colonies held them "merely as the caretaker of the ultimate naval Power," which might take them whenever it wished.[30] The following year, 1894, Thursfield denied the contention of the Jeune Ecole that the naval warfare of the future would be a war of coasts: it would be, rather, "a struggle for command of the sea."[31] If England only maintained the strength of the Royal Navy, she had nothing to fear.[32]

No longer, as Admiral Sir Cyprian Bridge was later to observe, were British statesmen led to a farcical "mimicking in a free England [of] the cast-iron methods of the Great Frederick," to demanding land fortifications for the island, thus throwing aside her advantages as the mistress of the sea. "In no small degree owing to the teachings of Mahan," Bridge declared, the British people now demanded that "a great maritime empire" must have a fleet adequate for the defense of "all that made its existence possible."[33] A writer on military strategy, Colonel C. à C. Repington, was to write similarly that after Mahan's work, "the secret of our world power stood revealed." The secret was the command of the sea.[34]

Mahan and commercial war

Despite some dissenting voices, the prevailing strategical conception in the 1880s and 1890s remained that of a decisive naval duel. The writings of the Colombs and Mahan, and of their followers of the blue-water school, extended this simpler formulation into that of the command of the seas, which Britain must secure by victory in such a duel. But in his magnum opus, which made the Victorian strategic consensus of a decisive battle between fleets almost canonical, Mahan had somewhat qualified this view, though this was not immediately noticed. For if the American had insisted that commerce-destroying could not be successful as a primary strategy, and must prove wholly ineffective when directed against Britain's vast trade, he none the less saw it as a useful secondary strategy – but *only* for a considerable naval power like England. Indeed, Britain's ability to wage successful war against the maritime trade of her enemies, Mahan observed, explained why for over two centuries she had been "most reluctant to concede the immunities of commerce and the rights of neutrals." "Regarded not as a matter of right but of policy," he asserted, "history has justified the refusal."[35]

In 1892, two years after the appearance of his first work, Mahan published a two-volume study of the role of sea power during the wars of the French Revolution. In these volumes, there was a clear shift in emphasis: in the conflicts with Napoleonic France, the naval historian saw the war against French trade as England's primary not secondary strategy. As in his earlier work, Mahan approved England's conduct toward neutral commerce, including the extra-legal innovations of the orders-in-council. Though an American whose country had denounced the Rule of 1756, he was convinced that the English "belligerent argument seems the stronger"; certainly the desire of the neutral for gain was hardly "a nobler motive" than the concern of "men who rightly believed themselves engaged in a struggle for national existence." Neither Napoleon's Berlin and Milan Decrees nor the British orders-in-council could be "justified at the bar, except by the simple plea of self-preservation – the first law of states even more than of men." True, England had alienated America by her maritime conduct, but Great Britain shrewdly calculated that a peace-minded Jefferson and Madison would put up with a great deal before turning to war as a remedy. When the United States did finally declare war, Napoleon was engaged in a hopeless struggle with Russia, and Britain had virtually assured victory.[36]

J. K. Laughton took note of Mahan's change of direction in an article in 1893: Mahan displayed what many historians had not previously understood, "how essentially the Napoleonic War was a war of commerce." Laughton believed that Britain would be wise to prepare to fight such a war in the future, and not weaken herself further by accepting the principle of immunity.[37]

In 1894, in an article concerning the possibility of "an Anglo-American reunion," Mahan explicitly argued the primacy of a future naval war against commerce. The English civil servant who was to become most prominently identified with questions of imperial defense, Sir George Sydenham Clarke, had suggested a closely-qualified immunity as an accommodation to traditional American policy, this in an article proposing a naval league with the United States. Mahan rejected Clarke's effort at compromise. Such an Anglo-American naval league would in all likelihood establish a maritime supremacy, Mahan observed, but if so, why should it concede immunity to enemy commerce? Why, after all, did navies exist? "Surely not merely to fight one another?" "If navies, as all agree, exist for the protection of commerce, it inevitably follows that in war they must aim at depriving their enemy of that great resource." The American strategist again condemned random naval actions "frittered away in the feeble dissemination of the *guerre de course*," the strategy followed by the French in the eighteenth century. What he now advocated was "commerce destroying (or commerce prevention) through the strategic control of the sea by powerful navies." In the French wars, the British navy "not only protected her own commerce, but also annihilated that of the enemy." This was the proper policy, for just as two armies could not agree to hold each other's communications inviolate, so a well-designed naval strategy must accept that "blows at commerce are blows at the communications of the state."

Great Britain had made her concessions to neutrals in 1856 because she was "no longer supreme at sea," Mahan continued in this 1894 article; "a mistaken humanitarianism," he added, might also have played a role in the abandonment of the old rule. Britain had believed that she needed to protect herself against the possibility of neutrals joining her enemies. Now the new rule was "forever secured," and "no one power would be strong enough at sea to maintain the contrary by arms." (Was Mahan suggesting that an Anglo-American naval league might possess such strength?) But "a nation or an alliance confident in its own sea-power" would never concede immunity to private property at sea. When a nation went to war, its so-called "private" maritime commerce was "sustaining the well-being and endurance" of the belligerent country. To strike at that commerce was to injure the enemy "to an extent exceeding all other sources of national power."[38]

In 1905, in a study of sea power during the War of 1812, Mahan was prepared to go still further in elevating the strategy of "commerce destroying," both by capture and blockade. It was "not only legitimate in principle, but particularly effective to seek the disorganization of his [the enemy's] financial system." That certain losses fell more "directly on individuals or a class, instead of upon the whole community" was merely an accident of war, just as "some men are killed and others are not." Property at sea, that is, maritime commerce, was like "money in circulation": it was "the life-blood of national prosperity, on which war depends, and as such is national in employment, and only in ownership private." The critical issue was not whether or not the property was private, but whether its seizure would help to end the war more quickly. Mahan warned American proponents of the principle of immunity that they "must logically" also denounce blockade, "so distinctly commerce-destructive in essence." The stronger maritime power, as in the American Civil War, would generally adopt the tactic of "commerce-destruction by blockade," he concluded, the weaker, that of "commerce-destruction by cruisers on the high sea."[39]

How can we explain these changes in Mahan's thinking? We cannot forget that the general climate of opinion was changing dramatically during the 1890s. Within that decade, for example, William Cunningham, a British historian writing an economic history of his country, moved from a free-trade position to a neo-mercantilist one, as did the economic historian W.J. Ashley, and soon afterward the geographer and geopolitician H.J. Mackinder.[40] Like these other students of history, Mahan perceived the end of an era when considerations of profit predominated, and a return to what these converts to protectionism viewed as the mainstream of development, with Imperial Germany as its harbinger and the primacy of power as its leading characteristic. As an American, Mahan may well have begun with the neutralist prejudices of his countrymen, but even the United States was turning to the expansion of her navy, and with the Spanish War in 1898 to the development of an empire. In a neo-mercantilist world, the traditional strategy of commerce destruction made more sense than it had in the liberal world, with its dream of a commercial peace in the midst of national war – an ideal whose strategical expression was the decisive duel between rival battle fleets.

In 1894, two years after his collaboration with Dilke, Spenser Wilkinson wrote a tract in which he pictured the developing naval doctrine of the blue-water school in an ideological contest with its liberal opponent. Mahan's writings, Wilkinson observed, were "little less than a revelation even to those who had specially devoted themselves to the study of maritime affairs," and confirmed what Englishmen long knew instinctively but had for some decades forgotten. British policy needed to be founded on "realities, not upon creeds." The country had to shed outmoded ideas, and awake from her "irresolute, aimless, ungoverned and unled" condition. Wilkinson called for the unity of the two parties in behalf of the national interest, with each lopping off "extreme men and crotchet-mongers." Such a political realignment must then repudiate the Declaration of Paris and return to the traditional strategy of the old rule. It did no good to close the sea to enemy merchantmen, if neutral ships supplied the foe. The only advantage to Great Britain in the 1856 treaty, the easing of food imports in neutral ships, might prove "illusory" if the enemy "felt strong enough" to treat food as contraband.[41] In an 1895 address to the Navy League, which he had helped to form, Wilkinson asserted that a nation supreme on the sea and living by trade was inescapably led to found colonies with which to trade, along uncivilized coasts, a restatement of the old mercantilist slogan of "Ships, Commerce, Colonies."[42]

But there was not to be the party realignment that Wilkinson desired. The Radical "crotchet-mongers" remained firmly entrenched in the Liberal party, a potent minority to which a moderate leadership felt at times obliged to respond; and many Tories, less comfortably perhaps, shared liberal preconceptions, notably free trade. In 1903, the colonial secretary Joseph Chamberlain began a campaign to convert the Tory party and the nation to a neo-mercantilist program of protection and imperial preference. He hoped that at least some Liberals would be drawn to this cause. However, the Liberal party – Radicals, a group of Liberal-Imperialists, and what we have called mainstream Liberals – in some disarray because of differences over the recent war in South Africa, united in defense of *their* palladium, free trade.

The naval strategists versus Loreburn and immunity

Shortly before the election of 1906, fought largely on the tariff issue, a prominent Liberal politician revived the campaign for the principle of immunity which he saw as the natural consequence of a free-trade policy. The barrister Sir Robert Reid, attorney general in the Rosebery government of 1894 to 1895, wrote a letter to *The Times* in mid-October 1905 on behalf of immunity. Reid deliberately omitted any appeal to humanitarian sentiment in his argument, stressing strategical considerations.

Maritime blockades of continental nations had proved useful in the past, Reid observed, but would no longer because railway networks now provided the "effective means" to blunt "the weapon of capture at sea." On the other hand, the maintenance of the right of capture would place island nations like England and Japan in extreme jeopardy: "If the sea is closed, we are half-starved," and without access to raw materials Britain would be "reduced to idleness." England's position as the leading maritime carrier put her especially at risk because war would bring higher insurance premiums and consequently higher prices, as well as the wholesale transfer of trade to neutral bottoms. Reid reiterated the Radical position that "our merchant marine is vulnerable in proportion to its size and its ubiquity," and warned his countrymen that England was therefore "not only liable to be ruined by naval defeat" but also by a "doubtful war." He urged the adoption of the principle of immunity "not upon any ground of sentiment or humanity," but rather because "the interests of Great Britain will gain much from a change long and eagerly desired by the great majority of other Powers."[43]

After the Liberal triumph in 1906, Reid joined the cabinet as lord chancellor with the title of Loreburn. Loreburn's determination to convert the Liberal government to immunity became the focus of controversy for a number of naval and military strategists in the years before 1914.

In mid-1906, Spenser Wilkinson, who by this time was probably the most respected British writer on military questions, took up the argument with Loreburn. All countries, including Germany, were becoming "more and more tributary" to overseas suppliers for "articles of primary necessity," Wilkinson observed, and these were "hostages to peace." How then could England give up "the tremendous insurance against war which we possess in our predominant navy, and our belligerent rights"? With the adoption of immunity, furthermore, the British public would be less interested in maintaining the Navy, which was "a better protection than all the Treaties in the world." Unless Britain remained "sufficiently armed," an "unscrupulous enemy engaged in a war of existence" might tear up "paper guarantees" and "fling them in our face." "Would our conscious sense of moral rectitude then atone for the loss of naval predominance?"[44]

In 1907 Mahan described Loreburn's portrait of the dangers to which the right of capture exposed Britain as "overdrawn; that to her enemies ... is underdrawn." The seizure of private property at sea was a powerful weapon that had made possible not only the British triumph over Napoleon, but the Union's victory over the Southern Confederacy. The liberal view of the issue was distorted, for there was "practically no such thing as private-individual-losses distinguished from the loss of the community to which the individual belongs." It was precisely because of the wide range of persons injured by capture at sea – "the producer, the transporter, the handler, the broker, the merchant, the banker," along with the national treasury – that the right of capture was so effective a weapon. Given the "permanent situation" in which the English-speaking powers found themselves as maritime powers, the right of capture was absolutely necessary to any effective British and American strategy.

If the nations soon to meet at The Hague for a disarmament conference abolished the Declaration of 1856, Mahan continued, "they would do a much better stroke for the world's peace than by granting immunity to the commerce of a belligerent." Enemy property on neutral ships must again become lawful prize. Mahan chided England for her original adherence to the Declaration of Paris: "The concession was in the air, as we say; which proves only that it was contagious, not that it was wise." Even the much-criticized rule of 1756 was "not only strictly just but wisely expedient": let the Hague Conference revive that rule and forbid "any enlargement of neutral tonnage, in the carriage for a belligerent, over that practised in peace." The forthcoming Hague Conference should also prohibit neutral loans to belligerents, and call for the condemnation of ships (with their cargoes) that attempted to run a blockade, as well as the imprisonment of their crews.[45] The American naval historian now fully and decisively embraced a strategy of a war against commerce as the most effective weapon of the sea powers against continental powers with, we shall see, Germany particularly in mind.

England's most perceptive naval strategist at this time was Julian Corbett, a Cambridge-educated barrister who became first a writer of adventure novels and then a journalist. It was not until the turn of the century that Corbett began to write naval history, and to contribute to discussions of strategic questions. On many issues, Corbett agreed with Mahan, as he happily acknowledged in a 1906 article on the right of capture.

To have yielded the right of capture to any degree, as England had in 1856, Corbett argued, put maritime states at a sharp disadvantage in a war against military states; indeed, British adherence to the new rule was an "almost quixotic sacrifice." To accept immunity, as Loreburn advocated, would mean to give up any hope "to produce that stagnation of the enemy's life at sea which an army is permitted to produce ashore by the conquest of territory." The right of capture was not, as liberal proponents of immunity claimed, merely a survival of a primitive piracy; it was "the right and necessity of controlling our enemy's communications," as Mahan had demonstrated in his study of the War of 1812. "No real and crushing defence" was "possible without attack," Corbett declared, and without the right of capture, a navy could not make war at sea. This was "a distasteful subject, above all to the higher Liberalism, where the desire to unarm is keenest." Corbett rejected the Radical argument that British commerce and merchantmen were particularly vulnerable to maritime predators: in fact, given the time- and coal-consuming character of a cruiser's activities, the greater the "ubiquity" of sea commerce and "the greater the bulk . . . the larger will be the percentage that is beyond the utmost capacity of the enemy's fleet." In reply to the argument that enemy trade might be carried on neutral ships or by rail, he observed that these "breezy generalizations" neglected the fact that "the capacity of neutral shipping and of inland communications is not unlimited," and ignored "the well-known difficulty of forcing trade to flow healthily out of the channels into which it has settled itself."[46]

Britain must entirely re-think her naval strategy, Corbett urged in a later work in 1911. She must adopt a system of commercial war and have the "right to forbid, if we can, the passage of both public and private property upon the sea." Britain must mount a distant "strategical blockade of the great trade routes," since the close tactical blockade – the only kind the 1856 treaty permitted – was "exhausting, and . . . tended to occupy a force greater than that against which it was acting." Corbett's ideal system, like Mahan's, was not the tactical commerce destruction of the eighteenth-century *guerre de course*, but a strategic "commerce prevention." Command of the sea meant not merely the ability to win "battles between . . . fleets," but the power "to exert pressure on the citizens [of the enemy state] and their collective life." For commerce and finance "now more than ever control or check" the foreign policy of a nation, and if these branches of the economy "stand to lose by war, their influence for a peaceful solution will be great."[47]

Following Mahan's line of reasoning, the naval writers were moving from a strategy of a decisive naval duel to one of a war of economic exhaustion. Consequently, these strategists doubted the wisdom of England's having subscribed to the new rule in 1856, and rejected the renewal of the Radical plea for immunity. While there continued to be disagreement on a number of issues, the chief naval strategists agreed that in a future war England must seek to destroy enemy commerce.

The strategical arguments, on both sides, reflected the conflict between the neutralist and free-trade world-view and the belligerent and neo-mercantilist outlook. We shall see that the officials in the chief governmental departments, intent on preserving both Britain's commercial interests and her strategic position, sometimes arrived at ambiguous conclusions. What, of course, would make the struggle over naval policy in the first decade of the twentieth century so impassioned was the growing fear that Europe was at the brink of war. More immediately, however, the Hague Peace Conference of 1907 was at hand, and its decisions would three years later produce the Treaty of London which the Liberal government would support as a "progressive" advance, and which the Tory opposition would denounce as a dangerous snare.

[7] Britannia Contra Mundum

The light is still in our eyes
Of Faith and Gentlehood,
Of Service and Sacrifice;
And it does not match our mood,
To turn so soon to your treacheries
That starve our land of her food.

Our ears still carry the sound
Of our once-Imperial seas,
Exultant after our King was crowned,
Beneath the sun and the breeze.
It is too early to have them bound
Or sold at your decrees.

Wait till the memory goes,
Wait till the visions fade,
We may betray in time, God knows,
But we would not have it said,
When you make report to our scornful foes,
That we kissed as we betrayed!

Rudyard Kipling, *The Declaration of London*, June 29, 1911

When Vice Admiral Sir John Fisher was the British naval delegate at the First Hague Peace Conference in 1899, he dismissed the hostility of the other powers toward Great Britain. An England that knew her interests could and would defend her position: "It's very hard work here," Fisher declared at the time; "it's a case of *Britannia contra mundum*!" but, he added, "we are more than holding our own."[1] Fisher had begun his naval career at the age of thirteen during the Crimean War; by the mid-1870s he had become the captain of the *Inflexible*, the model man-of-war of the period, and by 1899 was clearly seen as a future sea lord. At The Hague, Fisher behaved with the bluster of the representative of a navy without a peer, on one occasion telling the German naval delegate Captain Siegel, as Siegel later reported to his superiors, that his "sole principle" was "that might is right" and that he would regard any agreement reached at The Hague as "null and void" if it ran counter "to the political and military interests of his country."[2] The head of the American delegation, A. D. White, a historian and former college president, and at this time ambassador to Germany, was upset that Fisher was "using the same arguments as regards the sea" that the Germans "made regarding the land."[3]

The United States delegation to The Hague presented a memorial to the conference in behalf of immunity. Ambassador White inveighed against the destruction of property belonging to the "most industrious and meritorious portion of our population." It was not because she might materially benefit as a neutral carrier that America supported immunity, White assured the conference, but because Americans were "idealists," thinking immunity "a question of right, of justice, of progress towards a better future for the entire world."[4] While not prepared to adopt the United States position, the Germans endorsed an uncertainly defined freedom of the seas, a slogan traditionally directed against England's naval power. With both the Germans and the Americans increasing the size of their war fleets, some in England began to fear the possibility of a German–American alliance on this issue.

But did England always know her interests, as Fisher believed. While Liberals saw Britain in a future war as a neutral merchant, Tories sought to preserve her maritime rights as a belligerent. Was England's primary strategy in the event of hostilities to be a battle between fleets or an economic war of exhaustion? Though these were substantially different and even contradictory conceptions, the admiralty at times held both simultaneously.[5] When the Liberal government in 1909 accepted new maritime rules that would further limit England's power to strike at the trade of her enemy, it rejected Fisher's intransigent posture ten years earlier, declaring, in the words of a foreign ministry official, that Britain could not play "the part of *Athanasius contra mundum*" and force her views on "the rest of the world."[6] But most Tories believed England must do just that to survive.

The world had changed dramatically since the mid-Victorian heyday of free trade, these Tories insisted. It was no longer realistic to base England's prosperity and security on an international division of labor. The nations of the continent, having returned to protection and imposed conscription on their peoples, were arming themselves for a struggle. The Tariff Reformers and a party of blue-water naval ultras warned that Germany saw England as an obstacle to the position to which her economic and military strength entitled her, and was building a navy to assert her claim. While Liberal free traders believed in England's future role as a center of finance and commerce, a brain in the body of a cosmopolitan economy, the Tory neo-mercantilists, in part converted by Joseph Chamberlain, saw her in the autarchic terms of a new age of commercial wars. Britain needed both the muscle of her steel industry that only a tariff could protect, and a supply of colonial food that a system of imperial preference would secure, as well as the strengthening of her navy and the preservation of her belligerent rights at sea.[7]

Sir George Clarke and the 1906 inter-departmental committee

The Liberal government that took office in 1906 was a coalition of Radicals, Liberal-Imperialists, and moderate mainstream Liberals. Sir Henry Campbell-Bannerman, the prime minister, a man of the Liberal mainstream, appointed in that year a top-level interdepartmental committee to consider the subjects that might come up for discussion at the Second Hague Conference scheduled to open in 1907.[8] The committee was composed of officials of government departments, among them Lord Desart, Eyre A. Crowe, and C.J.B. Hurst from the foreign office, Captain C.L. Ottley representing the admiralty, and Sir George Clarke, the secretary of the Committee for Imperial Defence (C.I.D.) One of the accomplishments of the previous Tory government was the formation in 1901 of a permanent C.I.D., an act inspired by a triumvirate who constituted a virtual brains-trust on military and naval questions – Lord Esher, a confidant of King Edward VII, Admiral Sir John Fisher, and Clarke.

Officials like Clarke were assigned leading roles in making strategy in the years before the war. Trained to assume office as a matter of duty, they (whether to the manor born, or newly admitted to the "governing" class) saw themselves as guardians of the long-term interests of the nation, and drew on a long corporate experience. By and large, they worked to contain an undue surrender of British belligerent rights by a commercial class seeking short-term advantages, or liberal idealists convinced that a cosmopolitan and pacifist world was at hand. A number of them, like Clarke, were conscious of the requirements of British industry and trade, as well as the need to satisfy the various interest groups (not only economic but also philanthropic) that composed the electorate, and they attempted a balance between the necessities of strategy and those of commerce and politics.

Clarke began his career as an army engineer whose speciality was building fortifications, and served as secretary to the Colonial Defence Committee from 1885 to 1892; a recent writer has described him as "the first defence 'bureaucrat.'"[9] During the 1890s, Clarke was awakened by Mahan and the Colombs to "the necessity – vital to the Empire – of holding the command of the sea."[10] Like them, he defended the right of capture and opposed immunity. As early as 1890 he insisted that England had nothing to fear from a *guerre de course*, but might employ such a strategy against the commerce of her enemies; not only did she have the largest fleet, but she also possessed harbors all over the world to which she could bring prizes, while a weak belligerent could only destroy captured ships and would have difficulty in disposing of their crews.[11] He rejected the Radical argument that "the vulnerability of a steam mercantile marine" was "directly proportional to its volume"; the critical question was "the strength of the attack which can be brought to bear against it."[12] "Warfare against commerce, attempted in the face of naval supremacy, never succeeded in sailing days," he observed; "steam has distinctly increased its difficulties, and has greatly simplified the task of a protecting navy well provided with coaling stations on main trade routes."[13]

That Clarke possessed an understanding of Britain's commercial interests as they affected strategy, one not always found among acolytes of the blue-water school, was apparent in his early support of a state system of marine insurance. In 1890, Vice-Admiral Sir George Tryon suggested such a system to offset the great rises in marine premiums expected in the early months of a conflict. There were also two rival proposals: Lord Charles Beresford, a naval officer of the blue-water school, did not wish state intervention in a commercial matter,[14] while Admiral Philip Colomb observed that "in spite of all our present ideas of free trade," the privy council might use the powers reserved by the 1849 bill repealing the navigation acts to prohibit a transfer of British ships to neutral ownership.[15] Clarke, characteristically, preferred Tryon's scheme, the bureaucratic solution, rather than either Beresford's laissez-faire or Colomb's mercantilist proposals. Such a system of state insurance would "avert panic and abate the unholy craving for an alien flag with which British shipowners are credited," he wrote, while agreeing with Beresford that "the only real insurance of the empire" was a strong Navy.[16]

When Clarke became secretary of the C.I.D. in 1904, he pressed for national maritime insurance because "I have never shared the prevailing contempt" in certain quarters "for 'the doctrine of commerce destruction by cruisers.'"[17] None the less, he believed that as soon as British sea power "made itself felt," captures of British merchantmen would rapidly diminish. This was clear to all familiar with maritime questions. But since "the commercial classes" were "not students of Naval history" and had "no experience of a Naval war" in which Britain participated, a state guarantee would calm their fears.[18]

In his views on contraband as well, Clarke demonstrated his concern for both commerce and strategy.[19] When asked in 1904 to report to the cabinet on the value to Great Britain of the belligerent right of search of neutral vessels for contraband, he concluded that on this question England's chief interest was as a neutral. What immediately spurred cabinet interest in this issue were the extensive contraband lists proclaimed by Russia during the Russo-Japanese war then in progress. When England was neutral, Clarke declared, such wide-ranging lists "might inflict considerable injury" on British commercial interests, and pose "a danger" to England's continued non-involvement. Moreover, "purely opportunist" lists of contraband posed a threat to an England at war. "An island Power" that was "dependent upon external sources for its food-stuffs and raw materials might suffer serious injury if its enemy adopted the Russian definition of contraband"; besides, the injury inflicted on an enemy by the right of search did not counterbalance the risk of provoking neutral hostility.[20] Clarke's report was circulated to both the board of trade and the admiralty, the departments principally concerned. The board of trade found his conclusions "sound";[21] but, perhaps not surprisingly, the admiralty opposed yielding the right to search for contraband.

Particularly revealing of the mood of the time was that even the admiralty developed its argument along business not strategic lines. The profits to Britain as a neutral carrier would be greater, the admiralty contended, if belligerents maintained the right of search for contraband, for this would justify neutral carriers, among whom England was pre-eminent, in charging "heavy premiums" for carrying contraband, premiums which came "ultimately out of the pocket of the belligerent." British insurers – and the greater part of marine insurers were British – could also secure "very handsome profits" since premiums on war risks were usually "considerably in excess of what is warranted by the proportion of war losses." Finally, so long as coal, one of Britain's chief exports, was "even conditionally contraband, our profits as a State, in a commodity which is desired by every maritime belligerent, and obtainable only from us, should be great also." For all these reasons, the admiralty concluded that there was no "clear evidence that we lose as a neutral more than we gain."[22]

When the 1906 inter-departmental committee issued its report, Clarke's views – as revealed in his writings of the 1890s, and his 1904 report on contraband – clearly prevailed. On the right of capture of enemy merchantmen, the 1906 committee agreed with "naval opinion" that given "our naval supremacy," assuring us not only of "unique powers of offence, but also adequate protection to our much greater commerce," acceptance of immunity involved "a surrender" that might be estimated "up to infinity," while conferring a gain which might be "depreciated down to nil." The retention of the right of capture by the power that possessed naval supremacy threatened an enemy with the "complete destruction" of its carrying trade, and should war come "the coercive pressure and industrial stress" would operate to shorten the conflict. "Capture for the sake of prize" was certainly obsolete, but a "more scientific policy" of ending enemy maritime commerce "by confining it to port" must be followed. The committee was critical of the restrictions on the right of capture in the Declaration of Paris, though there was no call for repudiation. Lord Brougham's mid-century description of the right of capture as belonging with "the practices of barbarous and obsolete warfare" had "little but rhetoric to recommend it," the report observed. Indeed, the opposite was more true; the "sacrifice of human life involved is almost nil," while property loss was "confined to those who risk it at sea," and such persons were generally insured. The report recorded with satisfaction that such statesmen as Mill, Derby, Russell, Harcourt, Northcote, and Holker had all opposed immunity.[23]

How would Germany and America regard Britain's continued insistence on the right of capture? German rhetorical support for immunity so as to cultivate American opinion was dismissed as unworthy of consideration. The 1906 committee assumed that Germany – "our great rival in maritime commerce, and possibly also in naval supremacy" – would be the most likely enemy in a future war, and the right to capture private property would be a powerful maritime weapon against her. Remembering the Napoleonic Wars, and employing mercantilist reasoning, the report observed that the British carrying trade would benefit by the confinement of German ships to port, thereby turning "the apprehended disaster" of commercial war into "a source of gain." British insurers as well as financiers and brokers involved with foreign shipping might suffer, but it was "impossible to escape serious sacrifices in a war with a great commercial Power." As for America, now that she had become "a great colonial and naval Power," the committee suggested that she would probably alter her views. Mahan's writings made it appear that a change of opinion was taking place. Without doubting the sincerity of American support for immunity "in the cause of an enlightened and progressive humanity," the committee suspected that the underlying issue had been America's material interests.[24]

If England were to yield the possibility of a naval war against enemy commerce in favor of a duel between fleets, the report warned, such a change "would be popularly regarded as a mode of fighting which revived the traditions of the tournament in an age of chivalry, and refined war to a point at which it almost ceases to be war." Any serious change in maritime rules, given "traditional national sentiment in regard to the Navy and the services to be expected from it in case of war," would invite an intense and adverse public reaction. In these matters, the committee expressed "with great diffidence our dissent" from "an authority of the eminence of Lord Loreburn."[25]

On the issue of contraband, the inter-departmental committee agreed with the conclusions of Sir George Clarke's 1904 memorandum that it would be "of great advantage" to England if the principle of contraband were abandoned. Most of the powers either manufactured their own war equipment, or could receive such goods by rail. On the other hand, England needed to import food and raw materials by neutral ships, and the wide application given to the term contraband in the Russo-Japanese War might "conceivably place those sources of national existence in some peril." Though the Royal Navy could protect the British merchant marine, yet given "the disadvantages attaching to our insular position" the "general estimation" of Britain's strength would rise significantly by abolishing the concept of contraband. With this accomplished, "we could insure that while neutral our mercantile marine would not be molested" and that when a belligerent neutral ships could "continue to assist in supplying us from the markets of the world."[26] The end of contraband would close a loophole the 1856 Declaration offered to naval force, and neutral trade would be restrained in no way other than by the right of visit to determine nationality, and an effective blockade. In a supplementary memorandum, Clarke again described the abolition of contraband as particularly valuable to "a belligerent island Power."[27]

There were three other matters which the 1906 inter-departmental committee brought to the attention of the cabinet. First, the committee wished the British delegation to The Hague to insist that a cruiser unable to bring a neutral prize into port must release that ship, and not be permitted to sink her as lesser sea powers wished. This "doctrine of release" was of special importance to Great Britain and the United States whose navies could with greater facility bring a prize ship into their ports for adjudication by admiralty courts without running the risk of being captured in turn. Secondly, the committee argued that it would be in the British interest if the three-mile coastal limit to national territorial waters were maintained. Certain of the lesser naval powers wished to extend this limit on the ground that modern coastal artillery had a longer range, but clearly such an increase would tend "to diminish the sphere of action of the strongest navy." Lastly, the continental powers, as well as British Radicals, had long argued for the establishment of an international prize court which would have appellate jurisdiction over national admiralty courts. The committee urged that England had best support the establishment of such a court, or else she would arouse the enmity of other nations.[28]

The board of admiralty – to whom a copy of the inter-departmental committee's report was sent – endorsed the assurance of Britain's naval capacity to protect the country and her commerce given by Captain Ottley, its representative on the committee. The admiralty was confident in "the power of the fleet to obtain command of the sea" in any "reasonably probable" war, and in this way guarantee British trade against attack by hostile fleets. This "British command of the sea" should also bring about "the practically complete disappearance of the enemy's flag from the high seas."[29]

The admiralty board understood that the Liberal government was committed to limitations on naval armaments, but this posed both political and strategic problems. Who could verify that the pledges of other powers to reduce naval strength were observed? If Great Britain, the United States, and France decided to limit armaments "while Governments as retrograde as those of Germany and Russia declined to do so," such a course "would be the supreme limit of human folly, and might jeopardize the cause of liberal progress and civilization throughout the world." Naval armaments, the board warned the Liberals, were a principal national industry, and arms limitation might have serious economic consequences. The admiralty was also opposed to proposals to reduce the tonnage of warships. That British ships were larger than foreign ships was a "corollary to the primary strategic principle that the British fleet exists for one purpose only, viz., to seek out and destroy the armed vessels of our enemies, wherever they may be." Britain needed bigger ships with greater power so as to insure victory in "naval duels" of single vessels, since "decisive naval action between organized battle fleets will be comparatively rare."[30] – a variation of the Victorian strategic consensus.

The committee's report was sent to lord chancellor Loreburn, who stood by his support of immunity. While the views of Clarke and the committee might well be correct in the event of a war with Germany, he conceded, what if Britain were at war with America or Japan? "We cannot police two oceans against distant powers." Sir George Clarke had "conveniently" taken for granted "the eternal supremacy of the British fleet," but what if the Royal Navy were diminished by "the risks and chances of war, or of the sea" or if foreign nations made a "sustained and combined effort" to build rival fleets? Under such circumstances, would not immunity be most useful to England? The opponents of immunity might well have agreed with parts of this analysis, though they would have found Loreburn's contingencies unlikely. The lord chancellor concluded by dismissing the report as the work of unworldly government officials, without even a single businessman to defend the practicalities of the case.[31]

In June, Sir Edward Grey, the foreign secretary, also memorialized the cabinet on the report. Though the foreign office was later to take what many regarded as an extreme position in its advocacy of the 1909 Declaration of London, Grey hardly supported the Radicals or Loreburn on immunity. That principle "if carried to its logical conclusion," Grey reminded the cabinet, would mean the end of commercial blockade. "The British navy is the only offensive weapon which Great Britain has against Continental Powers," while these powers had "a double means of offence," their navies and "their powerful armies." Britain's delegates to the Hague Conference must always keep this in mind.[32]

The 1907 Hague Conference and the Declaration of London

That the prime minister was more Palmerstonian than Radical in his view of the Royal Navy became clear in a 1907 article written in the midst of an Anglo-German naval race and just before the opening of the Second Hague Conference. Campbell-Bannerman wrote the piece for the first issue of a new Radical weekly, *The Nation*, and used this forum to call for the reduction of military and naval expenditures, even as he eulogized the philanthropic disinterest of British sea-power. The Liberal government had just unilaterally scrapped plans for a dreadnought, but foreigners derided this concession as signifying nothing, since "our preponderant naval position" would "remain unimpaired." How could sensible men believe such a canard? For one thing "the sea power of this country implies no challenge to any single State or group of States"; everywhere, "that power is recognised as non-aggressive, and innocent of designs against the independence, the commercial freedom, and the legitimate development of other States." British maritime preponderance was consequently no obstacle to a truce in the armaments race. "The truth appears to me to lie in the opposite direction," the prime minister observed. England's support of "those two dominant principles – the independence of nationalities and the freedom of trade" entitled her to maintain "that if our fleets be invulnerable, they carry with them no menace across the waters of the world"; they bore, rather, "a message of the most cordial good will, based on a belief in the community of interests between the nations."[33]

The French historian Elie Halévy, an Anglophile and a liberal, described Campbell-Bannerman's *Nation* article as a "quaint manifesto which began with a pacifist act of faith" and concluded by subscribing to "the creed of Mahan." The prime minister's strange juxtaposition was as puzzling to Halévy as Brougham's expectations in the 1840s that France would happily accept Britain's naval campaign against the slave trade had been to Tocqueville. "When it confused in this way the freedom of mankind with the naval supremacy of England," Halévy asked, "was the British Government deceiving itself or with an even greater simplicity trying to deceive other countries?"[34]

Shortly after the appearance of the article, the government dropped still another dreadnought from its naval-building program in a gesture of conciliation to Germany. This move activated a body of naval "ultras" among the Tories. With the support of papers like the *Daily Mail* and journals like the *National Review*, these ultras denounced the Liberals and an "effete" Admiral Fisher, now first sea lord, for underestimating the seriousness of the German threat, even as Fisher, aided by some journalists whom he had attached to his person and policies, complained of Tory efforts to panic the public in the interests of party rather than patriotism.[35]

The Second Hague Conference met from June through October 1907. At The Hague, the Germans endorsed the American proposal for immunity, joining in the neutral demand for freedom of the seas. Since the architect of German naval expansion Admiral von Tirpitz opposed immunity on strategical grounds, it was apparent that his country's support for the United States initiative was founded on the hope of forming a diplomatic coalition against England. Admiral Fisher was worried. Writing to King Edward in 1907, Fisher observed that "Germany has collared the United States absolutely at The Hague! The only *one* thing in the world that England has to fear is Germany and the United States combining against England," since "the

German army and the American Navy would certainly make it hot for us."[36] The proposal in favor of immunity, however, was rejected by the conference. Supported by the lesser naval powers, England then argued in favor of the complete abolition of contraband of war. This effort was defeated by the opposition of Germany, France, and the United States. The British proposed to ban all floating mines, but other nations saw such weapons as a means of defending weaker powers against the Royal Navy; a compromise was however effected. The conference also decided to create an international prize court to preside over a new international maritime code.[37]

The Hague Conference called for a committee of experts to meet in London in 1908 to flesh out the principles accepted in 1907. The experts of the ten leading naval powers assembled at the British foreign office in December 1908, and in meetings that continued through February 1909 framed a treaty concerning "the laws of naval war." This Declaration of London contained a chapter on blockades, with 22 articles detailing just what constituted an effective blockade and how it might be legally enforced. A second chapter specified the articles included in three classes of goods: arms, ammunition, explosives, and the like were declared "absolute contraband"; into the class of "conditional contraband," articles "susceptible of use in war" as well as in peace, fell such goods as foodstuffs, clothing, communications materiel, and fuel; raw materials such as raw cotton and rubber, and industrial and agricultural machinery were non-contraband. Food and other conditional contraband could be confiscated if bound for a military or naval destination or if intended for the use of the armed services or the government itself, otherwise not. The agreement accepted the British doctrine of "continuous voyage" in the case of absolute contraband, making it liable to capture if it could be proved to be destined for enemy territory, whether directly or through trans-shipment by sea or land. Contrary to the wishes of both Britain and the United States, a cruiser might now destroy a neutral vessel liable to condemnation, if taking her into port "would involve danger to the safety of the warship or to the success of the operations in which she is engaged at the time." However, all persons aboard the captured ship were to be taken to safety. A transfer of an enemy ship to a neutral flag before the outbreak of war was to be valid unless it were proved that the transfer had been made to avoid capture.

Other issues festering for over a century and a half were put to rest by the 1909 agreement. The flag a ship was entitled to fly was declared to be decisive as to its character, though the case of a neutral ship chartered to engage in a trade closed to neutrals in time of peace remained unaffected by this provision; the British, thus, could revive, albeit in qualified form, the rule of 1756. The Armed Neutralities of the past triumphed, however, in the Declaration's provision that neutral vessels under national convoy were exempt from search.[38] Sir Edward Grey at the foreign office noted in a memorandum to the cabinet in November 1908 that "the divergence on this point between the old continental system that convoy exempts from visit and search and the English practice admits of no reconciliation," and England felt obliged to yield.[39]

Lord Desart, Britain's plenipotentiary at the London conference, signed the treaty on 26 February 1909; the question arose as to whether it was necessary to have parliamentary sanction in order to make the new rules binding. The Liberal government took the view, as had Palmerston's government in 1856, that a treaty did not require parliamentary ratification. The Crown's law officers, however, advised that although ratification of the naval provisions of the 1909 Declaration would not be necessary, parliament would have to accept the convention concerning the establishment of an international prize court before it could become effective.[40] A bill to consolidate the acts relating to naval prizes of war was framed by the foreign secretary, with the support of the first lord of the admiralty Reginald McKenna and the Crown's law officers. This piece of legislation was to become the focus of discussion in both houses of parliament and throughout the country.

T. G. Bowles, and the public debate

The leading figure in the fight against the Declaration of London was the journalist Thomas Gibson Bowles, the acknowledged illegitimate son of T. Milner Gibson, and the founder of the magazine *Vanity Fair*. Gibson, we recall, had been a follower of Cobden and an advocate of liberal maritime policies. Bowles, on the other hand, had for some decades associated himself with the Urquhartite opposition. As Conservative candidate for Darlington in 1875, he urged Englishmen to repudiate the 1856 Declaration if they were to avoid both an un-English system of conscription and universal military service, and being "a willing prey" to the military powers of the continent.[41] In the following years, he reminded his countrymen that it was "madness to suppose that now, for the first time in the history of the world," there was no one who would seek to acquire his "neighbour's property by methods of fraud or of violence,"[42] warning that the 1856 Declaration "neutralizes the sea and renders real maritime warfare impossible," a situation not to the advantage of a naval England. In an article in 1885, Bowles argued that so long as Britain was "predominant at sea," English merchant carriers need have no fear;[43] the piece attracted the attention of Captain Mahan, who asked Bowles for information on commerce-destroying for his forthcoming work.[44] In 1892, Bowles became the Conservative MP for King's Lynn, and began a single-handed campaign in the Commons against the new rule.[45]

Bowles published a book on the Declaration of Paris in 1900, calling for its immediate repudiation. "Conscription and universal military service never should be and never can be established in England," but what was the alternative after the "secret surrender" of 1856? British sea power could not defeat an enemy by battles like Trafalgar, as so many Victorians believed, but could triumph only by the "capture of property and stoppage of trade." The traditional British strategy of commercial war was "as merciful as it was effectual"; it "touched the Pocket rather than the Person of the enemy." Bowles denounced the Radical view that there could be "at one and the same time a national war and a commercial peace."[46]

Bowles's parliamentary career was cut short because he chose to support free trade during the election of 1906, when the bulk of his fellow Conservatives endorsed Chamberlain's program of protection and imperial preference. Faithful to a substantial part of his father's political legacy, he was determined to uphold the fiscal policies which he believed had made England the premier power. He went over to the Liberals, as did other Conservative free traders like Winston Chuchill. (Churchill saw free trade as essential to England's financial pre-eminence and preferred a cosmopolitan capitalism to a narrow and retrograde protectionism.)[47] Bowles stood as a Liberal candidate in the City of London in early 1906, charging that "the Protection System" would be "a deadly blow at the commercial and financial supremacy" of Great Britain,[48] but was defeated by the outgoing Tory prime minister, Arthur Balfour.

In 1909, Bowles began a campaign to rouse the nation to oppose the Declaration of London. Denouncing Sir Edward Grey for having gone over to the neutrals "bag and baggage," he declared the 1909 Declaration "all against a naval England" and "all for a military Germany." "In exchange for a small and unlawful profit to a few individuals in time of peace, it paralyses the power of the whole nation in time of war"; the "few unprincipled and selfish shipowners" who were "greedy for the high freights of contraband and enemy goods" were "enemies of the State."[49]

In 1910, Bowles published his *Sea Law and Sea Power* in which he observed, following his mentor Urquhart, that the seaborne trade of the continental powers was "in pawn to Great Britain," and at London in 1909 those powers joined "to take it out of pawn." He condemned the agreement's narrow view of contraband, its exemption of convoyed vessels from capture, its readiness to permit the destruction of a neutral ship, and its failure to prevent enemy steamers from being converted into warships on the high seas. The establishment of an international court was "a renewal of the conspiracy against British naval supremacy" begun by the Dutch in the seventeenth century; but now there was no Cromwell, Chatham, or Pitt to repel the enemy, only "a bleating Foreign Office" which chanted slogans of peace and denounced "all war as barbaric and sinful." Britain – as in 1856 – surrendered her essential maritime rights to "those insinuating foreigners who mouth philanthropy to the simple British emotionalists." Bowles called upon parliament to reject the international prize court, with its majority hostile to Britain, and thereby render the remainder of the Declaration inoperative.[50]

Bowles occupied the leading position in the debate on the 1909 agreement. In January 1910, he was returned to parliament as a Liberal from King's Lynn, the constituency he had formerly represented as a Tory, but in a second general election in December of that year, he was defeated. His campaign to convince parliament to reject the prize court, however, was to prove a powerful influence on those who opposed the measure in the debate of 1911.[51] A liberal barrister referred to him as "the Rupert of the battle," praised or excoriated, but regularly invoked.[52]

Since the opponents of the Declaration of London saw it as favoring mercantile interests, the opposition of the more important chambers of commerce was to prove both surprising and dismaying to the Liberal government. The Tories, by intensive efforts, persuaded officials of the chambers of London, Glasgow, Edinburgh, and Belfast among others, that the Liberals were endangering naval supremacy and the nation's very existence. In 1910 and 1911, one chamber of commerce after another memorialized their disapproval in virtually identical terms: they opposed listing food as conditional contraband, the destruction of neutral prizes, and the conversion of merchantmen on the high seas into warships; they were particularly disturbed because the Declaration's definition of "base of supply" to which conditional contraband could not be sent would include the majority of British ports.[53] For these reasons, they urged the submission of this agreement, so "destructive to the essential rights and contrary to the great trade interests of Great Britain," to full parliamentary debate.[54] The Chamber of Shipping, composed of thirty-one shipping associations, cited the same grounds for opposition, objecting particularly to shippers being compelled "when neutrals, to exchange the certainty of the support of our Government for the uncertainties" of "a hybrid Prize Court."[55]

This apostasy of the chamber officials, from whom a more "progressive" stand was expected, obliged T. McKinnon Wood, the under-secretary for foreign affairs, to chide those straying from the true interests of commerce. Though granting that the London agreement was not perfect but rather a useful compromise, Wood warned that its rejection would not only "gravely and lastingly" impair British influence in the world, but would also provide "a new stimulus" for the increasingly burdensome naval arms race, making necessary further taxes on trade and traders. When Britain was neutral, the 1909 Declaration, like that of 1856, would bring "enormous gains" to shipowners and merchants.[56] This was an undeniable advantage since "to preserve our commerce" was "a war interest as well as a peace interest"; the adoption of the Declaration would consequently enable Great Britain to better "sustain the economic strain of war."[57] Wood reminded the men of commerce that Bowles, the leader of the opposition campaign, wished to repudiate even the 1856 agreement which had proved so advantageous to British carriers. Bowles desired "international anarchy in time of war";[58] his position was "very simple, very drastic, very reactionary."[59]

Two committees waged vigorous public campaigns. On one side, the issue was presented as liberal progressive principle in opposition to Tory reaction, on the other, as a defense of the national interest against commercial greed. The Committee for Furthering the Ratification of the Declaration of London included representatives of all wings of liberalism, as well as of the new Labour Party: Lord Courtney, a friend and biographer of Mill, and the positivist barrister Frederic Harrison, as well as Noel Buxton, representing a later generation of the philanthropic family, were members, as were the journalist and Radical MP, J. M. Robertson, such Quaker pacifists as Sir Edward Fry and A. S. Rowntree, liberal businessmen like Sir Alfred Mond, and a number of trade-unionist Labour MPs, among them G. N. Barnes and G. M. Roberts.[60] The committee's publications cast Gibson Bowles as chief villain,[61] and stressed the advantages of the Declaration to the commercial community.[62] In reply, the publications of the Imperial Maritime League, founded in 1908 "to avert the passing of our naval supremacy," warned against pernicious Liberal efforts to reduce armaments.[63] Since the defenders of the Declaration, virtually all free traders, accused Tory protectionists of wishing to cut off the supply of the cheap white bread so prized by the working classes, the Tories returned the charge: the League denounced "Sir Edward Grey and his 'Liberal' friends," for having "betrayed the National Trust" by permitting liberal naval policies to endanger the safe entry in time of war of "the People's Food."[64]

The Hankey episode

Within the government, a similar debate was taking place among the officials of the C.I.D. and the admiralty. Sir George Clarke had resigned his position as the C.I.D.'s secretary to become Governor of Bombay, and was replaced in 1907 by the director of naval intelligence, Captain Charles Ottley. Ottley, knighted that same year, had represented the admiralty on the 1906 interdepartmental committee, and was among the framers of the Declaration of London. In 1910 and 1911, naval Captain Maurice Hankey, the C.I.D.'s assistant secretary since 1908 and a protégé of Ottley's, became increasingly uncomfortable with that agreement.

When Hankey first saw the 1909 Declaration, he was to report years later, "I was absolutely horrified" that "my beloved chief and benefactor" had approved its terms. Since in recent wars "the weapon of sea power as a means of putting economic pressure" upon a naval inferior had had no role, Hankey believed the Liberals had forgotten the essential lesson of the Napoleonic Wars – that Britain could only impose its will upon a continental enemy by destroying its trade. The principles of the Declaration "could not fail to impair the efficacy of sea-power as a weapon for the exercise of economic pressure." How could naval officers like Ottley, "privy to our most secret war plans," have accepted "so dubious an instrument"?[65]

Like most of the naval journalists and official strategists at this time, Hankey regretted the signing of the Declaration of Paris. But that agreement had two loopholes: the first, that contraband was not defined, and the second, the retention of the right of blockade. Yet because of the pressure of commercial interests, a Liberal government foolishly yielded these advantages. Though "fortunately for the future of sea-power" the Hague Conference of 1907 had rejected the British motion to abolish the concept of contraband, the lists of conditional and unconditional contraband in the London agreement "closed effectively" this "loophole for the exercise of sea-power." Moreover, the British delegates to the 1909 Conference had agreed to a definition of blockade that made a distant blockade, so necessary to a war against Germany, if not impossible, at least open to legal objections.[66]

In February 1911, before the opening of a parliamentary debate on the international prize court, Hankey, with Ottley's consent, wrote a long memorandum in which he surveyed the difficulties these concessions would pose in the event of a conflict with Germany. The supporters of the 1909 agreement believed a war against commerce "unthinkable." They argued that the Royal Navy no longer possessed an "unchallenged supremacy," that neutral navies were "more powerful and numerous," and that "a new and more powerful 'Armed Neutrality' would be formed." Hankey, however, was convinced that but for the limitations imposed by the London treaty, Germany's overseas "trade would be diminished and harrassed as was the trade with France in the wars of a century ago." The admiralty had already decided that a naval blockade of the Baltic coast of Germany must put the fleet at risk; and the 1909 agreement would cripple what remained of British naval effectiveness against the commerce of Germany's North Sea ports. There was a way out of these difficulties, a recourse to the spirit of "the fierce trident": if the Navy destroyed German sea power in early fleet action, Hankey observed, what neutral would dare to "challenge the right of Great Britain to fight the war in her own way and to declare contraband any article she desired?"[67] But Hankey stressed the rejection of the Declaration of London, and not this ultimate appeal.

Sir Charles Ottley forwarded his subordinate's memorandum to both the admiralty and the foreign office while warning in a covering note of dreadful international repercussions were Britain now to reject the London treaty. This would bring into doubt "all the neutral immunities for which civilized nations have struggled during the last century." To thus "overawe an entire world of powerful neutrals and terrorize them" would stir them "to the pitch of taking up arms in support of their rights." Hankey's "extreme contraband proposals quite transcend in rigour" the orders-in-council of the Napoleonic Wars; "motives of prudence and national self-interest" pointed elsewhere. Ottley found the solution in Hankey's ultimate appeal. There was no reason to reject the Declaration of London "to obtain the liberty of action which Captain Hankey desires." Britain merely needed to adhere formally to both the Paris and London agreements "until fortune had declared unmistakably in our favour at sea." Then she could proclaim that only a repudiation of their restrictions could bring a war to an end, and neutrals would have no alternative but to accept.[68]

A scrupulous foreign office rejected both Hankey's memorandum and Ottley's note "somewhat contemptuously," Hankey was later to write,[69] but the admiralty did not. The first lord Reginald McKenna, a barrister and City man known as a bit of a Radical before coming to the admiralty, called a conference in late February 1911 with both Hankey and Ottley. The minutes of the conference report that the first sea lord shared Ottley's lubricious view of the "binding" character of international agreements. Although naval actions might seem "theoretically hampered" by the Paris and London Declarations, McKenna observed that "international treaties are easily evaded." If the British fleet were victorious over the German, "some pretext" would readily be found and both agreements "swept away." "Meanwhile, however," he declared, "we should benefit from these Declarations when we were neutral."[70]

After the three-way conversation, Hankey noted that there now appeared to be "very little difference" between Ottley and himself. Both naval officers were prepared to violate the Declaration of Paris "in spirit if not in letter." But Hankey continued to argue that since the 1856 agreement had never been ratified by parliament, and had been signed "more than 50 years ago at a time when men believed an era of universal peace to have set in," it might well be thought obsolete. Ottley wished to repudiate both the 1856 and 1909 treaties "*after ratification*" of the latter, "notwithstanding that this Declaration renews and sets the seal" on the 1856 agreement. "Which policy is the more calculated to give offence to neutrals"?[71] For Hankey, the difference may not have been so much one of morality as of simple prudence. The difficulties of repudiation were clear to him, and after the war of 1914 he was to chide Grey for having underrated how "we were hampered morally" by the government's acceptance of the 1909 treaty.[72]

The parliamentary debate

The years 1909 and 1910 were marked by a number of political conflicts, some of which influenced the debate on the Declaration of London. The question of free trade or neo-mercantilism continued to be a leading issue, but there were related questions, among them the Radical insistence on the primacy of social reform while Tories saw the building of dreadnoughts to meet the German naval threat as more immediately necessary. The Liberal government was determined to satisfy the demands for naval expansion *and* social reform, and the budget of 1909 called for a system of progressive taxation, the taxation of unearned land values, and a rise of inheritance levies, measures aimed at the rich and the landowners. It was a provocative gesture and the Tory-controlled House of Lords rejected the measure. The issue was debated in two elections in 1910, and the Liberals won both. In 1911, threatened with being swamped by newly-created peers, the upper house conceded. Humiliated at their surrender, the Tory peers viewed the battle over the prize court bill as one in which they might again be seen as guardians of the true interests of the country.

The subjection of British maritime courts to an international court was a sensitive issue. In 1907, *The Times* – representing conservative opinion generally – denounced the proposal as "nothing less than the surrender" of essential British "rights and interests," and of Britain's strategic options. "All our sailors and all our statesmen have taught us that our power to destroy the commerce of our enemies is one of our most trenchant weapons in war and in diplomacy." An international court composed of foreigners who "always repudiated English doctrines of maritime law" would give "foreigners *carte blanche* to make laws for our fleet, and to shorten at their discretion our arm upon the seas."[73]

Each side enlisted prominent legal authorities in favor of its position. John Westlake, formerly Whewell professor of international law at Cambridge, was content with the Declaration, describing it as the product of an "atmosphere of scientific impartiality,"[74] while Oxford law professor T. E. Holland strongly disapproved of it as hostile to the national interest.[75] L. A. Atherley-Jones[76] and Leslie Scott,[77] both well-known international lawyers, the first a Liberal and the second a Tory, opposed the agreement; on the other side, a barrister of Lincoln's Inn, Norman Bentwich, wrote a learned defense,[78] as did the distinguished jurist, Arthur Cohen. Cohen saw the treaty as a compromise: while approving the codes on blockades and contraband, he shared the doubts of its opponents on, for example, the destruction of neutral prizes.[79] Yet, all in all, Cohen urged passage of the bill, and his support was particularly welcome to the Liberal attorney general.[80]

The foreign secretary was given the responsibility for seeing the prize court bill through parliament. Grey's frustrations were apparent in his memorandum to the cabinet in February 1911. A long-simmering resentment of the 1856 agreement had merged with opposition to that of 1909, Grey observed, and "the Declaration [of London] is being ignorantly, or perversely, accused" – he complained particularly of Bowles – "of creating the state of things which existed before it came into being, and for which ... it provides ... a partial remedy." It was "impossible to reproduce the conditions of the Napoleonic wars or for this country to enforce as against neutrals the belligerent rights which Great Britain enforced a century ago," for foreign nations were "sufficiently powerful at sea" to prevent such a policy. "What is essential" was that "the code of rules agreed [upon] should not diminish the belligerent rights which this country is in a position to enforce in a war under present conditions." An international prize court would protect belligerents against neutral hostility, and Grey cautioned that the "risk of such complications must be greater for the Power with the command of the sea than for her enemy."[81]

The upper house debated not merely the international prize court, but all the provisions of the London agreement. The leading theme of the opposition was the possibility that every major British port might be regarded "a base of supply" to which food shipments would be prohibited. The writings of Gibson Bowles formed a quarry from which the Conservatives drew their arguments. (The Tory protectionist Lord Desborough praised Bowles as "one of the few people in the country" who had mastered the facts of the case.)[82] The principal objections made by the opponents of the Declaration have already been discussed, but the debate did offer the surprising revelation by the Earl of Desart (who had signed the 1909 agreement on behalf of the government) that he joined Bowles in opposing the 1856 agreement, but believed it not possible "that we should go back on it." The 1909 Declaration substituted "fixed rules for what now approaches to chaos," Desart added, and "we shall benefit from it largely as neutrals" without sacrificing the right to capture enemy ships.[83]

The terms of the debate followed lines similar to the parliamentary encounters of the 1850s, 1860s, and 1870s. The confrontation was again between liberal principle and a concern for power. When Lord Loreburn observed that to persist in a maritime code constructed "under conditions of British naval supremacy" would be "a defiance of the world,"[84] the octogenarian Halsbury, the leader of the Tory fight against the Liberal budget, invoked the position of John Stuart Mill, and denounced the Liberals of 1911 who like those of the 1850s disregarded "the authority of Grotius ... [and] of Pufendorf." The Liberals were "very fond of peace and believe in the perfect goodness of human nature," but human nature "I am afraid is too strong for them."[85] The Liberal Lord Weardale, chairman of the committee which sought ratification, looked forward to the acceptance of immunity to which the 1909 agreement was "an absolutely necessary preliminary step."[86] Another Liberal peer, Lord Ritchie, warned against the possibility of an England at war with "half the civilised world" on account of her return "to the tactics we adopted 100 years ago."[87] Viscount Morley, the Radical essayist and journalist now serving as lord president of the council, saw ratification as necessary to preserve Britain's "moral influence" – "a valid, practical and substantial asset" which "it would be madness to throw overboard."[88] The Tory Lord Ellenborough, a distinguished soldier, while complaining that international lawyers do "a great deal of mischief" when they "interfere with the strategy and tactics of our naval campaigns," was relieved that their deliberations would prove meaningless, for a belligerent was "sure to justify his breaches of the Treaty by accusing his enemy of some technical breakage."[89]

By a party vote, the Lords rejected the prize court bill, and with it the Declaration of London. The government announced that it would make the issue a party question in the Commons, applying the whips to insure unanimous Liberal support. The Conservatives condemned this tactic, and renewed their effort to arouse a public clamor. Just as the Liberals neglected the national interest and undermined British industry by loyalty to an outmoded free trade, the Tories argued, so were they abandoning the belligerent rights at sea necessary to England's security.

The days before the debate scheduled in the lower house were marked by public meetings, press harangues, and even a Kipling poem. One meeting, with Lord Charles Beresford in the chair, launched a petition of 102 admirals, many of them retired, which proclaimed that the Declaration sacrificed "those maritime rights which had preserved our Empire for centuries and renders far more difficult the Navy's task of protecting the trade routes in time of war."[90] The day before the opening of debate, Bowles persuaded Arthur Balfour, the leader of the Tory opposition, to join him in a great public meeting in the City, whose theme was that the agreement posed a threat to Britain's food supply, and whose dominant tone was that of hostility to foreigners.[91] (Bowles was later to write of an international court composed "of defaulting Dagoes and Negro neologists.")[92] At this time also, the Tory *Morning Post* published a long poem by Rudyard Kipling warning against liberal "treacheries that [would] starve our land of her food."[93]

The House of Commons was to support the international prize court by a vote of 301 to 231. The press reported "some opposition cries of 'Traitors.'" Only one Liberal, the international lawyer L. A. Atherley-Jones, and one Labour member voted against the proposal, although there were five Liberal abstentions.[94] Atherley-Jones, a barrister who had written extensively on wartime commerce, insisted that "no question of Liberal principle" was involved.[95]

Bowles' example proved that a free trader might still reject the Declaration, but for most Liberal MPs principle (in various forms) necessarily led to support. The real issue was war or peace, one Liberal insisted, and England must show that like the United States she favored "arbitration and not war"; acceptance of the international prize court would be a vote for peace.[96] Other Liberals saw the question in terms of a "progressive" humanitarianism as against a "retrograde" opposition to the court.[97] Beneath the surface of the Tory opposition, the Liberals saw the jingoism of men like Lord Charles Beresford, who declared that if a naval officer saw food-bearing ships moving to enemy ports, he would sink them even if "hanged for putting them down." The Liberals were "pulling out" England's "teeth and claws, and you think other nations are going to do the same"; such a method had never worked in all of world history.[98] To Liberals, such bellicose sentiments exemplified what they had come to expect of Tory reactionaries – whose "teeth and claws" they indeed wished to extract.

Winston Churchill, the Liberal home secretary, described the debate in a letter to the king, whom he regularly kept informed of happenings in the Commons. Churchill noted that McKenna had assured the House that both Admiral Fisher and his successor as first sea lord, Sir Arthur Wilson, favored the treaty: "the Admiralty view is that the declaration is of small practical significance, but on the whole beneficent." Churchill agreed, and was dismayed at the "un-Parliamentary" conduct of Tories who had accused Liberals of being traitors. "We cannot stand outside the general movement of international agreements except for reasons of the utmost gravity," and no such reasons existed. Indeed, the English stood to benefit "as neutrals" by the replacement of an international for a national prize court. "As belligerents," of course, Churchill added, "we must rely not on any paper instrument, but on our own naval strength."[99]

In much this tridentine spirit, many navy men, among them admirals Sir Reginald Custance and Sir Cyprian Bridge, welcomed the Declaration of London, as bringing order to what had been maritime chaos without interfering with essential strategic needs. As the "most authoritative statement of International Law," ratified or not, it was "a great boon to belligerents and neutrals alike," Admiral Custance wrote in a Liberal quarterly in 1912. While conceding that the new rules made naval action against commerce more difficult, Custance followed the Victorian consensus in seeing a war against trade as "secondary to" and unable to "reverse, the decision by battle."[100] (Two years earlier, Admiral Bridge had also argued that these further restrictions in commercial warfare did not obstruct the "true objective" of naval warfare, battle with "the enemy's navy"; that navy "must be destroyed or decisively defeated, or intimidated into remaining in its ports.")[101] In 1914, a few months before the beginning of war, replying to Lord Loreburn and other proponents of immunity, Custance defended the right of capture of enemy merchantmen as "essential to an island State," yet continued to urge a strategy "of fixing the gaze on the attack on the enemy's armed ships."[102]

At the end of 1911, Churchill exchanged cabinet posts with McKenna and became first lord of the admiralty. Some weeks later, the foreign secretary wrote to reassure the new first lord that the Declaration of London was "not only innocuous, but positively advantageous to this country,"[103] although we have seen that Churchill needed no reassurance. Soon Churchill, who was one of Fisher's most loyal supporters, was to join Fisher as one of the two chief targets of Bowles and the naval ultras, this because of his role in March 1914 in abolishing prize money as "not compatible with the highest conception of the naval or military profession."[104] Forty-eight hours before the war of 1914 began, the first lord would also push through a bill providing for state insurance for war losses to British shipping, as Admiral Tryon and Sir George Clarke had advocated nearly a quarter of a century earlier.[105]

In 1911, Admiral Fisher derided the agitation of Bowles, the ultras of the Maritime League, and the Tory party:

> These d—d fools who talk about invasion and about our commerce being destroyed and the Declaration of London being an awful catastrophe . . . are of inestimable value, though asses, because they keep the pot boiling! I wouldn't have them contradicted for the world! They keep up the Navy estimates!

Fisher continued to see international politics as a pitched battle, much as he had when writing from the First Hague Conference in 1899 of *Britannia contra mundum*. Britain would easily win such an encounter. Writing a friend in June 1911, he declared:[106]

> Don't you worry about either the British Empire or the British Navy! (THEY ARE SYNONYMOUS TERMS!) We are the Lost Ten Tribes of Israel! WE CAN'T GO UNDER! . . . in spite of the idiots who govern us, *we never were so absolutely paramount as now*! WHY? Because our Navy at this moment could take on all the Navies of the world! "Let 'em all come!"

The admiral's attitude toward international agreements was as it had been at The Hague in 1899 when he told the German naval delegate that "might is right." In 1911, he reassured Hankey about the consequences of the Declaration of London that, as Hankey was later to paraphrase Fisher's view, "all these agreements would tumble down as soon as the guns went off."[107]

[8] The Politics of Pacifism, Parsimony, and Redistribution

The men of the nineteenth century were under the illusion that the world in which they carried on business was held together by the so-called laws of political economy . . . But in fact . . . that control was supplied . . . by the supremacy of Great Britain, exercised through the Navy . . . The naval supremacy of Great Britain . . . may prove to be the most significant contribution made by that century of economic progress to the life of mankind.

Sir Alfred Zimmern, *Quo Vadimus?*, 1934

The liberal tradition in thinking about war and peace . . . has been often marred by naivete, by intellectual arrogance, by ignorance, by confused thinking and sometimes, alas, by sheer hypocrisy.

Michael Howard, *War and the Liberal Conscience*, 1977

When Radicals, on the left of the Liberal mainstream, wished to proceed beyond protection of neutral trade to granting immunity to enemy private property and outlawing commercial blockades, the mainstream Liberals (as well, of course, as Tories) rallied to defend what remained of the traditional strategy. Yet though the Radicals constituted only a small, but highly articulate, minority, even moderate Liberals who believed them impractical were obliged to treat them with a measure of deference if only because Radical ideals represented the liberal creed in its purest form. For Radical Cobdenites, free trade was not merely practical policy, as it was for Liberals generally, but the necessary basis for world harmony, and immunity and the end of blockade would enable commerce to fulfill its providential role in securing a perpetual peace. Although prepared to make use of commercial greed when convenient, the Radical pacifists were at times as contemptuous of the capitalist Mammon as they were of the feudal gods of battle. They stood for a true Christian ethic. For them "strategy," any plan for exerting or projecting military or naval force, was *ipso facto* wrong.

Twentieth-century Radicals differed from their mid-Victorian predecessors in their perception of domestic politics. Laissez-faire and economy in government had been leading principles of the earlier Cobdenites, who associated state intervention and great expenditures with sinister interests, particularly those of the aristocracy in sinecures and war. Their successors continued to hit at wasteful expenditure; however, when the working classes became not merely a passive electoral majority but an increasingly well-organized and demanding constituency, one that might threaten social stability by extra-parliamentary acts, the Radicals abandoned laissez-faire. Seeing a working class still in the grip of instinct, as its enthusiasm for the war in South Africa had recently demonstrated, they acted to block labor support for a neo-mercantilist and aggressive Tory policy by promising such reforms as old-age pensions and sickness and unemployment insurance. This was necessary, they believed, not only to thwart the risks of socialism and even revolution, but also to enlist the interest of the trade unions against the alternative use of available tax revenues for armaments.

In the decade before the First World War, advancing both practical and moral arguments, Radicals renewed their earlier efforts to make immunity part of the law of nations. They were convinced that with immunity granted Germany would no longer seek a great fleet, and England no more require a navy superior to that of her two closest rivals, the standard accepted in 1889. Wasteful naval expenditure could be eliminated, and the costs of social reform more easily borne. But the opponents of immunity, seeing Germany as a determined rival for predominance, denied the Radical premise and maintained their resistance to immunity on strategic grounds. When Radicals turned from more pragmatic considerations to insist that immunity was dictated by international custom and morality, they found that even international jurists often appeared more conscious of strategy than of ethics.

International law and strategy

International law had exerted an influence in world politics at least since the time of Grotius, but it had not always served as an effective restraint on political conduct. For Carl von Clausewitz, the "self-imposed, imperceptible limitations" on force "known as International law and custom" were "hardly worth mentioning."[1] There were British politicians and civil servants who agreed but who proceeded more discreetly. A readiness to subscribe to lofty abstractions of uncertain meaning so as to satisfy liberal or continental prejudices had become a part of British diplomatic practice by the mid-nineteenth century. The instructions given to the chief British delegate to the 1874 Brussels conference on war advised him not to under-rate the importance the continental mind attached to "abstract statements." While "nothing should induce us to surrender any mode of warfare which we believe to be essential to our safety," he was told, it might on occasion be useful to indulge the continental and American taste for pious platitudes. Britain might well accept "a proposed International Declaration" that "may strike us as superfluous or ill-expressed" if she thought it "a step towards that mutual good understanding of the nations, which is the best safeguard of peace."[2] Such declarations ought not to be taken too seriously.

But liberal-minded Englishmen did take them seriously. And not only liberals believed that once Britain subscribed to a rule, once the general opinion of civilized mankind had come to some agreement, explicit or implicit, such a rule became part of the *ius gentium* and binding. For many Englishmen international law was synonymous with morality, though for others it still smacked too much of the doctrine that might made right. Although Kant anticipated both those positions, he stressed the duty of good men to obey a public law of nations. Many Tories doubted whether the new rule of the Paris Declaration would hold up in wartime, but few denied that accepted international law would play some limiting role in the event of war. In 1907, Admiral Sir Cyprian Bridge wondered whether the nature of man could be "altered by the formulation of rules or the signing of conventions"; he believed that powers like the United States would probably get their way, while weaker neutrals would not. You cannot "stop a dogfight by singing a hymn," he observed. None the less, in the coming war "the strategist may have to reckon with the international jurist as well as with the enemy."[3]

In the Franconia Case of the 1870s, the question of how seriously England was limited by an international consensus was debated in a British court. The issue was simple: was England bound by the almost universal acceptance of the three-mile zone, once the range of a cannon shot from shore, which distinguished national from international waters? Many Englishmen saw no reason why Britain's warships should be excluded from any waters. Lord chief justice Cockburn, speaking for the majority of the Court of Criminal Appeal, argued that since there was no positive act by the government, the parliament, or a British tribunal, English law recognized no such limit. The "mere assertions" of the "writers on the public law" or "even the assent of other nations" were not binding on Great Britain. Lord Coleridge, speaking for the minority, observed that in England as in other civilized nations "treaties and acts of state" as well as "a consensus of jurists" could expand the law of nations to which a state owed obedience. For men did not obey laws merely out of fear of punishment. They might be coerced by religious or moral feelings, or by the sanction of public opinion. The question was settled in 1878 when the parliament passed a territorial waters act to bring British law and practice into conformity with that of the rest of the civilized world.[4] Cockburn and Coleridge represented two different views of English jurisprudence: Cockburn's was that of the nineteenth-century legal philosopher John Austin who insisted that a valid law required a sovereign capable of compelling obedience, and that without a supra-national sovereign international law fell utterly to the ground; that of Coleridge stemmed from the natural rights and natural law tradition of which Sir William Blackstone, in England, and Kant, more generally, were the leading eighteenth-century spokesmen. Liberal opinion preferred the latter, and stressed an overriding natural rights and obedience to an enlightened international morality.

By the eighteenth century, liberal public opinion had emerged as a force to be reckoned with, and the articulate middle classes (in their newspapers and journals, in their trade and professional associations, in their religious and humanitarian societies) were its principal source. In countries where these classes were numerous and politically influential – in the United States and in Western Europe – this liberal opinion, in maritime as in other affairs, set unwritten limits on the rule of might. Moreover, this morality was seen as a progressive affair: the rules of war would be judged by a continually improving standard. The Declaration of Paris was a considerable effort to lay down a new moral consensus concerning maritime war, but for liberals far from the final one.

Lord Loreburn in a 1913 work on the law of maritime capture complained that "we do not sufficiently discriminate between questions of strategy, in which naval officers speak with conclusive authority, and questions of policy, upon which they cannot claim to be experts." Let "mercantile men" not admirals address themselves to "questions of policy." Among policy questions Loreburn included not only immunity but also blockade and contraband. Only "imperative military necessity" ought to overcome "the principle" of non-interference with the lives and property of private persons. But even in stating this moral principle, Loreburn could not avoid the strategic conclusion that by accepting the principle of immunity, "we should prevent its [the Royal Navy's] strength being dissipated upon secondary enterprises which cannot determine the issue of a war."[5] (For Radicals like Loreburn, the decisive naval duel continued as the primary strategy until the time of the war of 1914, when it was replaced by one of a speedily negotiated peace.)

It was difficult for international lawyers to avoid discussing strategy.[6] "International Law at sea is merely the will of the most powerful maritime State at a given moment," a prominent British barrister declared at a meeting of the Royal United Service Institution in early 1906.[7] Although the writers on international law shared common assumptions, most saw themselves – implicitly if not always explicitly – as barristers defending their country's interests. (Sir William Harcourt was appointed Cambridge's first Whewell professor of international law in 1869 in good part because of his defense of British maritime policies against French legal opinion.[8] It is also noteworthy how often the legal officers of the Crown served as the government's spokesmen in debates on naval policy.) By the time W. E. Hall published his *Treatise on International Law* in 1880 – a work which a generation later the Oxford professor of international law called "unquestionably the best book upon the subject in the English language"[9] – uncertainties about British interests were quite pronounced, and Hall's argument against immunity was equivocal. He dismissed the so-called "fundamental principle" of war as existing only between states: Capture was certainly not harsher than other practices of war; while causing relatively "little individual misery," its role in deranging trade placed it "among the most formidable of belligerent weapons." Yet though "legally and morally" unexceptionable, for Hall the wisdom of the right of capture had become questionable. It was a matter "for grave consideration whether it is not more in the interest of England to protect her own than to destroy her enemies' trade"; and a sufficiently strong "set of opinion" in the world against capture might confront a belligerent England with "an unfriendly neutrality" on the part of other nations.[10]

A contemporary was to describe legal opinion on the right of capture at the time of the Second Hague Conference and afterward as "hopelessly divided."[11] While Cambridge professor Westlake argued that since the Royal Navy was no longer supreme, English interest dictated that she reject capture and see herself as a neutral,[12] T. E. Holland, professor of international law at Oxford, praised the campaign of Gibson Bowles as having prevented "overhasty acts" in favor of neutral trade that would seriously damage Britain's position as a belligerent.[13] A number of international lawyers, on both sides of the question, invoked the testimony of strategists, like Mahan and Corbett, in support of their different views on the state of the law.[14]

In 1908, in a comic tussle between ideals and temperament, Rev. T. C. Lawrence, who had earlier taught international law at Cambridge and now lectured at the naval college at Portsmouth, argued for immunity in a warlike spirit. Since Britain was both "the greatest naval Power" and "the greatest commercial Power," he declared, she was "entitled, not, indeed, to dictate the law, but to have the most influential voice in reshaping it." "A vast quantity of antiquated legal *débris* should be shot into the sea," he concluded, in a martial metaphor. When an army man, Lord Ellenborough, replied that "if any one of our admirals allowed the supremacy of our Navy in the Channel or North Sea to be imperilled by a slavish obedience" to a Hague Conference resolution, he might be lynched, Lawrence, somewhat confusedly recollecting his clerical vocation, responded that this was "going back to something like barbarism."[15]

Liberals and the Navy: peace, retrenchment, reform

Liberals, even Radicals committed to a cosmopolitan policy, were convinced of the usefulness of sea power in an unredeemed world, but were reluctant to endorse any expansion of naval forces that might prove unnecessarily large for Britain's defensive requirements. Though Cobdenites at times vied with

Tories in rhetorical support of the Royal Navy, Liberals were sufficiently devoted to the ideal of a parsimonious state that they begrudged any considerable expenditure for the services. P. H. Colomb complained in 1878 of the difficulties of maintaining a powerful fleet in "a constitutional soil," one "adverse to the production" of such a force. A liberal democracy was prepared to think of the protection of commerce but not the projection of power: given a parliament "driven by the eager but uninstructed opinions of the least informed and most pre-occupied people," he noted that "the greatest caution is necessary not to push a theory of naval force too much into prominence."[16]

A decade later, fears of France united both parties, with the exception of the Radicals, in an effort to strengthen the Navy. In 1889, the Tory and Liberal front benches agreed, in the words of the Tory first lord of the admiralty Lord George Hamilton, that "our [naval] establishment should be on such a scale that it should at least be equal to the naval strength of any two other countries." England's "whole social and constitutional policy" forbade her to compete with the continental powers "in the magnitude of their land forces," but she intended to maintain "our naval supremacy."[17] Speaking for the Liberals, Henry Campbell-Bannerman accepted this doctrine, insisting that England held naval supremacy its "traditional possession," with "the consent of, and without any injury or grievance to, neighbouring countries."[18] Even Gladstone, who had become more of a Radical as he grew older, joined in support, though with some show of reluctance.[19] But a new crop of Radicals as well as some mainstream Liberals revived the old cause of maritime morality and of economy, and even the cry of "outdoor relief for the aristocracy."[20]

Among them were working-men Liberal (labelled "Lib-Lab") MPs such as W. R. Cremer[21] and George Howell[22] as well as middle-class Radicals like Henry Labouchere. Labouchere observed that when Britain possessed naval supremacy she "misused it in order to bully neutrals."[23] A Wolverhampton Radical H. H. Fowler, while proclaiming that "the Liberal party – I may go further and say, the Radical party – has accepted during a long series of years Cobden's doctrine that the Navy is our first, second, and third line of defence," expressed grave doubts as to the expense of a two-power standard.[24] Given the ambivalence of these occasional Radical bursts of maritime pride, it was not difficult for Admiral Field, a Tory MP, to blame the unsound condition of the Navy on "the weak-kneed and flabby Liberal Governments in the past."[25]

Pacific-minded Radicals preferred a force with fewer ships and a more limited function, and resisted efforts to add to naval estimates. Britain possessed a sufficient advantage on the sea, they said, particularly if naval wars were to be confined to duels between fleets. When Tory governments called for increased expenditures, Liberals demanded a reduction of waste in the shipyards, in the fleet itself, and, their ultimate thrust at the landed classes, in the service-lists. In 1893, after a Liberal government again came to power, the former Tory chancellor of the exchequer G. J. Goschen protested that the Liberals had done nothing to make up certain naval losses. The Liberal chief secretary for Ireland John Morley answered that "everybody knows, Liberals as well as Tories, that it is indispensable that we should have not only a powerful Navy, but I may say an all-powerful Navy."[26] Yet there was no haste in providing for the deficiency of which Goschen complained.

During what Radicals called a "naval panic" in 1907, a Tory journalist writing under the pseudonym Dreadnought described the Liberal view of England's place in the world. Liberals did not believe that any power "seriously" intended to seize British possessions because "the certainty of financial loss and the disturbance of trade" would "act as a sufficient check to ambition." They were convinced that "war, as war, is out of date," and if armies were disbanded and naval ships laid up, as it was to almost everyone's interest to do, wars would be no more. Since such a "scheme is not yet entirely practicable," they were prepared "to compromise": they would maintain forces sufficient to provide against what they saw as "those trifling emergencies which may occur while the world is passing through the transitional stage from periodical or incessant war to universal peace and the 'calico millennium.'" Any money saved by reducing the forces, the writer observed, was "vaguely intended" for "distribution among the poor."[27]

But all Liberals were not of one mind. The naval journalist and Liberal MP Carlyon Bellairs remarked that the Liberal party had "always been divided into extreme Radicals and Liberal imperialists";[28] Admiral E. J. W. Slade, a writer on strategic questions, identified the groups in the 1908 cabinet as the Radical "economists," Lloyd George, the new chancellor of the exchequer, and Churchill, "standing for a general reduction [of naval expenditures] all round so as to get money for old age pensions," and the Liberal-Imperialists, "Asquith, Grey, and Haldane standing for keeping up our strength."[29] Bellairs viewed the social reformers as a "little Navy party."[30]

A Liberal writer more sympathetic to "the warnings of the economists" than to "the clamour of the jingos [*sic*]" lamented in 1912 that the economists in the party were "negligible while the jingos are formidable."[31] In fact, of Liberal-Imperialists proper – members of the former Liberal prime minister Lord Rosebery's imperial-minded Liberal League – there were fifty-nine returned at the 1906 election; a 1907 petition to cut naval expenditure was signed by 136 Liberal MPs, and a similar one in 1908 received eighty-two signatures, though as actual votes against the naval estimates would suggest, hardly all were "extreme" Radicals.[32] A recent scholar has argued that the Radical pacifists were better able to form a cohesive school because they more clearly knew their own position; that there was a Radical "collective mind" might be seen in the views of some cabinet ministers (Loreburn, Morley, and Sir William Harcourt's son Louis), a number of civil servants (particularly at the treasury and the board of trade), "certain City financiers and Nonconformist businessmen, Liberal backbenchers and a cluster of Radical journalists."[33]

The bulk of the Liberal party continued to hold a moderate not a Radical nor an imperialist position on naval questions; they did not regard naval policy as their primary concern. A supporter of Fisher's admiralty, the Liberal journalist Archibald Hurd, described the thrust of the mainstream view in a 1908 article: "We want to provide a Navy as cheaply as possible," and "every penny spent above the necessary standard dictated by activity abroad is money wasted" for "in these times of falling trade, we cannot afford to waste our resources."[34] The chief interests of mainstream Liberals were in the field of domestic not foreign affairs. The party was a coalition of groups concerned with Irish home rule or social reform, with improving the status of the trade unions or of the non-conformist churches, with free trade or pacifism – most often with more than one of these goals. Except for certain Radicals whose first commitment was to pacifism, each group understood that his special interest or interests depended on the survival of the Liberal government.

After the Liberal victory of 1906, it was the mission of the Liberal-Imperialists – of chancellor of the exchequer and later prime minister H. H. Asquith and foreign secretary Sir Edward Grey particularly – and of first sea lord Fisher to reassure a public opinion increasingly worried, as we shall see, about the German naval challenge. They served to guarantee that a Liberal government would not permit its MPs, whose constituents supported the party because of a dedication to special interests, to neglect the national interest. If, in the middle decades of the nineteenth century, such Whig grandees as Russell and Palmerston had provided this assurance, now it was most of all Sir Edward Grey, a country gentleman and amateur tennis champion, whom as one MP noted "the country trusts above all others" to maintain the superiority of the Royal Navy.[35]

The chief instrument in the services of this Liberal guarantee was Admiral Sir John Fisher. Fisher understood that the Liberal government had constituencies that demanded economy in armaments and made himself a spokesman for economy in opposition to the demands of the Tories and the ultras for vastly increased programs of naval construction. The first sea lord was confident of the superiority of the Royal Navy. Writing to the king in 1907, he observed that the Radical industrialist "Sir John Brunner, M.P., and 150 Members of the House of Commons who are Sir Henry Campbell-Bannerman's warmest supporters and have been his steadfast friends in adversity have sent him quite recently one of the best papers I have read, convincingly showing that we don't have to lay down any new ships at all – *we are so strong*. It is quite true!"[36] The navalist *Daily Express* in March 1909 was critical of Fisher's seeming connivance with the Radical "economaniacs," and the first sea lord became a prime target of the ultras of the Imperial Maritime

League.[37] When the Germans accelerated their naval program in 1908–9, the new Liberal prime minister Asquith proposed the building of further dreadnoughts; this unexpected move to expand the fleet gave the admiralty "perhaps the greatest triumph ever known!," Fisher wrote Esher in May 1908. "You may tell Lloyd George" that "he can rely on my parsimony."[38]

But if the ultras thought Fisher a Liberal puppet, the Radicals and the Germans believed him to be a roaring jingo, a model reactionary. One journalist described him as "a bit of a barbarian who talked like a savage at times."[39] And it was Fisher that Germany's Admiral von Tirpitz particularly feared.

Immunity, social reform, and the German naval challenge

Germany was determined to attain the place in the sun to which she believed her economic and military strength entitled her. Only by securing a fleet that rivaled the British, many Germans came to believe, could she pursue a fitting world-political role, and both protect her colonies and commerce and restrain British actions in Africa or Asia. This was Admiral von Tirpitz's justification of the naval laws of 1898 and 1900, incorporating a long-term shipbuilding program. But what if during Germany's period of naval inferiority Fisher launched a pre-emptive strike, following the model set by Nelson in 1801 and repeated in 1807, when the Danish fleet was surprised and defeated at Copenhagen? Admiral Fisher and certain elements of the Tory press were believed to favor such a course. An influential section of German opinion saw England as determined to destroy Germany as a trade rival, and regarded a repetition of the Copenhagen assault as probable, and even justifiable in terms of *realpolitik*.

Tirpitz was pleased by the Liberal victory of 1906: he was confident that the Liberals would work to reduce naval estimates, waste time in seeking international naval disarmament, and be less likely than the Tories to fight a preventive war.[40] Certainly the Liberal triumph at the polls revived the campaign for immunity. Radicals believed that the adoption of immunity would persuade Germany that she no longer needed to challenge Britain's naval superiority, making possible reduced naval expenditures and essential social reform. The Radicals were puzzled as to why not even the economists in the cabinet could understand this.

In 1908, while both press and parliament debated a response to increased German naval armaments, a "Universal Congress of Peace" met in London in which speakers presented the adoption of the principle of immunity as the certain solution to the problem of war. Delegates urged Great Britain, "the chief sinner," to accede to the entreaties of the "whole world" and yield the right of capture, describing it as "the ancient practice of marine privateering" and "the old plunder policy of the past."[41] After Asquith addressed the conference, the Radical Lord Courtney called the attention of the prime minister to the fact that international law still barbarously sanctioned the capture of private property at sea, and suggested that this alone justified German naval expansion.[42] Another delegate H. S. Perris, the secretary of the British National Peace Council and of the Universal Peace Congress, declared that the adoption of immunity would go to "the root of the matter" of war and peace, and undermine "the militarists" who demanded a big navy to protect British commerce.[43] Another delegate, Dr G. B. Clark, added that "I hope Lord Courtney made Mr Asquith a convert," for if he had, peace would be assured.[44]

The Radicals, like the peace-congress pacifists, appeared convinced that the adoption of immunity was all that was required for ending war. In 1909, Brunner insisted that immunity was not irrelevant, as the government believed, but central to the German naval build-up.[45] The Radical *Economist* urged the protection of "peaceful commerce by naval convention" as essential since Germany's fleet was rapidly achieving parity with the Royal Navy.[46] If private property at sea were immune from capture, another Radical journal, the *Nation*, declared, the "taxpayer's gold" would not be wasted in useless expenditure for naval expansion.[47] Yet C. P. Scott, the editor of the Radical *Manchester Guardian*, had complained in 1908 that Lloyd George was "unhappily as much opposed as any of the Jingoes" to the abolition of the right of capture, "the real key of the situation."[48]

In 1910, the *Nation* published an address by the German liberal economist Lujo Brentano to the Antwerp Free Trade Congress in which Brentano spoke of "the humiliation of search at the hands of British cruisers" when England was at war. Such a maritime system, now confirmed by Chamberlain's "Neo-mercantile policy," flattered "the meaner passions of Englishmen" while it "outraged the feelings" of other nations against "England's military despotism." Brentano was critical of the Radicals, whom he saw as much the heirs of the doctrine of maritime supremacy as other Englishmen, for failing to demand more insistently that their country adopt the principle of immunity.[49] Vernon Lee, writing for the *Nation*, agreed that "the English Radical . . . turns a deaf ear (has turned ever since 1856!) to any suggestions that England should forego the use of her buccaneer weapons against private property, that is to say the one concession which might justify Germany in disarming."[50] But we know that Radicals had vigorously promoted immunity in the 1860s and 1870s, though they failed to convert even fellow Liberals. The effort continued. In 1912 Brunner, now president of the National Liberal Federation, called for an "enlightened patriotism" in "the best traditions of Liberal policy," and again argued that England's failure to accept immunity had compelled Germany, "our chief European customer and our best commercial friend," to arm "nervously and rapidly in order to protect her own mercantile marine from the menace of our greatly superior fleet."[51] The *Economist* observed further at this time that German taxpayers only tolerated the increase in naval budgets because both Liberal and Tory governments, "ill-inspired by their naval experts," had "clung to the so-called Right of Capture."[52]

There were other grounds for Radical unhappiness with the Liberal government's program of naval expansion. Henry Vivian, a leader in the co-partnership movement and a Radical MP from Birkenhead, observed in a 1906 speech in the Commons that high naval budgets lessened "national commercial credit," and at the same time increased unemployment (he did not specify how) and reduced "resources available for social reform." Calling for a revival of "the great traditions of the [Liberal] Party," and noting particularly the "task of retrenchment" in the service estimates, Vivian saw the country's renewed interest in armaments as "discreditable to a so-called Christian nation."[53] The following year, in 1907, Brunner and the Radical MP Murray Macdonald framed a vigorous manifesto to Campbell-Bannerman – signed by 136 members of parliament – urging a reduction in naval expenditures which they believed "excessive and injurious." The Radical manifesto deplored oversized naval budgets which served to destroy "the financial elasticity" of the nation and depleted "those financial reserves upon which success in war so largely depends." The "well-being of our people" was "at least as essential" for victory in a conflict as "a great Army or a great Navy," and "every penny" spent on "excessive armaments was at the expense of resources necessary to promote national welfare."[54] Radicals believed social reform not naval expansion was the most pressing need of the day. The *Nation* noted in 1913 that "every principle of the Liberal Party, and nearly every problem of democracy, are involved in the approaching struggle between the two conflicting types of expenditure."[55]

In mid-1910, the *Nation* chastised the Liberal government for having increased "warlike expenditure" on no grounds other than "suspicion, and only suspicion," of Germany's intentions.[56] Asquith and his colleagues were captives of the "Generals and Admirals" who had pointed pistols at their heads, the weekly charged the following year; Liberal politicians must regain the "power of the purse" for if Germany forced the pace of arms expansion "even our great financial and political reserves" might "begin to totter."[57] Surely "any British Imperialist" not "a victim of the mania of persecution nor a shareholder in an armament firm" should be content with England's naval superiority, the journal wrote in early 1913.[58]

The Radicals agreed with Fisher's ultra opponents that it was foolish for the mistress of the seas to have developed a new and expensive class of warship, the dreadnought, making it possible for other fleets to compete from a position of near equality.[59] The ultras had more serious strategic objections, we shall see, but for the Radicals the chief issue was expense. In 1913, the *Economist* called the adoption of the dreadnought "either an act of treachery or a piece of madness," or perhaps "a skilful device" for stimulating the international armor-plate industry. Given the effectiveness of torpedoes, mines, and submarines, the admiralty would not dispatch "these 'capital ships' down the channel" in wartime, no less approach the enemy coast.[60] Five years earlier, the journal had doubted that either Germany or Britain would in time of war "dare to send a battleship that cost it from £1,500,000, to £2,000,000 into the North Sea."[61] The *Nation* also pointed to the waste of the admiralty's program of "bigger docks, bigger guns, costlier fuels, more men."[62]

What had happened to the great traditions of the Liberal party, the *Economist* inquired. The editor of the journal F. W. Hirst was a complete Cobdenite. The Radical weekly believed that England was more to blame for the threat to peace than Germany, and that Britain's efforts to meet what jingoes mistakenly saw as a naval challenge were highly provocative. Moreover the journal usually preferred the word of the Germans on the state of British and German naval strength to that of the British government.[63] The *Economist* was pained by the conversion of reasonable men to the hysteria of naval panic. Almost as soon as Reginald McKenna was appointed first lord of the admiralty, the paper noted, he was converted "from the Treasury and the Manchester School" into a kind of jingo. If the Liberal party abandoned "the last relic of its traditions as a moderating and peaceful factor, its moral force will disappear," and "many of its best elements" would turn to socialism. What was needed was social reform, not increased budgets "to promote the machinery of human destruction and to enlarge the already excessive profits of the contractors." The journal chastised the support of naval building by City financial circles and contrasted Germany's "straightforward and moderate conduct" with McKenna's "unfounded suspicions."[64]

The *Economist* in 1911 had hoped that the new first lord Winston Churchill might set matters right, only to be disappointed. In 1913, the journal decried the light cruisers requested in the naval estimates. These were "presumably intended for privateering or cruising for prize money, a vocation upon which we shall hope for some public explanation by Mr. Churchill, in view of the condemnatory resolution lately passed by the committee of the National Liberal Federation."[65] A year later the paper noted that Churchill – "this ardent disciple of Bright and Cobden" – had also been converted to jingoism and indeed had "broken all records in naval extravagance."[66] In 1913, Hirst wrote a book on "the six panics," adding three subsequent alarms (naval in 1884 and 1909, and an airship panic in 1913) to Cobden's original three. England was forcing the pace in naval construction. Only in the unlikely event that Germany continued her naval program after the adoption of immunity would Hirst support a larger fleet.[67]

Liberalism was the preserve of not merely the Liberal party, for British public opinion generally was liberal during much of the nineteenth and early twentieth centuries – if by public opinion we mean the views prevailing in most of the respectable newspapers and in the more important weeklies and quarterlies. The grand issue for this liberalism often seemed to be one of "progress," on the one hand, and "retrogression" or "reaction" on the other. In virtually all such journals, whichever party they supported, it was assumed that a conflict between advanced nations was economically irrational and consequently unlikely. Enlightened opinion saw the institution of war as doomed by the progressive advance of industry, science, and civilization. In this sense, such papers as *The Times* and the *National Review*, in seeing the German threat in the primitive and irrational terms of a will-to-power were truly *ultra* – in that their views were beyond the ordinary conceptions, perhaps, of even many middle-class English Tories. While the average reader of the influential periodicals might not subscribe to the pacifistic views of the Cobdenites, neither was he prepared to listen to the "reactionary" ones of the ultras.

Radical politicians and journalists, unlike moderates of both parties, were almost always prepared to think of Germany as unfairly maligned. Radicals continued to see their primary political opponent as internal – an alliance of a feudal military class and corrupt capitalists and armaments manufacturers who awaited an opportunity to reassert the old authority. (As early as the 1880s, the liberal social theorist Herbert Spencer feared that England's peaceful "industrial" society was already reverting to a "militant" quasi-feudal one.)[68] To join, then, in an effort to arouse suspicion against Germany was to play a retrogressive game. Moderate liberals, in contrast to the Radicals, were more likely to see the threat of aggression as external, though still as feudal and reactionary: For example, the liberal American social theorist Thorsten Veblen, a disciple of Spencer, saw an industrial Germany still governed by a Junker military class as the prime warlike power.[69] But Radicals preferred to see their own much weaker and more poorly positioned feudal "governing" classes as evil, sinful, and driven by violent passions, and insisted that Germany – unless forced onto a bellicose path by British moral and strategic intransigence – was more amenable to the appeal of rational interest. If the fault and guilt were one's own, or residing in one's own society, they might be more readily dealt with. Of course, one might also argue that a Tory projected inner difficulties as well as domestic conflicts onto foreigners – the French, the Russians, and the Germans, successively – and often saw aggressive behavior where there was none.

What united the special interests, quasi-pacifistic Radicals, and imperialists of the Liberal party was the need to support a Liberal government without which no good could be realized. This was why – as Cobden had observed a half century earlier – the various sections of the party, with the exception of a small group of passionate pacifists, saw other concerns frequently overriding their unhappiness with increasing naval estimates. In the winter of 1913 and 1914, for example, some hundred Radical and moderate Liberal MPs combined to take action against the naval estimates that first lord of the admiralty Churchill – now fully converted to naval expansion – was expected to present to parliament the following March. These Liberals met with prime minister Asquith in December to proclaim their unhappiness; public meetings were held, and certain chambers of commerce (including that of Manchester) supported the effort. A number of members of the cabinet, among whom was Lloyd George, still a naval economist, were unhappy with Churchill's determination to increase the size of the fleet. None the less, as on former occasions, only 35 MPs, some of whom belonged to the Labour party, were to vote against the naval estimates. Not only had fears of German aggression risen, but the country now faced the prospect of unemployment in the shipyards if the naval budget were cut.[70]

British Liberals were hopeful about the preservation of peace until the end. About a week before England entered the war of 1914, the chancellor of the exchequer David Lloyd George prophesied that there would be a cut in navy estimates the following year because "the financial interests of the world are getting alarmed" at the "menace" posed by increasing armaments expenditures "to capital, to property, to industry, to the prosperity of the world." One nation acting alone could of course do nothing so long as other nations were spending huge amounts for weapons "which are not merely weapons of defence, but are equally weapons of attack." But the new movement against increased armaments was happily "a cosmopolitan one and an international one." Relations between Great Britain and Germany, Lloyd George reported, were definitely improving.[71]

[9] Offense and Defense: The Historical and Materiel Schools

> Not long after Fabius laid down the dictatorship ... those who immediately succeeded observed the same method in managing the war, and avoided all occasions of fighting Hannibal in a pitched battle ... But afterwards, when Terentius Varro ... very popular and bold, had obtained the consulship, he soon made it appear that by his rashness and ignorance he would stake the whole commonwealth on the hazard. For it was his custom to declaim in all assemblies, that, as long as Rome employed generals like Fabius, there never would be an end of the war ... and when his turn came, he posted his army close to Hannibal, at a village called Cannae ... In this battle ... fifty thousand Romans were slain ... And ... the counsels and actions of Fabius, which, before the battle, they had branded as cowardice and fear, now, in the other extreme, they accounted to have been more than human wisdom.
>
> Plutarch, *Lives*

British politicians and admirals before and during the war of 1914 debated the effectiveness of two naval tactical systems and strategies: one of attack, of seeking a decisive battle; the second, a more cautious one, of defense which while not denying the ultimate necessity of battle wished to choose the moment, the place, and the conditions. The proponents of the first saw themselves following the tactics of Nelson and the will to victory without which any strategy must fail. Their opponents believed themselves calculating the requirements of overall strategy, and balancing these against the undeniable risks that naval battle (even under the most favorable conditions) posed. For the latter, the risks of engagement for Britain were formidable, particularly when a victory at sea would probably not bring about the final defeat of the enemy.

These differences were prefigured three generations earlier in Carl von Clausewitz's classic work. Clausewitz described two strategical systems: the first, with which he would later be identified in military circles, was that of an "absolute war" to crush the enemy by decisive battle; the second was that of a war limited in means and intensity, in duration and goal. But Clausewitz cautioned that absolute war existed only in the realm of theory; in the real world, war was "an act of policy" and not "a complete, untrammeled, absolute manifestation of violence (as the pure concept would require)." The political object was to be taken into account in determining whether a war would be one of "extermination" or, at the other extreme, one of "simple armed observation" designed "*to bring about a gradual exhaustion of his* [the enemy's] *physical and moral resistance*." Combat was, of course, at the heart of war but "at the right time and the right place"; an army might even secure its objective "without any fighting at all." War was a gamble at best, for it dealt with "living and with moral forces." While this "margin of uncertainty" must be balanced by "courage and self-confidence," he warned against allowing "a headlong rush" to "triumph over skilful caution," for "blind aggressiveness would destroy the attack itself, not the defense."[1]

Clausewitz's disciple, the German military historian Hans Delbrück, at the turn of the twentieth century, wrote similarly of two basic forms of strategy. The first he called *Niederwerfungsstrategie*, the Napoleonic strategy of annihilation by decisive battle; the second, *Ermattungsstrategie*, Frederick the Great's strategy of exhaustion, one that might involve both battle and maneuver, the occupation of enemy territory and the destruction of crops, or blockade and the destruction of commerce. The German officer corps was at this time devoted to a war of annihilation and saw both Frederick and Napoleon as successful practitioners of this method.[2]

These questions were debated in French military circles, where the Napoleonic model would also prevail. In 1867, General L. J. Trochu attacked the military psychology of the army of Louis Napoleon's middle-class empire as exemplifying the "esprit capitaliste" which made it parsimoniously unwilling to risk either lives or positions. Ardant du Picq, a French officer influenced by Trochu, insisted that only a strategy of attack could prove victorious and that morale not weapons was decisive in battle; the army with the more disciplined "will" and "resolution" would put to flight a better-equipped but less-determined enemy.[3] Another French officer, Ferdinand Foch made du Picq's doctrine that of France's armies during the war of 1914. A devout Catholic and an admirer of Joan of Arc, Foch insisted on the spiritual force in war, while the France of the bourgeois republic, true to its middle-class faith in accumulation and scientific rationality, stressed material and technological factors. Foch's *Principles of War* in 1903 sought to restore "the living element of war," the "divine part" that Jomini's deductive "positivist teaching of a scientific theory" had routed. Before Napoleon, the strategy of the mercenary armies of the dynastic states was necessarily one of position and maneuver, of avoidance of battle; modern wars would reach a decision by battle, and the victorious general would seek out the enemy's armies and destroy them.[4]

There were, similarly, two schools of British naval strategy. The men of the so-called "historical school" wished to return to the tactics of Nelson even as their French and German military counterparts hoped to emulate those of Frederick and Napoleon. For Admiral Fisher, a leading exponent of what was to become known as the "materiel school," those who sought their strategy in history were hopelessly condemned to error.[5] Only superiority in numbers and in technology would bring naval victory in modern warfare, this school insisted. In the materiel school, we may see the ethos of what Schumpeter called bourgeois consolidation and minimization of risk, the doctrine of a war of defensive caution. In its rival, we have a reversion to an earlier period of heroic naval and military enterprise, of attack and seeking engagement even with a materially superior enemy.

The brothers Colomb eulogized Nelson's spirit of heroic risk taking. "In none of her former naval wars did England begin with any tangible support in her favour," Philip Colomb observed in 1878: "When she won . . . she did it by the stubborn daring of her navy leaders, and by the superior moral and physical strength of her seamen"; indeed, "her forces at any menaced point, seldom exceeded the nominal power of those of her enemies."[6] But did not such technological innovations as steam-driven iron-clads, torpedoes, and submarines make a change in tactics necessary? The army reformer Edward Cardwell had observed in 1871, with torpedoes in mind, that "scientific defence" was "gaining on scientific attack."[7] But Colomb insisted that none of the "new inventions" had "modified the leading principles of Naval Warfare."[8] His brother, now Sir John Colomb, agreed, and in 1902 urged the nation "to reject passive defence as a principle, and to adopt offensive defence as a practice," that is, to "seek out and eliminate, or paralyse, the fleets, squadrons, or ships of the enemy in preference to using our naval power to directly guard our shores." "The naval policy for the great sea Empire of to-day," Sir John concluded, "does not, and cannot differ from the policy of an island a hundred years ago."[9]

The naval journalist F. T. Jane described the issue in 1906 as one between "superior materiel" or "superior weapons" on the one hand, and a primitive Darwinian fitness on the other. Jane believed that Nelson had won not because his ships or strategy were better than those of the French but because he and his men had "a crude desire to kill the enemy" and thus passed the "survival of the fittest test."[10] Encapsulating this difference was the division in naval opinion in the 1890s on the uses of the ram and the gun: the future hero of the historical school Admiral Beresford believed the ram, usable only in close, one-to-one duels, was the most effective weapon in naval warfare, while Fisher preferred the tactical luxury of long-range guns.[11]

Lord Sydenham, the former Sir George Clarke, was in 1927 to write of "psychological causes preexisting" in a liberal state that imposed a defensive naval strategy upon England during the war of 1914. A spirit of excessive caution, Sydenham felt, had nearly brought the country to ruin.[12] Similarly, Mahan saw liberal democracies as inclined to pacifism; but while they might react only defensively in their politics, he urged that their naval strategy be one of attack.[13] This had been the lesson of England's naval triumphs, as he had described them in his great work.[14] The men of the historical school denounced their opponents – timidly devoted to numbers, speed of maneuver, thicker armor, and longer-range guns – as seeking a way of avoiding the gamble of battle.

Marx's colleague Friedrich Engels, who prided himself on his knowledge of military matters, commented in 1878 on the "competitive struggle between armour-plating and guns" that marked the naval race of the last generation of the nineteenth century. The warship was being "developed to a pitch of perfection" and was consequently becoming "both outrageously costly and unusable in war." Engels was convinced that bourgeois states would never expose such expensive ships to the risks of battle.[15] A peroration to a 1912 address to the Commons by first lord of the admiralty Winston Churchill, an admirer of the wisdom of the financial circles of the City,[16] seemed to confirm Engels's analysis. Noting the immense cost of naval building, Churchill saw the new dreadnoughts as being "the modern substitute" for what might earlier have been wars: "Just as credit transactions have in the present day so largely superseded cash payments," he observed, "so the jealousies and disputes of nations are more and more decided by the mere possession of war power without the necessity for its actual employment."[17] (In this, Churchill was revising Clausewitz's observation that "the decision by arms" in war is "what cash payment is in commerce," regardless of "how rarely settlements actually occur.")[18]

The battle of schools

The naval officer presiding over Britain's effort to meet the German challenge on the seas was Admiral Fisher, who served as first sea lord from 1904 to 1910, and again in the first year of the war of 1914. Though he moved in the highest social circles, and was a friend of King Edward VII, he regarded himself as a democrat and a radical, and initiated reforms that antagonized the more traditionally-minded of the service. As first sea lord, for example, he promoted the principle of "inter-changeability" to end the separation – constructed largely along class lines – of executive and engineering officers. He remodelled the service to rid the Navy of "our redundancies in useless ships and unnecessary men," which he declared would make it "thirty percent more fit to fight." "The income-tax payer will worship it, and the Navy will growl at it!"[19] He combined managerial talents with an interest in economy, which both Tories and Liberals thought necessary for the country and the Navy. On his last day in office in December 1905, Conservative prime minister Balfour observed that "at the very moment when the changed conditions of naval sea-power rendered administrative revolution necessary, in Sir John Fisher was found a man of genius peculiarly fitted to aid in its execution."[20]

For much of Fisher's service as first sea lord, Lord Charles Beresford led an opposition of naval officers and ultra politicians and journalists against him. An aristocrat, Beresford saw Fisher as a brash upstart, and a rival who had been niggardly in giving him the ships he needed in his post as admiral of the newly-formed channel fleet. Beresford easily became the leader of those naval officers injured or about to be injured by Fisher's reforms, and of the Tory naval ultras who believed that the Liberal program of social reform was depriving the country of its strength. Fisher's reassurances that England could easily absorb Liberal cuts in the naval building program and still vanquish her maritime rivals only convinced the ultras that the first sea lord was unreliable.

The strategist who led the attack on Fisher was Admiral Sir Reginald Custance, the most systematic and perceptive spokesman for the historical school. Custance, an officer well-acquainted with naval history, served as director of naval intelligence between 1899 and 1902 and as second-in-command (to Beresford) of the channel fleet in 1907 and 1908. In May 1905, soon after Fisher's installation as first sea lord, Custance wrote the first of six anonymous articles that appeared in *Blackwood's* in 1905 and 1906. Since the 1870s when the naval college at Greenwich opened, Custance observed, the admiralty had given up the study of strategy. Since that time, "undue importance" was assigned to "great size and thick armour," and to "superior speed" – climaxing in Fisher's dreadnought building program. For Custance, "the spirit of the men in the ships" was "more important than the ships themselves"; in believing that victory depended on size rather than on "superior skill and a lofty spirit," the materiel school had abandoned the "principles and practices of our forefathers." "Bad will be the day for Britain when her Navy falls away from their great traditions."[21]

Custance believed Fisher's decommissioning of smaller, slower, more lightly-armored cruisers and destroyers in the interest of economy was a strategical blunder. While "command of the sea can only be decided by hostile fleets meeting and fighting," he conceded, wars against commerce remained feasible and useful, and an attack on trade as well as a defense of British merchantmen required "a large number of small ships and not a small number of large ones."[22] Custance warned that "when the next war comes, want of cruisers will be found written in the hearts of British admirals."[23] In advocating the retention of smaller ships, Custance was also defending the interests of the professional naval officers whose active commissions were in jeopardy.

Custance and the naval professionals also opposed the plan to end the separation between officers in charge of the ship and subordinate engineering officers who ran the engine-room. The first group tended to be gentlemen who went to sea at an early age and acquired "the habit of command." The prime duty of these gentleman-officers was to study the art of war, Custance wrote, and devote themselves "to tactics, to strategy, to the discipline and spirit of the crews." The engineers, who had foregone "this practical training in favour of mere book knowledge," were "skilled mechanics" without the habit of command. Custance wished the gentleman-officer to have a general knowledge of mechanics: when "the military caste is predominant" (as "in feudal England" or in "modern Germany or Japan"), the executive officer needed to know nothing of the engine room, but in modern England he must know enough to exercise full control of the ship, though without becoming a "mere mechanic."[24]

In an article in early 1906, Custance described the Japanese victory over the Russian fleet at the 1905 battle of Tsushima as a vindication of the views of the historical school which stressed the importance of Nelson's strategy of the hail of fire in attaining the "great object in battle" – "to upset the moral equilibrium" of the enemy. The Japanese Admiral Togo accomplished this by hurling a great many six-inch shells at the Russian fleet rather than a relatively few armor-piercing twelve-inch ones, as Fisher's admiralty preferred. What was wanted, therefore, was not the admiralty's program of dreadnoughts and heavy cruisers, with their heavier guns, but more smaller ships to carry greater numbers of medium caliber guns capable of faster firing. Concentrated fire would always prove decisive. The admiralty was sacrificing "fighting power" to speed, which was not useful except "in running away." Nor was it useful to arm ships with long-range guns, as the admiralty intended: "when one side means business," as the Japanese did at Tsushima, "fleets rapidly close to decisive ranges" of no more than 5,000 yards "unless the other side runs away." Unlike the policy of the present admiralty, the Japanese relied on strategy and tactics, not speed or size, on seeking a close encounter, not "an attitude of mind defensive rather than offensive – a disposition to exalt the ship above the man."[25]

Elsewhere, Custance observed caustically that the new "monster warships," the dreadnoughts, fired fewer shots than Nelson's "old 100-gun *Victory*."[26] Foch, not surprisingly, also insisted on the importance of laying down a hail of "offensive fire" in land warfare in order to demoralize an enemy;[27] and anticipating Custance, Mahan in his account of Tsushima was critical of long-range firing as "diametrically opposed to the teaching of Nelson" and "destructive" of "the mental attitude which keeps offensive power in the foreground."[28]

Admiral Sir Cyprian Bridge, a director of naval intelligence from 1889 to 1894 and commander-in-chief of both the Australian and China stations, presented the historical school's arguments in a 1907 work. Bridge, like Mahan and Custance, insisted on the superiority of a large number of guns and a concentration of fire (to "pour a nearly simultaneous fire on a part" of the enemy fleet) over fewer if heavier guns. He even advocated the use of the sailing-ship tactic of "crossing the T" as a means of accomplishing this. Never doubting that the coming war would include attacks on commerce, regardless of the views of international jurists, he called for more light cruisers. Among the errors of certain naval journalists was the "deplorable ... modern habit" of favoring "imposing material" over what history taught of strategy and tactics. Strategy belonged to "the moral or intellectual world," while "speed superiority" was "the refuge of the bad strategist." Like Custance, Bridge objected to naval officers "who are primarily mechanics." "Sturdy pugnacity" was what an officer most required, and pugnacity could defeat mere genius, for success in war depended on the will, on the combination of "courage and intelligence." Bridge questioned the usefulness of a shipbuilding policy that was "a mere contest of extravagant pecuniary expenditure," and, finally, warned against the "heresies" that came from mere "commentators" on naval questions.[29]

Who were these commentators? One of Fisher's opponents called attention to the admiral's use of "inspired writers in the Press" to defend his position against both Liberal and ultra opponents.[30] There were a number of journalists to whom Fisher made available sometimes privileged information, and who served to enlist public opinion in his favor. Among them were J. K. Thursfield, J. L. Garvin, and Archibald Hurd. When Garvin became editor of *The Observer*, he made that weekly an organ of the Fisher policy of naval reform.[31] These journalists saw naval traditionalists as the prime enemy, and defended Fisher against attacks from the right. For the naval writer Archibald Hurd, writing for the Liberal *Fortnightly* in 1906, the issue was "progress or reaction in the Navy." Many naval officers so valued "tradition and custom" that they were "constitutionally opposed to change," and more concerned with "paint and polish" than effective gunnery. Interchangeability and the cutting of obsolescent ships had in the past few years "converted" the Fleet into "an instrument of unparalleled power." "In these days of progress," he concluded, the critics of the new policy were "the apostles of inefficiency and retrogression."[32]

A number of naval writers supported the "retrogressive" historical school. The journalist H. H. Wilson, for example, denounced "the sacrifice of sea power to 'economy'" in the Admiralty's "jettisoning" of large numbers of smaller warships.[33] Carlyon Bellairs agreed,[34] as did John St Loe Strachey, the editor of the Conservative (although Free Trade) *Spectator*. That journal was to observe in 1910 that Britain had won at Trafalgar "because our Fleet, inspired by a great tradition and a great man, recognized that to win you must attack – go for, fall upon, fly at the threat of, hammer, pulverise, destroy, annihilate – your enemy."[35] Writing as "Civis" in 1907, the well-known naval designer Sir William H. White charged the Fisher program with posing "serious dangers" to naval efficiency. "Civis" particularly noted the admiralty's "fictitious economies," such as the weeding out of so-called obsolete ships.[36] The following year, White denounced the dreadnought building program as "the cult of the monster warship." This "policy of Goliath" conflicted with all sound principles of naval warfare that a study of naval history offered. Expensive dreadnoughts made it difficult to provide the numbers of ships needed to protect the widespread interests of the empire.[37]

Corbett and a defensive strategy

The naval strategy that Britain pursued in the war of 1914 had been set down almost a decade earlier. In November 1906, Julian Corbett and Admiral Slade prepared for the war course of the Portsmouth naval college what became known as the Green Pamphlet. Its central message was that the Royal Navy's primary object was no longer to seek out the enemy's fleet in order to destroy it. The true guiding rule, it argued, was to secure communications, and to do battle only if the enemy threatened these communications. Corbett distinguished between an offensive strategy necessary if a nation wished to assert a claim at an enemy's expense, and a defensive strategy if the object was merely to deny an enemy claim. Corbett and Slade accepted the need of a decisive battle of fleets for general control – for a general command of the sea – but insisted that local and temporary control, all that was usually necessary, could be secured and maintained by defensive action.[38] (In the years before the war, Corbett defended certain controversial aspects of Fisher's naval-building program against critics, among them the admiralty's interest in dreadnoughts and in speed.)[39]

The Green Pamphlet's apparent preference for a defensive strategy distressed naval traditionalists, and when Corbett revised and expanded his views in 1911 he qualified his opinions to disarm his critics. But his position remained essentially the same. Britain was a "have" power contending with aspiring "have nots," he argued, and since possession was "nine points of the law, it is easier to keep money in our pocket than to take it from another man's." He granted that an "unduly prolonged" strategy of defense tended "to deaden the spirit of offence," and that the "moral stimulation of attack" gave rise to a "strength and energy" that had immense "practical value." Yet Britain stood to gain most not by seeking battle but by exerting sufficient "pressure" upon the enemy on shore as to "strangle the whole national life," to cripple an enemy's finances and to cut his commerce. "Finance is scarcely less important" than military and naval force in deciding wars, for "when other things are equal, it is the longer purse that wins."

Corbett observed – in the spirit of Clausewitz, to whom he acknowledged a debt – that it was certainly "an amateurish notion that defence is always stupid or pusillanimous, leading always to defeat, and that what is called 'the military spirit' means nothing but taking the offensive." If a nation's political aim was "negative, and we simply seek to prevent the enemy wresting some advantage to our detriment, then the war in its general direction will be defensive." "Rightly conceived," defense was not "passive" but "an attitude of alert expectation" in which "we wait for the moment when the enemy shall expose himself to a counterstroke." A defensive posture enabled Britain to "choose our own ground for the trial of strength," when the enemy would be "most dangerously exposed." In the past, Britain's enemies, notably France, had employed such a strategy so as to make it "almost impossible for us to attack him with decisive result"; the enemy could remain "in his own waters and near his own bases ... and whence he always threatened us with a counter-attack at moments of exhaustion." All in all, Corbett insisted that such a strategy was not "the mere pestilent heresy it is generally represented."[40] (This was the strategy of the fleet-in-being, previously thought useful only for inferior naval powers; Sir John Colomb had in fact considered such a posture for England in the 1890s but Spenser Wilkinson had persuaded him that it would not do.)[41]

In this 1911 work, Corbett predicted the scenario of the coming war. Germany as the inferior naval power would seek "to substitute commerce destruction for the clash of squadrons." But if the superior power adopted "a reasonably sound" system of defense, the German fleet would be brought to battle long before its commerce raiders could have much impact. In the end a decision by battle would come to pass. "That was the old British creed," and "it is still our creed." Indeed, any impugning of its claim would "be held dangerous." We "feel instinctively" that the seeking of battle expressed "the secret of British success at sea," and consequently "we cannot do without it." Yet, Corbett added, "we cannot do with it in its nakedness." "For all its moral exhilaration, for all its value as an expression of high and sound naval spirit," sea encounters in both the Spanish–American and the Russo-Japanese wars made such a strategy doubtful. If Britain accepted the maxim "in its nakedness," she would allow the enemy to choose the time and place of battle. What the maxim really meant was that the Navy must not seek contact with the enemy fleet until it was "in the best position for bringing about a complete decision in our favour, and as soon as the other parts of our war plan, military and political, will permit."[42]

Wartime strategy

Though by the 1890s bested in the industrial and technological spheres, England continued to serve as the model of naval development. Despite the Jeune Ecole and its strategy of trade war, England's past successes and long superiority at sea had imprinted a strategy of naval battle upon her rivals.

England could thus enlist her superior financial resources, extended by her avoidance of the elaborate military expenditures of continental powers, in the building of expensive battleships, and after 1905 of even more costly dreadnoughts. When Tirpitz became the German navy minister in 1897, he set aside his predecessor's program for building commerce-raiding cruisers in favor of battleships which, like Mahan, he saw as essential to exercising world power. The Kaiser advised his naval chief to explore the usefulness of submarine warfare, but Tirpitz declined his counsel.[43] This decision was to leave Germany (like Britain) short of both cruisers and submarines when war came in 1914. A French naval writer in 1902, a proponent of a war against commerce, saw all the European naval programs as established on "the great English doctrine," of decision by battle. England gained a "complete and decisive victory" in the wide acceptance of this strategy: "she triumphs over the whole world, for her security and her power at the present time depend less upon her formidable squadrons than upon this universal spirit which she has created, and which is indeed the masterpiece of her policy."[44]

But what in fact was Britain's strategy at sea? Fisher's critics believed that the admiralty possessed no well-thought-out plan. Not even the character of the blockade to be mounted was certain. The navy's chief strategist Admiral Sir Arthur Wilson advocated a close blockade of German ports on the North Sea, and prescribed such a blockade in the 1909 war orders.[45] But a close blockade was out of keeping with the navy envisioned by Fisher, for it would require a much greater naval force than the force contained; for Britain to build her navy up to the level necessary for such a watch on continental ports, Corbett observed in 1911, would be "to march to economic ruin" and "to seek a position of maritime despotism which, even if it were attainable, would set every man's hand against us."[46]

A naval officer K. G. B. Dewar, in a prize-winning essay in 1912, urged a more economical open blockade, a "defensive" policy of controlling the North Sea exits rather than what the admiralty labelled an "offensive" close blockade. Mines, torpedoes, and submarines made a close blockade too hazardous, and might bring about "the gradual attrition of our naval power" and with this "the end of the Empire." The policy of closing the North Sea exits, he argued, would oblige the weaker German fleet to come out for battle. By the summer of 1914, Dewar's plan of an open blockade had become admiralty policy.[47]

Another long-debated issue was the relationship of the fleet to a military force, and the related question of a continental strategy. In 1871, John Colomb stressed the importance of maintaining maritime communications so as to enable an army "to carry the war into the enemy's country";[48] "the fleet is the shield to guard" and "the army is the spear to strike," he observed in 1902, and "only an army" could "decide the final issue of war." At this later time, however, Colomb saw the fleet as Britain's while "the spear was in the hands of her allies."[49] A strategy of relying on the military forces of an ally, at times useful in the eighteenth century, became questionable when the population of the French ally was substantially outnumbered by that of the German enemy.

In 1908 and 1909, there was a controversy between the admiralty and the army concerning the effectiveness of a purely maritime strategy against Germany. The admiralty believed that a blockade of German ports accompanied by amphibious raids along the enemy's shores would not only compel the German fleet to fight but divert sufficient military strength to insure German defeat on the land front. The army, supported by the foreign office and the French, believed a British military force to occupy the left flank along the French–German frontier necessary to defeat Germany. After conducting detailed studies in 1908, the foreign office concluded that only if neutral Dutch and Belgian ports were closed might blockade prove useful. But even with such an extension, which neutrals would protest, Germany's well-developed road and railroad system would make food and raw materials shipment by land possible, and new transport patterns might well deprive England of her Baltic trade.[50]

Corbett in 1911, noting that naval pressure alone worked by a lengthy and exhausting process disturbing to commerce and to neutrals, called for surprise attacks on Germany's coast and even the occupation of an offshore enemy island to compel the German fleet to come out and fight.[51] Fisher was known to favor such a strategy, and the first sea lord approvingly quoted Sir Edward Grey as seeing the army as "a projectile to be fired by the Navy" against "the outlying possessions of the enemy."[52] Both Radicals and many in the blue-water school were wary of a continental strategy and agreed that British maritime supremacy made non-involvement in land wars possible, relatively inexpensive, and consequently desirable. When war came Fisher, supported by certain blue-water opponents of a full-scale continental involvement, like Hankey, lost out to the generals and to the demands of the French.

In 1914, first lord of the admiralty Winston Churchill recalled Fisher to his former position of first sea lord, and together they applied the strategy of the Green Pamphlet. In a memorandum dated 25 January 1915, Fisher observed that Britain must husband her strength until "the gradual pressure of sea power" compelled the enemy "to attack us at a disadvantage." This called for "great patience," and the Navy ought not to risk "its present superiority" by exposing itself to the "present great strength and splendid gunnery efficiency" of the German fleet. Fisher spoke of "the supreme necessity and difficulty of remaining passive" until the enemy exposed its fleet "to a general action."[53]

The Germans also pursued "a strategy of reserve and of waiting," as the navy minister Count Ernst zu Reventlow described it in a July 1915 letter to an American newspaper. Reventlow complained that older and smaller

British ships – armed merchantmen, light cruisers, an earlier vintage of battleships, and torpedo boats – were illegally maintaining an open North Sea blockade, while the main British fleet with its "great battleships" was held in readiness for naval action. (This disposition of naval ships had been set in the Dewar plan of 1912). But despite her naval superiority, Britain wished to avoid a "serious encounter" with the German fleet "except under especially favourable conditions." Germany, however, refused to accept battle at a disadvantage. Reventlow concluded that "the motives for holding back the main fleets on both sides are similar."[54]

After the war Winston Churchill was to describe Fisher as primarily "a constructor, organiser, and energiser" rather than a strategist. The admiral's enthusiasm was "mainly confined to the material sphere," and his temper prevailed at the admiralty both before and during the war. When he returned to the admiralty in 1914, his main concern was the building of warships. The "doctrine widely inculcated among our senior naval officers," Churchill continued, was "that the Navy's task was to keep open our own communications, blockade those of the enemy, and to wait for the Armies to do their proper job." This was a clearly defensive sea strategy, and Fisher resisted using "the naval forces more directly in the main shock of war," as Churchill at times wished him to do. "In all matters where naval fighting was concerned," Fisher was "more than usually cautious": "he could not bear the idea of risking ships in battle."[55] While at the admiralty, however, Churchill supported Fisher's policies.

After the failure of the amphibious campaign at Gallipoli in mid-1915, Balfour replaced Churchill at the admiralty, but continued Fisher's and Churchill's defensive strategy. While not blaming Germany for declining battle with a superior force, the new first lord congratulated the Royal Navy for having avoided the enemy strategy of "continued attrition" by which Germany hoped "to reduce the superior British Fleet ship by ship until an equality was established." Balfour saw the Royal Navy as having already achieved victory, even though no battle had taken place. There were "only seven functions" a fleet could accomplish:

> It may drive the enemy's commerce off the sea.
> It may protect its own commerce.
> It may render the enemy's fleet impotent.
> It may make the transfer of enemy troops across the sea impossible, whether for attack or defence.
> It may transport its own troops where it will.
> It may secure their supplies, and (in fitting circumstances) it may assist their operations.

All had been "successfully performed" by the British fleet; indeed, "no fleet has ever done more."[56] No longer in office, Churchill in a speech to the Commons in early 1916 criticized the "attitude of pure passivity" displayed by the admiralty during the previous year as not necessarily "the path of greatest prudence"; he could not understand why "with resources far greater than those Lord Fisher and I ever possessed" the Navy had not taken a more active role.[57]

Among the senior naval officers who accepted the doctrine of defensive caution preached by Fisher and Corbett was Admiral J. R. Jellicoe, who became the commander-in-chief of the Grand Fleet with the coming of war in 1914. Like Fisher, Jellicoe was an organizer and a disciple of the materiel school, a gunnery expert who believed that the palms in battle went to the fleet that could hit the enemy hardest at the greatest range.[58] After the war, Lloyd George was to write of Jellicoe's "disbelief in the offensive power of our Fleet."[59] Like Fisher again, Jellicoe was not disposed to take risks with the fleet under his command. He was convinced that such new weapons as mines, torpedoes and submarines (in all of which he believed Germany superior) gave a considerable advantage to a retreating fleet, which might lead an enemy into dangerous waters. In October 1914, Jellicoe charted a strategy of caution, warning that "if a false move is made," the enemy might disable "half of our battle fleet ... by under-water attack before the guns opened fire at all."[60]

These cautionary views pervaded the strategy adopted on 31 May 1916, when the Germans at last provided an opportunity for a Grand Fleet action. At the battle of Jutland off the Danish coast, a superior British fleet commanded by Jellicoe encountered the German fleet of Admiral Scheer. In an article half-a-dozen years later, Captain A. C. Dewar described the battle as "characterized by excessive caution," and "dominated by a fear of the submarine or torpedo." Jellicoe had not even made an effort to pursue Scheer's fleet when it turned away. Dewar observed that such tactics undermined the strategy upon which the Grand Fleet had been constructed – that of "dealing a decisive blow." For Dewar, as for Victorian consensus and the historical school, "battle represents in war the economy of the decisive blow." Other imperative naval duties – "commerce defence, convoy and anti-submarine work" – had "all been sacrificed" to enable the fleet to strike this blow. Proponents of the defensive strategy were to argue that Jellicoe had won in compelling the enemy to return to harbor. Dewar saw the result differently, for after Jutland, the German Fleet remained intact: "If, as Foch said, there can be no victory without a battle," and "if Nelson's teachings are sound – the battle of Jutland ... must rank merely as a great and unique opportunity for the British fleet, of which advantage was not sufficiently taken."[61]

In July 1916, in a statement to representatives of the dominion governments, first lord of the admiralty Balfour defended the strategy at Jutland as essential to preserve from needless risk a fleet upon whose superiority so much depended, and his one-time critic Churchill agreed. Without the Royal Navy to protect supplies from America, the Allied war effort "would have broken down like a house of cards," Balfour declared. Moreover, America would not have granted the credits necessary to pay for the munitions so essential to Allied success "had it not been for our credit, and our credit equally depends upon our Fleet."[62] In a magazine article in October 1916, Churchill came to the defense of Balfour and the admiralty. Although the "opportunity of decisive battle" had been "denied them," the British "command of the sea" could not have been "more effective" had all German battleships been sunk. If the Germans desired battle, let her fleet come out and "fight for a final decision." It was for the Royal Navy "to determine where and under what conditions the battle shall be fought." "Without a battle we have all that the most victorious of battles could give us," Churchill concluded, and "we are content."[63]

Churchill's article provoked a flurry of letters to *The Times* by critics of admiralty policy. Among the first, on 4 October 1916, was one by Lord Sydenham, who, putting earlier concerns for commercial interest or neutral opinion behind him, had become an ultra. Sydenham saw Churchill as overly concerned about "British interests" as "measured in lives and pounds sterling": this was why the fleet did not seek a decisive encounter. If England refused to hazard the chances of battle, "we may bid farewell to the dominion of the seas."[64] Admiral Custance, now retired, wrote on 9 October to attack Corbett's (although he was not named) "theory which omits all reference to battle, with its immense mental and moral consequences." This was not the strategy of Drake, Hawke, and Nelson.[65] The following day, Sydenham joined in attacking "recent theories destructive" of "the spirit on which all the most glorious traditions of the Royal Navy have been built."[66] Admiral Sir Nathaniel Bowden-Smith replied in defense on 11 October that because of changes in naval warfare it was "unfair" to compare the admiralty's strategy with that of Nelson.[67]

At a press conference on 7 November 1916, first lord of the admiralty Balfour once again defended the Navy's strategy. The Germans intended to present their fleet as "a kind of bait" with which to tempt the British fleet into minefields infested by submarines – dangers "unknown in the happier days of Nelson, which no modern Admiral can afford to forget." They hoped to induce "a succession of small misfortunes" whose "cumulative effect might be serious." "Our business" was "to avoid falling into the trap." The admiralty was accused of lacking "enterprise." In fact, thc fleet was prepared to battle but only under "fair conditions." To permit "our strength" to be "whittled away with no good military object whatever is bad strategy." "We are, therefore, necessarily thrown on what appears to be the defensive." Critics charged the admiralty with "lack of policy"; if so, Balfour concluded, "it is a lack of policy which I do not think anybody on serious reflection would say does not carry out the real traditions of the British Navy."[68] Archibald Hurd, writing on "sea heresy" for the Liberal *Fortnightly Review* a month later, declared that battles were fought for "a specific purpose" not "for the sake of fighting," and cautioned that "we have little to gain from a victory at sea, but everything to lose by a reverse."[69]

In a debate in the House of Lords on 15 November 1916, Lord Sydenham, supported by the ultras, called on the government to adopt a policy of attack, as well as a more vigorous campaign against enemy commerce. Churchill's position particularly angered Sydenham, who believed "a defensive naval policy" to be "the absolute negation of all the finest traditions of the British Navy." The theory of control of enemy maritime communications was "in effect the teaching of Clausewitz misunderstood and misapplied to naval warfare."[70] Admiral Beresford, having also been translated to the upper house, agreed, observing that "all previous wars have been won ... by attack." In calling for a more effective commercial blockade, he again denounced "the Dreadnought policy" of the prewar Liberals which "left us short of destroyer patrol vessels and cruisers when we went to war."[71] Earl Lytton, the civil lord of the admiralty, disassociated the admiralty from the Churchill article,[72] and the Marquess of Crewe, the lord president of the council, while observing that "gladiatorial combats on the open sea" could not be an exclusive strategy, agreed that "the destruction of the enemy's fleet must ... remain the prime object of our naval policy."[73] Lytton and Crewe reassured Sydenham that England intended to "follow the policy and precepts of St. Vincent and Nelson."[74]

The controversy subsided for the moment, to be revived by a renewal of letters to *The Times* by Custance and Churchill seven months later. In early May 1917, Churchill defended himself against Custance's charge that as first lord of the admiralty he had failed to support an offensive strategy. Churchill saw himself as having always "strongly" agreed with Custance's "military conception of naval strategy," and therefore "I am the last person on whom he should seek to fasten his present quarrel." Somewhat obscurely, Churchill put the blame "for the paralysis of the naval offensive" on "those whose senseless outcry at the loss of a few obsolete ships checked naval enterprise and quenched Admiralty initiative."[75] It is difficult to guess at Churchill's meaning. Had the prewar criticism of Beresford and the historical school undermined the admiralty's morale? In reply, Custance noted that earlier that year Jellicoe in a public speech had suggested that a ship must fire on its enemy beyond the 10,000 yard effectiveness of a torpedo. This reasoning was the "logical result" of the doctrine conceived by the "directing naval minds" that "the safety of our ships is more important than the destruction of the enemy." "Of what use is a greatly superior Fleet if no part of it is to be risked when the decisive moment arrives"?[76] A week later, Custance wondered why, since it was "universally admitted that the destruction of the German army is a matter of decisive and primary importance," the "same principle" was not "equally true at sea."[77] (A few days earlier, the Tory first lord of the admiralty from 1886 to 1892 Lord George Hamilton had addressed this question: "the defensive in warfare, both on sea and land," he observed, "has of recent years obtained a mastery over the offensive"; "the old slap-dash methods of attacks" brought only disaster.[78] This was the message borne, no doubt, by the early battles of the Somme.)

Spenser Wilkinson summed up the controversy, also in a letter to *The Times*. For Wilkinson, as for other opponents of the admiralty's strategy, the difficulty began with the appointment of "a great shipbuilder as First Sea Lord." Under Fisher's auspices "the destruction of the enemy's fleet," up to this point considered sound strategy, was subordinated to what was mistakenly understood as command of the sea – mistakenly because such command was not possible until the enemy fleet had been destroyed. At the cost of "a good deal of money," the Navy had built ships, but did not know how to use them. There had been naval officers who followed Napoleon's advice to study past battles – what the French emperor called "the high parts of war." In America, there was Mahan, in England, the brothers Colomb, Sir Cyprian Bridge, and Sir Reginald Custance. "But none of these men of knowledge was ever given power at the Admiralty." This was because democratic governments resisted thinking through military and naval problems, which made it difficult for them "to conduct a war against an absolute Government." "In a word," Wilkinson concluded, a liberal state "did not believe in strategy for the Navy."[79]

The debate was to continue for a long time after the war. In 1924, Churchill published his history of the war years. Once again he defended Jellicoe's tactics at Jutland as having been made necessary by the weapons that gave "new advantages to a retreating fleet." If the stronger British fleet had forced a battle, the result might have been a decisive defeat that would have invited the risks of "starvation and invasion" and of "ruin utter and final." Jellicoe and the admiralty had acted wisely in avoiding such risks.[80] Lord Sydenham, in a 1927 article replying to Churchill, described Jutland as "the most momentous failure in our naval history." The battle-cruiser – a fast ship that might fire at long range and therefore "with a minimum of risk" – was for Sydenham a symbol of the ruinous design of Fisher's navy. "Defensive ideals had for some years prevailed at the Admiralty, where monster ships and guns had seemed more important than the study of war." Consequently "psychological causes pre-existing made a Nelson or a Togo victory impossible."[81]

Corbett again became a target of the historical school – which Churchill in 1924 described as now "the dominant school of naval thought and policy."[82] In a 1923 obituary article on Corbett, his admirer Sir Herbert Richmond stressed Corbett's opinion that it was foolish to assume "that the defeat of the enemy's fleets solves all problems." Nelson's victory at Trafalgar had been important because it made possible Wellington's victories on the continent. The importance of sea power to Britain in the First World War was that it had facilitated the transfer and supply of the armies on the Western front. Command of sea meant the control of communications, and therefore also the ability to protect or to destroy commerce, and Britain had maintained this command.[83] In 1931, Sydenham denounced the school of Corbett and Slade as "translating the conduct of War in terms of metaphysics," a misconstruction of Clausewitz, by whom Sydenham felt "repelled." The overriding purpose of the navy was battle; "our main and first duty" was "to seek out and destroy the enemy fleet." Fisher had wished to intimidate the German fleet by material superiority in battleships, not by seeking to fight and to destroy it. Sydenham once again urged a return to the "sound sea doctrine" of Nelson and Trafalgar.[84]

The policy of intimidation by greater numbers of dreadnoughts may, of course, be seen as a bloodless variation of the naval duel. Clausewitz had written that "decision by arms" was what "cash payment is in commerce": though both might occur only rarely, the probability of such a settlement if sought had to be real to be effective. In the most estimable burgher style, through the years of 1914 through 1918, both the British and German navies were prepared to accept each other's credit-worthiness. Each of these navies had been constructed for battle; each, for similar reasons, declined to seek it.

In 1917, Tirpitz declared that "the British fleet fulfilled its *raison d'être* simply by lying quietly at Scapa Flow."[85] Writing after the war, he condemned the unwillingness of the German High Sea Fleet, superior in both "*personnel* and *materiel*" to the British, to do battle. The German admiralty was betrayed by "the defensive spirit" of a "mistaken" and "exhausting guerrilla warfare" that depressed the navy's morale. In seeking to avoid battle, and consequently losses at sea, the German navy committed a "fundamental error," and Tirpitz regretted that the German naval staff had not formed its plans in the light of the "experience of Nelson's day." Inferior fleets might triumph because in the encounter of ship against ship, one ship established "superiority of fire," destroying the morale of the men on the other.[86] But despite this echoing of the historical school, before the war Tirpitz had seemed more responsive to the ideas of the materiel.

A writer has compared Tirpitz and Fisher, seeing them both as products of middle-class professional and service families, generally liberal in their politics, and strong advocates of the materiel school.[87] In both Germany and England the middle classes were well-represented among the chief officers of the navy. Although the generals on both sides (the Napoleon-intoxicated French following Trochu and Foch, and the Junker aristocrats misunderstanding Clausewitz) were profligate in risking men and materiel on the Western Front, frugality prevailed in the war at sea. Sydenham in 1928 suggested that the German fleet, though "highly trained and technically efficient," was "without naval traditions" and consequently "disinclined to risk";[88] we know his psychological explanation of the British strategy. It is tempting to think of a "feudal" strategy of chivalric battle versus one of defensive restraint on the part of tight-fisted and timid burgesses, as a number of contemporary observers did. Russian Marxist writers during the wars of the Russian Revolution were similarly quick to denounce the "defensive positionalism" of the Western Front as effete bourgeois strategy, while arguing that one of "offensive maneuver" was genuinely proletarian.[89] However, what these Marxists lauded as proletarian was a duplication of the strategy the tzarist General Kutuzov had used against France in 1812. This proved suited to the realities of Soviet military circumstances in 1919–20, even as Kutuzov's had been to Russia's war against Napoleon, and Fabius's to Rome's against Hannibal.

Though a spirit of parsimony may have affected the thinking of certain admirals and politicians – as Nelson's heroic tactics helped to shape that of their critics, anxious to avoid the bourgeois taint – other forces were probably decisive; those of geography and naval technology, for example, favored a strategy of restraint. An observer has speculated that where Tirpitz and the German admiralty went wrong was to imagine that the British fleet would assume the unnecessary risks of an offensive strategy – of a costly close blockade or a chancey seeking out of the enemy for battle.[90] Corbett's (and the admiralty's) defensive caution proved successful – helped no doubt by the readiness of the German fleet to emulate the Royal Navy's line of inaction.[91]

[10] America and Freedom of the Seas

> [The American] Blenkiron was a different matter ... The first thing the sportsman did was to write a letter to the papers ... He said our blockade of Germany had broken all the laws of God and humanity, and he reckoned that Britain was now the worst exponent of Prussianism going ... He said that Germany was right in wanting the freedom of the seas, and that America would back her up, and that the British Navy was a bigger menace to the peace of the world than the Kaiser's army.
>
> John Buchan, *Greenmantle*, 1916

> England is to the populations of Europe the representative, by no means perfect but still the representative, of the same principles of social & political freedom which Americans so justly cherish. Any weakening of her influence would be simply so much additional discouragement to popular institutions & to liberty of thought, speech, & action throughout the old continents & strengthening of the hands of despotism, temporal & spiritual, all over the world.
>
> John Stuart Mill, 1865, in a letter to an American critic of English policy

The cause of freedom of the seas had been the established position of the United States from the first years of the republic. Bred in the doctrines of the enlightenment, and born under the protection of the Armed Neutrality of 1780, America saw herself as a perpetual neutral in European conflicts, with a neutral's antipathy to wars against commerce. The threatened loss of United States trade during the Napoleonic Wars had spurred Brougham and Baring to oppose the orders-in-council; the growth of American power on the seas, as Palmerston acknowledged, had exerted a perhaps decisive influence on Britain's adoption of the Paris Declaration; fears of a conflict with the United States had compelled England to yield her practice of visit and search in the late 1850s. Whenever an English statesman suggested that the enforcement of traditional belligerent rights would make enemies of powerful neutrals, he had a neutral America primarily in mind. It was important to England that an overly vigorous display of her naval predominance should not drive the United States into an enemy's arms, as it had in 1812.

In 1823 the American secretary of state John Quincy Adams, citing both interest and morals, strongly supported freedom of the seas and the principle of immunity. England's "great national interests," he observed, indeed "maritime war itself ... *must* be affected by the downfall of the colonial system," for what was the use of the rule of 1756 when "the colonies yet existing, Britain's own included, are open to foreign commerce and shipping, *in time of peace*?" "The abolition of private War upon the Sea" was a goal as "congenial to the true spirit of Christianity" as that of the suppression of the slave trade.[1] Adams noted that the advantages of immunity would be shared by maritime Nations "in proportion to the interest" they had "at stake upon the Ocean," and consequently the "greatest share" would be England's: first, by the "entire security" given her commerce, and secondly, "by relieving her from the necessity of maintaining that immense naval force which preys upon all her resources and aggravates the burden of her debt." While neutrals like the United States might lose "the considerable and alluring profits" of a wartime trade, they would gain that "comfort, tranquility and peace" which were "better than wealth." Adams concluded that there was therefore no real obstacle to the adoption of a liberal maritime code.[2]

Future American secretaries of state were not so optimisitc. In 1826 Henry Clay, although hopeful that the new rule advanced by neutrals would be "merged in the more liberal and extensive rule" of immunity, judged that "the slow progress of civilization" and the "tenacity with which power ever clings to advantages which it conceives itself to possess" made "a speedy, universal concurrence" unlikely.[3] In 1830, an even less sanguine secretary Martin Van Buren instructed the American minister to St Petersburg to explore a naval entente with Russia as a means of "counterbalancing" English maritime preponderance. In case of a renewal of British arrogance on the oceans, Van Buren suggested, the "combined fleets" of Russia and the United States could maintain jointly that "defence of neutral rights and the freedom of the sea" that "the Law of Nations have given them the right to enforce."[4]

In 1856, after secretary of state Marcy had insisted on immunity as the price for United States acceptance of the Paris Declaration, Richard Cobden observed that the day had passed when "any one nation can 'rule the seas' with an arbitrary sceptre." Since Nelson's time "a people have grown up beyond the Atlantic who lay claim to equal rights ... with ourselves on the ocean." The English Radical scoffed at "the transient ascendancy" of Great Britain that depended on "the costly display" of physical force. The new and "powerful empire" in America, never having known the corrupting rule of a feudal aristocracy, espoused principles Radicals believed correct and Britain's commercial classes thought practical. The American imperium would not seek to assert "a supremacy over any other people," he concluded, but would be established "on principles of moral right and equal justice to all, totally irrespective of their material strength."[5]

Would America's new imperial interests at the end of the nineteenth century – her growing naval power, expanding overseas commerce, and colonial possessions – shake her loyalty to her traditional policy? Although the United States disappointed Cobden in not embracing free trade, the English Radical was confident that the new American empire would not lose her liberal and humanitarian faith in the free seas. Any realistic observer would have disagreed.

Sir George Clarke in his 1906 report to the British cabinet insisted that "humanitarian considerations" played no real role in moulding American policy, for every power regarded such questions "solely in the light of its own interests, real or assumed." In 1870 before she had acquired a navy, Germany favored the immunity principle; in 1892, a Germany in possession of a navy repudiated this position. The Americans had inherited their maritime views from the country's founders "who contemplated a peaceful commercial commonwealth standing wholly aloof from the quarrels of the Old World." With the growth of American naval and colonial interests, Clarke prophesied change: "Already Captain Mahan, as a result of his studies in English naval history," argued "that the abandonment of the right of maritime capture would reduce the efficiency of the national navy in war," and that therefore the country ought not to persist in policies spawned by an irrelevant ideology.[6]

Mahan, Roosevelt, and the Second Hague Conference

Mahan was an Anglophile, an admirer of the uses to which British naval power had been put and an advocate of an Anglo-American naval alliance as the basis for a future world peace. In the early 1890s, he entered into a correspondence with a number of Englishmen (including Clarke) who thought in similar terms.[7] Such a naval alliance would be a guarantee against "outside barbarians" who though they might "readily assimilate our material advance" would take very long to reach "the general spirit" of modern Christianity. While liberals placed their hopes in arbitration as a substitute for war, Mahan could imagine "no greater misfortune" than the abandonment by civilized nations of military preparations in favor of an arbitration that would permit the barbarians to triumph.[8] When England was at war with the Boer republics in South Africa, he supported Great Britain, as he told J. R. Thursfield, because "on broad general principles" he was "satisfied of the right and duty of great Powers, when occasion offers to put an end to gross evils at their door."[9]

When Theodore Roosevelt succeeded to the presidency in 1901, it was reasonable to suppose that Mahan's political realism would replace idealistic rhetoric on maritime questions. A writer on the naval war of 1812 himself, Roosevelt was an early admirer of Mahan and an advocate of the strengthening of the American fleet. Moreover, he identified himself with the position that America ought to take a role in world affairs more consonant with her growing powers. Yet on the question of immunity, Roosevelt held fast to traditional policy.

In a message to Congress in December 1903, the president described freedom of the seas as "a matter of humanity and morals." With "the modern system of corporate ownership," a good deal of "American capital is now invested in foreign ships," and it was difficult to say to which nation any ship belonged. To cosmopolitan economics, Roosevelt added the strategic analysis associated with Mahan but which the American strategist had sought to qualify: "as a practical matter," Roosevelt observed, "all of our naval experts" believed that while a war against commerce might bring "serious loss and great annoyance," it was merely "a subsidiary factor" in winning naval wars; what was critical was "the fighting ship, not the commerce destroyer."[10] From the standpoint of morals, economics, and naval efficiency, the president argued that commercial wars were obsolete. The United States Congress in the spring of 1904 unanimously passed a joint resolution calling for all powers to accept immunity. As its chief sponsor, R. R. Hitt, an Illinois Republican and chairman of the House foreign affairs committee noted, this was "a doctrine for which we have striven for one hundred and twenty years."[11]

Before the opening of the Second Hague Conference, Mahan set out to convince Roosevelt that changing American interests made a new policy desirable and perhaps vital. In a letter in late 1904, the admiral (for he now held this reserve rank) urged Roosevelt to give up "the traditional policy" on immunity which had "lost the fitness it possibly once had to national conditions." While insisting that he had not changed his "known position" that commerce-destroying was a secondary operation, Mahan warned that "the power to control commerce, – the lawful right [that] international precedent now hampers – may be of immense, of decisive importance." Mahan sent Roosevelt pages from his forthcoming study of the war of 1812 to convince him that immunity was "inexpedient and illogical." "The question is one of expediency, and what was expedient to our weakness of a century ago is not expedient to our strength today." Mahan even wished "to withdraw from our position" of "free ships, free goods," which he believed was no longer suited to American needs. Britain and the United States were moving toward "a silent cooperation" at sea. "We need to fasten our grip on the sea," and with a change in maritime policy "our united naval strength can *probably* control the seas."[12]

The president's reply was somewhat equivocal. It was "a big subject," but with the advance of civilization there had grown up "a strong tendency to protect private property and private life on sea and land," which Roosevelt did not feel himself able to oppose.[13] While Roosevelt was reluctant to alter the traditional policy abruptly, in a letter to the admiral a few months later he agreed with Mahan's warnings about "the danger" posed by "extreme peace men" to "the cause of civilization": "We have to watch them quite as much as the demagogues of war."[14]

In 1906, with the Second Hague Conference nearer at hand, secretary of state Elihu Root forwarded Mahan's recommendations on immunity to the general board of the Navy. Root was sympathetic: the maintenance of the right of capture, he observed in a covering letter, insured "a strong and powerful class in every commercial country" interested in preserving peace, the shippers and merchants. American policy ought not "to result in sacrificing human life in order to save merchandise."[15] In reply, and in agreement with Mahan, the board reported that America's position on immunity was established on "moral" and no longer on "military or practical considerations." In the past, immunity would have been advantageous since the United States had a large merchant marine and a small navy; "at the present time, conditions are reversed," and America ought unhesitatingly to oppose the principle. Attached to this report was a letter written by the hero of the 1898 war against Spain, Admiral Dewey, the president of the naval board. Dewey urged America to persuade Britain, with whom "our interests are now so closely bound up," not to surrender the "great advantage" she held over the German empire by joining the United States in its "previous mistaken policy" of immunity. Unfortunately the British public was "still doubtful" of the ability of the Royal Navy to protect her commerce, Dewey observed; hence the sentiment in favor of a principle that would deprive England of the advantages of her superior fleet.[16]

Since military and naval officers were restricted in public discussions of sensitive issues, in mid-1906 Mahan requested the president's permission to write for the press on immunity. There was a strong pacifist tendency in advanced countries, he observed, and the present Liberal government in England with "its huge heterogeneous majority to keep placated" was "a special element of danger." If the Conservatives were in power, the United States might safely persist "in our old national policy" for the Tories would have blocked a move toward immunity. With a Liberal government, "you will . . . be playing with fire." The Royal Navy was well-placed to interfere with the German carrying trade: this was "the strongest hook in the jaws of Germany." To adopt the principle of immunity was consequently to yield "a principal gage for peace."[17] Roosevelt gave Mahan "a free hand" to discuss "the so-called peace proposals." Given Mahan's "deserved reputation as a publicist," it was important that he "write just what you think of the matter." This last, penned by the president onto a typewritten note, seemed more encouragement than routine permission.[18] Two months later, Roosevelt wrote to Mahan that he would recommend the admiral's study of the War of 1812 for the "general reading" of the Congress.[19]

But despite such signs of change – the intimations of the president, the secretary of state's letter to the Navy, and the opposition to immunity of the Navy's general board – there was no alteration in policy. On the day that Root dispatched his letter, and without waiting for the Navy's reply, the secretary of state wrote to Mahan that although he himself "already entertained and in private expressed serious doubts" on immunity, "the subject is no longer an open one for us." The United States had "so long and so positively" advocated the principle that it was not possible "to make a *volte face* at the Hague."[20]

The American delegation to The Hague in 1907 unanimously favored immunity as a moral necessity. Secretary Root charged the delegates to "maintain the traditional policy of the United States": whatever "the apparent specific interest" of any country "at the moment," the principle of immunity was of "such permanent and universal importance" that "no balancing of the chances of probable loss or gain in the immediate future on the part of any nation" could "outweigh the ... common benefit to civilization" of its adoption.[21] The chief American delegate Joseph Hodges Choate, a prominent Republican lawyer who had served earlier as ambassador to Great Britain, wrote to his son about the foolishness of the position Britain held "so obstinately" when immunity seemed "so manifestly for her interest."[22] In his address to the conference Choate – observing that those "generally in favour" of immunity were not only "the merchants," but "the statesmen, the jurists and the majority of the press" – rejected the argument that the end of capture would soften the opposition of the commercial classes to war. A nation's merchants and ship-owners were by nature peaceful men; "comerce and trade are always opposed to war." Wars were waged because of "passion, the lust of conquest, revenge for supposed affront." With the end of capture, nations could concentrate their naval building on battleships, not on commerce-destroyers or protectors, and war would be confined, quite properly, "to a test of strength between the armed forces and the financial resources of the combatant on sea and on land," a contest between nations, not individuals. The seas must always remain "free for innocent and unoffending trade and commerce."[23]

But there were counter-currents at The Hague that made other powers doubtful of the sincerity of the American position. Encouraged by the president to speak his mind, Mahan denounced immunity in an article for the ultra *National Review*, which like himself was highly suspicious of Germany's intentions. The admiral intimated in a letter to its editor that he did not believe "our Government will seriously regret the rejection" of Choate's immunity proposal.[24]

The powers divided on the question. The Norwegian delegate reminded the conference that in supporting immunity his country was "merely continuing a policy ... inaugurated in the eighteenth century by the kingdoms of the North" and the Armed Neutralities of 1780 and 1800.[25] On the other hand, the Colombian delegate observed that his country's circumstances did "not permit us to indulge in this great luxury of the abstract principles of justice and humanity": it was his duty to defend his country's "interests," and to forward the principles "of international policy, not of philanthropy"; Colombia therefore opposed immunity.[26] The major powers were skeptical. "Commercial interests have often prevented a declaration of war," Russia's delegate Nelidow declared.[27] Louis Renault, a French jurist, agreed, adding that in naval warfare "a belligerent must have the means of arresting the economic life of his adversary by hindering, or even by suppressing his commerce with the outside world."[28] The German delegate Baron Marschall von Bieberstein expressed sympathy for the American proposal, but declared that until both contraband and blockade were more clearly defined the present system ought to continue.[29]

Sir Ernest Satow, representing Great Britain, warned that the adoption of immunity "carried to its logical conclusion" would mean the abolition of commercial blockade. While granting that certain earlier British statesmen had favored the principle, he stressed that such views "date back to a rather remote period, when the conditions of commerce and of naval warfare were entirely different from what they are today." More appropriate to the present were the opinions of "a contemporary trans-Atlantic writer, whose eminent authority in this matter is universally recognized"; this writer – clearly Mahan, although his name was not, nor did it need to be, mentioned – was "unequivocally" in favor of the right of capture.[30]

The American proposal failed. When the vote was taken, immunity received the support of Germany, with the reservations outlined by Bieberstein, for that country wished to identify herself with America's cause without running the risk of seeing it successful. Austria–Hungary, Belgium, as well as a number of the smaller powers joined in forming a block of twenty-one nations in support of immunity. Among the eleven opponents of the principle, however, were such naval powers as Great Britain, France, Russia and Japan;[31] probably not coincidentally, England had signed an alliance with Japan in 1902, and "ententes" with France in 1904 and Russia in 1907 – agreements that implicitly recognized Germany as a target.

Wilson and freedom of the seas

When hostilities began in 1914, American naval strategists anticipated a successful British war against German commerce. In late July 1914, before England had actually entered the war, Mahan outlined the probable course of the conflict: if "the first German rush" should prove "indecisive or prolonged," British "financial pressure" would "determine the issue." Such pressure would "force the German fleet to fight," but if not, the Royal Navy had the power "to prevent all commerce under the German flag" and to close all German rivers except those emptying into the Baltic.[32] In early January 1915, a similar analysis appeared in the *New York Times* under the authorship of "Naval Officer." This writer observed that "as long as the sea is open to the Allies and closed to the Germans, the certainty of German defeat can be safely presumed," adding that "as this war will eventually be one of economic, financial, and military exhaustion, Germany, lacking control of the sea, is bound to be the first belligerent to become exhausted." The naval officer also remarked that "in spite of the peace croakers in Parliament," so grand a ship-building program had been mounted in the preceding decade that the Royal Navy was now vastly superior to the German.[33]

Even as American naval strategists forecast the economic exhaustion of the Central Powers, the United States government worked to restrict the effectiveness of the British blockade. Although the Declaration of London had not been formally ratified by any of the powers, America urged all belligerents to adopt it in practice. Foreign secretary Grey suggested to American secretary of state Lansing that because of "strong opposition" in parliament, England's position with respect to the agreement was similar to that of the United States in the case of a treaty to which the Senate refused consent[34] – a very different constitutional view from the one the Liberal government had argued in 1909. However, Britain was compromised by the Liberal government's support of the 1909 treaty, and in fact the provisions of the naval agreement were part of the prize manual issued to British naval officers by the time war came.[35]

The United States felt justified in pressing for whatever advantages the new code offered neutral commerce. By an order-in-council in August 1914, the British government put into force most of the principles of the Declaration, though not its contraband lists. The American state department placed Britain under pressure in the fall of 1914 to comply with these, and president Woodrow Wilson and his secretary of state repeatedly urged the American ambassador Walter Hines Page, who was sympathetic to the Allied cause, to admonish the British on "our continued insistence on the Declaration of London." Noting "England's positive declination three times to accept it *in toto*," Page cautioned in October 1914 that "Great Britain is our friend" not "an opponent in court, whom we are fighting and propose to fight."[36]

Even a friendly Page was a determined advocate of his country's policies. On 28 December 1914, for example, he wrote Sir Edward Grey to complain of the "frequent seizures and detentions of American cargoes destined to neutral European ports." Page defended "neutral rights," the "peaceful pursuit of lawful commerce," and "the freedom of the seas," and reminded the Liberal government that England, "usually the champion of the freedom of the seas and the rights of trade" in time of peace, had no right to interfere with neutral commerce "unless such interference is manifestly an imperative necessity to protect ... national safety." America protested the seizure of foodstuffs and cotton bound for neutral ports, not permitted by the London treaty, as an interference with the livelihoods of Midwest farmers and Southern planters "denied long established markets in European countries which, though neutral, are contiguous to nations at war." England would awaken hostile feelings in the United States, Page warned, if she did not abide by the provisions of the 1909 agreement.[37]

The British ambassador to the United States Sir Cecil Spring-Rice reported in mid-July 1915 that American hostility to England was "growing very serious." Since Britain must depend on American war supplies for at least another year and a half, it was necessary "to conciliate public opinion" in the United States, "even at great sacrifice." He suggested that British financial combines must somehow manage to placate Southern planters, disturbed at cotton being declared contraband, by keeping cotton prices high. Americans believed that the belligerents were "deliberately flouting" them, Spring-Rice cautioned, and such an opinion "may very easily, as in 1812, be turned against us."[38]

After the war, Sir Edward Grey wrote of the dilemma Britain had faced. "Blockade of Germany was essential to the victory of the Allies, but the ill-will of the United States meant their certain defeat"; "the object of diplomacy, therefore, was to secure the maximum of blockade that could be enforced without a rupture with the United States." Because America saw herself as "the trustee for the right of weaker neutrals," the foreign secretary noted, Britain was obliged to forego the advantages of her superior sea-power.[39] The question was complicated by the German claim, like that of Napoleon a century earlier, that she was fighting for freedom of the seas against British maritime tyranny.

In Woodrow Wilson, a former professor of politics and history, the traditional maritime policy of the United States found one of its most faithful and persistent advocates, and Wilson's friend and closest advisor Edward House, an adept Texas politician, shared the president's strong commitment. Cobden had observed over a half century earlier that the Democratic Party had a greater devotion to liberal principle, to free trade for example, than the Whigs or (later) Republicans,[40] much as the English Liberal party was more reliable on such questions than the Tories. Wilson was very much Cobden's kind of Democrat, a stalwart proponent of both free trade and freedom of the seas. In 1918, General Sir Henry Wilson was to describe him as a "super Gladstone" and a "dangerous visionary."[41] Gladstone was in fact one of the president's heroes. With the coming of war in 1914, Wilson asked his countrymen to remain netural in heart and mind, and the president led the way by seeming to see little difference between Prussian militarism and English navalism.[42]

In the early months of 1915, Wilson asked Colonel House (the title was an honorary one) to bring about a negotiated peace between Britain and Germany on the basis of freedom of the seas. Statesmen of both belligerent countries wished to persuade a neutral United States, whose friendship they sought, that they shared many of her maritime views, but were blocked from fully accepting them by fear of enemy perfidy. Yet there may well have been as much confusion as deception in the wavering opinions of the British and German foreign offices.

In early February 1915, Grey told House that England would be prepared "to agree that all merchant shipping of whatever nature, belligerent or neutral would be immune [from attack]." House was pleased and surprised that Great Britain "stood ready to go so far." The following day, House lunched with Sir William Tyrrell, the senior clerk of the foreign office and Grey's private secretary, who spoke of "the absolute freedom of merchantmen of all nations to sail the seas in time of war unmolested" – the end of searches for contraband. The submarine had so changed the character of maritime war, Tyrrell observed, that Britain would be "better protected" by such a policy than "by maintaining an overwhelming navy."[43] (Tyrrell's wife, it may be of some interest to mention, was a daughter of David Urquhart.) Believing that an insular Britain had more to gain from freedom of the seas than Germany, House was persuaded of the good faith of the foreign office.

House then approached German statesmen, intimating to them, as he wrote Wilson, that "when the end comes you will insist on this [Britain's acceptance of the new maritime rules] being done."[44] The German foreign minister Zimmermann was "exceedingly sympathetic" when the American assured him that the United States believed England had no right to a navy greater than what was "sufficient to prevent invasion."[45] The German chancellor Bethmann-Hollweg was "surprised when I told him the idea was to go far beyond the Declaration of Paris or the proposed Declaration of London."[46] What "we had in mind," House told the Germans, was "the absolute freedom of commerce in future warfare." Germany wanted peace but needed to save face, he reported to the president, and if America persuaded England to accept freedom of the seas Germany could tell its people "that the great cause they have been striving for" had been achieved, and English public opinion could be made to understand that "in the long run and looking at the matter broadly," the proposal was also in Britain's interest.[47]

House's diplomacy gave renewed hope to British Radicals like Lord Loreburn and F.H. Hirst, spokesmen for the "peace party," as House described them in early 1915.[48] Loreburn was the kind of Englishman the president's emissary found compatible: he was "a man that can be thoroughly trusted," House wrote Wilson in early May; "I believe he is my friend."[49] But Radical hopes were disappointed. When the German foreign office publicly and vociferously took up the demand for freedom of the seas, British opinion rejected the overture with scorn and Grey retreated. In April, House warned

Grey of "the dangers of a world-wide coalition against her."[50] The Radical "peace party" wished to encourage the United States to defy "a paper blockade" against Germany, or alternatively to halt exports to all belligerents, as she had done in 1809. If Wilson did this, Hirst told House, "he could force this Government to do practically what he desired," and "lay down a new international code of laws and insist upon every nation living up to it."[51] Former lord chancellor Loreburn told House that "if we could bring about the Freedom of the Seas, it would be the greatest act of statesmanship that had been accomplished in centuries." While such a state of things would be more valuable to England than to other countries, Loreburn observed, it would be hard to get "the English mind to see this."[52]

The blockades

The Royal Navy had more ships than Germany when war began, and increased naval building widened the gap; this superiority was to prove decisive. The German High Seas Fleet remained in home waters and relied on blockading Britain by submarines. Given British maritime dominance, the Germans did not dare follow the legal course of warfare against merchant ships, that is, the examining of ships, sinking them only after warning, and making provision for safety of passengers and crew. Their campaign of "unrestricted" submarine warfare launched in early 1915 was ostensibly a reply to Britain's having declared food contraband, an inhumane "hunger blockade." (The United States protested, and American ships were for a time exempted from attack.) This and other German violations of international treaties provided Britain with the excuses she required, as Ottley, McKenna, and others had foreseen, to extend the blockade in ways contrary to the Declarations of 1856 and 1909.

Britain mounted a "distant blockade" to seal off the sea routes from the North Sea to the ocean. The only way to make blockade truly effective, she insisted, was to apply it to enemy trade through neutral ports, and by an order-in-council in March 1915 she announced that her naval vessels would "take into port ships carrying goods of presumed enemy destination, ownership, or origin." When the German naval command renewed its submarine campaign in late 1915, Britain tightened her blockade by limiting imports by neutrals to commodities purchased for their own use before the war, to forestall re-shipment to Germany; this, of course, was the variation of the rule of 1756 that Mahan had suggested in 1907. The United States objected, as it had over a century earlier, that this was merely a device to gain a monopoly of neutral markets for British goods.[53]

There were grounds for such a suspicion. Britain's long-term commercial interests became a central issue for a number of interdepartmental committees. As in the wars against Napoleon plans were put forward – in mercantilist fashion – to use the blockade to take over parts of the trade not only of enemy but also of neutral competitors, notably the United States. Though it ran against English tradition to wage war against private persons and their businesses, a 1916 memorandum conceded, an inter-departmental committee none the less prepared a statutory list of firms of enemy nationality or association doing business with Germany so as to exclude them from British trade channels. This would bring "home the effects of sea-power to neutrals," as well as "wreck German trade prospects after the war"; this last could better be achieved by "belligerent action" during a conflict rather than by "trade-war" after peace was restored.[54] But exceptions to these restrictive rules were allowed in Britain's overall interest. It was sometimes necessary to license certain exchanges with the enemy, for example, the buying of German aniline dyes so British calico printers might continue to supply foreign customers. (The granting of such licenses, a foreign office memorandum noted, was of "some historical interest as being modelled on the licenses granted by the Crown during the Napoleonic Wars.") Although many merchants did not "realise that war had any relation to commerce," and saw any government interference as "unwarranted and officious," the "bulk of the traders" had at times to be persuaded that trade with the enemy – as in China and South America where German firms controlled the merchandising of British goods – was essential "to avoid injuring our export trade."[55] Indeed, continuing to trade with these German firms in many parts of Central and South America would avert the acute "danger of trade passing into American hands" permanently.[56] With all this, E. M. Pollock, the chairman of the Contraband Committee, could yet complain in a June 1917 statement of the regrettable tendency among Americans "to suspect that our policy is directed to selfish ends."[57]

The need to satisfy the commercial and ideological requirements of a neutral United States set uncomfortable limits on the Royal Navy. In early 1915 Hankey, who succeeded Ottley as secretary of the C.I.D. in 1912, urged the prime minister to continue to attack Germany's food supply, the enemy's "Achilles heel," and warned against abandoning England's most powerful weapon to secure neutral approval.[58] But we know that foreign secretary Grey tried to accommodate the United States, and other members of the cabinet wished to proceed even further. (In June 1915, Crewe, the lord president of the council, advised the lifting of the blockade against foodstuffs,[59] as did the ambassador to the United States, Spring-Rice). England felt herself injured by the "legal niceties" on which the Americans insisted, Grey wrote House in 1915, and acceptance of further American complaints would so cramp British operations "that Germany could evade them wholesale." British belligerent rights at sea "would be mere paper rights, quite useless in practice." By her intransigence, Grey concluded, the United

States would "strike the weapon of sea power out of our hands" and "ensure a German victory."[60]

By 1916, an England hard-pressed by America pledged herself to accept the full doctrine of freedom of the seas, but only after the war. Grey informed Colonel House that this concession must be accompanied by "the elimination of militarism," and by the United States joining in "a general covenant to sustain it." This seemed a considerable victory to House, who, with Wilson, had become increasingly committed to the doctrine.[61]

Though unaware that Grey had gone quite so far in his post-war concessions, the naval ultras were outraged by what they regarded as the Liberal government's pusillanimity in enforcing the blockade. The Tory *Morning Post* in mid-February 1916 denounced Grey and the Liberal ministry. "Long before the war, in the year 1907," the paper observed, it had been "made quite clear by the Foreign Office that in war by sea the interests of the neutrals were to be placed first all the time." This had proved to be the case. The paper opposed the release of neutral ships that violated the orders-in-council, and urged that "the full power of the Fleet" be used "to besiege Germany." The "nervous hallucination" that a firm policy would push neutrals into a war against England merely reflected "the mind of the Foreign Office." If the government had been "less afraid" and exercised the "legitimate enforcement of belligerent rights" – if only the admiralty had been "in supreme command" not the foreign office – the *Morning Post* was convinced that "the war ere now would have been over."[62]

A week later the dispute erupted in the upper house. Sydenham attacked the foreign office for its adherence to the unratified Declaration of London, and took up the demand for a tighter blockade.[63] Beresford supported Sydenham, noting that "the Foreign Office prepared for peace, not for war," and presumed "this great Empire" was "always going to be neutral."[64] In reply, Lord Loreburn revived the Cobdenite goal of "national war and commercial peace": a commercial blockade would injure "the nations" not their governments, he observed, clearly seeing governments as still largely in the hands of the traditional landed and military classes, yet "the Governments not the nations of Europe" had brought about the war and were "responsible for its continuance."[65]

In the early months of 1917, after the Germans re-opened a campaign of unrestricted submarine warfare, losses of Allied shipping increased perilously. Convoys had been successfully employed in previous wars, but the admiralty believed that under modern conditions – with steam navigation, the almost constant flow of traffic, and the stealthiness of submarine tactics – such a system would not work. The 1879 Royal Commission's decision against convoys, Lord Sydenham argued half a century later, was prompted by "the great steamship owners who resented the slowing down entailed" by mixed convoys of steam and sail vessels, and the inescapable delays in assembling the ships.[66] Admiral P. H. Colomb in 1893 had observed that mercantile "opinion and not mechanical or physical fact" gave rise to "the greatest resistance to the revival of convoy in the old sense." The issue was whether at the outbreak of war insurance underwriters would believe sailing with or without a convoy constituted the greater risk. "What Government will be asked to do if we are unhappily involved in a naval war will now, as then [in 1801 to 1815] depend upon the views of the underwriters." The "idea of convoy" was "abhorrent" to the business community "now in peace-time," he had noted; it was to prove equally distasteful in naval circles.[67]

Colomb had described patrolled routes as an alternative to convoys, and when war came such a system was instituted. Though strategists like Colomb and Mahan had advocated convoys, the prevailing admiralty view in the decade before the war was set down by the naval writer F. T. Jane who described convoys as "a splendid prize already prepared for the enemy."[68] Admiralty fears proved fanciful when Lloyd George, now prime minister, and Hankey finally persuaded the Navy to install a convoy system in 1917, though the admiralty in its anxiety to avoid risks retained its patrols of sea lanes.

Exasperated by attacks of German submarines on merchant and passenger ships, the United States entered the war in April 1917, and was now prepared to allow the blockade to proceed well beyond the restrictive provisions of the agreements of 1856 and 1909. By the last month of 1917, all foreign supplies to Germany (except some Dutch and Scandinavian produce) were effectively halted. In early 1918, an American embargo on goods the United States sent to Scandinavia and Holland forced those countries to reduce their exports to Germany; on the other hand, Britain, seeing herself as more dependent on Dutch and Scandinavian trade, believed she could not afford so grand an effort, and continued to export to the continental neutrals. None the less, the naval blockade was now having an undoubted effect on the German war effort.

After the war, the virtually unanimous view was that the blockade had proved critical to victory. In July 1916 in a confidential statement to dominion representatives, Balfour defended the blockade policy as "not a purely naval problem" but one of "trying to induce neutral and independent countries ... to manipulate their commerce – or allow us to manipulate it – so that they should not receive goods at their ports in transit to Germany." Such a task had "never been attempted before in the history of the world," and the "amazing measure of success" was "a marvel of improvised administration."[69] By the end of 1917, Lloyd George would write in his memoirs, the British blockade was bringing about a shortage of essential foodstuffs and "gradually breaking down the morale of the German nation." The Allies needed only to stay the course until the blockade "completed its terrible work" and fresh American troops were rushed over "to help in the final overthrowing of a debilitated enemy."[70] In 1932, the military writer Basil

Liddell Hart was convinced that blockade had proved "more decisive" than the armies on the Western Front in defeating the Germans.[71]

Liddell Hart, in fact, doubted the usefulness of Britain's military involvement on the continent, and urged a return to "the British way of warfare." "Our historic practice," he observed, was the exercise of "economic pressure" by means of sea power – the mounting of blockades and amphibious thrusts against the enemy's "vulnerable extremities." This was one of the "two arms" of British policy; the other was a financial arm – "the subsidizing and military provisioning of [continental] allies." Between 1914 and 1918, the country adopted "a revolutionary innovation" in raising a mass army and using it "for direct action in the main theatre of war." "The cost is known," Liddell Hart concluded, "the benefit doubtful."[72]

The strategist and naval historian Sir Herbert Richmond would also blame the exhausting length of the war on "the dominance of the 'continental' school of thought": "Largely under French influence," the generals and politicians showed themselves "unable to understand the use and influence of sea power." Richmond condemned England for having given "sanction" in 1856 to the neutral position, arguing that the war might have ended earlier if the Royal Navy were free from the start to apply maximum economic pressure against Germany.[73] (That an exclusively maritime strategy would have proved sufficient during the war of 1914 was perhaps the dominant British strategical view in the period between the wars; more recent writers have stressed the critical importance of Britain's continental commitment.)[74]

Freedom of the seas at Versailles

Although yielding reluctantly to the necessities of blockade, Wilson was not prepared to surrender his nation's traditional maritime policy. In January 1918, the president announced the fourteen points which he expected to be the basis of the coming peace. The second was "freedom of the seas alike in peace and in war." The fourteen points as a whole were well received in England, but even Liberal papers like the *Manchester Guardian* and the *Westminster Gazette* were suspicious of Wilson's stress on this second point.[75]

By October 1918 it was clear that a defeated Germany must soon sue for peace, and Wilson and House intensified their campaign to persuade Britain, indeed to bludgeon her, to accept freedom of the seas. The United States refused to "submit to Great Britain's complete domination of the seas any more than to Germany's domination of the land," Colonel House informed Lord Reading, Spring-Rice's successor as British ambassador; House warned another British official that "if the British were not careful they would bring upon themselves the dislike of the world," and "all hope of Anglo-Saxon unity would be at an end."[76] "I again repeated," he wrote in his journal, "that our people would not consent to allow the British Government . . . to determine on what terms our ships should sail the seas, either in time of peace, or in time of war."[77] In early November, before the signing of the armistice, Wilson authorized House to advise the British that if England did not accept freedom of the seas, the United States would "build up the strongest navy that our resources permit and as our people have long desired."[78]

Lloyd George refused to accept what he saw as an American ultimatum. Though House believed the doctrine of freedom of the seas would do no more than make the principle of immunity sacrosanct, Lloyd George saw it as destroying the power of commercial blockade that in his view played a decisive role in the Allied victory.[79] On this question, "the nation is absolutely solid," Lloyd George declared, noting further that Britain was determined to "spend her last guinea" if necessary to maintain her naval superiority.[80] Fear of the United States as a naval rival had surfaced earlier in the war when the 1916 program to expand the American fleet appeared to one liberal naval writer as "more ambitious and sensational" than even the German prewar expansion; it was possible that the Americans thought the war an "opportunity of seizing the trident."[81] Sir William Wiseman, a diplomat who served as an intermediary between House and the foreign office, was later to write that the phrase "freedom of the seas" was "so vague and yet so far-reaching and vital" that it inevitably produced dissensions: while many of Britain's Liberal politicians were "in general agreement" with Wilson, and prepared to accept the doctrine as an ideal, the admirals were "breathing fire."[82]

The admiralty demanded the rejection of the American demands. A memorandum by Admiral Wemyss, the first sea lord, insisted on "the British idea" of freedom of the seas in time of peace; "in time of *war* this privilege must be fought for by belligerent navies." Were Wilson's proposal accepted, England would not be able to use "our strongest weapon," while "the value of military power, both for attack and defence, would be enhanced." Nor did Wemyss believe that Britain ought to surrender to any league of nations, as many Liberals urged, "the sea-power we have for centuries maintained and have never yet misused."[83] Lord Lytton, the additional parliamentary secretary to the admiralty, agreed, and declared that if the government made "a gesture of acceptance," the admiralty would ignore any such commitment in time of war. Britain ought "to take her stand" in favor of her belligerent interests, Lytton urged, counting on the Navy to apply pressure on belligerents when England was neutral.[84] The leading strategists supported the official view. Julian Corbett again warned that immunity would make naval warfare impossible,[85] and Spenser Wilkinson cautioned his compatriots against changes in naval policy that would weaken England's "power of self-defence and her strength for upholding the cause of freedom."[86]

Here was an impasse in Anglo-American relations that might have proved insurmountable; but now there was a new division among American politicians. Most of the American public, of course, continued to cheer Wilson's insistence on the traditional doctrine of freedom of the seas, and like the New York *World* encouraged the president not to permit the United States to "be false to its entire history."[87] In late November 1918, however, Theodore Roosevelt took the step he had resisted in office, and endorsed the view taken over a decade earlier by Mahan and the Navy's general board. Wilson's "abstract policies" on contraband and blockades were "utterly impossible," he declared, and had they prevailed, the war would have brought about "the enslavement of mankind" to the German empire. "Whatever were our views prior to the great war, we are fools, indeed, if we have not learned the lessons these last four and a half terrible years have taught." The former president urged Americans to prevent Wilson from bringing on the country "such outrageous potentiality of disaster" as the international adoption of "the so-called freedom of the seas."[88] In early December, Roosevelt wrote to Lloyd George denying that Wilson was fully supported by American opinion on this issue. Roosevelt's close friend, Republican senator Henry Cabot Lodge, who would in a few weeks become chairman of the Senate's foreign relations committee, backed Roosevelt's stand.[89]

During the Versailles conference, the powers expected a confrontation between Wilson and Lloyd George on freedom of the seas. This was one of the "clouds on the horizon" that a member of the British delegation, the economist J. M. Keynes, foresaw. But Wilson never raised the question, "presumably," observed Keynes, "the price he deemed it judicious to pay" for Lloyd George's support on other matters.[90] Having become aware not only of a now divided American opinion but also of British determination to resist, Wilson found a way of side-stepping the issue while still remaining committed to the ideal. The President's non-conformist conscience was quieted by the conviction that since the new League of Nations would banish war forever, the problem need never rise again.[91]

Epilogue: naval alliance versus freedom of the seas

In the last months of the war, Sir Francis Piggott, a prominent barrister and an admirer of David Urquhart, became the leading non-governmental spokesman for England's belligerent rights. Like Urquhart, Piggot denounced the pacifists, the shipowners, and the Manchester School who followed the views of "a certain set of Radicals" and were ready "to adopt anything which smacked of philosophy," as well as "the remnant" of the great Whig party which, like Lord Clarendon in the 1850s, regarded the great days of Pitt and Nelson as an "age of barbarism." Though the German empire now saw defeat as inevitable, the Germans hoped to renew their effort to dominate the world; and their "most potent weapons" would be "the doctrines of 'free ships, free goods,' " and "immunity of private property at sea." Were such principles accepted, the German would "have the world at his mercy." Piggott recognized that the Pax Britannica was no more, but hoped that England's maritime "pax" would be replaced by a naval alliance of the Allies.[92]

An Anglo-American naval alliance had been for some time a goal of statesmen and strategists on both sides of the Atlantic. In the early 1890s, Andrew Carnegie suggested that the forces of the two English-speaking peoples be joined in the interests of peace, and Sir George Clarke supported an Anglo-American "naval league of armed neutrality."[93] In a letter in 1904 to the journalist Valentine Chirol, soon to visit the United States, Clarke (then secretary of the C.I.D.) urged Chirol to spark President Roosevelt's interest in a naval alliance so that Roosevelt might in turn "inspire the [British] Foreign Office to action." The United States had "a very powerful & an increasing Navy," Clarke noted, more than she needed for her own defense. If it were understood that "in certain contingencies the fleets of G. B. & U. S. would act together to dominate the naval situation," the two, constituting "so tremendous" a power, might impose "peace on the seas."[94] We recall that Mahan and his disciples in the Navy also found the prospect of an Anglo-American alliance attractive, since they saw the external interests of the two countries converging. But the United States was not prepared for so bold a step. In the postwar years, America continued as spokesman for liberal doctrine and neutral rights, and took up the apparently diverse goals of freedom of the seas and the maintenance of naval parity with Britain.

George Young, a civil servant who served in the admiralty during the war, wrote in 1928 an article for a liberal monthly on the usefulness of an Anglo-American naval alliance. Ought Britain to give up command of the sea or fight America for predominance and probably lose, Young asked. There was hardly "sufficient security" in the proposals of " 'legalist' voluptuaries" who "would 'scrap the navy' and accept in return 'scraps of paper' " from the League of Nations. Genuine security rested only in England's and America's accepting "a common naval policy." Britain must recognize that her naval supremacy was no more, and that she must "formally" renounce any blockade that did not have American approval. An Anglo-American "Armed Neutrality," he observed, using Clarke's label of nearly forty years earlier, would be a way-station to a general naval disarmament, first under the hegemony of the English-speaking nations and then, perhaps, under the authority of the League. There was no "difference in principle" between the rival British and American conceptions, the conflict between which had been going on for over a century. Britain's command of the seas was "the only material 'sanction' " for freedom of the seas, while the principle of freedom of the seas was "the only moral sanction" for the command of the seas.[95]

The following month Colonel House replied, rejecting Young's proposal and reiterating traditional American policy. House demanded "the sanctity of private property at sea," observing that with the adoption of immunity, there would be "no incentive" to maintain large navies. England might have a navy large enough to prevent invasion, but no larger, and that navy must pledge itself not to "blockade or interfere with enemy or neutral commerce in time of war." Freedom of the seas would moreover "eliminate the terrors" submarine warfare might in the future impose on England's food supply. House dismissed the prevailing view that the Allied blockade had defeated Germany in 1918. That the blockade had any effect was because the "circumstances were unusual": it was extremely unlikely, he concluded with something less than prescience, that there would be another conflict in which a coalition of England, Russia and France would be pitted against Germany.[96]

Colonel House's article renewed British discussion of freedom of the seas. The Labour party, an heir to the Radical cosmopolitan tradition, welcomed the Wilson-House position and called for "the complete renunciation of the right of private war and private blockade," though both instruments would be permitted the League.[97] Lord Eustace Percy, a prominent defender of the League of Nations, noted the "risks [of] being regarded as one of those facile and naive policy-mongers" when he agreed with this Radical and Labour view.[98] A dissenting voice on the left, Lieutenant-Commander J. M. Kenworthy, a former naval adviser to Lloyd George and first a Radical and then a Labour MP, joined Young in calling for a naval alliance between the two powers.[99] Admiral Sir Herbert Richmond prepared for the C.I.D. a memorandum on House's article which warned against the dangers of accepting what the United States called freedom of the seas. The C.I.D. secretary Sir Maurice Hankey called Richmond's statement "the finest thing" he had ever read on the subject.[100]

Yet fear of American rivalry, and even enmity, brought a number of influential Conservatives to favor – albeit only briefly – yielding belligerent rights at sea. The matter arose a number of times in the Tory cabinet between 1927 and 1929. Lord Cushendun, the parliamentary under-secretary of foreign affairs, suggested in 1927 that it was now opportune "to abandon, or modify our traditional doctrine of blockade."[101] The foreign secretary Austen Chamberlain favored this recommendation, believing that "the rise of United States naval and financial power" made it necessary to change British policy, or else a future war with America was "probable." Chamberlain observed, in a by now familiar refrain, that international politics had "altered to our disadvantage, and what was possible in the past may have become impossible in the future."[102] Winston Churchill, having rejoined the Conservative party and now chancellor of the exchequer, noted that in a war with either the United States or Russia "a convention protecting seaborne commerce from attack would be a priceless help to a small over-crowded island and a scattered Empire."[103] A cabinet subcommittee on belligerent rights, chaired by Chamberlain, was formed to discuss the issue in January 1928. By 1929, however, both Chamberlain and Churchill had returned to what Hankey described as "high Belligerent Rights," the result of a vigorous campaign waged by Hankey and the C.I.D.[104]

When the issue first arose in late 1927, Hankey wrote a memorandum to the cabinet in which he reminded the Tory leaders that their party in 1911 had "saved" an England "on the edge of the abyss" from "the final catastrophe" of ratification of the Declaration of London. Even unratified, the commitment of the Liberals to the treaty made it "not easy to shelve." For almost two years of war it "exercised a baneful influence on our policy," for its restrictions were "incompatible with the full exercise of sea power." An effective blockade of Germany had been essential to victory, and acceptance of the 1909 agreement would have made this impossible. The maintenance of belligerent rights might again prove vital to Britain's existence. The war of 1914 like that against Napoleon, Hankey concluded, gave evidence that neutrals would suffer much before taking up arms.[105]

In early January 1929, there was a debate on naval questions in the United States Senate in which Senator Borah of Idaho warned Britain that America would build "not 15 but 50 cruisers" unless England agreed to the principle of freedom of the seas. Hankey described Borah's warning as "political blackmail!" What right had America to attempt to intimidate Britain on this "great question of international controversy" now "more than a century old"? Hankey might "stomach" the "odious term" freedom of the seas "if it means nothing," but the Americans continued to expand its meaning. The C.I.D. secretary was not ready to discuss the question "with a pistol at my head." Though the Tories were in office, Hankey was worried: "I don't trust any Government nowadays to stand up to American threats."[106] The prime minister Stanley Baldwin, an industrialist from the midlands, like his predecessor Bonar Law and the foreign secretary Austen Chamberlain belonged to that group of businessmen in the party that Loreburn described as "practical";[107] Loreburn believed that such Tories were prepared to accept a progressive maritime policy while the reactionary, landed class would continue to resist.

When a Labour government took office in 1929, president Herbert Hoover, spurred no doubt by his wartime role as provider of food for Europe's starving, and probably encouraged by Colonel House, saw an opportunity to revive what seems, again, to have become a bipartisan American policy of freedom of the seas. Hoover urged that foodstuffs be excluded from any future blockade. Hankey however persuaded the pacifist Labour prime minister Ramsay Macdonald and his cabinet that any such action would cause a popular uproar.[108] During the Second World War, the United States would take a very different view of blockade and economic warfare.

[11] Radicals, Reactionaries, and Power

> It would now be broadly true to say that most Liberals deplore, and many condemn, increasing expenditure upon armaments; while most Tories obstinately demand and extol it, feeling that they thereby appeal to a still prevalent instinct in the mass of the people ... Toryism, broadly speaking, voices loudly the animal jealousy felt by the foreigner-hating Briton of the old type ... As the attitude of the Labour party is still more markedly internationalist, it may be safely inferred that the democratic tendency is more and more toward peace. But while both in the Liberal and the Labour ranks there are men ready to make or risk 'war to prevent war' and to intervene unwarrantably in the affairs of foreign States on the side of popular rights, it cannot be said that British Liberalism has cast off the ancient British tendency to take part in other people's quarrels. Even as in international morals, so in international politics, reason and equity are of a slower growth than in the relations of individuals within a community.
>
> J. M. Robertson, *The Meaning of Liberalism*, 1912

> But what this generation did not fully appreciate was how far these values, the fine flower of Victorian Liberalism, were tied up with the social order and national institutions which might continue to need power, and in the last resort *military* power, for their survival.
>
> Michael Howard, *Ethics and Power in International Politics*, 1978

The liberal ego, though devoted to peace, was long prepared to accept the view of *Si vis pacem, para bellum*; the liberal conscience came more and more to insist that those who wished for peace must abandon not merely preparations but even the thought of war. War to liberals was "an evil aberration," and strategy "not a worthy subject for a serious mind of high moral tone," a recent writer has observed.[1] The historian Sir Lewis Namier wrote of "the underlying emotions, the music, to which the ideas are a mere libretto." Namier had little respect for ideas "high and dry," which "become doctrine, or at best innocuous cliches" once "the emotions have ebbed."[2] But ideas in doctrinal form, that is, after they have been incorporated in a system, may be more influential than they were at birth. Such a system – like that of modern liberalism – evokes an enchantment of its own, mobilizing emotional forces generated by inner psychological as well as socio-economic conflicts long after the realities to which these may once have corresponded have faded.

If the three motives of economic interest, the prevailing ideology, and power were in accord in England of the eighteenth century, this was less true in the nineteenth, and even less the case by 1914. In the wars against Napoleon, liberal principle and the interest of the Liverpool merchants were opposed to the traditional use of British maritime might. With peace was to come the re-establishment of some harmony: liberal ideology and commercial interest might without too pronounced jarring employ naval power to advance progress and civilization in the effort to destroy the slave trade. A generation later this naval crusade produced a new dissonance as pacifistic free traders denounced the use of naval force as a brutal atavism, immoral as well as futile, and hurtful to economic interests. Briefly in the 1850s, the three motives again seemed united by the Declaration of Paris, as England saw herself primarily as a neutral trader, and war as soon to become extinct. Almost immediately, Radical liberalism – the quintessence of the liberal ideology and the voice of its conscience – moved further along the pacifist road and enlisted the mercantile interest in an effort to make all (even enemy) private property at sea free from naval capture. This shocked those concerned with power, particularly after continental nations turned to military and naval expansion.

From the late 1880s to 1914, the advocates of naval power fought to free themselves from the restraints imposed by interest and the liberal ideology. But the merchants and industrialists understood rather better than the advocates of power that war would undermine the international economy upon which the welfare, and, ultimately, the national strength, of a free-trade Britain depended. It would certainly have been self-defeating to neglect economic well-being in the effort to maintain military or naval power, and a well-conceived strategy had to seek a judicious accommodation between the two.[3] There was a similar tension between power and the demands of the liberal conscience: Despite the strength of nationalism among the middle classes elsewhere, the Radical burgesses of the Pax Britannica continued to see themselves first of all as Christians and cosmopolitans, devoted to international peace and progress as inseparable moral touchstones; in the twentieth century, a more secularized version of this faith established itself in the public opinion of the advanced nations of the West. To fail to accommodate these tensions between the prevailing liberal outlook and power could prove equally self-destructive in democratic states where so much depended on morale.

Kant foresaw a world in which, in all the advanced states, compassionate citizens, not irresponsible rulers, made critical decisions. Nations would then be disposed to avoid aggressive war. By the middle of the nineteenth century a liberal English (and American) public opinion believed such a world had already arrived. One historian has suggested that in part because of the evangelical spirit of the public schools, violence and arrogance gave way to gentleness and kindness in the character of the English governing class. Liberal precepts furthered the Christian belief that all men, regardless of their different historical developments, were cast in the same moral image. And bourgeois affluence confirmed liberal and Christian conviction. "Like an enchantment, liberal doctrine seemed to blind British eyes and paralyse British will power" in the years before 1914, this writer observed; the upper-middle and upper-class men who governed the nation, the "flowers of English liberalism and romanticism," possessed "a set of unpractical idealistic attitudes."[4] In the period before the First World War, the German chancellor von Bülow declared that "in their artless egoism" the British "find difficulty in believing in really evil intentions in others"; "the country exhales wealth, comfort, content, and confidence," and the "people have never seen an enemy ... and simply cannot believe that things could ever go really wrong, either at home or abroad."[5]

A different view dominated governing circles on the continent. A German writer on naval questions observed in 1911 that "war and not peace are part of the nature of things and of life itself"; the liberal advocates of "perpetual peace" assumed quite erroneously that "all conflicts of interest and all differences of outlook can be reconciled," a view that "contradicts the nature of man, and is incompatible with human societies."[6] After the First World War, the pre-1914 dynastic monarchies of the continent were replaced by regimes even less concerned with morals or rational interest and even more with brute power.[7]

The ideal types: radicals and reactionaries

When Lord Devlin, a high court judge, delivered the Rede Lecture at Cambridge in 1968, he took for his subject the rejection by the House of Lords of the naval prize bill of 1911. Had he been a young MP at that time, Devlin declared, he would have supported the Declaration of London as "a great step forward towards a better international order," even if this meant the end of British maritime supremacy. Now, however, he saw what might have been the consequences of ratification, for if the Lords had passed the bill, America would have insisted on the fulfillment of the agreement's every provision during the early years of the war; "at the very least, the Declaration would have been a weighty and perhaps fatal encumbrance." While the "nineteenth-century mind" sought to subject war to law, that of the twentieth century agreed with the pre-1914 Tory opponents of maritime reform that the two were fundamentally "irreconcilable." While reason might dominate in discussions of legal questions, war was the province of power. In surveying the probable consequences of British acceptance of the 1909 treaty, the jurist concluded that "the reactionaries in this case were right."[8]

Others had earlier agreed on the good fortune of the bill's failure, and denounced the unrealistic assumptions of liberal opinion in much the same terms. Even the cabinet's chief sponsor of the Declaration, Sir Edward Grey, was prepared in 1925 to concede that if the peers had not prevented ratification, the treaty's "rules would have hampered us" during the war, and the bill's opponents were "entitled on this account to take credit for their action."[9] Another supporter David Lloyd George observed that had the Declaration not been "luckily rejected," England would have been deprived of "our most effective weapon against Germany."[10] And, of course, naval ultras like Lord Charles Beresford had been delighted at the time of the bill's defeat that the Lords resisted the "amiable visionaries" who aimed to "substitute for effective force a series of paper safeguards"[11] because they did not understand "the essential elements of sea power."[12] A writer for a Tory organ condemned "our sentimentalists and Pacifists" who assured the nation "that war had become obsolete,"[13] and an admiral charged Liberals with longing "to be embraced by any suitor who whispers the magic word 'peace.'"[14] Denouncing those who feared that "a vigorous line" would mean "trouble with Germany," a Tory journalist described liberalism as wishing "to pursue right – but only when it involves no risk," while making an exception of the free trader T. G. Bowles because Bowles was "something more than a Liberal; he is a patriotic man."[15]

We have considered two "ideal-types" – the first the radical-liberal, the second the reactionary-conservative – but we must do so cautiously. The two have been distinguished in a number of ways: a free trader confronting a mercantilist; a cosmopolitan and internationalist opposing a nationalist and patriot; an advocate of liberal maritime policy versus an upholder of belligerent rights at sea. While the radical-liberal saw himself in the vanguard of progress, and all men as necessarily becoming, like himself, rational and peace-loving, the reactionary-conservative insisted that men were as they always had been and would be, ruled by passion, anxious for power, and prepared if practicable to seize the possessions of their neighbors. But however useful as a conceptual tool, such a simple polarization must be guarded against.

Cobden and his followers were almost precise incarnations of the radical model, just as the naval ultras, another comparatively small group, represented the reactionary position in virtually all its purity. By the beginning of the twentieth century, more qualified and practical versions of these types, and of the maritime positions they espoused, had imprinted themselves on the bulk of the Liberal and Tory parties.

A naive Cobdenite outlook survived the heyday of Victorian optimism, though fewer people took its more extreme effusions seriously. In an important naval debate in 1889, for example, a Radical member for Leicester denied that we are "living in a world of pirates" and that foreign countries were "nothing but dens of robbers," and confessed himself to having "more faith in human nature." At this point, the parliamentary report recorded "*Ministerial laughter*," which caused the speaker to observe that Tories "forget altogether the advance of the world" and that what the country required was not naval but "moral supremacy."[16] The Tory civil lord of the admiralty remarked that the "exaggerated descendants of the old 'Manchester school' used to be in the ascendancy," but now this "peace at any price party," while "weak enough in Parliament" was still "weaker in the country," thanks to the "clearer insight" and "purer patriotism" of the working-class electorate.[17]

Yet though the mood of the 1850s had passed, the liberal concern for a "progressive" morality in the conduct of maritime war persisted. An insurance underwriter with liberal sympathies defended immunity because war might be "virtuous or vicious in its conduct," and "if tainted with mercenary plunder it is vicious."[18] Morality and progress were regularly invoked: in 1906, the *Nation* hoped that when the Second Hague Conference ended, "our delegates will not be found to have voted or spoken as reactionaries," stressing that "nothing could be more damaging to our influence as a Liberal Power" than to permit "the destruction of innocent merchant ships."[19] Nor did liberal businessmen lack the courage of their convictions. In the course of a discussion at the National Liberal Club in 1909, Sir John Brunner adopted a high moral posture in replying to Julian Corbett's suggestion that England ought not to rely for her safety on a mere treaty guaranteeing immunity: "Speaking as a man of business," Brunner declared, "I would rather have the protection of the public law of the world than the protection of our own Navy," for no nation would dare to break "a law adopted by the world."[20]

The readiness of the admiralty to support the Declaration of London, even though it would seriously inhibit the Navy's planned strategy, has puzzled historians.[21] Fisher believed that a decisive naval duel could be managed and won, and given the readiness of the Liberals to increase the size of the battle fleet, there was no reason to deny what was politically important to them. But more significantly, many naval officers as well as ministers presiding over the admiralty saw the agreements of London and Paris as mere words to be abandoned if Britain became a belligerent. Nor was the Hankey–McKenna episode of 1911 an isolated incident.[22] Was the naval ultra like Hankey who wished to repudiate these treaties, or someone like Ottley or McKenna who performed lip-service to them while intending to throw them overboard in war closer to the ideal-type reactionary?

The charge of "navalism" made by German propagandists during the war was probably justified. Julian Corbett's 1915 defense of England and his eulogy of Britain's use of its naval supremacy were plausible, and even persuasive, but the admiralty was no more ready to be seriously hampered by the laws of war than was the German army or U-boat squadrons.[23] In 1914, the Fabian playwright Bernard Shaw shocked British opinion by describing as "Junkers" the scions of the traditional governing classes who he believed retained control of the foreign office, the war office, and the admiralty. Shaw saw these landed gentlemen as being as much the relics of feudalism as their German counterparts.[24] This was an exaggeration, for we know that even in offices most directly concerned with power, the liberal ethos had had its effect. Yet there were "Junkers" in high places who determined, with the coming of war, to loosen the shackles that a progressive public opinion imposed, and, as they saw it, save a nation naively devoted to utopian principles and a short-sighted interest in mercantile profit.

The spokesmen for modern liberal society, rational and pacifist, were concerned with wealth and welfare and shunned the making of a strategy based on immoral force. The economic ideal of this liberalism was a free and harmonious international division of labor and its political goal a cosmopolitan republic. The traditional governing classes, on the other hand, could not believe that modern circumstances or liberal moralizing would destroy envy and the wish to predominate. They sensed that although liberals from Jeremy Bentham and Richard Cobden to Norman Angell were quite likely correct in arguing that advanced nations would lose economically by waging war against each other, irrational aggressive sentiments would, as always, produce violent conflicts.

What helped to make liberals opponents of strategy may have been a false analogy between economic interest and power. The earlier mercantilists had understood the international competition both for wealth and for power as zero-sum games in which one nation might profit only by another's loss. But the coming of the new industry proved the possibility of increasing absolutely and many-fold the wealth to be shared. On the other hand, since power is the ability to make others conduct their affairs as you would wish them to, one nation can only gain when another loses. Power remains a zero-sum game. One can speak only of being relatively more powerful than another, and, less certainly, by how great a factor. The pursuit of power, moreover, is continuous, and given its ever-changing components a perfectly-balanced world of stable power relations is remote if not unattainable.[25]

Industrial society rejected many of the values of traditional society to which the landed and military classes were still to some extent loyal. The landed classes were certainly more easily roused to patriotic self-assertion. But heroism, moral as well as physical, and honor, not uncommon motives in traditional society, had little place in one founded on the precept that all good would come from the increase of wealth. John Stuart Mill, in wishing to use English power to defend the liberty of the repressed nations of the continent, found a bourgeois England not prepared for such a sacrifice: if pre-industrial society was too profligate with life, Mill complained, modern society tended to value it too highly.[26]

Wars not only dislocated and distorted economic life, they revived primitive emotions that modern civilization wished to suppress. To speak of war as a likely event was personally threatening, as well as a threat to civilization. Freud wrote of a cultural super-ego, a conscience whose ethical prescriptions were "a therapeutic attempt" to rid mankind of "the greatest hindrance to civilization – namely, the constitutional inclination of human beings to be aggressive towards one another." This conscience made the impossible demand that we love our neighbors as ourselves, and "admonishes us that the harder it is to obey the precept the more meritorious it is to do so." But Freud warned that one who follows this rule "only puts himself at a disadvantage *vis-à-vis* the person who disregards it," and one may have only "the narcissistic satisfaction of being able to think oneself better than others." He conjectured that cultural conflicts of this kind might well produce a neurotic civilization.[27] Ideology, interest, and power appear in a perpetual tug-of-war. Actions take place half-heartedly, doomed to failure from the start; and often, no action can be taken.

Liberalism and democracy versus strategy

In 1871, with a stereotypically-liberal Gladstone in office, John Stuart Mill wrote to Cliffe Leslie on the threat liberalism posed for national survival. The Franco-Prussian War seems to have defeated Leslie's earlier optimism, and the Irish economist had come to believe that something like the Swiss system of military training and conscription was now necessary for England. Mill agreed, but he observed that given the prejudices of the public, it would be "an uphill fight" to achieve this. The liberal philosopher denounced as "smitten with imbecility" those who believed Britain could defend her shores or realize her national objectives without well-prepared armed forces.[28] Mill also dismissed the Radical illusions of the death of nationalist feelings or the imminence of world government.[29] He saw such misconceptions as among the defects of the liberal outlook. In a letter later that year to another Irish economist (and also a supporter of conscription) J. E. Cairnes,[30] Mill expressed his "contempt" for England's military and naval weakness, and, noting other faults of the Liberals in office, declared that "I shall henceforth wish for a Tory Government."[31]

Although the naval policies of the pre-1914 Liberal government would probably not have gained Mill's wholehearted approval, he would have welcomed the thrust of a speech made in 1909 by the Liberal foreign secretary, Sir Edward Grey. Speaking to the Commons, Grey declared that England's "very existence would be at stake" were she to lose her naval superiority. There was no evidence for the Radical view that Germany would alter her naval program if England accepted immunity, and therefore England had no choice but to arm herself, despite the real danger that were such "preparations to kill each other" to increase, they would "sooner or later" doom civilization. But if England unilaterally "gave up the competition and sank into a position of inferiority," her "self respect is gone"; she would "fall into a state of apathy," and the spirit of "enterprise . . . essential both to the material success of industry" and to achieving "great ideals of social reform" would be no more. "We should cease to count for anything amongst the nations of Europe, and we should be fortunate if our liberty was left, and we did not become the conscript appendage of some stronger Power." "The martial spirit," Grey concluded, had a "proper place, in the life of a nation."[32]

But could a liberal and democratic public opinion be made to understand the harsh necessities of the world-wide struggle for power? In 1913, Captain Ottley saw "our Empire's destinies" as "now in the hands of the masses of the people"; "heavy sacrifices" by the taxpayers were necessary to maintain the fleet upon which the national security and welfare depended. "The moral factor," he noted, "in all cases and at every epoch dominates and controls the material."[33] The strategists Admiral Mahan and H.J. Mackinder agreed, though, less sanguinely, they feared that the democratic liberalism of the maritime, industrial societies was the enemy of any sound military or naval preparedness.

Admiral Mahan in 1910 saw England as fortunate in possessing "the popular tradition of the national need for a great Navy"; this provided "a steadying hand" in her politics. But he cautioned that this "conviction is less operative" now than formerly. The long peace had brought about "a practical disbelief in the possibility of war," and this had resulted in "insular democracies" like Britain and the United States being unduly optimistic concerning foreign dangers, and "lax and inefficient in preparation for war." England could maintain, proportionally, as large an army as that of Germany, but maritime democracies shunned military training and conscription, and preferred a navy in which "the mass of citizens are paying a body of men to do their fighting for them." The electorate even shied at the cost of the naval predominance so necessary to maintain Britain's defenses.[34]

H. J. Mackinder, in his 1919 study of "democratic ideas and reality," examined "the moral factor" after four years of war. There were two kinds of men, the geopolitician observed at this time – democratic idealists, and organizers: the idealists were cosmopolitans and internationalists while the organizers were patriots; the thinking of the organizer was "essentially strategical," while that of the "true democrat" was "ethical." The educated class of a landed and military Germany was indoctrinated with a "strategical mentality": this élite understood that Germany's geographical position made strong government as well as universal military training and conscription necessary to national survival. The "strategical German mind" knew how to organize not only armies but also the economy, and the latter not merely for profit but to increase national strength. In this, they were unlike the "honest

Cobdenites" of England who refused "to think strategically"; the Radicals considered only "principles," luxurious "habits of thought" that prospered "under the insular protection of Britain." This was why democracy was "incompatible with the organization necessary for war against autocracies," Mackinder concluded, in a melancholy confirmation of his earlier prediction that future global rule belonged to the landed, military powers of the Eurasian heartland.[35]

What averted a more complete abandonment of the advantages of Britain's maritime superiority during the time of the Pax may have been the survival of the pre-liberal ethos, the martial spirit which at critical moments subdued Radical challenges. The habit of deference to the old governing classes probably helped to provide popular support for what Lord Devlin called the reactionary position;[36] and it may also have been that much of the middle and working-class electorates had never been truly converted to the liberal cosmopolitanism of a commercial, maritime society. Therefore, despite the fears of Mill and Mahan and Mackinder, liberal nations – powerfully assisted by favorable geographical placement, demographic and economic superiority, and good fortune – managed in the course of two world conflicts to emerge victorious in struggles against continental despotisms. Given new forms of warfare, however, such advantages have diminished in importance.

We have seen that a liberal public opinion, in good part converted to the moral prescriptions of Kant and Cobden, thought first of principle – and of commercial profit – rather than of preparations for a possible, even probable war, or of a strategy by which such a war might be averted, or, if this failed, conducted. Though "panics" intermittently roused voters and parliaments, England continued to pursue courses whose chief recommendation was that they were relatively economical. In their rejection of power and preferred identification with powerlessness, British and American liberals were suspicious of a Pax based on naval predominance, and often pictured the Royal Navy as an obstacle to world peace. A foreign policy erected on what liberals believe a specious fear of an external opponent was the chief enemy of the social reform policies that promoted domestic tranquillity; for them, the principal threat to peace came from social conflicts within, not from aggressive and expansionist states abroad. Liberals rejected violent means on principle, and insisted that all actions by democratic states be subject to an exacting standard – of morality, international law, or approval by progressive opinion – even if barbarous or despotic governments conducted themselves without any such restraints. To an observer of present-day Anglo-American societies, it is startling to see how little has changed, even if details have altered.

Today, a still predominantly liberal public opinion understandably believes that present-day ultras, like their predecessors, are hardly reliable guides in foreign policy, particularly when the nuclear bomb serves as a warning that "success" might mean the end not only of material comforts, but of life itself. But while being properly cautious of extreme solutions, liberals appear as unwilling as ever to confront questions involving power and strategy. Democratic society, moreover, now seems less willing to see any transcendent meaning even in the liberty which was its early ideal. Though the naive Cobdenism of the past has largely dissolved, it has been replaced by a political cynicism – not always without a basis in fact – whose exaggerations endanger the morale required by a free society. Many of today's radical-liberals denounce the West's "capitalist imperialism," a label that has taken the place reserved for feudalism by nineteenth-century Radicals, and not unlike the Radicals of the Pax Britannica who saw steel and armaments manufacturers in a selfish alliance with generals and admirals, they at times seem to see their country's "military-industrial complex" as their principal enemy; again like their Radical predecessors, and despite recent experience with Hitler's Germany or Stalin's Russia, they scoff at the existence of rogue empires – whose bona fides they too readily accept – as exploded fallacies invoked by bellicose interests.

Liberals are increasingly turning to the passivity that Mill, Brooks Adams, and Schumpeter, found characteristic of their psychology, and the pacifism implicit in their creed. The historian Edward Gibbon placed the responsibility for the defeat of the civilization of the Roman world by the barbarians on an other-worldly Christianity. Is there a danger that present-day liberalism in Western Europe and America, continuing its long association with commerce, will in the coming decades play a similar role? No community can long survive profound disharmonies in its ideology, interests, and instruments of power. Under such stress, even if the democracies maintained their physical existence, free institutions would be seriously impaired, and their economic base, so much the consequence of these institutions and so important to social cohesion, undermined. But now, as earlier, liberalism is a field of contending ideas and emotions. A great deal depends on which of the rival conceptions of the liberal ideal prevails, today as in the time of Mill and Grey.

Notes

Chapter 1: *Sea Power, Commerce, and Liberalism*

1 One such article by the Dutch-born H.W. Van Loon, later to become a well-known writer of popular history, appeared in late May 1915 in the *New York Times*, and was quickly brought to the cabinet's attention. The cabinet memorandum noted that "it would not be an exaggeration to say that 'British Navalism' ... is the strongest card in the German Propaganda game, because the daily events of the British Blockade offer a practical commentary on it, which can always be interpreted in an anti-British sense." See Public Record Office, CAB 37/130, no. 34, pp. 1, 7–8. [Cited hereafter as PRO.]

2 Julian S. Corbett, "The bugbear of British navalism", *New York Times*, 25 May 1915, 14: 7–8; reprinted as *The Spectre of Navalism* (London, 1915).

3 Thucydides, *The Complete Writings of Thucydides* (New York, 1951), especially pp. 40–50.

4 See J. W. Konvitz, *Cities and the Sea* (Baltimore, 1978), especially pp. 74–8, 123–4.

5 See discussion in Elie Halévy, *England in 1815* (New York, 1949), pp. 45–67.

6 F. List, *The National System of Political Economy* (London, 1885; first published, 1841), pp. 108–9.

7 A. T. Mahan, *The Influence of Sea Power Upon History, 1660–1783* (New York, 1957; first published, 1890), pp. 45–6, and 43–77 *passim.*

8 List, *National System of Political Economy*, pp. 46–7.

9 Mahan, *Influence of Sea Power*, especially pp. xi–xiii, 11–21.

10 Brooks Adams, *America's Economic Supremacy* (New York, 1900), pp. 68, 190–2; see also pp. 60–1, 142–9.

11 H. J. Mackinder, "The geographical pivot of history" (1904), in *Democratic Ideals and Reality* (New York, 1962), pp. 256–62.

12 Norman Angell, *The Great Illusion; A Study of the Relation of Military Power to National Advantage* (New York, 1913; first published, 1909), p. 71, and *passim.* See H. S. Weinroth, "Norman Angell and the 'Great Illusion'; an episode in pre-1914 pacifism", *Historical Journal*, vol. 17 (1974), pp. 551–74.

13 William James, "The moral equivalent of war" (1910), in R. A. Wasserstrom (ed.), *War and Morality* (Belmont, Calif., 1970), p. 5.

14 Brooks Adams, "War as the ultimate form of economic competition", *Proceedings of the US Naval Institute*, vol. 29 (1903), pp. 829–81.

15 I. Kant, "Idea for a universal history with a cosmopolitan purpose" (1784), *Kant's Political Writings*, ed. H. Reiss (Cambridge, 1970), pp. 44, 46, 50–1. For useful discussions of Kant's theory of international relations, see F. H. Hinsley, *Power and the Pursuit of Peace; Theory and Practice in the History of Relations Between States* (Cambridge, 1963), pp. 62–80; and W. B. Gallie, *Philosophers of Peace and War; Kant, Clausewitz, Marx, Engels, and Tolstoy* (Cambridge, 1978), pp. 8–36.

16 I. Kant, "On the common saying: 'This may be true in theory, but it does not apply in practice'" (1793), *Kant's Political Writings*, pp. 90–2.

17 I. Kant, "Perpetual peace: a philosophical sketch" (1795), ibid., pp. 94–6, 99–100, 103, 106–7. Kant (no doubt with some assistance from David Hume) pre-

figured a later Keynesianism when he suggested that the "ingenious" British funding of the national debt provided a military treasury whose payment might be postponed for a long time "by the commercial stimulus which industry and trade receive through the credit system" (p. 95).

18 I. Kant, "The metaphysics of morals" (1797), ibid., p. 174.

19 I. Kant, "The contest of faculties" (1778), ibid., pp. 188–9, 183; and "Perpetual peace", ibid., p. 114.

20 Richard Cobden, *England, Ireland, and America* (Edinburgh, 1836), p. 11.

21 Leoni Levi, *War and Its Consequences: Economical, Commercial, Financial, and Moral* (London, 1881), p. 35. The English social theorist Herbert Spencer was also to describe the traditional society as "militant," in contrast to the "industrial" society of nineteenth-century England. (See below.) See also Adam Ferguson, *An Essay on the History of Civil Society* (Philadelphia, 1819; first published, 1767), pp. 385–418; Benjamin Constant, *L'Esprit de conquête* (Paris, 1918; first published, 1814), pp. 11–15; Auguste Comte, *The Positive Philosophy of Auguste Comte*, ed. Harriet Martineau, Vol. 2 (London, 1875), p. 144; and Ferdinand Tönnies, *Community and Society* (New York 1963; first published, 1887), especially pp. 33–102, 211–18.

22 W. E. H. Lecky, *History of the Rise and Influence of the Spirit of Rationalism in Europe*, Vol. 2 (New York, 1893; first published, 1865), pp. 219–20.

23 H. T. Buckle, *History of Civilization in England*, Vol. 1 (London, 1871; first published, 1857), pp. 190–3, 198. See also Bernard Semmel, "H. T. Buckle: the liberal faith and the science of history", *The British Journal of Sociology*, vol. 27, no. 3 (September 1976), pp. 370–86.

24 Otto Hintze, "Military organization and state organization", *The Historical Essays of Otto Hintze*, ed. F. Gilbert (New York, 1975), pp. 182–3, 214–15.

25 *The Times*, 24 January 1900, 7 b, c.

26 P. Muret, *La prépondérance anglaise, 1714–1763* (Paris, 1937).

27 See, for example, *Parliamentary Debates*, House of Commons, 3rd series, vol. 53 (7 April 1840), pp. 670–2, 703–4; also ibid., 8 April 1840, pp. 816–19. [Cited hereafter as *PD*, HC.]

28 For the term "Schumpeter," covering the three Kondratieffs: H. A. Innis' review of J. A. Schumpeter, *Business Cycles*, in *The Canadian Journal of Economics and Political Science* (1940), pp. 91–2.

29 See J. A. Schumpeter, *Business Cycles; a Theoretical, Historical, and Statistical Analysis of the Capitalist Process* (New York, 1939), especially Vol. 1, pp. 220–448, 692–731. See also J. A. Schumpeter, *Capitalism, Socialism and Democracy* (New York, 1947), especially pp. 111–16. Among more recent work on the relationship of economic cycles (principally the Kondratieff) and politics are Raimo Väyrynen, "Economic cycles, power transitions, political management and wars between major powers", *International Studies Quarterly*, vol. 27 (December 1983), pp. 389–418; and George Modelski, "Long cycles, Kondratieffs, and alternating innovations: implications for US foreign policy", in C. W. Kegley and P. McGowan (eds), *The Political Economy of Foreign Policy Behavior* (Beverly Hills, 1981). See also W. W. Rostow, "Kondratieff, Schumpeter, and Kuznets: trend periods revisited", *Journal of Economic History*, vol. 35, no. 4 (December 1975), pp. 719–53, especially p. 753 n.

30 Schumpeter, *Business Cycles*, Vol. 1, p. 312; see also J. A. Schumpeter, *Imperialism and Social Classes* (New York, 1951), especially pp. 9–30, 83–130.

31 Carl von Clausewitz, *On War*, eds M. Howard and P. Paret (Princeton, NJ, 1976), p. 75.

32 See also the discussion in Michael Howard, "The forgotten dimensions of strategy", *Foreign Affairs*, vol. 57, no. 5 (Summer 1979), pp. 975–86.

Chapter 2: *The Fierce Trident*

1 Hugo Grotius, *The Freedom of the Seas or the Right Which Belongs to the Dutch to Take Part in the East Indies Trade* (New York, 1916), pp. 3–5, 61, 70, 74–6.
2 *The Duke of Newcastle's Letter by His Majesty's Order, to Monsieur Michell, the King of Prussia's Secretary of the Embassy* (London, 1753). A penned notation in the British Library's copy of the pamphlet reads: "This able and Masterly Report was drawn by Mr. Murray the then Sollr General (now Earl Mansfield) and was justly admired by every State in Europe. See Montesquieu's Letters 5 March 1753 & Vattels Droit des Gens lib. 2, C. 7 & 84." The notation was initialed (though it is difficult to decipher whose initials they were) and dated 1779.
3 ibid., pp. 10, 15–16, 37.
4 ibid., pp. 4–5, 11, 13.
5 [Charles Jenkinson], Earl of Liverpool, *A Discourse on the Conduct of the Government of Great Britain in Respect to Neutral Nations* (London, 1801; first published, 1757), pp. 107, 10, 16, 108.
6 *Parliamentary History of England from the Earliest Period to the Year 1803*, 1 June 1780, vol. 21, pp. 632–4, 636–7. [Cited hereafter as *PH*.]
7 ibid., vol. 21, p. 650. The Earl of Mansfield commended Camden's views, but none the less opposed Shelburne's motion of censure (p. 654).
8 ibid., pp. 645, 647–8.
9 ibid., p. 654.
10 ibid., p. 653.
11 *PH*, 20 March 1801, vol. 35, pp. 1198–9.
12 *PH*, 2 February 1801, vol. 35, p. 886.
13 *PH*, 20 March 1801, vol. 35, p. 1199.
14 *PH*, 25 March 1801, vol. 35, p. 1062.
15 ibid., pp. 1127–8.
16 ibid., pp. 1138–9, 1134.
17 ibid., p. 1167.
18 Robert Ward, *An Enquiry into the Foundation and History of the Law of Nations in Europe, from the Time of the Greeks and Romans, to the Age of Grotius* (London, 1795), 2 vols. Curiously, there is no discussion of maritime law in these volumes.
19 See Hon. Edmund Phipps, *Memoirs of the Political and Literary Life of Robert Plumer Ward, Esq.*, Vol. 1 (London, 1850), p. 47, and *passim*.
20 Robert Ward, *A Treatise on the Relative Rights and Duties of Belligerent and Neutral Powers in Maritime Affairs: On Which the Principles of Armed Neutralities, and the Opinions of Hübner and Schlegel Are Fully Discussed* (London, 1801), pp. ix, xiii–xiv, 7, 18, 21, 172, viii–ix.
21 *PH*, 13 November 1801, vol. 36, p. 193.
22 ibid., pp. 201, 229–30, 255, 245.
23 ibid., pp. 271, 277.
24 ibid., p. 280.
25 ibid., p. 196.
26 ibid., pp. 256, 258–9.
27 ibid., p. 198.
28 ibid., p. 262.
29 ibid., p. 260.

30 [Henry Brougham], "On the speech of James Stephen in the House of Commons March 6th 1809", *Edinburgh Review*, vol. 14, no. 28 (July 1809), pp. 447–8.
31 Lord Brougham, *The Life and Times of Henry Lord Brougham*, Vol. 2 (Edinburgh, 1871), p. 290.
32 [James Stephen], *War in Disguise; or, the Frauds of the Neutral Flags* (London, 1806; first published, 1805), pp. 4, 7–9.
33 ibid., pp. 125–6, 41, 70, 99, 153–5.
34 ibid., pp. 172–3, 196–7.
35 ibid., pp. 196–7, 181.
36 [Gouverneur Morris], *An Answer to "War in Disguise"; or, Remarks upon the New Doctrine of England, concerning Neutral Trade* (New York, 1806), pp. 9, 67–8.
37 [James Madison], *An Examination of the British Doctrine Which Subjects to Capture A Neutral Trade Not Open in Time of Peace* (London, 1806), pp. 167–9, 4–5, 192.
38 [James Stephen], *The Dangers of the Country* (London, 1807), pp. 81, 79, 84–6.
39 *The Speech of Henry Brougham, Esq. Before the House of Commons, Friday, April 1, 1808, in Support of the Petitions from London, Liverpool and Manchester, Against the Orders in Council* (London, 1808), pp. 80–1, 32, 69. See Bradford Perkins, *Prologue to War; England and the United States, 1805–1812* (Berkeley, 1961), especially chapter 5; and G. J. Marcus, *The Age of Nelson* (London, 1971), *passim.*
40 *PD*, HC, 6 February 1809, vol. 12, p. 376.
41 *Parliamentary Debates*, House of Lords, 17 February 1809, vol. 12, pp. 780–1, 773, 774. [Cited hereafter as *PD*, HL.]
42 *PD*, HC, 6 March 1809, vol. 12, pp. 1163, 1167, 1169, 1174, 1181.
43 ibid., p. 1194.
44 ibid., p. 1201.
45 ibid., pp. 1203–4.
46 ibid., pp. 1187–8, 1190.
47 *PD*, HL, 17 February 1809, vol. 12, pp. 794–5.
48 Joseph Phillimore, *Reflections on the Nature and Extent of the License Trade* (London, 1811), pp. ii, 58.
49 Joseph Phillimore, *A Letter Addressed to the House of Commons on the Subject of the Notice Given by Mr. Brougham for a Motion Respecting the Orders-in-Council and the License Trade* (London, 1812), pp. 9, 66–7.
50 *The Speech of Henry Brougham, Esq. M.P. in the House of Commons, on Tuesday, the 16th of June 1812, Upon the Present State of Commerce and Manufactures* (London, 1812), pp. 39–41, 43–5, 55.
51 *PD*, HC, 16 June 1812, vol. 23, pp. 531–3, 536–7.
52 ibid., pp. 542–4.
53 ibid., p. 547.
54 ibid., pp. 538–42.
55 Brougham, *Life and Times*, Vol. 2, pp. 11–14.
56 *PD*, HC, 16 June 1812, vol. 23, pp. 546.
57 ibid., p. 548.

Chapter 3: *Christianity, Liberalism, and the Trident*

1 James Stephen to Lord Grenville, 5 May 1806, Grenville Correspondence, British Library, Add. Mss. 58,998, f.37; also 3 September 1806, ff.124, 127–31. [Cited hereafter as BL.] See also [James Stephen], "Letter on the slave trade", *Edinburgh Review*, vol. 7 (July 1806).

2 Stephen to Spencer Perceval, 19 October 1807, Spencer Perceval Papers, BL, Add. Mss. 49,183, f.5.
3 Stephen to Perceval, 13 November 1807, Spencer Perceval Papers, BL, Add. Mss. 49,183.
4 Quoted in Christopher Lloyd, *The Navy and the Slave Trade; the Suppression of the African Slave Trade in the Nineteenth Century* (London, 1968), p. 44.
5 [Henry Brougham], "Foreign slave trade", *Edinburgh Review*, vol. 36 (October 1821), pp. 41, 51, 49.
6 Quoted in H. G. Soulsby, *The Right of Search and the Slave Trade in Anglo-American Relations, 1814–1862* (Baltimore, 1933), pp. 17, 18, 31–2.
7 For details of the efforts to end the slave trade, see Soulsby, *Right of Search and the Slave Trade*, and W. E. B. Du Bois, *The Suppression of the African Slave Trade to the United States, 1638–1870* (New York, 1965).
8 [African Institution], *The Foreign Slave Trade, A Brief Account of Its State*, Vol. 1 (London, 1837), pp. 50–1, 58, 60–1.
9 T. F. Buxton to Lord Palmerston, 29 May 1837, Broadlands Papers, Papers and Correspondence of Palmerston, Historical Manuscripts Commission [cited hereafter as HMC], SLT/8.
10 [African Institution], *The Foreign Slave Trade*, Vol. 2 (London, 1838), pp. 43–4.
11 Stephen to Grenville, n.d. 1807, Grenville Correspondence, BL, Add. Mss. 58,998, f.161.
12 Stephen to Perceval, 2 December 1807, Spencer Perceval Papers, BL, Add. Mss. 59,183.
13 *Lord Brougham's Speech in the House of Lords, Monday, January 29, 1838, Upon the Slave Trade* (London, 1838), pp. 20–1.
14 *PD*, HL, 29 January 1838, 3rd series, vol. 40, pp. 613–14.
15 ibid., p. 614.
16 Remarks, 13 February 1838, Broadlands Papers, Papers and Correspondence of Palmerston, HMC, SLT/12.
17 *PD*, HC, 8 March 1839, 3rd series, vol. 46, pp. 145–6.
18 *PD*, HC, 10 May, 1838, 3rd series, vol. 42, pp. 1136, 1134.
19 ibid., p. 1138.
20 ibid., p. 1142.
21 *PD*, HL, 26 July 1839, 3rd series, vol. 49, p. 1058.
22 ibid., pp. 1065, 1067.
23 ibid., pp. 1068, 1071.
24 ibid., pp. 1073–4.
25 *PD*, HL, 2 August 1839, 3rd series, vol. 49, pp. 1128–9.
26 ibid., pp. 1133–4.
27 ibid., p. 1130.
28 ibid., pp. 1131–2, 1135.
29 ibid., pp. 1137–8.
30 *PD*, HL, 15 August 1839, 3rd series, vol. 50, p. 310.
31 ibid., p. 327.
32 ibid., pp. 313, 322.
33 ibid., pp. 334–5, 336.
34 *PD*, HC, 8 August 1839, vol. 50, pp. 125, 127.
35 *PD*, HC, 9 August 1839, vol. 50, pp. 157–8.
36 *PD*, HC, 24 July 1845, 3rd series, vol. 82, pp. 1047, 1049–50. With the coming of free trade in 1846, discriminatory tariffs against slave-grown produce were abolished, but the philanthropists continued to press for their re-instatement. Brougham, for example, urged in 1855 the end of "our unhappy policy [of] nine

years ago when, by a gross perversion of the doctrines of free trade, we resolved to obtain cheap sugar at the heavier cost of piracy, and torture, and blood." *Lord Brougham's Speech Upon the Slave Trade. House of Lords, 26th June 1855* (London, 1855), pp. 6–7.

37 *PD*, HC, 24 July 1845, 3rd series, vol. 82, p. 1058.

38 ibid., pp. 1066–70.

39 ibid., p. 1074. Palmerston's defense of the bill included an ingenuous reply to the Radical charge that Englishmen would not yield to such exactions by a foreign power; he observed that "I have such an opinion of the honour of this country, that I know we should submit to any inconvenience, however galling to the national pride, if bound by treaty to do so"! See ibid., p. 1059.

40 *PD*, HC, 31 July 1845, 3rd series, vol. 82, pp. 1290, 1293.

41 *The Times*, 26 July 1845, 5 b, c, d.

42 Palmerston's reply to an Anti-Slavery Society Address, 18 October 1842, Broadlands Papers, Papers and Correspondence of Palmerston, HMC, SLT/19.

43 Palmerston, Private Memorandum, n.d. [1845?], ibid., SLT/26.

44 Quoted in Leslie Bethell, *The Abolition of the Brazilian Slave Trade; Britain, Brazil and the Slave Trade Question, 1807–1869* (Cambridge, 1970), pp. 153–5.

45 *PD*, HC, 24 June 1845, 3rd Series, vol. 81, pp. 1156, 1158, 1171–2.

46 ibid., pp. 1175–6.

47 *Twelfth Report of the Directors of the African Institution* (London, 1819), p. 11.

48 *Thirteenth Report of the Directors of the African Institution* (London, 1820), p. 11.

49 [James Stephen], *The Speech of James Stephen, Esq. at the Annual Meeting of the African Institution, 26 March, 1817* (London, 1817), p. 86; see also pp. 32–46, 55. Indeed, Stephen observed, "the man who gains a thousand pounds in that trade, will be a more effectual benefactor to the African people, than if he had charitably subscribed a hundred thousand for their instruction in the arts and sciences or any other direct means of their improvement." On this occasion, Stephen was also obliged to defend himself against the charge that he had procured a job in the colonial office for his son. This son, later Sir James Stephen, was to pursue the Institution's philanthropic purposes as under-secretary for colonies in the 1830s and 1840s.

50 T. F. Buxton, *The African Slave Trade and Its Remedy* (London, 1968; first published, 1840), pp. 518, 284, 529.

51 *PD*, HC, 16 July 1844, 3rd series, vol. 76, pp. 957–8, 966.

52 *PD*, HL, 25 July 1844, 3rd series, vol. 76, p. 1379.

53 ibid., p. 1382.

54 Buxton, *African Slave Trade*, pp. 283, 285–6.

55 *PD*, HC, 16 July 1844, 3rd series, vol. 76, pp. 942–5.

56 ibid., p. 960.

57 *PD*, HC, 24 June 1845, 3rd series, vol. 81, pp. 1172–4.

58 ibid., p. 1181.

59 Hon. Captain Denman, R.N., *The African Squadron and Mr. Hutt's Committee* (London, n.d.), pp. 9, 57. Denman urged America to declare the slave trade piracy, for if England did this on her own the world would see the act as "an insidious attempt on the liberty of the seas" (p. 68).

60 Commander H. J. Matson, R.N., *Remarks on the Slave Trade and African Squadron* (London, 1848), pp. 1–2.

61 Lt. Henry Yule, *The African Squadron Vindicated* (London, 1850), p. 30. Other authorities endorsed the view of the naval officers and the philanthropists, from a variety of perspectives. See, for example, James Richardson, *The Cruisers: Being a Letter to the Marquess of Lansdowne, Lord President, &c., &c., &c., in Defence of Armed*

Coercion for the Extinction of the Slave Trade (London, 1849). Richardson, an African explorer, noted the "inexhaustible resources" of Africa, to which Britain's naval Squadron gave her access, concluding, in quite another strain, that England must end the slave trade to make reparations for the "uncompensated, unrequited toil of Africans" which had "maintained for us a colonial empire during two centuries." See pp. 6–7, 18–23, 31, 36–8. A missionary to Africa wrote of the necessity of the Squadron to Christian missions on the coast which he thought vital to the undermining of the slave trade; see Rev. J. L. Wilson, *The British Squadron on the Coast of Africa* (London, 1851), pp. 26, 28, 31. See also the well-argued tract in defense of the in-shore system by a Middle Temple barrister, J. S. Middleton, *Remarks on the African Squadron* (London, 1851), pp. 6, 11, 15, 20–2.

62 Richardson, *The Cruisers*, p. 5. See also *The Times*, 4 March 1845, 5 f, and 8 August 1845, 7 f.

63 [British and Foreign Anti-Slavery Society], *The Slave Trade and Its Remedy* (London, 1848), p. 2.

64 Quoted in Soulsby, *Right of Search and the Slave Trade*, pp. 67–8.

65 Quoted in W. B. Lawrence, *Visitation and Search; or An Historical Sketch of the British Claim to Exercise a Maritime Police Over the Vessels of All Nations in Peace as Well as in War* (Boston, 1858), pp. 78–9.

66 An American [Lewis Cass], *An Examination of the Question Now in Discussion Between the American and British Governments, Concerning the Right of Search* (n.p., 1842), pp. 10, 21, 8, 75–6.

67 *PD*, HC, 2 February 1843, 3rd series, vol. 66, pp. 88–9, 91.

68 *PD*, HC, 3 April 1843, 3rd series, vol. 68, pp. 324–7.

69 Alexis de Tocqueville, *Oeuvres Complètes*, ed. G. de Beaumont, Vol. 9 (Paris, 1864–6), pp. 389–90, 399.

70 *PD*, HL, 2 February 1843, 3rd Series, vol. 66, pp. 40–1.

71 Tocqueville to Mill, 9 February 1843, in Alexis de Tocqueville, *Oeuvres Complètes*, ed. J.-P. Mayer, Vol. 6, pt. 1 (Paris, 1851), p. 339.

72 Tocqueville to Brougham [March 1843], ibid., pp. 341–2.

73 See Mill to Tocqueville, 20 February 1843, ibid., p. 340.

74 Tocqueville to Mill, 12 March 1843, ibid., pp. 343–4.

75 J. S. Mill to Gustave d'Eichthal, 12 November 1839, *Collected Works of John Stuart Mill*, Vol. 13, pp. 412–13.

76 Mill to W. E. Hickson, 16 May 1849, *Collected Works*, Vol. 14, p. 24.

77 See Mill to Louis Blanc, 2 December 1865, *Collected Works*, Vol. 16, pp. 1123–4.

78 Americanus, *Comments on Lord Brougham's Attack upon General Cass* (Harrisburg, Pa, 1843), pp. 8, 11, 13.

79 *PD*, HC, 14 July 1857, 3rd series, vol. 146, pp. 1493–5.

80 Quoted in Soulsby, *Right of Search and the Slave Trade*, p. 162; see also *PD*, HC, 17 June 1858, 3rd series, vol. 150, pp. 2207–8.

81 In his memoirs, Malmesbury was to recall having told the Brazilian minister in 1852 that Palmerston "in his zeal to destroy slavery" had taken "a high handed line" in compelling Brazil "to submit to a right of search in her own waters." Malmesbury had clearly forgotten that Peel's Tory government had passed the Brazil Act in 1845! Earl of Malmesbury, *Memoirs of an Ex-Minister; An Autobiography*, Vol. 1 (London, 1884), p. 358.

82 Quoted in Soulsby, *Right of Search and the Slave Trade*, p. 16.

83 *PD*, HL, 26 July 1858, 3rd series, vol. 151, pp. 2087–8.

84 ibid., pp. 2079–80.

85 Quoted in Soulsby, *Right of Search and the Slave Trade*, p. 166.

86 *PD*, HC, 18 June 1858, 3rd series, vol. 151, pp. 52, 53–4.

87 *PD*, HL, 17 June 1858, 3rd series, vol. 150, pp. 2200–1, 2203–4.
88 *PD*, HC, 18 June 1858, 3rd series, vol. 151, pp. 50–1.
89 *PD*, HC, 12 July 1858, 3rd series, vol. 151, p. 1321.
90 *PD*, HC, 18 June 1858, 3rd series, vol. 151, p. 47–8.
91 ibid., pp. 41–2.
92 *PD*, HC, 12 July 1858, 3rd series, vol. 151, p. 1287.
93 ibid., p. 1311.
94 ibid., p. 1342.
95 ibid., pp. 1344–5.
96 ibid., pp. 1295, 1327. Admiral Napier recommended an even larger number of steamers for the Squadron, and hoped that in the future there would be no call "to apologize for every trifling excess of duty on the part of English captains."
97 ibid., p. 1334.
98 ibid., p. 1328.
99 ibid., pp. 1349–51.
100 ibid., pp. 1345–6.
101 Lawrence, *Visitation and Search*, pp. 3–4.
102 Quoted in ibid., pp. 191–2.

Chapter 4: *The Maritime Revolution*

1 Jeremy Bentham, *Plan for a Universal and Perpetual Peace* (London, 1927; first written *c.* 1789), pp. 11–12, 25–6, 18–21, 28, 37–9. See Hinsley, *Power and the Pursuit of Peace*, pp. 81–91.
2 Quoted in Leoni Levi, *The History of British Commerce* (London, 1880), pp. 294–5.
3 See Bernard Semmel, *The Rise of Free Trade Imperialism; Classical Political Economy, the Empire of Free Trade, and Imperialism 1750–1850* (Cambridge, 1970), *passim.*
4 See, for example, J. S. Mill, "De Tocqueville on democracy in America" (1840), *Collected Works*, Vol. 18, especially pp. 196–200.
5 *PD*, HC, 15 March 1838, 3rd series, vol. 41, p. 140.
6 *PD*, HC, 1 April 1840, 3rd series, vol. 53, pp. 383–4.
7 *PD*, HC, 9 June 1848, 3rd series, vol. 99, p. 646.
8 Quoted in Levi, *History of British Commerce*, p. 1030. *The Times*, on the other hand, saw repeal as the way England might "gain and secure for herself that naval pre-eminence which Nature undoubtedly intended." *The Times*, 10 June 1848, 5 d, e; see also 2 June 1848, 5 a, b, and 3 June 1848, 5 b, c.
9 Adam Smith, *The Wealth of Nations* (New York, 1965; first published, 1776), p. 431.
10 *PD*, HL, 7 May 1849, 3rd series, vol. 104. See discussion in Semmel, *Rise of Free Trade Imperialism*, pp. 198–201; also J. H. Clapham, "The last years of the Navigation Acts" (1910), in *Essays in Economic History*, Vol. 3, ed. E. M. Carus-Wilson (London, 1963), pp. 163–5, 178, and *passim.*
11 For the quotation and details of the commercial regulations during the Crimean War, see O. Anderson, *A Liberal State at War; English Politics and Economics during the Crimean War* (London, 1967), pp. 16–18, 139–52, 248–74.
12 *PD*, HC, 17 March 1854, 3rd series, vol. 131, pp. 955, 957, 965; see also pp. 959–63.
13 ibid., pp. 971–2.
14 ibid., p. 973.
15 [Henry Reeve], "The orders in council on trade during war", *Edinburgh Review*, vol. 100, no. 203 (July 1854), pp. 193–5, 206, 216, 221–2.

16 *PD*, HC, 4 July 1854, 3rd series, vol. 134, pp. 1100–4, 1108, 1129.
17 ibid., p. 1138.
18 ibid., pp. 1094–5.
19 ibid., pp. 1133–4.
20 *PD*, HC, 20 February 1855, 3rd series, vol. 136, p. 1670.
21 Quoted in Sir Francis Piggott, *The Declaration of Paris, 1856* (London, 1919), pp. 29–35.
22 ibid., p. 35.
23 Quoted in Sir Herbert Richmond, *Sea Power in the Modern World* (London, 1919), p. 29; see also C. I. Hamilton, "Anglo-French seapower and the Declaration of Paris", *International History Review*, vol. 4, no. 2 (May 1982), pp. 182–6, 189; and Olive Anderson, "Some further light on the inner history of the Declaration of Paris", *Law Quarterly Review*, vol. 76 (1960), pp. 379–85.
24 Herbert Paul, *A History of Modern England*, Vol. 2 (New York, 1904), p. 13.
25 *PD*, HL, 22 May 1856, 3rd series, vol. 142, pp. 486–7.
26 ibid., pp. 503, 506.
27 ibid., pp. 508–10.
28 ibid., pp. 532, 533, 536–7, 539.
29 ibid., pp. 491, 494–6, 500–1.
30 ibid., pp. 507–8.
31 ibid., pp. 515–16.
32 ibid., pp. 544–5.
33 ibid., p. 547.
34 ibid., pp. 516–17.
35 ibid., pp. 547–9.
36 *PD*, HC, 14 July 1857, 3rd series, vol. 146, p. 1490.
37 ibid., p. 1484.
38 ibid., p. 1492.
39 *PD*, HL, 6 February 1862, 3rd series, vol. 165, p. 115.
40 Richard Cobden, *Russia* (Edinburgh, 1836), *passim*.
41 For Urquhart and his activities, see Gertrude Robinson, *David Urquhart: Some Chapters in the Life of a Victorian Knight-Errant of Justice and Liberty* (Oxford, 1920), *passim*; Margaret Lamb, "The making of a Russophobe: David Urquhart – the formative years, 1825–1835", *International History Review*, vol. 3, no. 3 (July 1981), pp. 330–57; and Richard Shannon, "David Urquhart and the foreign affairs committees", in P. Hollis (ed.), *Pressure from Without in Early Victorian England* (London, 1974), pp. 239–61.
42 David Urquhart, *The Right of Search: Two Speeches by David Urquhart, January 20 and 27, 1862* (London, 1862), pp. 88–9, 40–1, 70–2, 54, 61, 76, 44–52; see also David Urquhart, *Naval Power Suppressed by the Maritime States* (London, 1874), pp. 13, 25, 29, and *passim*. In this, Urquhart described Russia's interest in abolishing the right of search as "the hidden spring of all the events of our epoch" (p. 15).
43 A Journeyman Shoemaker [A. Smith], *The Defences of England; Nine Letters* (London, 1862), pp. 3, 18–20.
44 Alexander Bain, *John Stuart Mill, a Criticism: With Personal Recollections* (London, 1882), p. 94.
45 J. S. Mill, "Grote's History of Greece", *Dissertations and Discussions; Political, Philosophical, and Historical*, Vol. 2 (London, 1859), pp. 531, 529–30.
46 J. S. Mill, "A few words on non-intervention" (1859), *Dissertations and Discussions*, Vol. 3 (London, 1867), pp. 153, 155–6, 170, 167, 175–7. See also J. S. Mill, "The Spanish question", *London and Westminster Review*, vol. 27 (July 1837), pp. 179–82.
47 Mill to J. G. Mawby, 17 March 1866, *Collected Works*, Vol. 16, p. 1153.

48 Mill to Mawby, 6 July 1866, ibid., Vol. 16, pp. 1181–2.
49 Mill to Mawby, 10 September 1866, ibid., Vol. 16, p. 1199.
50 *PD*, HC, 5 August 1867, 3rd series, Vol. 189, pp. 878–80.
51 ibid., pp. 878–80.
52 ibid., p. 880.
53 ibid., pp. 886–8, 889–90.
54 Marx to Dr Kugelmann, 11 May 1869, in Karl Marx, *Letters to Dr. Kugelmann* (London, n.d.), p. 90.
55 Karl Marx, *Secret Diplomatic History of the Eighteenth Century and the Story of the Life of Lord Palmerston* (London, 1969), pp. 214–15, and *passim*.
56 Marx to Kugelmann, 13 December 1870, in *Letters to Dr. Kugelmann*, p. 116 [wording amended after consulting original German].
57 *PD*, HC, 21 April 1871, 3rd series, vol. 205, pp. 1497–8.
58 ibid., p. 1479; see also pp. 1473, 1476–7.
59 ibid., p. 1501.
60 *PD*, HC, 13 April 1875, 3rd series, vol. 223, pp. 827–9.
61 ibid., pp. 837–8, 844.
62 ibid., pp. 857, 859, 860–1. In an earlier debate, Charles Buxton had suggested that were Britain to go to war "with some small Power," that power would immediately place its trade into neutral ships "while our ships in all parts of the globe would be in the utmost peril of capture"! See *PD*, HC, 2 March 1866, 3rd series, vol. 181, CLXXXI, p. 1439.
63 *PD*, HC, 2 March 1877, 3rd series, vol. 232, pp. 1269–70. Wyndham paid tribute to "Mr Mill – than whom hon. Members opposite would admit there had not been a greater authority in that house" (p. 1275).
64 ibid., pp. 1314–15.
65 ibid., p. 1285.
66 ibid., p. 1296.
67 ibid., p. 1311.
68 ibid., p. 1320.
69 ibid., pp. 1289–90.

Chapter 5: *The Cobdenite Conscience: National War and Commercial Peace*

1 J.-J. Rousseau, *The Social Contract and Discourses* (London, 1946), p. 9.
2 James Mill, *Essays on Government, etc.* (London [1828]), pp. 24–5, 27–33.
3 J.S. Mill, "Civilization" (1836), *Collected Works*, Vol. 18, pp. 130, 125–6, 129–31.
4 See Auguste Comte, *The Positive Philosophy*, Vol. 2, pp. 2–4, 11–15, 17, and *passim*. For a discussion of the relationship between liberalism and Dissent, see Bernard Semmel, *The Methodist Revolution* (New York, 1973); for relationship between religious and secular pacifism, see Peter Brock, *Pacifism in Europe to 1914* (Princeton, NJ, 1972), especially pp. 367–406.
5 See the discussion in Sigmund Freud, "An autobiographical study" (1925), and "Postscript" (1935), *Complete Psychological Works*, Vol. 20, ed. J. Strachey (London, 1962), pp. 72, 59.
6 Sigmund Freud, "Civilization and its discontents" (1930), *Complete Psychological Works*, Vol. 21, pp. 125–6.
7 See, for example, Goldwin Smith to C. E. Norton, 18 October, 1865, Goldwin Smith Papers, Cornell University; and discussion in Bernard Semmel, *Jamaican Blood and Victorian Conscience* (Boston, 1963), pp. 61–62, and *passim*.

8 See discussion in Alma Latifi, *Effects of War on Property; Being Studies in International Law and Policy* (London, 1909), pp. 4–5, 118–21, and *passim*.

9 John Bright, *The Letter of John Bright, Esq., M.P., on the War; to Absalom Watkin* (London, 1854), p. 2; see also John Coleman, *A Reply to Mr. Bright's Letter on the War* (London, 1855), pp. 1–2, 6–7, 15, 169–70, 184, and *passim*. English merchants knew, Coleman declared, that it was by the "memorable victories our fleets have gained that the ocean is laid open like a peaceful lake for the transit of their countless argosies."

10 *PD*, HC, 4 July 1854, 3rd series, vol. 134, p. 1129.

11 T. E. Cliffe Leslie, "Marine captures and commercial blockades", *Journal of the Dublin Statistical Society*, July 1855, vol. 1, pp. 105, 101, and *passim*. Leslie argued further that England must never break the commercial ties connecting her with "the peaceful subjects even of hostile and despotic states" like Russia; for only by linking the tzar's empire to Western Europe by bonds of peaceful trade could Britain "hope to quench the lust of conquest, and belief in their destiny to overcome the world which animate the Russian people" (p. 105). See also Alfred Waddilove, "The effect of the recent orders in council in relation to English, Russian, and neutral commerce", *Journal of the Statistical Society of London*, 1855, vol. 18, pp. 21–33.

12 J. L. Ricardo, *The War Policy of Commerce* (London, 1855), pp. 10, 4, 12.

13 See W. H. Dawson, *Richard Cobden and Foreign Policy* (London, 1926), pp. 170–4.

14 Cf. Paul M. Kennedy, *The Rise and Fall of British Naval Mastery* (New York, 1976), p. 175.

15 R. Cobden, "A Letter to Henry Ashworth, Esq." (1862), in *The Political Writings of Richard Cobden*, Vol. 2 (London, 1903), pp. 392, 388–90.

16 *The Times*, 11 December 1856, 5 e.

17 Richard Cobden to W. S. Lindsay, 29 August 1856, quoted in W. S. Lindsay, *Manning the Royal Navy and Merchant Marine; also Belligerent and Neutral Rights in the Event of War* (London, 1877), p. 116.

18 *The Times*, 8 November 1856, 7 a, b. Parts of the address were quoted by T. B. Horsfall in the 1862 debate on immunity; see *PD*, HC, 11 March 1862, 3rd series, vol. 165, p. 1364.

19 *The Times*, 10 November 1856, 6 c.

20 Lord Brougham to Henry Reeve, 28 January 1862, in Sir J. K. Laughton, *Memoirs of the Life and Correspondence of Henry Reeve*, Vol. 2 (London, 1898), p. 78; see also Vol. 1, p. 394.

21 Cobden to Lindsay, 4 July 1857, quoted in Lindsay, *Manning the Royal Navy*, p. 120.

22 *PD*, HC, 14 July 1857, 3rd series, vol. 146, p. 1491. W. S. Lindsay was to write a four-volume *History of Merchant Shipping and Ancient Commerce* (London, 1874). Its theme was that "it is alike vain and presumptuous for weak man to interpose obstacles in the way of securing to large masses of people articles absolutely requisite for them, and which, so far as we can divine the inscrutable ways of Providence, are produced for the general use and welfare of mankind" (Vol. 2, pp. 343–4).

23 *PD*, HC, 14 July 1857, 3rd series, vol. 146, p. 1489.

24 Cobden to Lindsay, 9 August 1860, quoted in Lindsay, *Manning the Royal Navy*, pp. 121–2.

25 John Bright, "On the foreign policy of England", Birmingham, 29 October 1858, in C. K. Adams, *Representative British Orations*, Vol. 3 (New York, 1884), pp. 161, 174, 190. In his study of *Imperialism* (London, 1948; first published, 1902), J. A. Hobson attributed to James Mill the statement that the colonies were "a vast

system of outdoor relief for the upper classes" (p. 51). Many scholars, myself among them, have followed Hobson's mistaken attribution of this image from Bright's 1858 address.

26 Cobden to John Bright, 31 October 1861, Cobden Papers, BL, Add. Mss. 43,651, ff. 276–8.

27 ibid., ff. 276–8.

28 Cobden to John Bright, 31 October 1861, Cobden Papers, BL, Add. Mss. 43,651, f. 274.

29 Cobden to M. Chevalier, 25 October 1862, quoted in J. A. Hobson, *Richard Cobden, the International Man* (London, 1968), pp. 299–300.

30 Cobden to John Bright, 31 October 1861, Cobden Papers, BL, Add. Mss. 43,651, f. 274. See also Cobden to Bright, 1 November 1861, Cobden Papers, BL, Add. Mss. 43,651, f. 280; and 4 November 1861, f. 288, and 6 November 1861, ff. 286–8.

31 Cobden to Bright, 31 October 1861, Cobden Papers, BL, Add. Mss. 43,651, f. 278.

32 Cobden to Charles Sumner, 27 November 1861, Cobden Papers, BL, Add. Mss. 43,676, ff. 184–5; see also 29 November 1861, ff. 186–7.

33 Cobden to Charles Sumner, 5 December 1861, Cobden Papers, BL, Add. Mss. 43,676, f. 191.

34 Cobden to Sumner, 6 December 1861, Cobden Papers, BL, Add. Mss. 43,676, f. 200.

35 Cobden to Sumner, 12 December 1861, Cobden Papers, BL, Add. Mss. 43,676, ff. 203–7.

36 Cobden to Sumner, 19 December 1861, Cobden Papers, BL, Add. Mss. 43,676, f. 209.

37 Cobden to Sumner, 12 December 1861, Cobden Papers, BL, Add. Mss. 43,676, f. 204. See also Cobden to Sumner, 23 January 1862, Cobden Papers, BL, Add. Mss. 43,676, ff. 216–17; and on 22 May 1863: "John Bull, you know, has never been a neutral when great naval operations have been carried on, and he does not take kindly to the task." (quoted in Hobson, *Richard Cobden*, p. 373). What are we to make of Bright's warning to Cobden that "to break the blockade is war, & war without the excuse of the 'outrage.'" Bright to Cobden, Bright Papers, 9 January 1862, BL, Add. Mss. 43,384, f. 287; see also 6 January 1862, ff. 285–6, and 10 January 1862, f. 289; 13 January 1862, ff. 291–2. Cobden's pacifism did not prevent his approval of the North's war against slavery, and it need not have inhibited his favoring naval action to break a commercial blockade, this in the interest of a more pacific future international order. But the evidence is insufficient for more than speculation.

38 Quoted in Urquhart, *Right of Search*, Appendix, pp. 95–8.

39 Sumner to Bright, 23 December 1861, Bright Papers, BL, Add. Mss. 43,390, f. 128.

40 [Henry Reeve], "Belligerents and neutrals", *Edinburgh Review*, vol. 115, no. 233 (January 1862), pp. 281, 265.

41 Cobden to Bright, 21 January 1862, Cobden Papers, BL, Add. Mss. 43,652, f. 17.

42 Cobden to Bright, 23 January 1862, Cobden Papers, BL, Add. Mss. 43,652, f. 24. Cobden feared that the Republicans, like their Whig predecessors, would not be like such Democrats as "the Jeffersons, Jacksons, & Marcys, & Casses who took broad views & enunciated great principles."

43 Cobden to Bright, 6 November 1862, Cobden Papers, BL, Add. Mss. 43,651, f. 288.

44 Cobden to Bright, 21 January 1862, Cobden Papers, BL, Add. Mss. 43,652, f. 18.

45 *PD*, HC, 11 March 1862, 3rd series, vol. 165, pp. 1363–4.

46 ibid., pp. 1374–5. Liddell was four years later to accuse his country of "the most

grinding despotism on the seas." *PD*, HC, 2 March 1866, 3rd series, vol. 181, p. 1426.

47 *PD*, HC, 17 March 1862, 3rd series, vol. 165, pp. 1651–2.

48 ibid., pp. 1599–1600.

49 ibid., pp., 1646–7.

50 ibid., p. 1668.

51 *PD*, HC, 11 March 1862, 3rd series, vol. 165, p. 1371.

52 ibid., p. 1388.

53 *PD*, HC, 17 March 1862, 3rd series, vol. 165, pp. 1671–3, 1676, 1681–2. In an 1866 debate, the future Marquess of Salisbury, an opponent of the Declaration of Paris which he saw as "a fatal blow to England's power on the ocean," was to listen carefully to such arguments by Liberal leaders, and to be content! See also *PD*, HC, 2 March 1866, 3rd series, vol. 181, p. 1458.

54 ibid., pp. 1692, 1696–9. If this principle of immunity were carried, Palmerston observed, French fishery boats with their 20,000 sailors "would pass with impunity through our blockading squadron to man the enemy's ships lying in port before us" (1697). Six days previously, in a brief contribution to an earlier debate, Palmerston anticipated his phrase of 17 March when he described the adoption of immunity as "a fatal blow at the naval power of this country," and "an act of political suicide." See *PD*, HC, 11 March 1862, 3rd series, vol. 165, p. 1392.

55 *PD*, HC, 17 March 1862, 3rd series, vol. 165, pp. 1703–4, 1700, 1701–3.

56 ibid., p. 1706.

57 For later debates, see *PD*, HC, 2 March 1866, 3rd Series, vol. 181, pp. 1407–80; 5 August 1867, 3rd series, vol. 189, pp. 876–94; 21 April 1871, 3rd series, vol. 205, pp. 1469–1505; 13 April 1875, 3rd series, vol. 223, pp. 822–64; 2 March 1877, 3rd series, vol. 232, pp. 1262–1344; 22 March 1878, 3rd series, vol. 238, pp. 1842–1909.

58 Lindsay, *Manning the Royal Navy*, p. 125.

59 David Urquhart, *Answer to Mr. Cobden on the Assimilation of War and Peace* (London, 1862), pp. 10, 38, and *passim*. See also, David Urquhart, *Sparing Private Property in War at Sea; Two Letters to Mr. Gregory on his Motion of March 2, 1866* (London, 1866), pp. 4, 11, 26–7, and *passim*.

60 Article reprinted in *Economist*, vol. 72, no. 3,517 (21 June 1911), pp. 95–6.

61 *PD*, HC, 29 July 1859, 3rd series, vol. 155, pp. 716–18.

62 *PD*, HC, 5 March 1863, 3rd series, vol. 169, pp. 1806–7.

63 *PD*, HC, 29 July 1859, 3rd series, vol. 155, pp. 713–14.

64 *PD*, HC, 7 July 1862, 3rd series, vol. 167, pp. 1557–8. In this debate, Palmerston described Cobden as being "in a state of blindness and delusion," rendering him "utterly unfit to be listened to" on matters of defense; by preparing for all contingencies, the prime minister added, "we shall have done more" for peace than Cobden had accomplished by "his free trade" (ibid., pp. 1561, 1564).

65 *PD*, HC, 5 March 1863, 3rd series, vol. 169, pp. 1086–7.

66 *PD*, HC, 5 March 1863, 3rd series, vol. 169, pp. 1071–2.

67 *PD*, HC, 7 July 1862, 3rd series, vol. 167, pp. 1556–7.

68 Richard Cobden, *Political Writings of Richard Cobden*, Vol. 2, p. 672; see also pp. 554, 580–1, 584, 696–9.

69 Cobden to Jonathan Slagg, 15 March 1862, Cobden Papers, BL, Add. Mss. 43,676, f. 109.

70 Cobden to Slagg, 28 July 1861, Cobden Papers, BL, Add. Mss. 43,676, f. 85.

71 Cobden to Slagg, 15 March 1862, Cobden Papers, BL, Add. Mss. 43,676, f. 109.

72 Cobden to Slagg, 3 February 1864, Cobden Papers, BL, Add. Mss. 43,676, f. 147.

73 Brooks Adams, *America's Economic Supremacy*, pp. 91, 111, 113, 146–7, 177–82.

74 Mill to J. E. Cairnes, 1 September 1867, *Collected Works*, Vol. 16, p. 1315.
75 See *PD*, HL, 9 March 1911, 5th series, vol. 7, pp. 389–92.
76 See R. Wemyss, *Memoirs and Letters of the Right Hon. Sir Robert Morier, G.C.B., from 1826 to 1876*, Vol. 2 (London, 1911), pp. 375–92.
77 *The Times*, 25 November 1856, 6 d.

Chapter 6: *The Strategists: Naval Duel or Commercial War?*

1 It was "highly beneficial" to England, Admiral Sir Cyprian Bridge observed, that the editor of so influential a journal should possess "so keen an appreciation and, for a civilian, so rare a knowledge of naval affairs." See Sir J. K. Laughton, *Memoirs of the Life and Correspondence of Henry Reeve*, Vol. 2 (London, 1898), p. 376.
2 Lt. Col. Chesney and Henry Reeve, *The Military Resources of Prussia and France and Recent Changes in the Art of War* (London, 1870), pp. 1–2.
3 [Henry Reeve], "The Declaration of Paris", *Edinburgh Review*, vol. 144, no. 295 (October 1876), pp. 361–7.
4 *PD*, HC, 11 March 1862, 3rd series, vol. 165, p. 1623.
5 *PD*, HC, 22 March 1878, 3rd series, vol. 238, p. 1871; see also pp. 1846, 1850.
6 *PD*, HC, 17 March 1862, 3rd series, vol. 165, p. 1623.
7 ibid., pp. 1676–8.
8 *PD*, HC, 2 March 1866, 3rd series, vol. 181, pp. 1465–6.
9 ibid., pp. 1457–8.
10 ibid., pp. 1466–7, 1471, 1477.
11 *PD*, HC, 5 August 1867, 3rd series, vol. 189, pp. 892–3.
12 *PD*, HC, 21 April 1871, 3rd series, vol. 205, pp. 1488–9.
13 See A. G. Gardiner, *The Life of Sir William Harcourt*, vol. 1 (London, 1923), pp. 125–48, 193–5, 199–200. In the early 1860s, Harcourt, under the name Historicus, wrote a series of letters to *The Times* on maritime issues proceeding from the Civil War in America.
14 See Sir William Harcourt, "The rights and duties of neutrals in time of war", *Journal of the Royal United Service Institution*, vol. 9 (1865), p. 328 [cited hereafter as *JRUSI*]. See also Sir William Harcourt, "Our naval and military establishments with reference to the dangers of invasion", *JRUSI*, vol. 16 (1872), pp. 574–632, where Harcourt insisted on the Navy's ability to defend the homeland against invasion.
15 *PD*, HC, 13 April 1875, 3rd series, vol. 223, pp. 855–6.
16 *PD*, HC, 2 March 1877, 3rd series, vol. 232, especially pp. 1331, 1337.
17 *PD*, HC, 22 March 1878, 3rd series, vol. 238, pp. 1858–62.
18 *PD*, HC, 22 March 1878, 3rd series, vol. 238, pp. 1895–70.
19 Captain [P. H.] Colomb, R.N., *Slave Catching in the Indian Ocean; A Record of Naval Experiences* (London, 1873). Colomb saw anti-slavery operations as hypocritical: by stopping the exports of slaves from Africa, England merely arranged for the blacks to be kept at home to produce ground nuts or palm oil. Working for white masters overseas, the blacks might achieve a measure of civilization, while in Africa they labored under black direction and a much more repressive discipline. African slavery, Colomb observed, had actually increased. "Does it, after all, make much difference to the negro slave whether we export him bodily or export only his labor," he inquired. "We save him a sea voyage by legitimate commerce – no more" (pp. 484–8, 501–3).
20 Captain J. C. R. Colomb, *Naval Intelligence and Protection of Commerce in War* (London, 1881), p. 14.

21 Captain P. H. Colomb, *The Naval Prize Essay, 1878: Great Britain's Maritime Power: How Best Developed, etc.* (London, 1878), pp. 10–12, and *passim.* For a discussion of Philip Colomb, see D. M. Schurman, *The Education of a Navy; the Development of British Naval Strategic Thought, 1867–1914* (Chicago, 1965), pp. 16–35; of John Colomb, see ibid., pp. 1–15.

22 J. C. R. Colomb, *Naval Intelligence and Protection of Commerce*, pp. 1–3, 3–5, 7, 20, 8–9, 16–18. See Bryan Ranft, "The protection of British seaborne trade and the development of systematic planning for war, 1860–1906", in *Technical Change and British Naval Policy, 1860–1939*, ed. B. Ranft (London, 1977), pp. 1, 12, 22, and *passim.*

23 See discussion in A. J. Marder, *The Anatomy of British Sea Power* (New York, 1940), pp. 76, 274–6, and *passim*; also Theodore Ropp, "Continental doctrines of sea power", in *Makers of Modern Strategy; Military Thought from Machiavelli to Hitler*, ed. E. M. Earle (Princeton, 1971), pp. 446–56; and idem, *War in the Modern World* (Durham, N C, 1959), pp. 190–4, 239 n., and *passim.*

24 Gabriel Charmes, *Naval Reform* (London, 1887), pp. vii, 58–60, iv–vi, xiii, 59–60, 62–4.

25 Quoted in Marder, *Anatomy of British Sea Power*, p. 87. The views of Aube and Charmes were set down in textbook form in 1893 in Henry Vignot's *Essai de Stratégie Navale*, so that the French navy would be prepared for war against "notre principal enemi: l'Angleterre." See Commandant Z. et H. Montechant [Henry Vignot], *Essai de Stratégie Navale* (Paris, 1893), p. 406, and *passim.*

26 Mahan, *Influence of Sea Power upon History*, pp. 480–1. For a discussion of the ideological background of Mahan's strategic ideas, see J. A. Field, Jr, "The origins of maritime strategy and the development of seapower", in *War, Strategy, and Maritime Power*, ed. B. M. Simpson III (New Brunswick, NJ, 1977), pp. 77–94.

27 Vice-Admiral P. H. Colomb, *Essays on Naval Defence* (London, 1893), p. 229.

28 Sir C. W. Dilke and Spenser Wilkinson, *Imperial Defence* (London, 1892), pp. 41, 49. The volume's discussion of naval tactics also owed much to Mahan's persuasive description of the utility of Lord St Vincent's close blockade, designed to keep a watch on Napoleon's fleet in French ports (pp. 71–2).

29 [J. K. Laughton], "Captain Mahan on maritime power", *Edinburgh Review*, vol. 172, no. 352 (October 1890), pp. 441–2. See Schurman, *Education of a Navy*, pp. 83–115 for a discussion of Laughton's contribution to the blue-water school.

30 J. R. Thursfield, "The command of the sea" (1893), in Sir G. S. Clarke and J. R. Thursfield, *The Navy and the Nation; or Naval Warfare and Imperial Defence* (London, 1897), pp. 149–51.

31 J. R. Thursfield, "The Jeune Ecole Française", (1894), in ibid., pp. 199–201.

32 J. R. Thursfield, "Navies and commerce", in ibid., p. 94.

33 Admiral Sir Cyprian Bridge, *Sea Power and Other Studies* (London, 1910), pp. 65, 252.

34 Lt. Col. C. à C. Repington, *Vestigia* (Boston, 1919), p. 277. For Mahan's influence, see especially R. Seager II, *Alfred Thayer Mahan: the Man and His Letters* (Annapolis, Md, 1977), and W. E. Livezey, *Mahan on Sea Power* (Norman, Okla, 1947).

35 Mahan, *Influence of Sea Power upon History*, pp. 481–2.

36 A. T. Mahan, *The Influence of Sea Power upon the French Revolution and Empire, 1793–1812*, Vol. 2 (New York, 1892), pp. 199–200, 200–2.

37 [J. K. Laughton], "Captain Mahan on maritime power", *Edinburgh Review*, vol. 177, no. 364 (April 1893), p. 485.

38 A. T. Mahan, "Possibilities of an Anglo-American reunion" (1894), in *The Interest of America in Sea Power, Present and Future* (Boston, 1897), pp. 126–9, 133, 130, 132.

39 A. T. Mahan, *Sea Power in its Relations to the War of 1812*, Vol. 1 (Boston, 1905), pp. 284–8.
40 See Bernard Semmel, *Imperialism and Social Reform* (London, 1960), especially chs. 8, 10, 11.
41 Spenser Wilkinson, *The Great Alternative; A Plea for a National Policy* (London, 1894), pp. 127, 322, 308, 318–19, 135–7, "At the mercy of whatever Power has acquired maritime supremacy," Wilkinson observed in a letter to *The Times* the previous year, England must either become a dependent or "herself command the sea." Quoted in H. Spenser Wilkinson, *Thirty-Five Years 1874–1905* (London, 1913), pp. 185–7.
42 Address included in Spenser Wilkinson, *War and Policy* (London, 1900), pp. 340–3.
43 *The Times*, 14 October 1905; text in "Report of the Inter-departmental Committee", 21 March 1907, PRO, CAB 37/87, Appendix, 5, pp. 55–8.
44 *The Times*, 23 July 1906; text in "Report of the Inter-departmental Committee", 11 April 1907, PRO, CAB 37/87, Appendix 6.
45 A. T. Mahan, "The Hague Conference: the question of immunity for belligerent merchant shipping" (1907) in *Some Neglected Aspects of War* (Boston, 1907), pp. 184, 162–3, 183, 192–3, 187, 191–2.
46 J. S. Corbett, "The capture of private property at sea" (1907), in Mahan, in *Some Neglected Aspects of War*, pp. 118–21, 130–1, 139–42, 151, 146, 149. Spenser Wilkinson had also dismissed the view that maritime trade could easily be diverted. See *The Times*, 23 July 1906; appended to "Report of the Inter-departmental Committee Appointed to Consider the Subjects Which May Arise for Discussion at the Second Peace Conference", 21 March 1907, PRO, CAB 37/87, no. 42, Appendix 6, p. 61.
47 J. S. Corbett, *Some Principles of Maritime Strategy* (London, 1911), pp. 90–1, 93, 190, 91–6, 284. Corbett attempted to adapt the principles of Clausewitz's *On War* to maritime warfare, and to British geopolitical circumstances. For example, while questioning the German military strategist's distinction between limited and unlimited war as "too shadowy and unstable" in wars between continental states, Corbett observed that "in wars between worldwide empires, the distinction at once becomes organic." A navy could isolate overseas territories so as to create conditions for a "true limited war," noting Britain's eighteenth-century conquest of Canada though England was militarily weaker than France. "Here, then, we reach the true meaning and highest military value of what we call command of the sea," Corbett proclaimed, "and here we touch the secret of England's success against Powers so greatly superior to her in military strength" (pp. 52–6). Also see D. M. Schurman, *Julian S. Corbett, 1854–1922: Historian of British Maritime Policy from Drake to Jellicoe* (London, 1981).

Chapter 7: *Britannia Contra Mundum*

1 Quoted in [J. A. Fisher], *Fear God and Dread Nought: The Correspondence of Admiral of the Fleet Lord Fisher of Kilverstone*, ed. A. J. Marder, Vol. 1 (London, 1952), p. 141.
2 Quoted in E. Halévy, *Imperialism and the Rise of Labour, 1895–1905* (New York, 1951), p. 64.
3 Quoted in ibid., p. 64 n.
4 See "Report of the Inter-departmental Committee Appointed to Consider the Subjects Which May Arise for Discussion at the Second Peace Conference", 21 March 1907, PRO, CAB 37/87, no. 42, Appendix I, pp. 36–7.

5 See Paul Haggie, "The Royal Navy and war planning in the Fisher era", in P. M. Kennedy (ed.), *The War Plans of the Great Powers, 1880–1914* (London, 1979), pp. 118–32.
6 *PD*, HL, 8 March 1911, 5th series, vol. 7, p. 345.
7 See Semmel, *Imperialism and Social Reform*, especially pp. 141–65.
8 See *PD*, HC, 10 May 1906, 5th series, vol. 161, p. 1494.
9 See John Gooch, *The Prospect of War; Studies in British Defence Policy 1847–1942* (London, 1981), p. 73. For the C.I.D., see N.d'Ombrain, *War Machinery and High Policy; Defence Administration in Peacetime Britain, 1902–1914* (London, 1973); also F.A. Johnson, *Defence by Committee; the British Committee of Imperial Defence 1885–1959* (London, 1960).
10 Lt. Col. Sir G. S. Clarke, *Imperial Defence* (London, 1897), p. 131.
11 G. S. Clarke, "National insurance" (1890), in Clarke and Thursfield, *Navy and the Nation*, p. 116. But Admiral Aube had suggested that crews could be summarily disposed of. "Whatever the late Admiral Aube may have written," Clarke declared, "the sentiment of the civilized world will not now stand the deliberate cold-blooded murder of unresisting non-combatants." A belligerent, as Britain had learned in the course of her naval history, "must not incur the moral reprobation of the civilized world," must not, indeed, "do anything to array a strong neutral against him."
12 Clarke, *Imperial Defence*, p. 136.
13 G. S. Clarke, "War, trade and food supply", *National Review*, vol. 29, no. 173 (July 1897), p. 756.
14 See discussion in Clarke, "National insurance", especially pp. 110–15.
15 P. H. Colomb, *Essays on Naval Defence*, pp. 253; and 246–57.
16 Clarke, "National insurance", p. 114. David French sees Clarke as a mercantilist in his *British Economic and Strategic Planning 1905–1915* (London, 1982), pp. 17–18, 52–4.
17 Sir G. S. Clarke to Sir C. W. Dilke, 16 June 1907, Dilke Papers, BL, Add. Mss. 43, 919, f. 230.
18 Memorandum to Lord Balfour of Burleigh, 4 July 1904, Sydenham Papers, BL, Add. Mss. 50,836, ff. 50–1.
19 See discussion in Clarke, "War, trade, and food supply" (1897), pp. 764–5.
20 [Sir G. S. Clarke], "The Value to Great Britain of the Right of Capture of Neutral Vessels", 12 December 1904, PRO, CAB 38/6 (C.I.D. 41B), no. 120, pp. 6, 1–2, 5–6. The question had emerged dramatically in 1885 when the then chancellor, Lord Selborne, the former Sir Roundell Palmer, described as "alarming" France's having declared rice contraband in the course of its war with China. Selborne saw this as a forecast of how the continental powers might deal with a Britain at war: they would expect England to observe all the concessions made in 1856, while they would "submit, as neutrals, to whatever law of contraband" Britain's enemy imposed. If England's imported food were declared contraband, Selborne warned, "we should have to denounce, and shake ourselves free from the Declaration of Paris." See Lord Selborne, Minute 24, April 1885, in "Report of the Inter-departmental Committee", 21 March 1907, PRO, CAB 37/87, Appendix, p. 54.
21 Board of Trade Memorandum, ibid., p. 10.
22 Admiralty Memorandum, ibid., pp. 9–10.
23 "Report of the Inter-departmental Committee", 21 March 1907, PRO, CAB 37/87, pp. 1, 3, 7, 5–6.
24 ibid., pp. 8, 10, 3–4; see also Appendix 8, p. 67.
25 ibid., pp. 2–3, 11, 6.

26 ibid., pp. 12–14.
27 ibid., "Memorandum on the Law of Contraband", of Sir George Clarke, pp. 13, 78–9.
28 ibid., pp. 26, 28, 17–18.
29 ibid., 4 February 1907, Appendix 7 (Admiralty Memorandum), p. 62.
30 ibid., 29 January 1907, Appendix 13 (Admiralty Memorandum on ... a Possible Limitation of Naval Armaments), pp. 88, 94, 88–9.
31 Memorandum from Lord Loreburn to Cabinet, PRO, CAB 37/88, 1907, no. 58, pp. 1–4, 5–6.
32 Memorandum from Sir Edward Grey, Foreign Office, to Cabinet, 3 June, 1907, PRO, CAB 37/89, pp. 1–2. For a discussion of these preparations for the Second Hague Conference, see J. W. Coogan, *The End of Neutrality; the United States, Britain and Maritime Rights 1899–1915* (Ithaca, NY, 1981), pp. 70–89.
33 The Prime Minister [H. Campbell-Bannerman], "The Hague Conference and the limitation of armaments", *The Nation*, vol. 1, no. 1 (2 March 1907), p. 4.
34 E. Halévy, *The Rule of Democracy, 1905–1914*, Vol. 1 (New York, 1952), pp. 223–4.
35 This is discussed in Chapter 8. See Memoranda from Admiral Fisher to J. R. Thursfield, 26 September 1906, and October 1906, Thursfield Papers, National Maritime Museum, THU/2/4.
36 Quoted in Marder (ed.), *Fear God and Dread Nought*, Vol. 2, p. 142.
37 *The Proceedings of The Hague Peace Conferences; The Conference of 1907* (New York, 1920). See Chapter 8, for details.
38 For text, see J. B. Scott (ed.), *The Declaration of London, February 26, 1909* (New York, 1919).
39 See Memorandum from Sir Edward Grey, Foreign Office, to Cabinet, 3 November 1908, PRO, CAB 37/95, no. 132, p. 7.
40 See Correspondence between Admiralty and Foreign Office, 26 June 1909 and 28 June 1910, PRO, ADM 1/8194. In 1909 and 1910, the foreign office began to make arrangements with foreign governments to fill in details of the Declaration, e.g., the method of verifying the flag of merchant vessels at sea. See Correspondence and Documents Respecting the International Naval Conference, March 1909, Miscellaneous no. 4 (1909), PRO, ADM 1/1800; and Correspondence Between France and England on Verification of the Flag, Foreign Office, 31 January 1910, PRO, ADM 1/8191.
41 T. G. Bowles, *The Forthcoming Congress at St. Petersburgh on the Laws of War; An Address delivered in the Central Hall, Darlington, on Tuesday, 5th January, 1875* (Newcastle-upon-Tyne, 1875), pp. 16–21.
42 T. G. Bowles, *Maritime Warfare* (London, 1877), pp. 2–3.
43 T. G. Bowles, "The Navy paralysed by paper", *Fortnightly Review*, N.S. vol. 37 (1 February 1885), pp. 260, 258.
44 See Leonard E. Naylor, *The Irrepressible Victorian: The Story of Thomas Gibson Bowles* (London, 1965), especially pp. 130–1.
45 See, for example, *PD*, HC, 26 February 1900, 4th series, vol. 79, pp. 1140–1; also 22 February 1900, 4th series, vol. 78, pp. 443–4.
46 T. G. Bowles, MP, *The Declaration of Paris of 1856* (London, 1900), pp. 2, vi–vii, 21, 102, 183.
47 See *PD*, HC, 28 May 1903, 4th series, vol. 123, p. 194; also, Liberal Publication Department, *Issues at Stake, A Speech Delivered by John Morley with One by Winston Churchill* (London, 1904), p. 19; and Beatrice Webb, *Our Partnership* (London, 1948), p. 269.
48 Quoted in Naylor, *Irrepressible Victorian*, p. 158.

49 T. G. Bowles, "The Declaration of London", *Nineteenth Century and After*, vol. 65, no. 387 (May 1909), pp. 745–8.
50 T. G. Bowles, *Sea Law and Sea Power* (London, 1910), pp. v, 51, 135–6, 56, 221–3; also pp. 154–63.
51 See Naylor, *Irrepressible Victorian*, especially pp. 165–7.
52 See Norman Bentwich, *The Declaration of London* (London, 1911), p. vi.
53 See Correspondence Respecting the Declaration of London, Miscellaneous no. 4 (1910), Cd. 5418.
54 Correspondence Respecting the Declaration of London, Miscellaneous no. 8 (1911), Cd. 5718, p. 17.
55 *Statement on Behalf of the Chamber of Shipping of the United Kingdom on the Subject of the Declaration of London* (London, 1911), p. 8. On the other hand, the Liverpool Steam Ship Owners' Association supported the Declaration; see *The Overseas Commerce of Neutral Nations in the Presence of Naval Warfare: The Declaration of London of 1909* (?, 1909); and *Annual Report of the Liverpool Steam Ship Owners' Association . . . For the Year . . . 1910.* (Liverpool, 1911), p. 4, and *Annual Report* (1911), pp. 3–5.
56 T. McKinnon Wood, *The Declaration of London* (London, 1911), pp. 3, 11.
57 T. McKinnon Wood, *British Commerce and the Declaration of London* (London, 1911), p. 19.
58 Wood, *Declaration of London*, p. 9.
59 Wood, *British Commerce*, p. 12.
60 Committee for the Ratification of the Declaration of London, *Statement* (London, 191?), *passim.*
61 Declaration of London Ratification Committee, *The Declaration of London Objections and Answers*, no. 1 (London, 191?), p. 6.
62 Declaration of London Ratification Committee, *The Position of the British Shipowner*, no. 2 (London, 191?), pp. 1–2.
63 Imperial Maritime League, *Keep the Flag Flying* (London, 1910), p. 13; see also L. G. Horton-Smith, *Sea Power: The Liberals and National Defence* (London 1911). See W. M. Hamilton, "The nation and the Navy: methods and organisation of British navalist propaganda 1889–1914", PhD, thesis, London, 1977; and Marder, *Anatomy of British Sea Power*, pp. 48–61.
64 Imperial Maritime League, *The Declaration of London: National Starvation in War and the Paralysis of Britain's Powers and Rights at Sea* (London, 1911), pp. 40, 46–7. For a discussion of the debate on the 1909 Declaration, see Coogan, *End of Neutrality*, pp. 125–47.
65 Lord Hankey, *The Supreme Command, 1914–18*, Vol. 1 (London, 1961), pp. 99, 95. See also C. L. Ottley, Director of Naval Intelligence, to Julian Corbett, 1 July 1905, Richmond Papers, National Maritime Museum, RIC/9/1.
66 Hankey, *Supreme Command*, pp. 95–7.
67 Hankey Memorandum, 17 February 1911, PRO, CAB 17/87.
68 Ottley Memorandum, 17 February 1911, PRO, CAB 17/87.
69 Hankey, *Supreme Command*, p. 99.
70 Memorandum of Conversation, 23 February 1911, PRO, CAB 17/87.
71 Hankey Memorandum, 25 February 1911, PRO, CAB 17/87. Ottley, in reply, repeated McKenna's argument that Britain might just as well profit by the 1909 rules as long as she remained a neutral in European wars. See Ottley Memorandum, 27 February 1911, PRO, CAB 17/87.
72 Hankey, *The Supreme Command*, pp. 100–1. See also Coogan, *End of Neutrality*, pp. 137–9.
73 *The Times*, 30 September 1907; text in Bowles, *Sea Law and Sea Power*, pp. 137–8.

74 J. Westlake, "The Declaration of London", *Nineteenth Century and After*, vol. 67, no. 397 (March 1910), p. 515.
75 T. E. Holland, *Proposed Changes in Naval Prize Law* (London, 1911).
76 See *PD*, HC, 28 June 1911, 5th series, vol. 27, pp. 489–98.
77 *PD*, HC, 29 June 1911, 5th series, vol. 27, pp. 662–4.
78 Bentwich, *Declaration of London.*
79 Rt Hon. Arthur Cohen, *Paper on the Declaration of London* (London, 1910), especially pp. 5–6 and 21–2.
80 See *PD*, HC, 29 June 1911, 5th series, vol. 27, p. 683.
81 Memorandum of Sir E. Grey, Foreign Office, to Cabinet, 1 February 1911, PRO, CAB 37/105, no. 6.
82 *PD*, HL, 8 March 1911, 5th series, vol. 7, p. 329. While the Foreign Office thought a wide definition of "base of supply" was "obviously absurd," it admitted that all depended on "what Power or Powers we are at war with." See Foreign Office Memoranda to Admiralty, "Definition of Certain Terms in the Declaration of London," 25 August 1910, and 11 August 1911, ADM 1/8526, 29310/10. In a Commons debate in 1902, Sir William Harcourt had observed that "I do not think, however, that neutral nations will ever allow provisions to be declared contraband of war." And Gibson Bowles had agreed. *PD*, HC, 28 January 1902, 4th series, vol. 101, pp. 1157–8.
83 *PD*, HL, 8 March 1911, 5th series, vol. 7, pp. 341, 346.
84 *PD*, HL, 9 March 1911, 5th series, vol. 7, pp. 377–8, 388.
85 ibid., pp. 389–92. To Halsbury's reference to Mill, Lord Morley replied that while his old friend Mill had criticized the 1856 Declaration, he had subsequently withdrawn that opinion; Halsbury drily observed, correctly as we know, that "I read Mr. Mill's denunciation but not his withdrawal."
86 ibid., p. 415.
87 *PD*, HL, 13 March 1911, 5th series, vol. 7, pp. 434–5.
88 ibid., p. 463.
89 ibid., pp. 397–9.
90 Admirals' Petition to Foreign Secretary, 26 June 1911, Sir Edward Grey Papers, PRO, FO 800/87, p. 245.
91 *The Annual Register*, 1911 (London, 1912), pp. 152–3.
92 Quoted in Naylor, *Irrepressible Victorian*, p. 184.
93 *Annual Register*, 1911, p. 152.
94 ibid., p. 158.
95 *PD*, HC, 28 June 1911, 5th series, vol. 27, p. 489.
96 See ibid., p. 593. (The speaker was R. D. Holt.)
97 ibid., p. 642.
98 ibid., pp. 631, 635.
99 See R. S. Churchill, *Winston S. Churchill*, companion Vol. 2, pt 2, *1907–1911* (Boston, 1969), pp. 1094–6.
100 Reginald Custance, "The naval case for ratifying the Declaration of London", *Nineteenth Century and After*, vol. 71, no. 421 (March 1912), pp. 444, 435.
101 Admiral Sir Cyprian Bridge, *Sea Power and Other Studies* (London, 1910), p. 252.
102 Admiral Sir Reginald Custance, "Capture of property at sea", *Nineteenth Century and After*, vol. 75, no. 444 (February 1914), pp. 231–2, 239.
103 Sir E. Grey to W. S. Churchill, 23 December 1911, Sir Edward Grey Papers, PRO, FO 800/87, f. 285.
104 *PD*, HC, 17 March 1914, 5th series, vol. 59, p. 1926.
105 See H. H. Asquith, *The Genesis of the War* (London, 1923), p. 117.
106 Quoted in Marder (ed.), *Fear God and Dread Nought*, Vol. 2, pp. 374–5.

107 Hankey, *Supreme Command*, Vol. 1, p. 100.

Chapter 8: *The Politics of Pacifism, Parsimony, and Redistribution*

1 Clausewitz, *On War*, p. 75.

2 Quoted in T. E. Holland, *A Lecture on the Brussels Conference of 1874* (Oxford, 1876), p. 23.

3 Admiral Sir Cyprian Bridge, *The Art of Naval Warfare: Introductory Observations* (London, 1907), p. 162.

4 See discussion in H. S. Maine, *International Law; a Series of Lectures Delivered Before the University of Cambridge, 1887* (New York, 1888), pp. 41–4, 47–50.

5 Earl Loreburn, *Capture at Sea* (London, 1913), pp. 154, 163, 161.

6 A recent study has declared that law "has been made to serve the purposes of sea power, and so had become a weapon in the naval armoury." See D. P. O'Connell, *The Influence of Law on Sea Power* (Manchester, 1975), p. 16.

7 T. Miller Maguire, "The development of international strategy since 1871 and its present conditions", *JRUSI*, vol. 50, no. 339 (May 1906), p. 641.

8 Gardiner, *Harcourt*, Vol. 1, pp. 193–5; see also [Sir William V. Harcourt], *Letters by Historicus on Some Questions of International Law Reprinted from 'The Times' With Considerable Additions* (London, 1863), pp. 55–56; for Harcourt, "beyond all other nations of the world, the traditionary policy of France has been to be violent when she is strong, and to be reasonable only when she is weak." (p. 73). In this work Harcourt denounced the French jurist Hautefeuille for his anti-English prejudices; Hautefeuille had called on the nations to construct a permanent armed neutrality against "le joug britannique."

9 T.E. Holland, "William Edward Hall", *Encyclopaedia Britannica* (11th edn; Cambridge, 1910), Vol. 12, p. 850.

10 W. E. Hall, *International Law* (Oxford, 1880), pp. 376–80, 380 n.

11 Rev. T. C. Lawrence, "The Hague Conference and naval war", *JRUSI*, vol. 52, no. 362 (April 1908), p. 479. See Clive Parry, "Foreign policy and international law", in *British Foreign Policy Under Sir Edward Grey*, ed. F. H. Hinsley (Cambridge, 1977), pp. 103–8.

12 J. Westlake, "The Declaration of London", p. 507. See also J. Westlake, "Notes on belligerent rights at sea", in Latifi, *Effects of War on Property*, p. 147.

13 T. E. Holland, *Proposed Changes in the Naval Prize Law*, especially p. 2.

14 See, for example, the professor of comparative law at the University of London, Sir John MacDonnell, *Some Plain Reasons for Immunity from Capture of Private Property at Sea* (London, 1910), especially p. 12; and his London colleague A. Pearce Higgins, *War and the Private Citizen; Studies in International Law* (London, 1912), pp. 68–70.

15 Discussion in Lawrence, "The Hague Convention and naval war", pp. 493–4; and discussion pp. 495–6, 503.

16 P.H. Colomb, *The Naval Prize Essay, 1878: Great Britain's Maritime Power*, pp. 10–12.

17 *PD*, HC, 7 March 1889, 3rd series, vol. 333, pp. 1171, 1187, 1190–1.

18 *PD*, HC, 1 April 1889, 3rd series, vol. 333, p. 1272.

19 *PD*, HC, 4 April 1889, 3rd series, vol. 333, p. 1636.

20 *PD*, HC, 1 April 1889, 3rd series, vol. 333, p. 1319.

21 *PD*, HC, 25 March 1889, 3rd series, vol. 333, pp. 774–7.

22 *PD*, HC, 1 April 1889, 3rd series, vol. 333, pp. 1288–9.

23 *PD*, HC, 6 May 1889, 3rd series, vol. 335, p. 1308.

24 *PD*, HC, 6 May 1889, 3rd series, vol. 335, pp. 1329–31.
25 *PD*, HC, 17 May 1889, 3rd series, vol. 336, p. 414.
26 *The Times*, 9 November 1893, 4 a.
27 Dreadnought, "Navy and Empire", *National Review*, vol. 53 (July 1909), pp. 739–40.
28 Carlyon Bellairs, MP, "The naval crisis", *National Review*, vol. 53 (March 1909), p. 34.
29 Quoted in R. F. Mackay, *Fisher of Kilverstone* (Oxford, 1973), p. 409.
30 Bellairs, "The naval crisis", p. 34.
31 Arthur Ponsonby, "Foreign policy and the Navy", *Contemporary Review*, vol. 102 (September 1912), p. 305.
32 See P. M. Kennedy, *The Rise of the Anglo-German Antagonism 1860–1914* (London, 1980), pp. 334–5.
33 P. M. Kennedy, *The Realities Behind Diplomacy: Background Influences on British External Policy, 1865–1980* (London, 1981), p. 65; see also A. J. A. Morris, *Radicalism Against War, 1906–1914; the Advocacy of Peace and Retrenchment* (Totowa, NJ, 1972), *passim.*
34 A. S. Hurd, "A British two-power fleet", *Nineteenth Century and After*, vol. 63, no. 373 (March 1908), p. 498.
35 Bellairs, "The naval crisis", p. 35; see also George Toulmin, "The Liberal Party and naval expenditure", *Contemporary Review*, vol. 102 (September 1910), pp. 314–16.
36 Marder (ed.), *Fear God and Dread Nought*, Vol. 2, p. 141; see also Mackay, *Fisher of Kilverstone*, p. 358.
37 Quoted in A. J. Marder, *From the Dreadnought to Scapa Flow; the Royal Navy in the Fisher Era, 1904–1919*, vol. 1 (London, 1961), p. 186; for a full discussion of the efforts of the navalists and ultras, see A. J. A. Morris, *The Scaremongers; the Advocacy of War and Rearmament 1896–1914* (London, 1984).
38 Marder (ed.), *Fear God and Dread Nought*, Vol. 2, pp. 175–6.
39 W. T. Stead quoted in Admiral Sir R. H. Bacon, *The Life of Lord Fisher of Kilverstone*, Vol. 1 (London, 1929), p. 121.
40 See E. L. Woodward, *Great Britain and the German Navy* (London, 1964; first published, 1935); also Marder, *Dreadnought to Scapa Flow*, *passim.*
41 *Official Report of the Seventeenth Universal Congress of Peace; held at Caxton Hall, Westminster, London, July 27th to August 1st, 1908* (London: National Council of Peace Societies, 1909), pp. 215, 114, 119.
42 ibid., pp. 214–16.
43 ibid., pp. 114, 242–3. A few years later, Perris was to write that "naval power is nothing but a clumsy temporary device which must give way before long, to the exemption of neutral commerce from capture and to the policing of the seas by an international force." See H. S. Perris, *Pax Britannica; A Study in the History of British Pacification* (London: Sidgwick & Jackson, 1913), p. 7.
44 *Seventeenth Universal Congress of Peace*, p. 243.
45 S. E. Koss, *Sir John Brunner, Radical Plutocrat 1842–1919* (Cambridge, 1970), p. 232.
46 *The Economist*, vol. 68, no. 3,421 (20 March 1909), p. 603.
47 *The Nation*, vol. 13, no. 1 (5 April 1913), p. 4.
48 Quoted in Koss, *Sir John Brunner*, p. 232 n.
49 Supplement: Vernon Lee, "The lines of Anglo-German agreement", *The Nation*, vol. 7, no. 24 (10 September 1910), pp. i–ii.
50 ibid., p. ii. See also Morris, *Radicalism Against War*, pp. 218–19, and *passim*; and K. G. Robbins, "Public opinion, the press, and pressure groups", in *British Foreign Policy*, ed. Hinsley, pp. 80–81, and *passim.*

51 See appendix, Koss, *Sir John Brunner*, pp. 295–6.
52 *The Economist*, vol. 75, no. 3,615 (7 December 1912), p. 1160.
53 *PD*, HC, 9 May 1906, 4th series, vol. 156, pp. 1383–4.
54 Quoted in appendix, Koss, *Sir John Brunner*, pp. 290–1.
55 *The Nation*, vol. 13, no. 1 (5 April 1913), pp. 4–5.
56 *The Nation*, vol. 7, no. 14 (2 July 1910), pp. 478–9.
57 *The Nation*, vol. 8, no. 20 (11 February 1911), pp. 791–2.
58 *The Nation*, vol. 12, no. 20 (15 February 1913), p. 804. Noting Radical arguments concerning a capitalist conspiracy to maintain a large navy, Balfour observed in 1906 (referring to remarks by the sociologist and Radical MP, J. M. Robertson), "I do not know whether that is sociology, but it strikes me as being nonsense." *PD*, HC, 9 May 1906, 4th series, vol. 156, p. 1408. See also *The Nation*, vol. 13, no. 1 (5 April 1913), pp. 4–5.
59 See for example, *The Nation*, vol. 8, no. 20 (11 February 1911), pp. 791–2. See also *The Economist*, vol. 72, no. 3,521 (18 February 1911), p. 305; and *The Economist*, vol. 75, no. 3,615 (7 December 1912), p. 1160.
60 *The Economist*, vol. 76, no. 3,626 (22 February 1913), p. 384.
61 *The Economist*, vol. 66, no. 3,366 (29 February 1908), p. 427.
62 *The Nation*, vol. 13, no. 1 (5 April 1913), pp. 4–5.
63 See "A survey and criticism of the growth of naval, military, and civil expenditure", *The Economist*, vol. 71, no. 3,508 (19 November 1910), Economist Supplement, November 1910, pp. iv–v, vii–viii. See also Woodward, *Great Britain and the German Navy*, pp. 494–8, and *passim*.
64 *The Economist*, vol. 72, no. 3,521 (18 February 1911), p. 305.
65 *The Economist*, vol. 76, no. 3,630 (22 March 1913), p. 695.
66 *The Economist*, vol. 78, no. 3,681 (14 March 1914), p. 647.
67 F. W. Hirst, *The Six Panics and Other Essays* (London, 1913), pp. 131–2.
68 Herbert Spencer, *The Principles of Sociology*, Vol. 1 (New York, 1887), pp. 567–75.
69 See Thorsten Veblen, *Imperial Germany and the Industrial Revolution* (New York, 1915), *passim*.
70 See discussion in Howard Weinroth, "Left-wing opposition to naval armaments in Britain before 1914", *Journal of Contemporary History*, vol. 6, no. 4, (1971), 98–9, 113–18.
71 *PD*, HC, 23 July 1914, 5th series, vol. 65, pp. 726–9.

Chapter 9: *Offense and Defense: The Historical and Materiel Schools*

1 Clausewitz, *On War*, pp. 75, 78, 87, 81, 93, 95–8, 86. For a similar view of Clausewitz's thought, see R. Aron, *Clausewitz, Philosopher of War* (Englewood, NJ, 1985).
2 See G. A. Craig, "Delbrück: the military historian", *Makers of Modern Strategy*, ed. E. M. Earle (Princeton, 1971), pp. 272–5. Clausewitz's view of Frederick's strategy had been much the same as Delbrück's: if Frederick had tried to fight as the wager of absolute war Charles XII had fought, "he would unfailingly have been destroyed himself" Clausewitz, *On War*, p. 94.
3 See S. T. Possony and E. Mantoux, "Du Picq and Foch: the French school", *Makers of Modern Strategy*, ed. E. M. Earle, pp. 206–18.
4 Ferdinand Foch, *The Principles of War*, trans. Hilaire Belloc (London, 1918), pp. 19, 4, 6, 34, 37–9, 42. For a discussion of Foch, see Possony and Mantoux, "Du Picq and Foch: the French school", pp. 218–33.
5 Quoted in Peter Padfield, *The Great Naval Race; The Anglo-German Naval Rivalry*,

1900–1914 (London, 1974), p. 114. Yet Nelson's strategy continued to be invoked and two years before the war an admiralty committee was charged to consider Nelson's tactics at Trafalgar. See G. Jordan, "Introduction", *Naval Warfare in the Twentieth Century, 1900–1945; Essays in Honour of Arthur Marder*, ed. G. Jordan (London, 1977), p. 13. For a discussion of the "materialist school of thought" that "dominated the Admiralty" between 1906 and 1913, see Stephen King-Hall, *My Naval Life 1906–1929* (London, 1952), pp. 93–4, 266, and *passim.* See also Vice-Admiral K. G. B. Dewar, *The Navy from Within* (London, 1939), pp. 243, 144–5, and *passim.*

6 Captain P. H. Colomb, "Great Britain's maritime power: how best developed" (Naval Prize Essay, 1878), Appendix in J. C. R. Colomb, *Defence of Great and Greater Britain*, p. 251.

7 Quoted in Howard d'Egville, *Imperial Defence and Closer Union; a Short Record of the Life-Work of the Late Sir John Colomb, in Connection with the Movement towards Imperial Organisation* (London, 1913), p. 17.

8 Vice-Admiral P. H. Colomb, *Naval Warfare; Its Ruling Principles and Practice Historically Treated* (London, 1895), p. 452.

9 Sir John Colomb, *British Dangers* (London, 1902), pp. 17–18.

10 F. T. Jane, *Heresies of Sea Power* (London, 1906), pp. 321, 323–4, 329, 332–4.

11 See Peter Kemp, "From Tryon to Fisher; the regeneration of a navy", in Jordan (ed.), *Naval Warfare in the Twentieth Century*, pp. 2, 23, 30 n.

12 A. T. Mahan, "Current fallacies upon naval subjects", in *Lessons of the War with Spain* (Freeport, NY, 1970, first published, 1899), pp. 282–8.

13 Mahan, *Influence of Sea Power*, pp. 7–11, 20–21 n., and *passim.*

14 Lord Sydenham of Combe [Sir George Clarke], "Mr Churchill as historian", in Colonel the Lord Sydenham of Combe, Admiral Sir R. Bacon, General Sir F. Maurice, General Sir W. D. Bird, and Sir C. Oman, *The World Crisis by Winston Churchill; A Criticism* (London, 1927), p. 32.

15 F. Engels, *Anti-Dühring; Herr Eugen Dühring's Revolution in Science* (Moscow, 1962), pp. 239–40.

16 Speech made in House of Commons, 18 March 1912, and reprinted in W. Churchill, *The Liberal Government and Naval Policy* (London, 1912), p. 23.

17 Clausewitz, *On War*, p. 97.

18 See Semmel, *Imperialism and Social Reform*, p. 145.

19 Quoted in Mackay, *Fisher of Kilverstone*, p. 310. My discussion of the naval race owes much to the classic account by Woodward, *Great Britain and the German Navy* as well as to Arthur Marder's superb *From the Dreadnought to Scapa Flow; The Royal Navy in the Fisher Era, 1904–1919*, 5 vols (Oxford, 1961–70). Peter Padfield has written a popular acount in his *The Great Naval Race; the Anglo-German Naval Rivalry, 1900–1914* (London, 1974). Also see R. F. Mackay, "Historical reinterpretations of the Anglo-German naval rivalry, 1897–1914" in Jordan (ed.), *Naval Warfare in the Twentieth Century*, pp. 32–4.

20 Quoted in Mackay, *Fisher of Kilverstone*, p. 348.

21 [Admiral R. Custance], "A retrograde admiralty", *Blackwood's Edinburgh Magazine* [hereafter cited as *Blackwood's*], vol. 177, no. 1,075 (May 1905), pp. 599–600, 603, 607.

22 [Custance], "The growth of the capital ship", *Blackwood's*, vol. 179, no. 1,087 (May 1906), p. 596; also [Custance], "A retrograde admiralty", pp. 603, 606–7; and *Blackwood's*, vol. 177, no. 1,076 (June 1905), pp. 738, 742, 746.

23 "Barfleur" [Sir Reginald Custance], *Naval policy: A Plea for the Study of War* (Edinburgh: Blackwood, 1907), p. 289. The book, a collection of Custance's articles, was dedicated to Vice-Admiral P. H. Colomb. Custance had been

Captain of the *Barfleur* from 1895 to 1898. See Marder, *From the Dreadnought to Scapa Flow*, Vol. 1, p. 91.

24 [Custance], "Naval education: its past and future", *Blackwood's*, vol. 178, no. 1,080 (October 1905), pp. 446–8; and "The naval officer – past and future", *Blackwood's*, vol. 178, no. 1,082 (December 1905), p. 745.

25 [Custance], "Lessons from the Battle of Tsusima", *Blackwood's*, vol. 179, no. 1,084 (February 1906), pp. 162–5.

26 "Barfleur", *Naval Policy*, pp. 289, 291.

27 See Possony and Mantoux, "Du Picq and Foch", pp. 226–7.

28 A. T. Mahan, in *U.S.N. Institute Proceedings*, June 1906; quoted in Padfield, *The Great Naval Race*, p. 144.

29 Bridge, *The Art of Naval Warfare*, pp. 222–3, 227–8, 160–2, 211–12, 242–3, 19, 233, 246–7.

30 "Civis" [pseud. Sir W. H. White], *The State of the Navy in 1907; A Plea for Inquiry* (London, 1907), pp. ix, 161.

31 See A. M. Gollin, *The Observer and J. L. Garvin 1908–1914; A Study in a Great Editorship* (London, 1960), pp. 28–92.

32 A. S. Hurd, "Progress or reaction in the Navy", *Fortnightly Review*, vol. 79, N.S., no. 473 (2 April 1906), pp. 707–9, 713.

33 H. H. Wilson, "The sacrifice of sea power to 'Economy' ", *National Review*, vol. 48, no. 286 (December 1906), pp. 714–15.

34 See Carlyon Bellairs, MP, "The naval crisis", pp. 33–44. In 1909, Bellairs was to move from the Liberal to the Unionist party.

35 Quoted in Marder, *Dreadnought to Scapa Flow*, p. 367; see also J. St L. Strachey, "Introduction" to "Civis" [Sir W. H. White], *The State of the Navy in 1907*, pp. 1–14.

36 ibid., pp. viii, 161, 83–97.

37 Sir W. H. White, "The cult of the monster warship", *Nineteenth Century and After*, vol. 63, no. 376 (June 1908), pp. 903, 922–3.

38 See D. M. Schurman, *Julian S. Corbett, 1854–1922; Historian of British Maritime Policy from Drake to Jellicoe* (London, 1981), pp. 51–5.

39 See, for example, J. S. Corbett, "Recent attacks on the admiralty", *Nineteenth Century and After*, vol. 61, no. 360 (February 1907), pp. 202–4.

40 Corbett, *Principles of Maritime Strategy*, pp. 28–30, 32–3, 35, 88, 90–1, 99.

41 See H. S. Wilkinson, *Thirty-Five Years 1874–1909* (London, 1933), pp. 186–8. [Letter 3–4 in exchange, 1893].

42 Corbett, *Principles of Maritime Strategy*, pp. 283, 169–73, 182.

43 See account in Grand Admiral von Tirpitz, *My Memoirs*, Vol. 1 (London, 1919), pp. 51, 58.

44 P. Fontin, *Revue Maritime*, October 1902, quoted in Padfield, *The Great Naval Race*, p. 99.

45 Winston Churchill, *The World Crisis 1911–1918* (London, 1938; first published, 1923–31), Vol. 1, p. 58.

46 Corbett, *Principles of Maritime Strategy*, pp. 284; also 190–6 *passim*.

47 Vice-Admiral K. G. B. Dewar, *The Navy from Within* (London, 1939), pp. 146–7, 149–50.

48 Captain J. C. R. Colomb, *Imperial Strategy* (London, 1871), p. 11.

49 Sir John Colomb, *British Dangers*, p. 20.

50 John McDermott, "Sir Francis Openheimer: 'Stranger Within' the Foreign Office", *History*, vol. 66, no. 217 (June 1981), pp. 204–7.

51 Corbett, *Principles of Maritime Strategy*, pp. 300–10, and *passim*; see also Mackay, *Fisher of Kilverstone*, pp. 385–6.

52 Marder (ed.), *Fear God and Dread Nought*, Vol. 2, p. 143. For a typical view of the Liberal position, see A. G. Gardiner, *The Life of Sir William Harcourt*, Vol. 2, (London, 1923), pp. 246–7; also ibid., vol. 1, pp. 233–4, 310–11, 201–2; and Sir William Harcourt, "Our naval and military establishments with reference to the dangers of invasion", *JRUSI*, vol. 16 (1872), p. 593 and *passim*.
53 Quoted in Churchill, *World Crisis*, Vol. 1, pp. 582–3.
54 For text, see A. J. Balfour, *The Navy and the War (August 1914 to August 1915)* (London, 1915), pp. 7–9.
55 Winston Churchill, *Great Contemporaries* (London, 1947), pp. 266–7.
56 Balfour, *The Navy and the War*, pp. 3–5.
57 *PD*, HC, 7 March 1916, 5th series, vol. 80, pp. 1429–30.
58 See Kemp, "From Tryon to Fisher", pp. 24–5.
59 D. Lloyd George, *War Memoirs*, Vol. 3, (London: Nicholson & Watson, 1934), p. 1174.
60 Quoted in Sydenham, "Churchill as historian", pp. 26–7.
61 A. C. D. [A. C. Dewar], "Jutland, Battle of", *Encyclopaedia Britannica*, 12th edn (London, 1922), Vol. 31, p. 667.
62 "Report of Statement made by The First Lord of the Admiralty to Overseas Parliamentary Representatives, 6th July, 1916." PRO, ADM 116/1681, item X, pp. 4, 16–17, 11.
63 W. S. Churchill, MP, "The war on land and sea", *The London Magazine*, N.S., vol. 37, no. 72 (October 1916), pp. 123, 126.
64 *The Times*, 4 October 1916, 6 d.
65 *The Times*, 9 October 1916, 6 d.
66 *The Times*, 10 October 1916, 6 d.
67 *The Times*, 11 October 1916, 6 d.
68 "Report of Proceedings at a Meeting held by the Right Hon. Arthur J. Balfour, O.M., M.P., with Representatives of the Press. 7th November 1916." PRO, ADM 116/1681, item XI, pp. 11–12, 18.
69 Archibald Hurd, "Sea heresy, invasion, and other matters", *Fortnightly Review*, N.S., vol. 100, no. 600 (1 December 1916), p. 927.
70 *PD*, HL, 15 November 1916, 5th series, vol. 23, pp. 510–12.
71 ibid., pp. 514–15.
72 ibid., p. 530.
73 ibid., pp. 524–5.
74 ibid., p. 536.
75 *The Times*, 5 May, 1917, 7 e.
76 *The Times*, 7 May 1917, 7 e.
77 *The Times*, 14 May 1917, 9 d.
78 *The Times*, 8 May 1917, 7 e; see also Custance's reply, 9 May 1917, 7 d.
79 *The Times*, 5 May 1917, 7 f.
80 Churchill, *World Crisis*, Vol. 2, pp. 1013–14; see also p. 1069.
81 Sydenham, "Mr. Churchill as historian", pp. 23–5, 31–2, and *passim*. On Fisher, the heavy cruiser, and fire-controlled long-range gunnery, see J. T. Sumida, "British capital ship design and fire control in the dreadnought era: Sir John Fisher, Arthur Hungerford Pollen, and the battle cruiser", *Journal of Modern History*, vol. 51, no. 2 (June 1979), pp. 205–30.
82 Churchill, *World Crisis*, Vol. 2, p. 1015.
83 [Sir H. Richmond], "The late Sir Julian Corbett", *The Naval Review*, vol. 11, no. 1 (February 1923), pp. 15, 17–18.
84 Lord Sydenham of Combe, "Sea heresies", *The Naval Review*, vol. 19, no. 2 (May 1931), pp. 226, 231–3, 234–5.

85 Tirpitz, *Memoirs*, Vol. 2, pp. 361, 366.
86 See ibid., Vol. 2, pp. 345, 353–4, 358, 366, 369–70, 444.
87 See P. M. Kennedy, "Fisher and Tirpitz: political admirals in the age of imperialism", *Naval Warfare in the Twentieth Century*, ed. G. Jordan, pp. 46–7, 52, 55–7. On the German naval officer corps having aped the "feudal" social standards of their military counterparts, see H. H. Herwig, *The German Naval Officer Corps: a Social and Political History 1890–1918* (Oxford, 1973), pp. ix, 59–60, 68–9, 101, and *passim*.
88 Lord Sydenham, Foreword to Vice-Admiral Sir H. W. Richmond, *Naval Policy and Naval Strength; and Other Essays* (London, 1928), p. ix.
89 See Bernard Semmel, "Marxism and the science of war: theory and praxis", in *Marxism and the Science of War*, ed. B. Semmel (Oxford, 1981), pp. 21–4, and *passim*.
90 See Kennedy, "Strategic aspects of the Anglo-German naval race", pp. 149–50 especially.
91 See Tirpitz, *Memoirs*, Vol. 2, p. 358. For critiques of Tirpitz's strategic planning, see Herbert Rosinski, *The Development of Naval Thought*, ed. B. M. Simpson III (Newport, RI, 1977), pp. 29–31, 53–7, 71–87 and Paul Kennedy; "Strategic aspects of the Anglo-German naval race", *Strategy and Diplomacy 1870–1945* (London, 1983), pp. 127–60.

Chapter 10: *America and Freedom of the Seas*

1 J. Q. Adams to Minister Rush, 28 July 1823, in *Policy of the United States Toward Maritime Commerce in War*, ed. Carlton Savage (Washington, 1934), Vol. 1 (1776–1914), pp. 306–7.
2 J. Q. Adams to Minister Middleton, 13 August 1823, in ibid., Vol. 1, p. 317.
3 Henry Clay to Delegates at Panama Congress, 8 May 1826, in ibid., Vol. 1, pp. 328–9.
4 Martin Van Buren to Minister Randolph, 18 June 1830, in ibid., Vol. 1, p. 345.
5 Cobden to Secretary of the Sheffield Foreign Affairs Committee, *The Times*, 19 December 1856, 9 a.
6 [Sir G. S. Clarke], "Report of the Inter-departmental Committee", 14 May 1906, PRO, CAB 37/87 (1907), Appendix 8, p. 67.
7 See, for example, A. T. Mahan to Sir G. S. Clarke, 5 November 1892, and 30 September 1894, Library of Congress [hereafter cited as L. of C.], Mahan Papers, Box no. 3.
8 Mahan to Colonel Sterling, 13 February 1896, L. of C., Mahan Papers, Box no. 3.
9 Mahan to J. R. Thursfield, 28 October 1899, L. of C., Mahan Papers, Box no. 3.
10 Theodore Roosevelt, Message to Congress, 7 December 1903, in Savage (ed.), *Policy of the United States*, Vol. 1, pp. 50–1.
11 Congressional Record, 58th Congress, 2nd Session, 1904, vol. 38.5, p. 4522; see also pp. 5633, 5696, 5846.
12 Mahan to Pres. T. Roosevelt, 27 December 1904, L. of C., Mahan Papers, Box no. 3. For the new perception of an Anglo-American common interest, see Bradford Perkins, *The Great Rapprochment: England and the United States, 1895–1914* (New York, 1968).
13 Roosevelt to Mahan, 29 December 1904, L. of C., Mahan Papers, Box no. 3.
14 Roosevelt to Mahan, 12 September 1905, L. of C., Theodore Roosevelt Papers, series 2.
15 Secretary of State Elihu Root to Secretary of the Navy, 21 May 1906, L. of C., Mahan Papers, Box no. 6.

16 General Board of Secretary of the Navy, 20 June 1906; and Admiral George Dewey to same (G.B. no. 438), L. of C., Mahan Papers, Box no. 6.
17 Mahan to Roosevelt, 14 August 1906, L. of C., Mahan Papers, Box no. 6.
18 Roosevelt to Mahan, 16 August 1906, L. of C., Roosevelt Papers, series 2.
19 Roosevelt to Mahan, 22 October 1906, L. of C., Roosevelt Papers, series 2. Coogan argues that Roosevelt believed neutral rights were in the US national interest, and that his work on the War of 1812 had given him an entrenched emotional position. See Coogan, *End of Neutrality*, pp. 62–5.
20 Root to Mahan, 21 May 1906, quoted in Livezey, *Mahan on Sea Power*, pp. 250–1.
21 Secretary of State E. Root to Hague Peace Conference Delegates, 31 May 1907, in Savage (ed.), *Policy of the United States*, Vol. 1, pp. 517–18.
22 Quoted in E. S. Martin, *The Life of Joseph Hodges Choate*, Vol. 2 (New York, 1920), p. 317.
23 *The Proceedings of the Hague Peace Conferences; The Conference of 1907*, Vol. 3 (New York, 1920), pp. 765–7. Uriah M. Rose, an Arkansas jurist and one of the United States delegates, defended immunity in the self-righteous manner of American liberalism that other delegations must have found particularly irritating. Rose protested against those who argued that the rules of land-warfare prohibiting pillage had not been established "chiefly for reasons of humanity" but rather "to prevent lack of discipline in the soldier." "We are not ignorant of the fact that a cynical philosophy holds that our best actions have their origins in selfish motives, but we are by no means disposed to accept a theory so revolting, which robs virtue of all that ennobles it and deprives it of what is often its last and only reward" (pp. 787–90). The British delegate Sir Ernest Satow, in reply, observed that "we seem to hear a voice, enjoining us to keep – with moderation however – the eighth Commandment, but when we open our ears to hear its counsels with regard to the sixth Commandment, that voice is silent" (p. 822).
24 A. T. Mahan to L. J. Maxse, 30 July 1907, *Letters and Papers of Alfred Thayer Mahan*, ed. R. Seager II and D. D. Maguire, Vol. 3 (Annapolis, 1975), p. 221. See also C. D. Davis, *The United States and the Second Hague Conference; American Diplomacy and International Organization* (Durham, NC, 1975), p. 229.
25 *Proceedings of the Hague Peace Conferences*, Vol. 3, pp. 779–80.
26 ibid., Vol. 3, p. 782.
27 ibid., Vol. 3, p. 768. Later the tzar's delegate in opposing immunity observed that it was "indisputable that in warfare on land the lower classes suffer more than all others, while at sea war reaches above all big corporations, and individuals are affected only indirectly" (p. 832).
28 ibid., Vol. 3, p. 783.
29 ibid., Vol. 3, pp. 778–9.
30 ibid., Vol. 3, pp. 778, 822.
31 ibid., Vol. 3, pp. 824–5.
32 Mahan Notes, July 1914, L. of C., Mahan Papers, Box no. 18.
33 *New York Times*, 3 January 1915, in PRO, CAB 37/123, no. 8. German strategists could only rely on "ignorant meddlers in Parliament" who might compel the Admiralty to divide the fleet, wrote this disciple of Mahan (who had died the previous month), thus enabling the German navy to make a sortie and concentrate its attack on one part of England's naval forces. The first lord of the admiralty, Winston Churchill, referred to the anonymous author as "a recognized authority" when he circulated copies of the article to the cabinet. On the blockade, see Arthur Marsden, "The blockade", in *British Foreign Policy*, ed. Hinsley; Gerd Hardach, *The First World War 1914–18* (Berkeley, 1977), pp. 11–34. See also M. C. Siney, *The Allied Blockade of Germany, 1914–1916* (Ann Arbor, 1959),

and the official A. C. Bell, *The Blockade of the Central Empires, 1914–1918* (London, 1937; confidential until 1961).

34 See *The Letters and Friendships of Sir Cecil Spring-Rice; A Record*, ed. Stephen Gwynn, Vol. 2 (Boston, 1929), pp. 107–10.

35 See Lord Devlin, *The House of Lords and the Naval Prize Bill, 1911* (Cambridge, 1968), p. 9.

36 Quoted in B. J. Hendrick, *The Life and Letters of Walter H. Page*, Vol. 3 (Garden City, NY, 1925), pp. 182, 186.

37 W. H. Page to Sir E. Grey, 28 December 1914; circulated to cabinet, 31 December 1914. PRO, CAB 37/122, no. 194.

38 Sir C. Spring-Rice to Foreign Office, 15 July 1915, PRO, CAB 37/131, no. 20.

39 Viscount Grey, *Twenty-five Years 1892–1916*, Vol. 2 (New York, 1925), pp. 107–10.

40 Cobden to Bright, 23 January 1862, Cobden Papers, BL, Add. Mss. 43,652, f. 24.

41 Quoted in M. G. Fry, "The imperial war cabinet, the United States, and the freedom of the seas", JRUSI, vol. 110 (1965), p. 365.

42 See discussion in Forrest Davies, *The Atlantic System; the Story of Anglo-American Control of the Seas* (New York, 1941), pp. 257–9. Coogan (in *End of Neutrality*, pp. 249–56, and *passim*) argues that Britain in the First World War was the first belligerent to break a viable international maritime law, and that Wilson, despite the accepted view to the contrary, permitted these violations. Some critics have found these conjectures without substance: see, for example, reviews of P. S. Holbo, *Journal of American History*, vol. 69, no. 2 (September 1982), pp. 482–3; R. Jeffreys-Jones, *History*, vol. 68, no. 224 (October 1983), p. 472.

43 *The Intimate Papers of Colonel House*, ed. C. Seymour, Vol. 1 (London, 1926), p. 376.

44 Col. House to Pres. Wilson, 23 February 1915, ibid., Vol. 1, p. 389.

45 House to Wilson, 20 March 1915, ibid., Vol. 1, p. 405.

46 House to Wilson, 27 March 1915, ibid., Vol. 1, p. 414.

47 Quoted in A. S. Link, *Wilson; the Struggle for Neutrality, 1914–1915* (Princeton, NJ, 1960), pp. 226–7.

48 Seymour (ed.), *Papers of Colonel House*, vol. 1, p. 390; for a discussion of the peace movement during the war, see Keith Robbins, *The Abolition of War; the Peace Movement in Britain, 1914–1919* (Cardiff, 1976).

49 House to Wilson, 3 May 1915, Seymour (ed.), *Papers of Colonel House*, Vol. 1, p. 432.

50 Quoted in ibid., pp. 229–30.

51 ibid., Vol. 1, pp. 459–60.

52 House to Wilson, 3 May 1915, ibid., Vol. 1, p. 432.

53 See A. J. Marder, *From the Dreadnought to Scapa Flow*, Vol. 2, pp. 372–7, and *passim*.

54 See Memorandum of 16 November 1916, PRO, FO 551/11, pp. 14–15. See also Minutes of Subcommittee "to consider the definition of the enemy", War Trade Advisory Committee [November] 1915, PRO, CAB 39/10, p. 24.

55 Foreign Office memorandum, May 1918, PRO, FO 551/11, p. 2.

56 Minutes, subcommittee, War Trade Advisory Committee [November] 1915, PRO, CAB 39/10, pp. 29, 31.

57 E. M. Pollock, "Memorandum on Trade War", 27 June 1917, PRO, FO 551/11, p. 27.

58 See Stephen Roskill, *Hankey, Man of Secrets*, Vol. 1 (London, 1970), pp. 158, 180.

59 ibid., pp. 184–5; and Lord Crewe to Cabinet, 18 June 1915, PRO, CAB 37/130, no. 15.

60 Grey to House, 11 November 1915, Seymour (ed.), *Papers of Colonel House*, Vol. 2, pp. 79–80.

61 House to Wilson, 17 January 1916, ibid., Vol. 2, p. 116; see also Vol. 2, pp. 328–9.

62 *Morning Post*, 14 February 1916, in Arnold White Papers, National Maritime Museum, WHI/14.
63 *PD*, HL, 22 February 1916, 5th series, vol. 21, pp. 74–5.
64 ibid., p. 88; see also pp. 84–6.
65 ibid., pp. 111–12.
66 Sydenham, "Sea heresies", p. 234 n.
67 P. H. Colomb, *Essays on Naval Defence*, pp. 245–6, 250, 256, and *passim*; see John Winton, *Convoy; the Defence of Sea Trade 1890–1990* (London, 1983), pp. 17–31.
68 Jane, *Heresies of Sea Power*, p. 177.
69 Report of the Statement made by the First Lord of the Admiralty to Oversea Parliamentary Representatives, 6 July 1916, PRO, ADM 116/1681, item X, pp. 12–13.
70 Lloyd George, *War Memoirs*, Vol. 3, pp. 1195–6.
71 B. Liddell Hart, *The British Way in Warfare* (London, 1932), p. 38. For a different view, see Kennedy, *Realities*, pp. 182–3; and Hardach, *First World War*, pp. 31, 33, 51–2.
72 Liddell Hart, *British Way in Warfare*, p. 37. See Brian Bond, *Liddell Hart; A Study of His Military Thought* (London, 1977), pp. 65–85.
73 Admiral Sir Herbert Richmond, *Statesmen and Sea Power* (Oxford, 1946), p. 283; also pp. 266–7. See also Admiral Sir Herbert Richmond, *British Strategy, Military and Economic; A Historical Review and its Contemporary Lessons* (Cambridge, 1941), pp. 128, 132–5, 137, 146, and *passim*.
74 See, for example, Michael Howard, *The British Way in Warfare; A Reappraisal* (London, 1975). Howard argues that military support for a continental ally "far from being alien to traditional British strategy, was absolutely central to it" (pp. 14–15); and David French, *British Economic and Strategic Planning 1905–1915* (London, 1982), who described the purely maritime strategy as "business as usual" and attributed the 1914 conversion of the nation to a continental strategy to Kitchener (pp. 98–137 *passim*). Avner Offer, "The working classes, British naval plans and the coming of the Great War," *Past & Present*, no. 107 (May 1985), argues that the upsurge of volunteers for Britain's armies during the first two months of the war settled the question in favor of a continental strategy (pp. 219–26). See also Hew Strachan, "The British way of warfare revisited", *Historical Journal*, vol. 26, pt 2 (1983), pp. 450–8.
75 See Seymour (ed.), *Papers of Colonel House*, Vol. 3, p. 355.
76 See House's Journal, 28 October 1918, ibid., Vol. 4, pp. 165, 179; see also Woodward, *Great Britain and the War*, p. 398 n.
77 House's Journal, 1 November 1918, Seymour (ed.), *Papers of Colonel House*, Vol. 4, p. 180.
78 Wilson to House, 4 November 1918, ibid., Vol. 4, p. 184.
79 House's Journal, October 1918, ibid., Vol. 4, pp. 168–9.
80 House's Journal, 4 November 1918, ibid., Vol. 4, pp. 189, 186.
81 Archibald Hurd, "America's new naval policy", *Fortnightly Review*, N.S., vol. 100, no. 599 (1 November 1916), pp. 744–5, 757.
82 Quoted in Seymour (ed.), *Papers of Colonel House*, Vol. 4, p. 184.
83 Quoted in D. F. Trask, *Captains and Cabinets; Anglo-American Naval Relations, 1917–1918* (Columbia, Mo., 1972), pp. 320–1. Trask has also described the American position during this period in "The American navy in a world at war, 1914–1919", in *In Peace and War; Interpretations of American Naval History*, ed. K. J. Hagan (Westport, Conn., 1978), pp. 205–20; and "William Shepherd Benson", in *The Chiefs of Naval Operations*, ed. R. W. Love, Jr (Annapolis, Md, 1980), particularly pp. 16–19.

84 Quoted in Fry, "Imperial war cabinet, etc.", p. 360.
85 Sir Julian Corbett, *The League of Peace and a Free Sea* (New York, 1917), pp. 3–5.
86 Spenser Wilkinson, *British Aspects of War and Peace* (London, 1920), p. 24.
87 Quoted in *Weekly Dispatch*, November 1918, in Arnold White Papers, National Maritime Museum, WHI/60.
88 *The Times*, 26 November 1918.
89 See Fry, "Imperial war cabinet, etc.", p. 360.
90 J. M. Keynes, *Essays in Biography* (New York, 1951), p. 33.
91 See Seymour (ed.), *Papers of Colonel House*, Vol. 4, p. 432; also Marder, *Dreadnought to Scapa Flow*, Vol. 5, pp. 238–42 and *passim*.
92 Sir Francis Piggott, *The Free Seas in War* (London, 1918), pp. 30–1, 35.
93 The Mahan papers include the letter written by Carnegie to Clarke, approving the latter's 1894 article on a federation of the English-speaking races. L. of C., Mahan Papers, Box no. 3.
94 Sir G. S. Clarke to Valentine Chirol, 11 November 1904, Sydenham Papers, BL Add. Mss. 50,831, ff. 262–7. See also G. S. Clarke, "Captain Mahan's counsels to the United States", *Nineteenth Century*, vol. 43, no. 252 (February 1898), p. 300 and *passim*.
95 George Young, "Anglo-American command of the seas", *Contemporary Review*, vol. 133 (March 1928), pp. 298–301. Young observed that it was foolish for Englishmen to insist that British use of sea power was not imperialistic while American activities in Latin America were, for "the American rulers are Anglo-Saxons like ourselves with the same capacity for sentimental humbug and for cynical self-help." (p. 297). Great Britain ought to seize the American offer of parity before the United States turned to a program of naval superiority. The offer of parity was "the result of a balance of power in America between, on the one side, an economic plutocracy and a pacifist public opinion and, on the other side, navalist ideals and imperialist interests. The latter are still immature but are steadily getting stronger" (p. 302).
96 Col. E. M. House, "The freedom of the seas", *Contemporary Review*, vol. 133 (April 1928), pp. 419–21.
97 Labour Party, *Freedom of the Seas, Old and New* (London, 192?), p. 12.
98 Lord Eustace Percy, *Maritime Trade in War; Lectures on Freedom of the Seas* (New Haven, Conn., 1930), pp. 113–14.
99 J. M. Kenworthy and G. Young, *Freedom of the Seas* (London, 1928), pp. 203–4; see also pp. 15–16, and 270.
100 Sir M. Hankey to Sir H. Richmond, *c.* 1928, Richmond Papers, National Maritime Museum, RIC/7/3(d). For his public discussion of the question, see Admiral Sir H. W. Richmond, *Imperial Defence and Capture at Sea in War* (London, 1932), especially pp. 167, 180–234, 254–82.
101 Quoted in Roskill, *Hankey, Man of Secrets*, Vol. 2, pp. 451–2.
102 See PRO, CAB 24/189, C.P. 258 (27), dated 26 October 1927.
103 Quoted in Roskill, *Hankey, Man of Secrets*, Vol. 2, p. 455.
104 Quoted in ibid., p. 451.
105 Memorandum by Sir Maurice Hankey, 14 November 1927, PRO, CAB 24/189, C.P. 286, ff. 4–7.
106 Hankey to Richmond, 31 January 1929, Richmond Papers, National Maritime Museum, RIC/7/3(d).
107 House to Wilson, 3 May 1915, in Seymour (ed.), *Papers of Colonel House*, Vol. 1, p. 432.
108 See Roskill, *Hankey, Man of Secrets*, Vol. 2, pp. 492–4. For a discussion of the

Anglo-American naval antagonism in the decade after the war, see S. W. Roskill, *Naval Policy Between the Wars*, Vol. 1, 1919–1929 (New York, 1969).

Chapter 11: *Radicals, Reactionaries, and Power*

1 Correlli Barnett, "Strategy and society", *JRUSI for Defence Studies*, vol. 121, no. 3 (September 1976), p. 12.
2 L. Namier, "Human nature in politics", *The Listener*, vol. 50, no. 1295 (24 December 1953), p. 1078.
3 P. M. Kennedy, "Strategy versus finance in twentieth-century Britain", *Strategy and Diplomacy*, pp. 105–6, and *passim*.
4 Correlli Barnett, *The Collapse of British Power* (London, 1972), pp. 98, 430, 62–4, and *passim*.
5 Quoted in Padfield, *The Great Naval Race*, p. 87.
6 Quoted in Woodward, *Great Britain and the German Navy*, p. 255.
7 See discussion in Michael Howard, *Ethics and Power in International Politics* (London, 1978), p. 9, and *passim*.
8 Lord Devlin, *The House of Lords and the Naval Prize Bill, 1911* (Cambridge, 1968), pp. 20–3, 26–7.
9 Viscount Grey, *Twenty-Five Years 1892–1916*, Vol. 2 (New York, 1925), pp. 105–6; see also pp. 108, 110.
10 D. Lloyd George, *War Memoirs*, p. 87.
11 Lord Charles Beresford, *The Betrayal* (London, 1912), pp. 149–50.
12 Lord Charles Beresford, *The Memoirs of Admiral Lord Charles Beresford*, Vol. 2 (London, 1914), pp. 386–7.
13 Ignotus, "Our sentimentalists and our sea-power", *National Review*, vol. 58 (November 1911), pp. 403–4.
14 Admiral Sir Hedworth Lambton, *The Times*, 28 June 1911; clipping in Arnold White Papers, National Maritime Museum, WHI/60.
15 H. H. Wilson, "Sea law made in Germany", *National Review*, vol. 56 (January 1911), p. 740.
16 *PD*, HC, 17 May 1889, 3rd series, vol. 336, pp. 406–8.
17 *PD*, HC, 6 May 1889, 3rd series, vol. 335, pp. 1322–3, p. 1327.
18 J. T. Danson, *Our Commerce in War Time; and How to Protect It* (London, 1897), p. 9.
19 *The Nation*, 6 July 1907, vol. 1 (no. 19), p. 682.
20 For Brunner's statement, see minutes of discussion, in Arthur Cohen, *The Immunity of Enemy's Property from Capture at Sea* (London, 1909), p. 31.
21 See, for example, discussion in S. R. Williamson, Jr, *The Politics of Grand Strategy; Britain and France Prepare for War, 1904–1914* (Cambridge, Mass., 1969), pp. 240–2; also M. R. Pitt, "Great Britain and belligerent maritime rights from the Declaration of Paris, 1856, to the Declaration of London, 1909", PhD thesis, University of London, 1964, p. 112.
22 See, for example, Evan MacGregor, at Admiralty, to E. Hertslet, Foreign Office, 13 April 1892, and Hertslet to MacGregor, 29 April 1892, PRO, FO 97/572, Letter M/2577, pp. 40–3, and 44–5, 47. I was alerted to this exchange by a discussion in Pitt, "Great Britain and belligerent maritime rights", p. 143.
23 See discussion in G. Best, "How right is might? Some aspects of the international debate about how to fight wars and how to win them 1870–1918", in *War, Economy, and the Military Mind* (London, 1976), pp. 131–2.

24 See Bernard Shaw, "Common sense about the war", *What I Really Wrote About the War* (London, 1931), pp. 22–110.
25 For a conservative view of the relativity of power, see J. L. Garvin, "The maintenance of empire: a study in the economics of power", in C. S. Goldmann (ed.), *The Empire and the Century* (London, 1905), especially p. 79.
26 See J. S. Mill, "Civilization" (1836), *Collected Works*, Vol. 18, especially pp. 122–4, 129–32.
27 Freud, "Civilization and its discontents" (1930), *Complete Psychological Works*, ed. James Strachey, Vol. 21, pp. 141–3.
28 J. S. Mill to T. E. Cliffe Leslie, 5 February 1871, *Collected Works*, Vol. 17, pp. 1805–6.
29 See J. S. Mill to T. E. Cliffe Leslie, 8 August 1860, *Collected Works*, Vol. 15, pp. 702–3.
30 See J. E. Cairnes, "Our defences: a national or a standing army?", *Political Essays* (first published, 1873; New York, 1967). Cairnes believed the Franco-Prussian War had invalidated "our peace-at-any-price principles" and "the doctrine of non-intervention, as interpreted by Manchester" (p. 198).
31 J. S. Mill to J. E. Cairnes, 21 August 1871, *Collected Works*, Vol. 17, pp. 1828–9. See E. P. Sullivan, "Liberalism and imperialism: J. S. Mill's defense of the British Empire", *Journal of the History of Ideas*, vol. 44, no. 4 (October–December 1983), pp. 599–617 *passim*.
32 *PD*, HC, 29 March 1909, 5th series, vol. 3, pp. 61, 69–70.
33 C. L. Ottley, "Introduction" to J. R. Thursfield, *Naval Warfare* (Cambridge, 1913), pp. vii–x.
34 A. T. Mahan, "Britain and the German Navy", *Daily Mail*, 6 July 1910, Appendix, C. C. Taylor, *The Life of Admiral Mahan* (London, 1920), pp. 310–13.
35 H. J. Mackinder, *Democratic Ideals and Reality* (New York, 1962), pp. 14–15, 19–23.
36 See Viscount Esher, *The Influence of King Edward* (London, 1915), p. 64.

Selected Bibliography

Newspapers, Serials, Periodicals, etc.

Annual Register
Chamber of Shipping, Annual Reports
Committee for the Ratification of the Declaration of London, Publications
Congressional Record
Contemporary Review
The Economist
Edinburgh Review
Fortnightly Review
Hansard's *Parliamentary Debates*
Imperial Maritime League, Publications
Liverpool Steamship Owners' Association, Annual Reports
The Nation
The National Review
The Nineteenth Century
The Nineteenth Century and After
Parliamentary History of England
The Times

Manuscripts

Admiralty Papers. Public Record Office.
Balfour Papers. British Library.
Bright Papers. British Library.
Broadlands Papers, Papers and Correspondence of Palmerston. Historical Manuscripts Commission.
Cabinet Papers. Public Record Office.
Campbell-Bannerman Papers. British Library.
Cobden Papers. British Library.
Dilke Papers. British Library.
Foreign Office Papers. Public Record Office.
Grenville Papers. British Library.
Sir Edward Grey Papers. Public Record Office.
Mahan Papers. Library of Congress.
Spencer Perceval Papers. British Library.
Sir Henry Richmond Papers. National Maritime Museum.
Theodore Roosevelt Papers. Library of Congress.
Sydenham Papers. British Library.
J. R. Thursfield Papers. National Maritime Museum.
Arnold White Papers. National Maritime Museum.

Primary Sources

Adams, Brooks, *America's Economic Supremacy* (New York: Macmillan, 1900).

Adams, Brooks, "War as the ultimate form of economic competition", *Proceedings of the US Naval Institute*, vol. 29 (1903), pp. 829–81.

[African Institution], *The Foreign Slave Trade, A Brief Account of Its State, etc.* (London: Hatchard, 1837).

[Americanus], *Comments on Lord Brougham's Attack upon General Cass* (Harrisburg, Pa: Argus, 1843).

Angell, Norman, *The Great Illusion; A Study of the Relation of Military Power to National Advantage* (New York: Putnam, 1913).

Asquith, H. H., *The Genesis of the War* (London: Cassell, 1923).

Balfour, A. J., *After A Year; Speech delivered by the Rt. Hon. A.J. Balfour, First Lord of the Admiralty, at the London Opera House, 4th August, 1915* (London: Darling & Son, 1915).

Balfour, A. J., *The British Blockade* (London: Darling & Son, 1915).

Balfour, A. J., *Essays Speculative and Political* (London: Hodder & Stoughton, 1920).

Balfour, A. J., *Imperial Defence; A Speech delivered in the House of Commons, May 11, 1905, with Corrections* (London: Longmans, Green, 1905).

Balfour, A. J., *The Navy and the War (August 1914 to August 1915)* (London: Darling & Son, 1915).

Balfour, A. J., *The No Bread Convention; Speech delivered at the Cannon Street Hotel, London, June 27, 1911* (London: National Union of Conservative and Constitutionalist Associations, 1911).

Balfour, A. J., *The Policy of the Unionist Party; a speech delivered ... at Nottingham on November 17, 1910* (London: National Union of Conservative and Constitutional Associations, 1910).

Bellairs, Carlyon, "The naval crisis", *National Review*, vol. 53 (March 1909), pp. 33–44.

Bentham, Jeremy, *Plan for a Universal and Perpetual Peace*, Grotius Society Publications, no. 6 (London: Sweet & Maxwell, 1927).

Bentwich, Norman, *The Declaration of London* (London: Effingham Wilson, 1911).

Beresford, Lord Charles, *The Betrayal* (London, 1912).

Beresford, Lord Charles, *The Memoirs of Admiral Lord Charles Beresford*, 2 vols (London: Methuen, 1914).

Bowles, Thomas Gibson, "The Declaration of London", *Nineteenth Century and After*, vol. 65, no. 387 (May 1909), pp. 744–54.

Bowles, T. G., *The Declaration of Paris of 1856: Being An Account of the Maritime Rights of Great Britain; A Consideration of Their Importance; A History of Their Surrender by the Signature of the Declaration of Paris; and An Argument for Their Resumption by the Denunciation and Repudiation of that Declaration* (London: Sampson, Low, 1900).

Bowles, T. G., *The Forthcoming Congress at St. Petersburgh on the Laws of War; An Address delivered in the Central Hall, Darlington, on Tuesday, 5th January 1875* (Newcastle-upon-Tyne, 1875).

Bowles, T. G., *Maritime Warfare* (London: Ridgway, 1877).

Bowles, T. G., "The Navy paralysed by paper", *Fortnightly Review*, vol. 37, N.S. (1 February 1885), pp. 253–61.

Bowles, T. G., *Sea Law and Sea Power; As They Would Be Affected by Recent Proposals; With Reasons Against Those Proposals* (London: John Murray, 1910).

Bridge, Admiral Sir Cyprian, *The Art of Naval Warfare; Introductory Observations* (London: Smith, Elder, 1907).

Bridge, Admiral Sir Cyprian, *Sea Power and Other Studies* (London: Smith, Elder, 1910).

Bright, John, *The Diaries of John Bright*, ed. R.A.J. Walling (New York: William Morrow, 1981).

Bright, John, *The Letter of John Bright, Esq., M.P., on The War; to Absalom Watkin* (London: Cash, 1854).

Bright, John, "On the foreign policy of England; delivered at a banquet given in honor of Mr Bright, at Birmingham, October 29, 1858", in *Representative British Orations*, ed. C. K. Adams, Vol. 3, pp. 159–203 (New York: Putnam, 1884).

[British and Foreign Anti-Slavery Society], *The Slave Trade and Its Remedy* (London: 1848).

Brougham, Henry, *The Life and Times of Henry Lord Brougham*, 2 vols (Edinburgh, 1871).

Brougham, Henry, *The Speech of Henry Brougham, Esq. Before the House of Commons, Friday, April 1, 1808, in Support of the Petitions from London, Liverpool and Manchester, Against the Orders in Council* (London: J. Ridgway, 1808).

[Brougham, Henry], "On the speech of James Stephen in the House of Commons, March 6th, 1809", *Edinburgh Review*, vol. 14, no. 28 (July 1809).

Buckle, H. T., *History of Civilization in England*, Vol. 1 (London: Longmans, Green, 1871; first published 1857).

Buxton, Thomas Fowell, *The African Slave Trade and Its Remedy* (London: Dawsons, 1868; first published, 1839–40).

Cairnes, J. E., *Political Essays* (New York: A. M. Kelley, 1967; first published, 1873).

[Cass, Lewis] An American, *An Examination of the Question, Now in Discussion, Between the American and British Governments, Concerning the Right of Search* (no publisher, 1842).

Charmes, Gabriel, *Naval Reform*, trans. J. E. Gordon-Cumming (London: W. H. Allen, 1887).

Chesney, Lt. Col. C. C., and Henry Reeve, *The Military Resources of Prussia and France and Recent Changes in the Art of War* (London: Longmans, 1870).

Choate, Joseph H., *The Two Hague Conferences* (Princeton, NJ: Princeton University Press, 1913).

Churchill, Winston S., *Great Contemporaries* (London: Odhams, 1947).

Churchill, W. S., *The Liberal Government and Naval Policy* (London: Liberal Publication Department, 1912).

Churchill, W. S., "The war on land and sea", *The London Magazine*, vol. 37, N.S., no. 72 (October 1916), pp. 119–29.

Churchill, W. S., *The World Crisis 1911–1918*, 2 vols (London: Odhams, 1938; first published, 1922–3).

Clarke, Sir George S., "Captain Mahan's counsels to the United States", *Nineteenth Century*, vol. 43, no. 252 (February 1898), pp. 292–300.

Clarke, Sir G. S., *Imperial Defence* (London: Imperial Press, 1897).

Clarke, Sir G. S., and James R. Thursfield, *The Navy and the Nation; or Naval Warfare and Imperial Defence* (London: John Murray, 1897).

Clarke, Sir G. S. [Lord Sydenham of Combe], "Mr. Churchill as historian", in *The World Crisis by Winston Churchill; A Criticism*, by Colonel the Lord Sydenham of Combe, Admiral Sir Reginald Bacon, General Sir Frederick Maurice, General Sir W. D. Bird, and Sir Charles Oman (London: Hutchinson, 1927).

Clarke, Sir G. S. [Lord Sydenham of Combe], "Sea heresies", *The Naval Review*, vol. 19, no. 2 (May 1931), pp. 222–36.

Clarke, Sir G. S., "War, trade, and food supply", *National Review*, vol. 29, no. 173 (July 1897), pp. 756–69.

Clausewitz, Carl von, *On War*, eds M. Howard and P. Paret (Princeton, NJ: Princeton University Press, 1976).

Cobden, Richard, *England, Ireland, and America* (Edinburgh: Tait, 1836).

Cobden, Richard, "A letter to Henry Ashworth, Esq." (1862), In *The Political Writings of Richard Cobden*, Vol. 2 (London: T. Fisher Unwin, 1903).

Cobden, Richard, *Russia* (Edinburgh: Tait, 1836).

Cobden, Richard, "The three panics", in *The Political Writings of Richard Cobden*, Vol. 2 (London: T. Fisher Unwin, 1903).

Cohen, Arthur, *The Immunity of Enemy's Property from Capture at Sea* (Speech at National Liberal Club, 9 November 1909), (London: The Eighty Club, 1909).

Cohen, Arthur, *Paper on the Declaration of London* (read at the Guildhall on 2 August 1910 at Conference of the International Law Association) (London: Flint, 1910).

Coleman, John, *A Reply to Mr. Bright's Letter on the War* (London: Hatchard, 1855).

Colomb, Sir John C. R., *British Dangers* (London: Swan Sonnenschein, 1902).

Colomb, J. C. R., *The Defence of Great and Greater Britain; Sketches of its Naval, Military and Political Aspects* (London: Edward Stanford, 1879).

Colomb, J. C. R., [Captain], *Imperial Defence: A Paper read at the Colonial and Indian Exhibition before a Conference of the Royal Colonial Institute, 18th June 1886* (London: Edward Stanford, 1886).

Colomb, J. C. R. [Captain], *Imperial Strategy* (London: Edward Stanford, 1871).

Colomb, J. C. R. [Captain], *Naval Intelligence and Protection of Commerce in War* (London: W. Mitchell, 1881).

Colomb, P. H., [Vice-Admiral] *Essays on Naval Defence* (London: W. H. Allen, 1893).

Colomb, P. H., [Captain], "Great Britain's maritime power: how best developed", printed as Appendix to J. C. R. Colomb's *Defence of Great and Greater Britain* (London: Edward Stanford, 1879), pp. 252–6.

Colomb, P. H. [Captain], *The Naval Prize Essay, 1878: Great Britain's Maritime Power: How Best Developed, etc.* (London, 1878).

Colomb, P. H. [Vice-Admiral], *Naval Warfare; Its Ruling Principles and Practice Historically Treated* (London: W. H. Allen, 1895).

Colomb, P. H. [Captain], *Slave Catching in the Indian Ocean; A Record of Naval Experiences* (London, 1873).

Corbett, Julian S., "The capture of private property at sea", in A. T. Mahan, *Some Neglected Aspects of War* (Boston: Little Brown, 1907).

Corbett, Julian S. [Sir], *The League of Peace and a Free Sea* (New York: Doran, 1917).

Corbett, Julian S., "Recent attacks on the admiralty", *The Nineteenth Century and After*, vol. 61, no. 360 (February 1907), pp. 195–208.

Corbett, Julian S., *Some Principles of Maritime Strategy* (London: Longmans, Green, 1911).

Corbett, Julian S., *The Spectre of Navalism* (London: Darling & Son, 1915).

Custance, Admiral Sir Reginald, "Capture of property at sea", *Nineteenth Century and After*, vol. 75, no. 444 (February 1914), pp. 225–39.

Custance, Sir Reginald, "Lessons from the Battle of Tsusima", *Blackwood's Magazine*, vol. 179, no. 1,084 (February 1906), pp. 151–65.

Custance, Sir Reginald, "The naval case for ratifying the Declaration of London", *Nineteenth Century and After*, vol. 71, no. 421 (March 1912), pp. 435–44.

Custance, Sir Reginald, ["Barfleur",] *Naval Policy, A Plea for the Study of War* (Edinburgh: Blackwood, 1907).

Custance, Sir Reginald, "The naval officer – past and future", *Blackwood's Edinburgh Magazine*, vol. 178, no. 1,082 (December 1905), pp. 735–46.

Custance, Sir Reginald [Anon.], "A retrograde admiralty", *Blackwood's Edinburgh Magazine*, vol. 177, no. 1,075 (May 1905), pp. 597–607.

Danson, J. T., *Our Commerce in War Time; and How to Protect It* (London: Blades, 1897).

Denman, Captain, R. N., *The African Squadron and Mr. Hutt's Committee* (London: John Mortimer, n.d.).

Dewar, Vice-Admiral K. G. B., *The Navy from Within* (London: Gollancz, 1939).

Dilke, Sir Charles Wentworth, and Spenser Wilkinson, *Imperial Defence* (London: Macmillan, 1892).

Dunraven, Earl of, *Past Times and Pastimes*, Vol.2 (London: Hodder & Stoughton, 192?).

Engels, Friedrich, *Anti-Dühring; Herr Eugen Dühring's Revolution in Science* (Moscow, 1962).

Esher, Viscount, *Modern War and Peace; A Lecture Delivered to the Cambridge University War and Peace Society, December 2, 1912* (Cambridge: Bowes & Bowes, 1912).

Esher, Viscount, *The Influence of King Edward* (London: John Murray, 1915).

Fisher, Sir John Arbuthnot, *Fear God and Dread Nought: The Correspondence of Admiral of the Fleet Lord Fisher of Kilverstone*, ed. Arthur J. Marder, 3 vols (London: Jonathan Cape, 1952, 1956).

Foch, Ferdinand, *The Principles of War*, trans. Hilaire Belloc (London: Chapman & Hall, 1918).

Garvin, J. L., "The maintenance of empire: a study in the economics of power", in *The Empire and the Century: a series of essays on Imperial Problems and Possibilities*, ed. C. S. Goldmann (London: John Murray, 1905).

Grey, Viscount, *Twenty-Five Years 1892–1916*, Vol. 2 (New York: F. A. Stokes, 1925).

Grotius, Hugo, *The Freedom of the Seas or the Right Which Belongs to the Dutch to Take Part in the East Indies Trade* (New York: Oxford University Press, 1916; first published, 1605).

[Hague Conference], *The Proceedings of the Hague Peace Conferences; The Conference of 1897* (New York: Oxford University Press, 1920).

[Hague Conference], *The Proceedings of the Hague Peace Conferences; The Conference of 1907*, 3 vols (New York: Oxford University Press, 1920).

Hall, W. E., *International Law* (Oxford: Oxford University Press, 1880).

Hankey, Lord, *The Supreme Command, 1914–1918*, 2 vols (London: Allen & Unwin, 1961).

[Harcourt, Sir William V.], *Letters by Historicus on Some Questions of International Law Reprinted from 'The Times' with Considerable Additions* (London: Macmillan, 1863).

Harcourt, Sir William, *Our Naval and Military Establishments Regarded with Reference to the Dangers of Invasion*, reprinted from *Journal of the Royal United Service Institution*, vol. 16 (Harrison & Sons, 1872).

Harcourt, Sir William, "The rights and duties of neutrals in time of war", *Journal of the Royal United Service Institution*, vol. 9 (1865), pp. 313–45.

Hart, B. Liddell, *The British Way in Warfare* (London: Faber, 1932).

Higgins, A. Pearce, *War and the Private Citizen; Studies in International Law* (London: King, 1912).

Hirst, F. W., *The Six Panics and Other Essays* (London: Methuen, 1913).

Holland, T. E., *A Lecture on the Brussels Conference of 1874* (Oxford: James Parker, 1876).

Holland, T. E., *Proposed Changes in Naval Prize Law* (London: British Academy, 1911).

Horton-Smith, L. G., *Sea Power: The Liberals and National Defence* (London: Imperial Maritime League, 1911).

House, Colonel Edward M., "The freedom of the seas", *Contemporary Review*, vol. 133 (April 1928); pp. 416–21.

House, Colonel E. M., *The Intimate Papers of Colonel House*, ed. C. Seymour, 4 vols (London: E. Benn, 1926).

Hozier, H. M., *Our Commerce in Maritime War*, Admiralty Intelligence Department (July 1902), no. 654.

Hurd, Archibald, "America's new naval policy", *Fortnightly Review*, vol. 100, N.S., no. 599 (1 November 1916), pp. 743–57.

Hurd, Archibald, "Progress or reaction in the Navy", *Fortnightly Review*, vol. 79, N.S., no. 473 (2 April 1906), pp. 707–19.

Hurd, Archibald, "Sea heresy, invasion, and other matters", *Fortnightly Review*, vol. 100, N.S., no. 600 (1 December 1916), pp. 920–35.

James, William, "The moral equivalent of war", in *War and Morality*, ed. R. A. Wasserstrom (Belmont, Calif.: Wadsworth, 1970).

Jane, Fred T., *Heresies of Sea Power* (London: Longmans, Green, 1906).

Kant, Immanuel, *Kant's Political Writings*, ed. H. Reiss (Cambridge: Cambridge University Press, 1970).

Kenworthy, J. M., and George Young, *Freedom of the Seas* (London: Hutchinson, 1928).

King-Hall, Stephen, *My Naval Life 1906–1929* (London: Faber, 1952).

Labour Party, *Freedom of the Seas, Old and New* (London: Labour Party, 192?).

[Laughton, J. K.], "Captain Mahan on maritime power", *Edinburgh Review*, vol. 172, no. 352 (October 1890), pp. 420–53.

[Laughton, J. K.], "Captain Mahan on maritime power", *Edinburgh Review*, vol. 177, no. 364 (April 1893), pp. 484–518.

Lawrence, Rev. T. C., "The Hague Convention and naval war", *Journal of the Royal United Service Institution*, vol. 52, no. 362 (April 1908), pp. 479–509.

Lawrence, William Beach, *Visitation and Search; or An Historical Sketch of the British Claim to Exercise a Maritime Police Over the Vessels of All Nations in Peace as well as in War* (Boston: Little, Brown, 1858).

Leslie, T. E. Cliffe, "Marine captures and commercial blockades", *Journal of the Dublin Statistical Society*, vol. 1, pp. 97–106.

Leslie, T. E. Cliffe, *The Military Systems of Europe Economically Considered* (Belfast: Shepherd & Aitchison, 1856).

Levi, Leoni, *The History of British Commerce and of the Economic Progress of the British Nation, 1763–1878* (London: John Murray, 1880).

Levi, Leoni, *The Rights and Duties of Neutrals and the Foreign Belligerent Act*, delivered 1 November 1870 (London: National Reform Union [1870]).

Levi, Leoni, *War and Its Consequences: Economical, Commercial, Financial, and Moral* (London: Partridge, 1881).

Lindsay, W. S., *History of Merchant Shipping and Ancient Commerce*, 4 vols (London: Sampson, Low, 1874).

Lindsay, W. S., *Manning the Royal Navy and Merchant Marine; also Belligerent and Neutral Rights in the Event of War* (London: Pewtress, 1877).

List, Friedrich, *The National System of Political Economy* (London: Longmans, Green, 1885; first published, 1841).

Liverpool, Earl of [Charles Jenkinson], *A Discourse on the Conduct of the Government of Great Britain in Respect to Neutral Nations* (London: J. Debrett, 1801; first published, 1757).

Lloyd George, David, *War Memoirs*, 3 vols (London: Nicholson & Watson, 1934).

Loreburn, Earl, *Capture at Sea* (London: Methuen, 1913).

Loreburn, Earl, *Commerce and Property in Naval Warfare; A Letter of the Lord Chancellor*, ed. F. W. Hirst (London: Macmillan, 1906).

MacDonnell, Sir John, *Some Plain Reasons for Immunity from Capture of Private Property at Sea* (London: John Murray, 1910).

Mackinder, H. J., *Democratic Ideals and Reality* (New York: W. W. Norton, 1962; first published, 1919).

Mackinder, H. J., "The geographical pivot of history" (1904), in *Democratic Ideals and Reality* (New York: W. W. Norton, 1962).

[Madison, James], *An Examination of the British Doctrine Which Subjects to Capture A Neutral Trade Not Open in Time of Peace* (London: J. Johnson, 1806).

[Madison, James], *Letters from the Secretary of State to Messrs. Monroe and Pinckney*, pt 3 (Washington, 1808).

Maguire, T. Miller, "The development of international strategy since 1871 and its present conditions", *Journal of the Royal United Service Institution*, vol. 50, no. 339 (May 1906), pp. 637–65.

Mahan, Alfred T., "The Hague Conference: the question of immunity for belligerent merchant shipping", *National Review* (July 1907); reprinted in *Some Neglected Aspects of War* (Boston: Little, Brown, 1907), pp. 157–93.

Mahan, A. T., *The Influence of Sea Power upon History, 1660–1783* (New York: Sagamore Press, 1957; first published 1890).

Mahan, A. T., *The Influence of Sea Power upon the French Revolution and Empire, 1793–1812*, 2 vols (Boston: Little, Brown, 1892).

Mahan, A. T., *Lessons of the War with Spain* (Freeport, NY: Books for Libraries, 1970; first published, 1899).

Mahan, A. T., *Letters and Papers of Alfred Thayer Mahan*, ed. Robert Seager II and D. D. Maguire, 3 vols (Annapolis, Md: Naval Institute Press, 1975).

Mahan, A. T., *Naval Strategy* (Boston: Little, Brown, 1911).

Mahan, A. T., "Possibilities of an Anglo-American reunion" (1894), in *The Interest of America in Sea Power, Present and Future* (Boston: Little, Brown, 1898).

Mahan, A. T., *Sea Power in its Relations to the War of 1812*, 2 vols, (Boston: Little, Brown, 1905).

Mahan, A. T., *Some Neglected Aspects of War* (Boston: Little, Brown, 1907).

Maine, Henry Sumner, *International Law; A Series of Lectures Delivered Before the University of Cambridge, 1887* (New York: Henry Holt, 1888).

Malmesbury, Earl of, *Memoirs of an Ex-Minister; An Autobiography* (London: Longmans, 1884).

Marder, A. J. (ed.), *Fear God and Dread Nought: The Correspondence of Admiral of the Fleet Lord Fisher of Kilverstone*, 3 vols (London: Jonathan Cape, 1952, 1956).

Marx, Karl, *Letters to Dr. Kugelmann* (London: Martin Lawrence, n.d.).

Marx, Karl, *Secret Diplomatic History of the Eighteenth Century and the Story of the Life of Lord Palmerston*, ed. Lester Hutchinson (London: Lawrence & Wishart, 1969).

Matson, Commander H. J., R.N., *Remarks on the Slave Trade and African Squadron* (London: Ridgway, 1848).

Middleton, J. S., *Remarks on the African Squadron* (London: Ridgway, 1851).

Mill, James, *Essays on Government* (London: J. Innes [1828]).

Mill, J. S., *Dissertations and Discussions; Political, Philosophical, and Historical*, vol. 2 (London: J. W. Parker, 1859); vol. 3 (London: Longmans, 1867).

Mill, J. S., *The Earlier Letters of John Stuart Mill, 1812–1848*, Vols 12–13 of *Collected Works*, ed. Francis E. Mineka (Toronto: University of Toronto Press, 1963).

Mill, J. S., *The Later Letters of John Stuart Mill, 1849–1873*, Vols. 14–17 of *Collected Works*, ed. Francis E. Mineka and D. N. Lindley (Toronto: University of Toronto Press, 1972).

Mill, J. S., *Essays on Politics and Society*, Vols 18–19 of *Collected Works*, ed. J. M. Robson (Toronto: University of Toronto Press, 1977).

Money, L. G. Chiozza, "British trade and the war", *Contemporary Review*, vol. 106 (October 1914).

[Morris, Gouverneur], *An Answer to 'War in Disguise'; or, Remarks upon the New Doctrine of England, concerning Neutral Trade* (New York: I. Riley & Co., 1806).

[Newcastle, Duke of], *The Duke of Newcastle's Letter by His Majesty's Order, to Monsieur Michell, the King of Prussia's Secretary of the Embassy* (London: Edward Owen, 1753).

Oliver, F. S., *Ordeal by Battle* (London: Macmillan, 1915).

Owen, Douglas, "Capture at sea", *Journal of the Royal United Service Institution*, vol. 49, no. 333 (November 1905), pp. 1233–61.

Percy, Lord Eustace, *Maritime Trade in War; Lectures on the Freedom of the Seas* (New Haven, Conn.: Yale University Press, 1930).

Phillimore, Joseph, *A Letter Addressed to a Member of the House of Commons on the Subject of the Notice Given by Mr Brougham for a Motion Respecting the Orders-in-Council and the License Trade* (London: 1812).

Phillimore, Joseph, *Reflections on the Nature and Extent of the License Trade* (London: Budd, 1811).

Piggott, Sir Francis, *The Free Seas in War* [with Appendix of extracts of the Writings and Speeches of David Urquhart] (London: P. S. King & Son, 1918).

Ponsonby, Arthur, "Foreign policy and the Navy", *Contemporary Review*, vol. 102 (September 1912), pp. 305–10.

[Reeve, Henry], "Belligerents and neutrals", *Edinburgh Review*, vol. 115, no. 233 (January 1862), pp. 258–92.

[Reeve, Henry], "The Declaration of Paris", *Edinburgh Review*, vol. 144, no. 295 (October 1876), pp. 352–69.

[Reeve, Henry], "The orders in council on trade during war", *Edinburgh Review*, vol. 100, no. 203 (July 1854); pp. 192–225.

Repington, C. à C., *Vestigia* (Boston: Houghton Mifflin, 1919).

Ricardo, J. L., *The War Policy of Commerce* (London: Effingham Wilson, 1855).

Richardson, James, *The Cruisers: Being a Letter to the Marquess of Lansdowne, Lord President . . . in Defence of Armed Coercion for the Extinction of the Slave Trade* (London: Hatchard, 1849).

Richmond, Admiral Sir H. W., *Imperial Defence and Capture at Sea in War* (London: Hutchinson, 1932).

Richmond, Vice-Admiral Sir H. W., *Naval Policy and Naval Strength; and Other Essays* (London: Longmans, Green, 1928).

Robertson, J. M., *The Meaning of Liberalism* (Port Washington, NY: Kennikat Press, 1971; first published, 1912).

Root, Elihu, "The real significance of the Declaration of London", *American Journal of International Law*, vol. 6 (1912), pp. 583–94.

Rousseau, J.-J., *The Social Contract and Discourses* (London: J. M. Dent, 1946).

[Smith, A.], A Journeyman Shoemaker, *The Defences of England; Nine Letters* (London: Robert Hardwicke, 1862).

Smith, Adam, *The Wealth of Nations* (New York: Modern Library, 1965).

Spring-Rice, Sir Cecil, *The Letters and Friendships of Sir Cecil Spring-Rice; A Record*, ed. Stephen Gwynn, Vol. 2 (Boston: Houghton Mifflin, 1929).

Stanley of Alderley, Lord, "Preface" to Robert Ward, *A Treatise of the Relative Rights and Duties of Belligerent and Neutral Nations in Maritime Affairs* (London: Diplomatic Review, 1875).

[Stephen, James], *The Dangers of the Country* (London: J. Butterworth, 1807).

[Stephen, James], "Letters on the slave trade", *Edinburgh Review*, vol. 7 (July 1806), pp. 365–85.

[Stephen, James], *The Speech of James Stephen, Esq. at the Annual Meeting of the African Institution, 26 March, 1817* (London: 1817).

[Stephen, James], *War in Disguise; or, the Frauds of the Neutral Flags* (London: J. Hatchard and J. Butterworth, 3rd edn, 1806).

Synnott, Nicholas, "Dangers to British sea-power under the present rules of naval warfare", *Fortnightly Review*, vol. 61, N.S., no. 364 (April 1897), pp. 568–81.

Thursfield, J. R., "The higher policy of defence", in *Nelson and Other Naval Studies* (London: John Murray, 1909).

Thursfield, J. R., *Naval Warfare* (Cambridge: Cambridge University Press, 1913).

Tirpitz, Grand Admiral von, *My Memoirs*, 2 vols (London: Hurst & Blackett, 1919).

Tocqueville, A. de, *Correspondance anglaise*, Vol. 2 of *Oeuvres Complètes*, ed. J.-P. Mayer (Paris: Gallimard, 1954).

Toulmin, George, "The Liberal Party and naval expenditures", *Contemporary Review*, vol. 102 (September 1912), pp. 311–16.

Urquhart, David, *Answer to Mr. Cobden on the Assimilation of War and Peace* (London: Hardwicke, 1862).

Urquhart, David, *Danger to England from the Congress at Brussels on the Laws of War* [Speech to Yorkshire Foreign Affairs Committees, 13 June 1874] (London: 1874).

Urquhart, David, *Naval Power Suppressed by the Maritime States* (London: 'Diplomatic Review', 1874).

Urquhart, David, *The Right of Search: Two Speeches by David Urquhart, January 20 and 27, 1862* (London: Hardwicke, 1862).

Urquhart, David, *Sparing Private Property in War at Sea; Two Letters to Mr. Gregory on his Motion of March 2, 1866* (London: Hardwicke, 1866).

[Vignot, Henry], *Essai de Stratégie Navale* (Paris: Berger-Levrault, 1893).

Waddilove, Alfred, "The effect of the recent orders in council in relation to English, Russian, and neutral commerce", *Journal of the Statistical Society of London*, 1855, vol. 18, pp. 21–33.

Walpole, Sir Spencer, *The History of Twenty-Five Years 1856–1880*, Vol. 3 (London: Longmans, Green, 1908).

Ward, Robert, *A Treatise of the Relative Rights and Duties of Belligerent and Neutral Powers in Maritime Affairs: In Which the Principles of Armed Neutralities, and the Opinions of Hübner and Schlegel Are Fully Discussed* (London: Butterworth, 1801).

Westlake, J., "The Declaration of London", *Nineteenth Century and After*, vol. 67, no. 397 (March 1910), pp. 505–15.

White, A. D., *Autobiography of Andrew Dickson White*, Vol. 2 (New York: Century, 1906).

White, Arnold, "Can we trust the admiralty", *National Review*, vol. 47, no. 277 (March 1906), pp. 68–76.

White, Sir W. H., "The cult of the monster warship", *Nineteenth Century and After*, vol. 63, no. 376 (June 1908).

White, Sir W. H. "Civis", *The State of the Navy in 1907; A Plea for Inquiry* (London: Smith, Elder, 1907).

Wilkinson, Spenser, *Britain at Bay* (London: 1909).

Wilkinson, Spenser, *British Aspects of War and Peace* (London: Duckworth, 1920).

Wilkinson, Spenser, *The Great Alternative; A Plea for a National Policy* (London: Swann Sonnenschein, 1894).

Wilkinson, Spenser, *Thirty Five Years 1874–1909* (London: Constable, 1933).

Wilkinson, Spenser, *War and Policy* (London: Constable, 1900).

Wilson, H. H., "The sacrifice of sea power to 'Economy'", *National Review*, vol. 48, no. 286 (December 1906), pp. 714–25.

Wilson, H. H., "Sea law made in Germany", *National Review*, vol. 56 (January 1911), pp. 740–54.

Wilson, Rev. J. L., *The British Squadron on the Coast of Africa* (London: Ridgway, 1851).

Wood, T. McKinnon, *British Commerce and the Declaration of London* (London: Liberal Publication Department, 1911).

Wood, T. Mckinnon, *The Declaration of London* (London: Liberal Publication Department, 1911).

Wyatt, H. F., "England's threatened rights at sea", *Journal of the Royal United Service Institution*, vol. 54, no. 383 (January 1910), pp. 5–33. [Lecture given at Institution.]

Young, George, "Anglo-American command of the seas", *Contemporary Review*, vol. 133 (March 1928), pp. 294–302.

Yule, Lt. Henry, *The African Squadron Vindicated* (London: Ridgway, 1850).

Zimmern, Alfred, *Quo Vadimus* (Oxford: Oxford University Press, 1934).

Secondary Sources

Anderson, Olive, *A Liberal State at War; English Politics and Economics during the Crimean War* (London: Macmillan, 1967).

Anderson, Olive, "Some further light on the inner history of the Declaration of Paris", *Law Quarterly Review*, vol. 76 (1969), pp. 379–85.

Aron, Raymond, *Clausewitz, Philosopher of War* (Englewood, NJ: Prentice Hall, 1985).

Bacon, Admiral Sir R. H., *The Life of Lord Fisher of Kilverstone*, 2 vols (London: Hodder & Stoughton, 1929).

Barnett, Correlli, *The Collapse of British Power* (London: Eyre Methuen, 1972).

Barnett, Correlli, "Strategy and society", *Journal of the Royal United Service Institution for Defence Studies*, vol. 121, no. 3 (September 1976), pp. 11–19.

Bartlett, C. J. (ed.), *Britain Pre-eminent: Studies of British World Influence in the Nineteenth Century* (New York: St Martin's Press 1969).

Bartlett, C. J., *Great Britain and Sea Power* (Oxford: Oxford University Press, 1963).

Bartlett, C. J., "The mid-Victorian reappraisal of naval policy", in *Studies in International History; Essays presented to W. Norton Medlicott*, eds K. Bourne and D. C. Watt (London: Longmans, 1967).

Beales, A. C. F., *The History of Peace; A Short Account of the Organised Movements for International Peace* (London: Bell, 1931).

Best, Geoffrey, "How right is might? Some aspects of the international debate about how to fight wars and how to win them, 1870–1918', in *War, Economy and the Military Mind* (London: Croom Helm, 1976).

Best, Geoffrey, *Honour among Men and Nations: Transformation of an Idea* (Toronto: University of Toronto Press, 1982).

Best, Geoffrey, *Humanity in Warfare: The Modern History of the International Law of Armed Conflicts*(London: Weidenfield & Nicolson, 1980).

Best, Geoffrey, *War and Society in Revolutionary Europe, 1770–1870* (New York: St Martin's Press, 1982).

Bethell, Leslie, *The Abolition of the Brazilian Slave Trade; Britain, Brazil and the Slave Trade Question, 1807–1869* (Cambridge: Cambridge University Press, 1970).

Bond, Brian, *Liddell Hart; A Study of His Military Thought* (London: Cassell, 1977).

Bourne, Kenneth, *The Foreign Policy of Victorian England, 1830–1902* (Oxford: Clarendon Press, 1970).

Bourne, Kenneth, *Britain and the Balance of Power in North America, 1815–1908* (Berkeley: University of California Press, 1967).

Brock, Peter, *Pacifism in Europe to 1914* (Princeton, NJ: Princeton University Press, 1972).

Brodie, Bernard, *Sea Power in the Machine Age* (Princeton NJ: Princeton University Press, 1941).

Churchill, Randolph S., *Winston S. Churchill*, Vols 1 and 2 (Boston: Houghton Mifflin, 1966).

Clapham, J. H., "The last years of the Navigation Acts", *English Historical Review*, vol. 25, July and October 1910; reprinted in *Essays in Economic History*, Vol. 3, ed. E. M. Carus-Wilson (London: Edward Arnold, 1963).

Coogan, John W., *The End of Neutrality; the United States, Britain, and Maritime Rights 1899–1915* (Ithaca, NY: Cornell University Press, 1981).

Craig, G. A., "Delbrück: the military historian", in *Makers of Modern Strategy; Military*

Thought from Machiavelli to Hitler, ed. E. M. Earle (Princeton, NJ: Princeton University Press, 1971).

Davies, Forrest, *The Atlantic System; The Story of the Anglo-American Control of the Seas* (New York: Reynal & Hitchcock, 1941).

Davis, C. D., *The United States and the Second Hague Peace Conference; American Diplomacy and International Organization* (Durham, NC: Duke University Press, 1975).

Davis, George T., *A Navy Second to None; The Development of Modern American Naval Policy* (New York: Harcourt Brace, 1940).

Dawson, W. H., *Richard Cobden and Foreign Policy; a Critical Exposition with Special Reference to our Day and Its Problems* (New York: Frank-Maurice, 1927).

d'Egville, Howard, *Imperial Defence and Closer Union; A Short Record of the Life-Work of the Late Sir John Colomb, in Connection with the Movement towards Imperial Organisation* (London: P. S. King, 1913).

Devlin, Lord, *The House of Lords and the Naval Prize Bill, 1911*, the Rede Lecture (Cambridge: Cambridge University Press, 1968).

Dewar, A. C., "Jutland, Battle of", *Encyclopaedia Britannica*, 12th edn (London, 1922), Vol. 31, p. 667.

d'Ombrain, Nicholas, *War Machinery and High Policy; Defence Administration in Peacetime Britain, 1902–1914* (London: Oxford University Press, 1973).

Dorpalen, Andreas, *The World of General Haushofer; Geopolitics in Action* (Port Washington, NY: Kennikat Press, 1966).

Du Bois, W. E. B., *The Suppression of the African Slave Trade to the United States 1638–1870* (New York: Russell & Russell, 1965).

Field, James A., Jr, "The origins of maritime strategy and the development of sea power", in *War, Strategy, and Maritime Power*, ed. B. Mitchell Simpson III (New Brunswick, NJ: Rutgers University Press, 1977).

Fiennes, Gerald, *Sea Power and Freedom; A Historical Study* (New York: C. P. Putnam, 1918).

French, David, *British Economic and Strategic Planning 1905–1915* (London: Allen & Unwin, 1982).

Fry, M. G., "The imperial war cabinet, the United States, and the freedom of the seas", *Journal of the Royal United Service Institution*, vol. 110 (1965), pp. 353–62.

Gallie, W. B., *Philosophers of Peace and War; Kant, Clausewitz, Marx, Engels, and Tolstoy* (Cambridge: Cambridge University Press, 1978).

Gardiner, A. G., *The Life of Sir William Harcourt*, 2 vols (London: Constable, 1923).

Gollin, A. M., *The Observer and J. L. Garvin 1908–1914; A Study in a Great Editorship* (London: Oxford University Press, 1960).

Gooch, John, *The Plans of War: The General Staff and British Military Strategy 1900–1916* (London: Routledge & Kegan Paul, 1974).

Gooch, John, *The Prospect of War; Studies in British Defence Policy 1847–1942* (London: Frank Cass, 1981).

Graham, G. S., *The Politics of Naval Supremacy: Studies in British Maritime Ascendancy* (Cambridge: Cambridge University Press, 1965).

Graham, G. S., *Sea Power and British North America* (Cambridge: Cambridge University Press, 1941).

Gretton, Vice-Admiral Sir Peter, *Maritime Strategy; A Study of Defense Problems* (New York: Praeger, 1965).

Gretton, Vice-Admiral Sir Peter, "The U-boat campaign in two world wars", in *Naval Warfare in the Twentieth Century; Essays in Honour of Arthur Marder*, ed. Gerald Jordan (London: Croom Helm, 1977).

Guinn, Paul, *British Strategy and Politics 1914 to 1918* (Oxford: Clarendon Press, 1965).

Haggie, P., "The Royal Navy and war planning in the Fisher era," in *The War Plans*

of the Great Powers, 1880–1914, ed. Paul M. Kennedy (London: Allen & Unwin, 1979).
Halévy, Elie, *England in 1815* (New York: Peter Smith, 1949).
Halévy, Elie, *Imperialism and the Rise of Labour, 1895–1905* (New York: Peter Smith, 1951).
Halévy, Elie, *The Rule of Democracy, 1905–1914* (New York: Peter Smith, 1952).
Hamilton, C. I., "Anglo-French seapower and the Declaration of Paris", *International History Review*, vol. 4, no. 2 (May 1982), pp. 166–190.
Hamilton, W. M., "The nation and the Navy: methods and organisation of British navalist propaganda 1889–1914". PhD thesis, London, 1977.
Hardach, Gerd, *The First World War 1914–1918* (Berkeley: University of California Press, 1977).
Hearnshaw, F. J. C., *Sea-Power and Empire* (London: Harrap, 1940).
Hendrick, B. J., *The Life and Letters of Walter H. Page*, 3 vols (Garden City, NY: Doubleday, 1925).
Herwig, H. H., *The German Naval Officer Corps: a Social and Political History, 1890–1918* (Oxford: Clarendon Press, 1973).
Herwig, H. H., *Luxury Fleet: The Imperial German Navy, 1889–1918* (London: Allen & Unwin, 1980).
Higham, Robin, *The Military Intellectuals in Britain: 1918–1939* (New Brunswick, NJ: Rutgers University Press, 1966).
Hinsley, F. H., *Power and the Pursuit of Peace; Theory and Practice in the History of Relations Between States* (Cambridge: Cambridge University Press, 1967).
Hintze, Otto, "Military organization and state organization", in *The Historical Essays of Otto Hintze*, ed. F. Gilbert (New York: Oxford University Press, 1975).
Hobson, J. A., *Richard Cobden, the International Man* (London: Fisher Unwin, 1918).
Hough, Richard A., *First Sea Lord: An Authorized Biography of Admiral Lord Fisher* (London: Allen & Unwin, 1969).
Howard, Michael, *The British Way in Warfare; A Reappraisal* (London: Jonathan Cape, 1975).
Howard, Michael, *The Continental Commitment; the Dilemma of British Defence Policy in the Era of the Two World Wars* (London: Temple Smith, 1972).
Howard, Michael, *Ethics and Power in International Politics* (London: Council on Christian Approaches to Defence and Disarmament, 1978).
Howard, Michael, "The forgotten dimensions of strategy", *Foreign Affairs*, vol. 57, no. 5 (Summer 1979), pp. 975–86.
Howard, Michael, "*Temperamenta Belli: Can war be controlled?*", in *Restraints on War*, ed. M. Howard (Oxford: Oxford University Press, 1979).
Howard, Michael, *War in European History* (London: Oxford University Press, 1976).
Hunt, Barry D., *Sailor-Scholar: Admiral Sir Herbert Richmond, 1871–1946* (Waterloo, Ont: Wilford Laurier University Press, 1982).
Jack, D. T., *Studies in Economic Warfare* (London: P. S. King, 1940).
Johnson, F. A., *Defence by Committee; The British Committee of Imperial Defence 1885–1959* (London: Oxford University Press, 1960).
Jordan, G. H. S., "Pensions not dreadnoughts: the Radicals and naval retrenchment", in *Edwardian Radicalism, 1900–1914*, ed. A. J. A. Morris (London: Routledge & Kegan Paul, 1974).
Jordan, Gerald (ed.), *Naval Warfare in the Twentieth Century 1900–1945; Essays in Honour of Arthur Marder* (London: Croom Helm, 1977).
Kemp, Peter, "From Tryon to Fisher: the regeneration of a navy", in *Naval Warfare in the Twentieth Century, 1900–1945; Essays in Honour of Arthur Marder*, ed. Gerald Jordan (London: Croom Helm, 1977).
Kennedy, Paul M., "Fisher and Tirpitz: political admirals in the age of imperialism",

in *Naval Warfare in the Twentieth Century, 1900–1945; Essays in Honour of Arthur Marder*, ed. Gerald Jordan (London: Croom Helm, 1977).

Kennedy, Paul M., *The Realities Behind Diplomacy: Background Influences on British External Policy, 1865–1980* (London: Allen & Unwin, 1981).

Kennedy, Paul M., *The Rise and Fall of British Naval Mastery* (New York: Scribner's, 1976).

Kennedy, Paul M., *The Rise of the Anglo-German Antagonism 1860–1914* (London: Allen & Unwin, 1980).

Kennedy, Paul M., *Strategy and Diplomacy 1870–1945: Eight Studies* (London: Allen & Unwin, 1983).

Konvitz, J. W., *Cities and the Sea* (Baltimore: Johns Hopkins University Press, 1978).

Koss, S. E., *Sir John Brunner, Radical Plutocrat 1842–1919* (Cambridge: Cambridge University Press, 1970).

Lamb, Margaret, "The making of a Russophobe: David Urquhart – the formative years, 1825–1835", *International History Review*, vol. 3, no. 3 (July 1981), pp. 330–57.

Latifi, Alma, *Effects of War on Property; Being Studies in International Law and Policy* (London: Macmillan, 1909).

Laughton, Sir J. K., *Memoirs of the Life and Correspondence of Henry Reeve*, 2 vols (London, 1898).

Link, A. S., *Wilson; the Struggle for Neutrality, 1914–1915* (Princeton, NJ: Princeton University Press, 1960).

Livezey, W. E., *Mahan on Sea Power* (Norman, Okla: University of Oklahoma Press, 1947).

Lloyd, Christopher, *The Navy and the Slave Trade; the Suppression of the African Slave Trade in the Nineteenth Century* (London: Frank Cass, 1968).

Luvaas, Jay, *The Education of An Army; British Military Thought, 1815–1940* (Chicago: University of Chicago Press, 1964).

Luttwak, Edward N., *The Political Uses of Sea Power* (Baltimore: Johns Hopkins Press, 1974).

Maccoby, Simon, *English Radicalism*, 6 vols (London: Allen & Unwin, 1935–61).

Mackay, R. F., *Fisher of Kilverstone* (Oxford: Clarendon Press, 1973).

Mackay, R. F., "Historical reinterpretations of the Anglo-German naval rivalry, 1897–1914", in *Naval Warfare in the Twentieth Century, 1900–1945; Essays in Honour of Arthur Marder*, ed. Gerald Jordan (London: Croom Helm, 1977).

McDermott, John, "Sir Francis Oppenheimer: 'Stranger Within' the Foreign Office", *History*, vol. 66, no. 217 (June 1981).

McNeill, W. H., *Pursuit of Power: Technology, Armed Force, and Society since AD 1000* (Chicago: University of Chicago Press, 1982).

Marder, Arthur J., *The Anatomy of British Sea Power: A History of British Naval Policy in the Pre-Dreadnought Era, 1880–1905* (New York: Knopf, 1940).

Marder, Arthur J., *From the Dreadnought to Scapa Flow; The Royal Navy in the Fisher Era, 1904–1919*, 5 vols (Oxford: Oxford University Press, 1961–70).

Marsden, Arthur, "The blockade", in *British Foreign Policy Under Sir Edward Grey*, ed. F. H. Hinsley (Cambridge: Cambridge University Press, 1977).

Martin, E. S., *The Life of Joseph Hodges Choate* (New York: Scribner's, 1920).

Morley, John, *Life of Richard Cobden* (London: Fisher Unwin, 1903).

Morris, A. J. Anthony, *Radicalism Against War, 1906–1914; the Advocacy of Peace and Retrenchment* (Totowa, NJ: Rowman & Littlefield, 1972).

Morris, A. J. A., *The Scaremongers; the Advocacy of War and Rearmament 1896–1914* (London: Routledge & Kegan Paul, 1984).

Naylor, Leonard E., *The Irrepressible Victorian: The Story of Thomas Gibson Bowles* (London: Macdonald, 1965).

O'Connell, D. P., *The Influence of Law on Sea Power* (Manchester: Manchester University Press, 1975).

Offer, Avner, "The working classes, British naval plans and the coming of the Great War", *Past & Present*, no. 107 (May 1985), pp. 204–26.

Padfield, Peter, *The Great Naval Race; the Anglo-German Naval Rivalry, 1900–1914* (London: Hart-Davis, MacGibbon, 1974).

Parry, Clive, "Foreign policy and international law", in *British Foreign Policy Under Sir Edward Grey*, ed., F. H. Hinsley (Cambridge: Cambridge University Press, 1977).

Paul, Herbert, *A History of Modern England*, Vol. 2 (New York: Macmillan, 1904).

Perkins, Bradford, *The Great Rapprochement: England and the United States, 1895–1914* (New York: 1968).

Perkins, Bradford, *Prologue to War; England and the United States, 1805–1812* (Berkeley: University of California Press, 1961).

Phillips, W. A., and A. H. Reede, *Neutrality: Its History, Economics and Law*, Vol. 2 (New York: Columbia University Press, 1936).

Phipps, Hon. Edmund, *Memoirs of the Political and Literary Life of Robert Plumer Ward, Esq.*, 2 vols (London: John Murray, 1850).

Piggott, Sir Francis, *The Declaration of Paris 1856* (London: University of London Press, 1919).

Pitt, M. R., "Great Britain and belligerent maritime rights from the Declaration of Paris, 1856, to the Declaration of London, 1909", PhD thesis, University of London, 1964.

Possony, S. T., and E. Mantoux, "Du Picq and Foch: the French school", in *Makers of Modern Strategy*, ed. E. M. Earle (Princeton, NJ: Princeton University Press, 1971).

Ranft, Bryan, "The protection of British seaborne trade and the development of systematic planning for war, 1860–1906", in *Technical Change and British Naval Policy, 1860–1939*, ed. Bryan Ranft (London: Hodder & Stoughton, 1977).

Ranft, Bryan, "Restraints on war at sea before 1945", in *Restraints on War*, ed. Michael Howard (Oxford: Oxford University Press, 1979).

Reynolds, Clark, G., *Command of the Sea; the History and Strategy of Maritime Empires* (New York: William Morrow, 1974).

Richmond, Admiral Sir Herbert, *British Strategy, Military and Economic; A Historical Review and its Contemporary Lessons* (Cambridge: Cambridge University Press, 1941).

Richmond, Sir Herbert, *National Policy and Naval Strength* (London: Longmans, Green, 1928).

Richmond, Sir Herbert, *Sea Power in the Modern World* (London: G. Bell, 1934).

Richmond, Sir Herbert, *Statesmen and Sea Power: The Navy as an Instrument of Policy, 1558–1727* (Oxford: Clarendon Press, 1946).

Robbins, Keith, *The Abolition of War; the Peace Movement in Britain, 1914–1919* (Cardiff: University of Wales Press, 1976).

Robbins, Keith, *John Bright* (London: Routledge & Kegan Paul, 1979).

Robbins, Keith, "Public opinion, the press and pressure groups", in *British Foreign Policy Under Sir Edward Grey*, ed. F. H. Hinsley (Cambridge: Cambridge University Press, 1977).

Robbins, Keith, *Sir Edward Grey; a Biography of Lord Grey of Fallodon* (London: Cassell, 1971).

Robinson, Gertrude, *David Urquhart; Some Chapters in the Life of a Victorian Knight-Errant of Justice and Liberty* (Oxford: Basil Blackwell, 1920).

Ropp, Theodore, "Continental doctrines of sea power," in *Makers of Modern Strategy*, ed. E. M. Earle (Princeton, NJ: Princeton University Press, 1971).

Ropp, Theodore, *War in the Modern World* (Durham, NC: Duke University Press, 1959).

Rosinski, Herbert, *The Development of Naval Thought*, ed. B. M. Simpson III (Newport, RI: Naval War College Press, 1977).

Roskill, Stephen, *Hankey, Man of Secrets*, 2 vols (London: Collins, 1970, 1972).

Roskill, Stephen, *Naval Policy Between the Wars*, Vol. 1: *The Period of Anglo-American Antagonism, 1919–1929* (New York: Walker, 1969).

Savage, Carlton (ed.), *Policy of the United States Toward Maritime Commerce in War*, Vol. 1, 1776–1914 (Washington: United States Government Printing Office, 1934).

Schmitt, B. E., *England and Germany, 1740–1914* (Princeton NJ: Princeton University Press, 1918).

Schumpeter, J.A., *Business Cycles; a Theoretical, Historical, and Statistical Analysis of the Capitalist Process*, 2 vols (New York: McGraw-Hill, 1939).

Schumpeter, J. A., *Capitalism, Socialism and Democracy* (New York: Harper & Brothers, 1947).

Schumpeter, J. A., *Imperialism and Social Classes* (Oxford: Blackwell, 1951).

Schurman, D. M., *The Education of a Navy; the Development of British Naval Strategic Thought, 1867–1914* (Chicago: University of Chicago Press, 1965).

Schurman, D. M., *Julian S. Corbett, 1854–1922; Historian of British Maritime Policy from Drake to Jellicoe* (London: Royal Historical Society, 1981).

Scott, J. B. (ed.), *The Declaration of London, February 26, 1909* (New York: Oxford University Press, 1919).

Seager, Robert, II, *Alfred Thayer Mahan: the Man and His Letters* (Annapolis, Md: Naval Institute Press, 1977).

Semmel, Bernard, *Imperialism and Social Reform: English Social-Imperial Thought 1895–1914* (London: Allen & Unwin, 1960).

Semmel, Bernard, *Jamaican Blood and Victorian Conscience; the Governor Eyre Controversy* (Boston: Houghton, Mifflin, 1963).

Semmel, Bernard, *John Stuart Mill and the Pursuit of Virtue* (New Haven: Yale University Press, 1984).

Semmel, Bernard, (ed.), *Marxism and the Science of War* (Oxford: Oxford University Press, 1981).

Semmel, Bernard, *The Methodist Revolution* (New York: Basic Books, 1973).

Semmel, Bernard, *The Rise of Free Trade Imperialism; Classical Political Economy, the Empire of Free Trade, and Imperialism 1750–1850* (Cambridge: Cambridge University Press, 1970).

Shannon, Richard, "David Urquhart and the foreign affairs committees", in *Pressure from Without in Early Victorian England*, ed. P. Hollis (London: Edward Arnold, 1974).

Soulsby, Hugh G., *The Right of Search and the Slave Trade in Anglo-American Relations, 1814–1862* (Baltimore: Johns Hopkins University Press, 1933).

Sprout, Harold and Margaret, *The Rise of American Naval Power, 1776–1918* (Princeton, NJ: Princeton University Press, 1939).

Sprout, Margaret, "Mahan: evangelist of sea power", in *Makers of Modern Strategy*, ed. E. M. Earle (Princeton, NJ: Princeton University Press, 1971).

Steinberg, Jonathan, *Yesterday's Deterrent: Tirpitz and the Birth of the German Battle Fleet* (London: Macmillan, 1965).

Steiner, Zara, *Britain and the Origins of the First World War* (London: Macmillan, 1977).

Steiner, Zara, "The foreign office under Sir Edward Grey, 1905–1914", in *British Foreign Policy Under Sir Edward Grey*, ed. F. H. Hinsley (Cambridge: Cambridge University Press, 1977).

Strachan, Hew, "The British way in warfare revisited", *Historical Journal*, vol. 26, pt 2 (1983), pp. 447–61.

Sullivan, E. P., "Liberalism and imperialism: J. S. Mill's defense of the British

Empire", *Journal of the History of Ideas*, vol. 44, no. 4 (October–December 1983), pp. 599–617.

Sumida, J. T., "British capital ship design and fire control in the dreadnought era: Sir John Fisher, Arthur Hungerford Pollen, and the battle cruiser", *Journal of Modern History*, vol. 51, no. 2 (June 1979), pp. 205–30.

Taylor, C. C., *The Life of Admiral Mahan* (London: John Murray, 1920).

Temperley, H. M. V., and L. M. Penson (eds), *Foundations of British Foreign Policy from Pitt to Salisbury, 1792–1902* (Cambridge: Cambridge University Press, 1938).

Trask, D. F., "The American Navy in a world at war, 1914–19", in *In Peace and War; Interpretations of American Naval History*, ed. K. J. Hagan (Westport, Conn.: Greenwood Press, 1978).

Trask, D. F., *Captains and Cabinets; Anglo-American Naval Relations, 1917–1918* (Columbia, Mo.: University of Missouri Press, 1972).

Ward, W. E. F., *The Royal Navy and the Slavers; the Suppression of the Atlantic Slave Trade* (New York: Pantheon, 1969).

Weinroth, H. S., "Norman Angell and the 'Great Illusion'; an episode in pre-1914 pacifism", *Historical Journal*, vol. 17 (1974), pp. 551–74.

Weinroth, H. S., "Left-wing opposition to naval armaments in Britain before 1914", *Journal of Contemporary History*, vol. 6, no. 4 (1971), pp. 93–121.

Wemyss, Rosslyn, *Memoirs and Letters of the Right Hon. Sir Robert Morier, G.C.B., from 1826 to 1876*, 2 vols (London: Edward Arnold, 1911).

Williamson, S. R., Jr, *The Politics of Grand Strategy; Britain and France Prepare for War, 1904–1914* (Cambridge, Mass.: Harvard University Press, 1969).

Winton, John, *Convoy; the Defence of Sea Trade 1890–1990* (London: Michael Joseph, 1983).

Woodward, E. L., *Great Britain and the German Navy* (London: Frank Cass, 1964).

Index